Translation and Rewriting in the Age of Post-Translation Studies

I0585721

In *Translation and Rewriting in the Age of Post-Translation Studies*, Edwin Gentzler argues that rewritings of literary works have taken translation to a new level: literary texts no longer simply originate, but rather circulate, moving internationally and intersemiotically into new media and forms. Drawing on traditional translations, post-translation rewritings and other forms of creative adaptation, he examines the different translational cultures from which literary works emerge, and the translational elements within them.

In this revealing study, four concise chapters give detailed analyses of the following classic works and their rewritings:

- *A Midsummer Night's Dream* in Germany
- Postcolonial *Faust*
- Proust for everyday readers
- *Hamlet* in China.

With examples from a variety of genres including music, film, ballet, comics, and video games, this book will be of special interest for all students and scholars of translation studies and contemporary literary and media studies.

Edwin Gentzler is a Professor of Translation Studies and Director of Comparative Literature at the University of Massachusetts Amherst. He is the author of *Contemporary Translation Theories* (Routledge, 1993) and *Translation and Identity in the Americas* (Routledge, 2008). He is the co-editor (with Maria Tymoczko) of *Translation and Power* (2002) and a series editor (with Susan Bassnett) of the "Topics in Translation" series.

New Perspectives in Translation and Interpreting Studies

Series editors:

Michael Cronin holds a Personal Chair in the Faculty of Humanities and Social Sciences at Dublin City University.

Moira Inghilleri is Director of Translation Studies in the Comparative Literature Program at the University of Massachusetts Amherst.

The *New Perspectives in Translation and Interpreting Studies* series aims to address changing needs in the fields of translation studies and interpreting studies. The series features works by leading scholars in both disciplines, on emerging and up to date topics. Key features of the titles in this series are accessibility, relevance and innovation.

These lively and highly readable texts provide an exploration into various areas of translation and interpreting studies for undergraduate and postgraduate students of translation studies, interpreting studies and cultural studies.

Cities in Translation
Sherry Simon

Translation in the Digital Age
Michael Cronin

Translation and Geography
Federico Italiano

Translation and Rewriting in the Age of Post-Translation Studies

Edwin Gentzler

Routledge
Taylor & Francis Group

LONDON AND NEW YORK

First published 2017
by Routledge
2 Park Square, Milton Park, Abingdon, Oxon OX14 4RN

and by Routledge
711 Third Avenue, New York, NY 10017

Routledge is an imprint of the Taylor & Francis Group, an informa business

© 2017 Edwin Gentzler

British Library Cataloguing in Publication Data
A catalogue record for this book is available from the British Library

Library of Congress Cataloguing in Publication Data
A catalog record has been requested for this book

ISBN: 978-1-138-66685-6 (hbk)
ISBN: 978-1-138-66686-3 (pbk)
ISBN: 978-1-3156-1919-4 (ebk)

Typeset in Sabon LT Std
by Out of House Publishing

Contents

List of figures and tables

Figures

Tables

Foreword by Susan Bassnett

The prefix 'post' has two meanings: it can signify ending, meaning that something is definitively over and behind you, even that something or someone is defunct. After all, a post-mortem can only be carried out on a corpse. Or it can have a much more positive meaning, it can signify the start of a new phase, of movement towards a next stage that builds on something that has been and is no more, but out of which comes new life and growth. In literary studies, we have had post-modernism, post-colonialism, post-structuralism, post-feminism and in each of these cases the prefix 'post' carries with it not so much a sense of ending, but rather a sense of excitement, of new beginning, of moving on to new ideas, new ways of thinking.

In coining the term 'post-translation studies' Edwin Gentzler is indeed seeking to create something new. It is, he acknowledges, not a term that everyone will find comfortable, but then terminology has been contentious throughout the four decades since translation studies came into existence, when a small group of angry young international researchers began to meet in Belgium and the Netherlands. They were angry back then because translation was sorely neglected in every field: literary studies looked down on translation as a secondary and derivative practice, unworthy of scholarly attention, while linguists were still arguing over what constituted equivalence and accuracy in translation, and history, philosophy, politics, theatre and cultural studies ignored translation altogether. Translators, those men and women working at the chalk face and actually producing texts were excluded from any scholarly discussion.

Gradually the new field grew, and translation has been undergoing a global explosion of interest since the dawn of the millennium. Inevitably, with expansion has come diversification, so that today there is little consensus as to what constitutes translation studies, other than that the subject (some have even called it a discipline) is concerned with the movement of texts across linguistic and cultural boundaries. Much contemporary work is technologically based, a necessary development but a long way from research into the theory, history, and transmission of literary texts which is where translation studies started. Interestingly, this kind of research is increasingly happening under the aegis of comparative and World Literature, where investigation into the cultural history of translation is starting to gain ground.

Edwin Gentzler is mindful of all this, but is also mindful of the fact that, despite the growing importance of translation in the world today, translation studies practitioners have not managed to reach out sufficiently to other fields and all too often talk only to one another. His notion of post-translation, or transdisciplinary translation studies, demands a questioning of older definitions of translation, and an end to trying to distinguish between so-called originals, translations, and rewritings. The various case studies he uses to argue for the breaking down of these distinctions point to the complexity of intercultural transmission and to the inadequacy of the old terminology that positioned translations and originals on either side of a linguistic divide.

His is by no means a lone voice: translators and translation scholars such as Sherry Simon, Lawrence Venuti, Haroldo de Campos, Josephine Balmer, Bella Brodzki, to name but a few, have all sought to expand the terminology of translation, as André Lefevere did in the early 1990s when he wrote about 'refractions' and then 'rewritings.' There is a current resurgence of interest in Gerald Genette's work from the early 1980s too, and to this we can add the growing interest in seeing translation as a plurivocal activity, since many other voices than those of translator and 'original' author combine in the actual translation process. Research into the production and dissemination of texts is central to World Literature scholarship and here the potential for collaboration with translation studies is enormous.

Gentzler invites us to see translation as a revolutionary act, in that it brings ideas and forms across cultural boundaries, offering life-changing possibilities. Translation, he suggests has infinite potential, and in a world of increased movement and migration, translation has a vital role to play in enabling people to cope with multilingual identities. Consequently, the study of translation should be alive to that role and should acknowledge that the time has come to rethink what we understand by translation and start to engage with it in new ways. His proposal is radical: he is not calling for an end to translation studies, but for expansion of its self-imposed boundaries, so that the field can reach out to other disciplines and become more open to ideas about translational issues coming from researchers who may not be primarily engaged in translation.

The repercussions of translation are to be seen everywhere and in every discipline, for translation 'finds itself on the cutting edge of time,' bringing the past back to life and pointing towards an exciting multilingual future. This book demonstrates how important translation is as a means of ensuring the circulation of texts across temporal and cultural frontiers. Translation studies is not moribund; post-translation studies is an exciting new phase for the subject. We have seen a great many 'turns' in translation studies; now is the time for the Outward Turn as the field redefines itself and begins to enjoy greater exchange with other disciplines in a mutually beneficial process of importing and exporting methodologies and ideas. Post-translation translation studies may annoy die-hards with overly rigid views about studying translation, but it may well prove the catalyst for taking the subject forward into a whole new stage of development and positioning translation as a fundamental cultural condition underlying communication in the twenty-first century.

Susan Bassnett
University of Glasgow,
University of Warwick

Preface and acknowledgments

The idea behind this project began in the fall of 2013 when I was invited by Simone Homem de Mello to the Casa Guilherme de Almeida to speak at their conference *Transfusão* [transfusion]. There I delivered a paper on "*Reescritura e tradução; Repensando André Lefevere*" and spoke on the panel on "*Transcriação e antropofagia.*" The conference was not an academic conference, but instead a gathering of poets, translators, musicians, visual artists, sculptors, as well as academics. Housed in Casa Almeida in the Pacaembu section of São Paulo, the Casa is the former home of Guilherme de Andrade de Almeida, a modernist poet, essayist, film critic, and children's book author. Today the museum hosts art and book exhibits, enjoys a wonderful archive or modernist works, and offers educational programs, including courses on translation. Directed by the poet, translator, and scholar Marcelo Tápia, the conference showed me the influence translation has in any number of the arts. Many of the performances were hybrid genres, combining, or shall I say *fusing*, text with illustrations, music with lyrics, poetry with visual art, classical works with modern ideas, and translation with film. One impressionable example was the musical translations-renditions of Cole Porter songs by Carlos Rennó. The translations were uncannily accurate—Rennó could spend up to six months translating one song—but they also were very localized, fitting into a Tropicalismo Brazilian musical movement. My sincere thanks are extended to Simone, Marcelo, Carlos, and all those attending the conference, including Paulo Henriques Britto, Roch Duval, John Milton, and Maria Teresa Quirino, for a transformative moment in my life.

In the winter of 2014, I was invited to speak at the Centre for Intercultural Mediation at Durham University in England, directed by Federico Federici and Zhang Binghan. On a cold and snowy night in February, I gave a version of the "*A Midsummer Night's Dream* in Germany" chapter to an audience of more Chinese graduate students than British. Many had never read *A Midsummer Night's Dream*, but all were familiar with it via other sources. Also in the audience was Siri Nergaard, who was in England meeting with publishers about her journal *Translation: A Transdisciplinary Journal*.

Afterwards she told me that the talk was more than a paper, but instead should be a book. Without her sage advice, I would have never turned to the project, and my gratitude is deep.

Siri is more instrumental than an advisor in the book that follows; her idea forms the theoretical basis for the book. In 2011, in the inaugural issue of *Translation*, she and Stefano Arduini coined the term "post-translation studies," redefining the field not in terms of national or linguistic borders, but within the larger entity of culture itself. I have always held that translation was a constitutive factor in cultural formation, consequently their idea much appealed to me. As an editorial member of the journal, I have had many discussions with Siri about possible new directions in translation studies, the hybrid nature of culture, and the transformational power of translation.

The journal itself is an outgrowth of the Nida Institute and the Nida School of Translation Studies in Misano Adriatico, Italy, where I have lectured annually for the past six years. The faculty and associates at the Nida School have thus heard several excerpts from the manuscript, and their feedback has been most welcome. Bible translators know more about the post-translation effects than any group. Bible translations have changed the religions, educational systems, and at times even the politics of many societies. My thanks for the opportunity to present my work and discuss the ideas in that beautiful venue on the Adriatic Sea goes to Phil Towner, Bob Hodgson, James Maxey, Stephano Arduini, Deborah Shadd, Roy Ciampa, and all the members of the Nida School of Translation Studies and San Pellegrino University Foundation.

Each year the Nida School brings two distinguished scholars as Nida Professors, and in the spring of 2015, one of those professors was Susan Bassnett. She heard an excerpt from the "Postcolonial *Faust*" chapter, and she and I have been in touch ever since. Her support and insight have proven instrumental in the manuscript's development and eventual final form. Susan was one of the founders of the cultural turn, to which I am devoted, and in her early work with André Lefevere, they talked about whether anyone today reads the seven volumes of *À la recherche du temps perdu*, or if they instead read abridgements or see film adaptations. Susan and André's thoughts and ideas can be felt throughout, but they are most prominent in the "Proust for everyday readers" chapter. While she perhaps has some issues with the term "post-translation," Susan has been very encouraging as I pursued the cultural ramifications that invariably follow translations. Without not just her pioneering ideas but her openness to contemporary approaches, this book would have been impossible. I thank her for her support and friendship, always.

I also thank my Chinese mentor Luo Xuanmin at Tsinghua University in Beijing, China, where in August of 2014, I was invited to give a series of lectures to graduate students in the Translation and Translation Studies Program at Tsinghua and to give a keynote address at the "11th Congress of the Chinese Association for Comparative Studies of English and Chinese" and the "International Conference of Comparative Studies of Translation and English-Chinese," also held at Tsinghua University. There I first presented a series of lectures on the topic of Post-Translation Studies, using many examples from the book. I thank many of the students in that course, including Yang Wendi, whose participation in the discussions about the ideas of the book was most helpful. My keynote address consisted of the second portion of the "*Hamlet* in China" chapter, and without that test drive and the many suggestions offered by the Chinese participants in attendance, that chapter would have been impossible. I thank all the conferences organizers, including Luo Xuanmin, Pan Wenguo, Wang Ning, and Sun Yifeng. A later version of that conference paper titled "*Hamlet* in China" has been published in the *Asia Pacific Translation and Intercultural Studies* Journal in July 2015, and I thank the editors, including Daisy Wong, for their help.

I thank the organizers of the Conference-Festival (Con-Fest) held in March 2015 at Indraprastha College for Women at the University of Delhi, India, especially Dean of the College Babli Moitra Saraf. The topic of the conference was "Plurilingualism and Orality in Translation," and the number of papers that dealt with new and innovative forms of rewriting and adaptation was invigorating. There I spoke briefly on "International Performances of *Faust*," and I felt my ideas about rewriting not only connected with many of the ideas circulating at the conference but also were pushed to new levels. For example, Harsh Bala Sharma gave the paper "One Ram; Many Ramayana," which looked at not just rewritings of Ramayana in India, but also international performances and film. She mentioned it being reshaped into more than 1,000 art forms, which makes my little project on *Faust* rewritings seem minuscule. My sincere thanks to all the conference organizers, including Babli, Vinita Sinha, Rekha Sethi, Poonam Trivedi, and Manasvini Yoga; I also thank the many artists who performed or presented, including Savitri Devi and Meera Jha, whose wall hangings embroidered with traditional narratives were magnificent. The "Con-Fest" at Indraprastha College was transformative for me, showing me the myriad forms translations can assume, in many ways similar to my experience at the "*Transfusão*" conference at the Casa de Almeida.

I thank my colleagues at the University of Massachusetts, including Julie Hayes, Dean of the College of Humanities and Fine Arts; William Moebius, Chair of the Department of Languages, Literatures, and Cultures; and my fellow faculty members in the Comparative Literature Program. They granted me an 11-month sabbatical during 2014–15 that gave me valuable time to write. I thank all my students in my International Shakespeare and Postcolonial Translation courses. Particular thanks go to Chandrani Chatterjee, Fulbright scholar from Pune, India, with whom I co-taught the postcolonial class in the fall of 2012. Her ideas about translation and genre, gender, caste, and class have proven enormously valuable. In March of 2015, she invited me to speak at an International Colloquium on Translation Studies at the Savitribai Phule Pune University, where interdisciplinary research projects on many post-translation topics were presented, including translational spaces in cities, translation in music and dance, several on translation in film, and even topics such as translation in fashion, food, and festivals. I feel as if Chandrani is a kindred spirit behind the formulation of the ideas that follow.

I also benefitted from not one but two International Shakespeare Conferences held at the University of Massachusetts Amherst, where I presented parts of the *"Midsummer"* and *"Hamlet"* chapters respectively in 2014 and 2015. We have now hosted more than 50 Shakespeare scholars or performers from more than 30 countries at UMass. I am grateful to all of the participants, with special recognition going to Jean-Michel Déprats, Peter Donaldson, Alexa Huang, Bill Worthen, Debra Ann Byrd, and all the performers of the Harlem Shakespeare Festival. I also thank my co-sponsor Arthur Kinney, director of the Renaissance Center at UMass, and the organizing committee of Marie Roche, Anna-Claire Simpson, Krzysztof Rowinski, and Santiago Vidales. The explosion of international Shakespeare films and performances in recent years underscores many of the points made in the book that follows.

Thanks go to colleagues who read individual chapters and gave me feedback, including Marie Roche, a postdoctoral fellow first at the Renaissance Center and currently in comparative literature, who gave the entire manuscript careful attention. I am grateful to my editors at Routledge, including Louisa Semlyen and Laura Sandford, who believed in this project and granted me leeway with the format and length. Every effort has been made to contact copyright holders of the images. I thank Reg Wilson and the Royal Shakespeare Company (RSC), Thomas Höckmann, Markus Marti, Ruphin Coudyzer and the Handspring Puppet Theater, the Bibiotheque nationale de France, Andy Warhol Foundation, Artists Rights Society (ARS), and Arts Resource, Inc. for their permissions. Any omission of acknowledgment is mine and will be rectified upon notification. All tables, unless otherwise noted, are my own. All quotations of Shakespeare's plays are taken from the latest Arden editions: *A Midsummer Night's Dream* (1979), edited by Harold Brooks; and *Hamlet* (2006), edited by Ann Thompson and Neil Taylor. All translations, unless otherwise noted, are my own.

While my daughter Megan is grown and works as a literacy coordinator in Washington, DC, I thank her for her love and affection throughout. My deepest gratitude goes to my wife Jenny Spencer, who not only read many of the drafts and offered suggestions but also lent me continuous support. I give her my love.

Introduction

In the field of translation studies, the term "post-translation studies" has been introduced to try to expand the kinds of texts and objects that scholars examine. The name was coined by Siri Nergaard and Stephano Arduini in "Translation: A New Paradigm" (2011), the introduction to the first issue of a new journal called *Translation*, founded in 2011. They wrote, "We propose the inauguration of a transdisciplinary research field with translation as an interpretive as well as an operative tool. We imagine a sort of new era that could be termed post-translation studies, where translation is viewed as fundamentally transdisciplinary, mobile, and open-ended" (2011: 8). They go on to suggest that the field open itself to investigations of translation from outside the discipline—from art, architecture, ethnography, memory studies, landscape, psychology, semiotics, philosophy, economics, gender studies, race, class, and ethnic studies. In *Death of a Discipline* (2003), Gayatri Spivak discussed opening up the field of comparative literature, which she viewed as Eurocentric and based on outdated comparative literary studies. Instead she called for a broader array of disciplinary investigations, which necessarily included gender, minority, and Third World discourses and their translation. In a similar fashion, some scholars find the field of translation studies too narrow, text-centric, and based upon European definitions and models derived in the 1970s and early 1980s. Research on translational phenomena need not be inscribed within a single discipline. Rather, translation phenomena appear in all languages, major and minor discourses, and in many forms of communication, not just written texts. These elements need to be allowed to flourish, inform, and instruct. Additionally, Nergaard and Arduini suggest that investigators be open to poststructuralist theory, gender, and border studies, demonstrating more attention to the happenings along the edges and interstices than what is going on in the center or mainstream. Their journal reflects that interest. Special issues of the journal *Translation* are forthcoming on the question of memory, edited by Bella Brodzki and Cristina Demaria; on space, edited by Sherry Simon; on conflict, edited by Emily Apter and Mona Baker; and economics, edited by Naoki Sakai and Jon Solomon. The shift in focus from translation as the center of a single discipline, to multidisciplinary analyses shows how translations impact many disciplines and signifies a new direction for the field. In addition, the discourse on translation from the *outside* field can help scholars better analyze the translational phenomena considered from within.

In my view, this post-translation concept is very helpful. The field of translation studies has accomplished a lot in the past 30 years, mapping out a disciplinary territory, developing translation histories in a variety of nations, coming up with better methodologies for better analyzing translations, and conducting important sociological work on the role of the translator. However, in many ways, the field strikes me as still restricted, primarily focused on written texts and two-way comparisons, and neglecting pre- and post-translation conditions and effects. Scholars have documented *how* texts differ and have shown that translators often make changes, adapt, and rewrite, but explaining *why* remains problematic. Additionally, many texts that are not referred to as translations but instead are often called rewritings, adaptations, or furtherings contain translational elements. In many cases, those borderline cases may tell us more about the nature of translation than the central paradigm. While scholars in the field largely dismantled traditional ideas of the translator's fidelity and pointed out degrees of difference, they have been less successful in the analysis of social and psychological reception matters or explored longer-term post-translation repercussions of translated texts.

While many translators strive for an accurate or acceptable reading of a text in one language to another, seeing their task as a craft and playing matching and mapping games, most translators I know translate because they want to *introduce a new idea* or aesthetic form into a culture. The revolutionary war leaders of the Americas were not translating Locke, Rousseau, or Montaigne because they wanted scholars at Harvard to review favorably their translations in learned journals; no, they wanted to introduce new ideas regarding democratic systems and human rights into their cultures that were not free and were still governed by European powers. Many of the translators cared little what the university professors thought about their translations; they wanted common men and women—farmers, sailors, shopkeepers, and craftspeople—to read their translations and think about and incorporate into their beliefs the new ideas being introduced. The purpose was not to better represent European texts but to *change* the receiving culture, to alter the way people think about politics, liberty, individual freedom, and their relationship to the absent monarchy. Which comes first, the pen or the sword? In many cases, more often than not, changing peoples' ideas about governing systems comes first, and the revolutionary fervor later. Indeed, the subsequent revolution in art, politics, literature, science, or any disciplinary analysis, may be interpreted as post-translation effects.

We see such a pattern of translation playing a major role in instituting cultural change frequently: the Germans translating Shakespeare as a way to break the hegemony of French theater in eighteenth-century Germany; Mao Zedong translating and adapting Marx and Engels to fit the Chinese situation, in which there was not a critical mass of working class to rebel against a capitalist society, but there was a massive peasant class that could be mobilized; Ezra Pound translating Tang dynasty poets in China to introduce a new way of imagining into American poetry, thereby changing the landscape of modern English-language poetry; Latin American revolutionaries translating Thomas Jefferson and Benjamin Franklin to help proclaim independence from the Spanish crown; Robert Bly translating European and Latin American poets to introduce surrealism into the American verse forms, thereby changing the landscape of North American verse; or Gary Snyder translating Native American poetry for ecological reasons in the hope of saving the planet. During World War II, when the American SOS (precursor to the CIA) landed in Vietnam to recruit a Vietnamese guerilla by the name of Ho Chi Minh to help fight against the Japanese, when they found him in the jungles of Northern Vietnam close to the Chinese border, he was not training a band of fighters, but translating the works of Lenin into Vietnamese. The post-translation repercussions are well known to all. Finding better methods to describe, inventory, or assess translations does not help measure whether or not the ideas contained within are understood and incorporated into the belief systems of the receiving cultures. This book serves as a call to begin that process.

To measure the success or failure of the ideas or the aesthetics of a translation, one has to look *beyond* translation and to begin to examine the cultural changes that take place *after* the translation, hence the move toward a post-translation analysis. If the Bible were translated into a new culture, did people convert to Christianity or were new churches built in subsequent years? If the translation Enlightenment philosophy introduced ideas of individual liberty, were despotic leaders deposed, new constitutions written, and people granted the right to vote? If new verse forms were introduced, did the conventions of poetry in the receiving cultures change for the next generation of "original" writers? If a feminist text were introduced into a culture with severe restrictions on women, did the dress codes, voting rights, driving rights, daycare availability, and job opportunities in the receiving culture change over the next decade? Sometimes the analysis of textual matters is not enough. I suggest that scholars in the future analyze both the initial reception of the translated text and the post-translation repercussions generated in the receiving culture over subsequent years. What are the changes in poetry and politics, art and architecture, education and the environment, and what role do translations play in effecting those changes? I argue that in conducting such an analysis, scholars will find that translation is not merely a footnote to history, but one of the most vital forces available to introducing new ways of thinking and inducing significant cultural change.

The other direction post-translation studies is moving, which is a bit deceptive given the "post" in its name, is taking a more detailed look at *pre*-translation culture that conditions not only the production of translated texts but *original* writing as well. Post-translation studies examines those conditions, socio-political and linguistic, that *create an environment* in which highly innovative, original writing can flourish. Thus, an original work, such as a Shakespeare play or a Proust novel, as I argue later in this book, can, in certain circumstances, be viewed as a *post-translation* effect. Often the very translation or multilingual environment serves as a stimulant for introducing new ideas or forms. Why does a writer such as the English playwright Ben Jonson (1572–1637), translator of Horace, succeed during the late Elizabethan Age in England? Why does an interest in World Literature emerge in late eighteenth-century Germany? What factors lead to a Czech Renaissance in the nineteenth century? Why did China open its doors for a flood of Western literary and social science texts in the early twentieth century? The polysystem theory suggestion that translation flourishes in weak or emerging cultures provides some explanation, but I suggest that the reasons are much more complex. It is not just that a vacuum exists and translations enter freely and uncritically. No, the cultural conditions are more complicated, sometimes involving a few strong individuals who champion translation, or a repressed linguistic minority breaking free, or a flourishing period of trade and expansion leading to an influx of foreign products and means of expression. Sometimes nation-states accept the fact that two or more linguistic groups must co-exist and allow for translation, such as in Belgium or Switzerland. Sometimes a repressed minority rises and forces the government's hand, as seen in Quebec and more recently in Catalonia. Much more work needs to be done on the environments in which translations flourish and why, and much more attention needs to be paid to those operating at the margins and linguistic minorities, facilitating not just linguistic communication, but economic and political cohesion as well.

Some of the pre- and post-translation investigations have begun. Gayatri Spivak teaches Karl Marx's *Das Kapital* to students at Columbia University, but she also adapts the text and conducts microeconomic courses for teachers in tribal and women's communities in impoverished villages in Bengal. Bible translators are perhaps the most aggressive regarding modifying a text to affect religious change. In poorer countries of Africa, Doctors without Borders cannot deliver health care or save lives without Translators without Borders, moving strategies of community translation and interpreting to the fore. Non-governmental organizations (NGOs) regularly translate material for community education in villages in Asia, Latin America, and Africa, and rewrite the texts to the educational and technical levels of their audiences. Interpreters and social workers are flocking to refugee camps in the Middle East to try to help relieve the plight of displaced peoples, but also to negotiate immigration rights and smooth transitions to more stable cultures.

Certainly the forces of globalization—mass media, new media, the Internet, and improved transportation infrastructures—have facilitated international communication. So too have the *goals* of translation shifted.

The aim of a new generation of translators is less to achieve linguistic accuracy and more to facilitate communication, open avenues for advancement, and to change the way many think about majority and minority encounters. Sales of religious texts have never been higher, and I would suggest it is *less* about the rigor of the translation—and if this new wave of Bible translation is indicative, the quality has never been lower, or shall I say more distant—and *more* about the spiritual rewards perceived to be contained within. Even news organizations are getting into the act, translating and rewriting in very politicized fashion in order less to communicate cultural difference and more to persuade viewers regarding the viewpoints held by the institutions for whom they work. Education, or re-education, has always been a motivating factor for translators. In this new global age, conditions have never been so fertile for growth in translation, but I suggest that so too has the *nature* of translation changed with the age, as has the media through which translations travel.

Some argue that studying pre-translation, translation, and post-translation texts would expand the field too much, and there is certainly some truth in that claim. However, I maintain that the cultural context for translation can tell us much about the translation itself. Further, many different kinds of texts contain translational elements that are seldom considered. To conduct such an analysis, translation studies scholars of necessity need to bring in academics from other disciplines such as politics, sociology, anthropology, and psychology; from linguistics and literary studies, cultural studies, gender, race, and class studies, to be able to see and measure the translational effects. Indeed, nearly *every* discipline derives from and depends upon translation, a dependency that will only increase in the future. Contemporary and increasingly interdisciplinary studies of translation suggest that the borders transgressed in translation tend to be more multiple and permeable than traditionally conceived. It can be argued that from this perspective, I am taking the idea of post-translation to the extreme, but in this book I ask, what if we erase the border completely and rethink translation as an always-ongoing process of *every* communication? What if translation becomes viewed less as a temporal act carried out between languages and cultures and instead as a *precondition* underlying the languages and cultures upon which communication is based? What if we consider the political, social, and economic structures as built upon translation? What if we view the landscape—the parks, buildings, roads, memorials, churches, schools, and government organizations—not as solely monocultural, but also as a product of post-translation effects?

In her book *Translating Montreal: Episodes in the Life of a Divided City* (2006), Sherry Simon questions the limits of traditional translation definitions and goes further, also focusing on the *cultural conditions conducive to translation*, such as the multicultural life of the city of Montreal and the hybrid forms of communication that take place there. She looks not just at translation in a synchronic sense, but also at the conditions *before* and *after* translation. Indicative of post-disciplinary translation studies, she offers a new definition: "I give translation an *expanded* definition in this book: writing that is inspired by the encounter with other tongues, including the effects of creative interference" (Simon 2006: 17, emphasis added). Simon analyzes translational and multilingual markers located all over the city: in creative writing, theater, art, and architecture, as well as the monuments, museums, churches, schools, stores, courts, even the signage in the streets, all of which offer a palimpsest of semiotic and translational elements that she felt were very positive and productive for artistic creation. She offers several new categories for translation analysis in the age of post-translation studies, including "transfiguration," "furtherings," and "creative interference" (Simon 2006: 120–40).

Simon has gone on to write a new book *Cities in Translation: Intersections of Language and Memory* (2012) in which she expands upon that notion, viewing translation in many places as the cultural foundation upon which *all* cultural constructions are founded. Some of the cities Simon discusses include Montreal, Trieste, Calcutta, Barcelona, Dhaka, and Manila, and again she looks at the translational nature of the post-translation forms in a variety of fields, including creative writing, art, and architecture. Plurilingualism is seen as a positive force: accents, code-switching, translations are enriching and facilitating. Translators are viewed as *cultural heroes*, ensuring the circulation of ideas and as agents initiating new forms of expression and ideas. Translators transform social and literary relations: major literary figures emerge, such as Nicole Brossard inventing a polyvalent feminist language in Montreal; Franz Kafka inventing German prose in Prague; and Paul Celan inventing a haunting multilingual poetic language in Czernowitz. Simon's list is persuasive: without translational culture as a foundation, no Tagore without multilingual Calcutta, no Joyce without Trieste, no Brossard without Montreal.

For example, in her discussion of the town of Czernowitz, Sherry Simon discusses the name changes from Tcernauti (Romanian), through Chernivtsi (Ukranian) to the Western Czernowitz (Austrian), which linguistically and culturally represent the palimpsest of the urban area. Many times the paths that translators travel are of forced displacement, which evolves in a writer such as Celan to a national and international displacement. Celan's German is ripe with indications of such alienation and dislocation, full of overtones of the Yiddish, Romanian, Ukrainian, French, and Russian languages he was familiar with, which continued in often suppressed fashions in his city. Sometimes the loss of culture is present by its very absence. Citing the Romanian/French/Quebec translation studies scholar Alexis Nouss [Nuselovic], author of *Paul Celan* (2010), Simon writes, "In Celan's poetry, the German language is shaped by other languages—and in this way distance, absence and loss become a mode of enunciation. The German language has survived, but it is now a 'meta-German,' a 'counter language,' a creation of 'uber-setzung,' a passage to the other side of history" (Simon

2012: 16; see also Nouss 2010: 38). Here Simon is talking about a singular language (German) that is layered on top of earlier languages, cultures, and community references, a monolingual language full of losses and absences, many captured hauntingly in Celan's writing/translating, the German language created in and by translation.

Rethinking translation, not as a short-term product or a process, but as a cultural condition underlying communication, or as a long-term cultural repercussion emerging after a translation, is, I admit, difficult, and certainly Simon's Celan example is particularly hard to comprehend. In such an analysis, "originals" and "translations" merge and distinctions between "home" and "foreign" tend to disappear. Premodern, modern, and postmodern forms are fluid. Indeed, the entire system of discourse upon which translations are described dissipates. What is it like to think of translation without a native language or homeland? How do people who have immigrated, emigrated, been displaced, absorbed, and expatriated conceive of translation? What are the allegiances of the young to nation-states and national languages? Despite the progressive nature of the new cultural studies programs, hyphenated designations describing the "new" subjects have never been enjoyed by those to whom the terms have been applied: the so-called Asian-American, Afro-American, Amer-Indian peoples have invariably found such labels limiting and discriminatory. Most just want to be referred to as everyday people. No "we" and no "they"; just the same for everyone.

The good news is that new categories of thought are emerging, internalizing the above system of distinctions and generating new ones, with highly creative results. In my research, which is derived from studying translation within the borders of the United States, but also influenced by ideas from abroad, I have found productive concepts generated by Latin American scholars, including Fernando Ortiz's concept of "transculturation," Octavio Paz's use of translation as "transformation" and "recreation," and especially Haroldo de Campos's various neologisms, including "transcreation," "transtextualization," "transparaization," "transillumination," and most provocatively, "transluciferation mefistofáustica." All of these neologisms allow for a certain degree of rewriting, often paying particular attention to the peoples and languages of the receiving culture. Thus, in this book, I loosely use the term "rewriting" to refer to such transgressive approaches. While many of these conceptual terms have been deemed marginal and exceptions to "standard" translation, I suggest that the margins may be larger than the center, that the exceptions may outnumber the norm, and that all translators transform texts to varying degrees.

Young people using new media have taken such "rewriting" processes to new heights: authoring blogs, spinning the news, adapting music and film, creating YouTube pastiches, devouring comics, playing games, expanding upon original characters in fan fiction, and crowd-sourcing translations, all taking standard texts, regardless of the original language, and rewriting them in new terms and genres. If European musicians want to riff on American jazz, they can adapt the "original" (which has probably undergone numerous versions already in source and target cultures) or merely consult any number of renditions already "translated" in their particular cultures. Or if an Asian theater director wants to produce a European classic, say by Goethe or Shakespeare, learning the source language is often optional, as many translations, productions, adaptations, films, abridgements, and educational versions saturate the receiving culture. Many systems of authority—publishing companies, governments, churches, established journals, and professional organizations—are being bypassed, breaking apart old structures that lent authority (and copyright legislation) to authors and translators and instead putting the power in the hands of a new and open generation. Indeed, there is a process of democratization going on in the translation industry, one that I find liberating. Small presses, Internet sites, and crowd-sourcing platforms proliferate. The description that works best for me is one in which translation is seen not as an uncritical form of importing a text from the outside, but rather listening to the outside and then drawing upon inward reserves and experiences from within each individual's experiences and multicultural heritage. Translation originates from abroad, yes, but it also resonates from within. In this context, translation is viewed as part of the very living substance of both the source and target text—a living, malleable, formable matter. Instead of thinking in terms of the self and other, in which the "other" is translated into the "same," instead of thinking in terms of the source and the receiver, instead of thinking in terms of the native and the immigrant being labeled "different" or "foreign," I suggest that we rethink translation by getting rid of the many dichotomies and reimagining the cultural foundation in terms of all peoples being rewriters.

Today, I suggest that scholars broaden their categorical thinking and learn from youthful discoveries, postmodern approaches, postcolonial evolutions, transnational migrations, and psychoanalytical investigations to see how such non-translational discourses and interdisciplinary fields inform translation studies. The intersections may be revealing. What if indigenous and immigrant struggles with adaptation, assimilation, and resistance were viewed not as the exception, but as *central* to cultural production? In this new global age, I suggest we all live in a translational culture, or better said, translational cultures, always in an ongoing process of movement and maneuvering, invariably traversing boundaries, changing and adapting as needed, buying, consuming, borrowing, interpreting, and translating. I argue that rather than thinking about translation as a somewhat secondary process of ferrying ideas across borders, we instead think about translation as one of the most important processes that can lead to revitalizing culture, a proactive force that continually introduces new ideas, forms or expressions, and pathways for change.

In this book, the theories underlying this investigation are multiple and admittedly eclectic. In *L'illusion de la fin* or *The Illusion of the End*, Jean Baudrillard suggests the current age is characterized by a period of "rewriting everything." (1994 [1992]: 12). Roland Barthes posited "The Death of the Author" (1968) and in "Des tours de Babel" (1985), Derrida locates original writing in an unlimited process of semiosis. All writing is increasingly viewed as a form of rewriting. While I plan to go into more detail in the chapters that follow, for those who know my work, concepts from deconstruction have been influential. Derrida's dismantling of the power and prestige of the original, directly and indirectly, figures prominently. As is well known in translation studies circles, in "Des tours de Babel" in which he discusses Benjamin's "The Task of the Translator" (1968a [1955]), Derrida destabilizes any concept of original writing, suggesting instead every text is a translation or better said a translation of a translation (of a translation). Derrida argues that no original can exist without its "other," in this case a multilingual yet untranslated voice, just as throughout his work, he cannot think of similitude without difference, presence without absence, truth without fiction, semantics without polysemy, a cure without poison, hospitality without hostility, or, repeatedly, an author without translation. Original texts, Derrida supposes, always carry with them their silent, deferred twin, the translational other, that unseen, unheard but always ongoing process of translation that occurs beneath the surface. In *Monolingualism of the Other; or the Prosthesis of Origin* (1998 [1996]), Derrida writes:

> —*We only ever speak one language* ...
> (*yes, but*)
> —*We never speak only one language*...
> is not only the very law of what is called translation. It would also be the law itself as translation.
>
> (Derrida 1998 [1996]:10, italics in original)

The kind of translation to which Derrida is referring is not the kind studied by translation studies scholars. Rather, it is a much deeper foundational *pre-original* condition located at the very roots of culture (see Gentzler 2008: 29–31). Perhaps the Simon example about the multilingual site of the city of Czernowitz comes closer to Derrida's definition. Translation is viewed as always present but nevertheless as an out-of-sight ongoing process, one that is admittedly difficult to discern, but one that Latin American immigrants to North America or North African immigrants to Europe only know too well. Derrida's definition has frustrated translation studies scholars over the years as this form of translation does not appear (at least on the surface) in any empirical text. Rather, as soon as a translator decides on one word, phrase, or concept, this ineffable translational aspect disappears, slipping away as the selected term or phrase crystallizes. Derrida posits the necessity of the possible-impossible nature of writing that always contains the forbidden yet nevertheless indirectly present nature of translation.

While Derrida's thinking about translation scares away some translation scholars, in many ways, his thinking about translation is hardly new to practicing translators. Every translator is faced with choices and has a myriad of options to draw upon from a multitude of linguistic possibilities from at least two and often more linguistic and cultural systems, all of which have advantages and disadvantages. Many translators feel that no translation is ever complete. For every single, monolingual word chosen, other alternatives are not selected and covered up. I suggest that rewriters, especially Third World writers translating/rewriting Western canonical works, or minority writers striving for acceptance under a dominant majority, have a sense of the deconstruction/reconstruction paradigm that both illuminates not just the translation process, but also the entire act of writing altogether. One of the reasons we see so many rewritings, adaptations, and furtherings in today's culture is that the translations to date have proven insufficient to the multiple possibilities offered by certain works. Today I suggest that all writing is rewriting, or better said, a rewriting of a rewriting of a rewriting, and translation—intralingual, interlingual, and intersemiotic—plays a significant role in that process.

To put it into psychological terms, the urge to rewrite is only natural. In the introduction to the anthology *Translation, Adaptation, and Transformation* (2012), Laurence Raw explores the psychological dimension to such underlying demands to rewrite and adapt. Going back to Freud's *Interpretation of Dreams* (1913 [1899]), he sees translators as both trying to bring a foreign text across a linguistic border, but also subjecting themselves to a complex process of wish fulfillment (Freud 1913 [1899]: 154; Raw 2012: 8). Since the wish to be fulfilled frequently conceals hidden thoughts, translators tend to disguise their texts with unconscious obfuscations, a process of self-censorship. Raw suggests that translators construct such a façade, manifest everywhere in terms of their self-effacement, in a belief that they are better serving the source language text. Issues of fidelity to the foreign source text, which often close off many options and creative solutions, are deeply embedded. Perhaps a healthier model may be for the translator to "look beneath the source-text's surface," to discover other levels of meaning and then to create an image of that text that may better represent the whole (Raw 2012: 9). In short, Raw recognizes that a certain degree of rewriting is acceptable. Translators, however neutral and impersonal they strive to be, cannot help but resort to their creative drives, drawing on their emotions, attitudes, and associations as they attempt to better represent the original. Turning to Jean Piaget's *The Origin of Intelligence in the Child* (1953), Raw suggests that translators might enrich their understanding by *not* being afraid to adapt the text to a new environment. Just as when children encounter new words and ideas, they learn to organize the new knowledge in and around structures already available to them. Piaget argued that restructuring data in one's own terms could lead to increased understanding of structures not only of the child's language but also new structural possibilities. Experimental processes, not copying or mimicry, are needed to allow for an open encounter with differences as well as the discovery of new terms with which to express that difference. Returning to Freudian terminology, the ego, as it were, establishes a defense mechanism that prohibits certain kinds of understanding of linguistic and cultural difference. Processes of rewriting and adaptation help break down such barriers, liberating the translator to limit the processes of repression and open the self up to forms of creativity and transformation that are not only fundamental to translation but allow the self to grow (Raw 2012: 10). Breaking the stranglehold of slavish adherence to the original text invariably results in *better* translations in many ways. Every translator, in a quite natural sense, consciously or unconsciously, engages in such rewriting practices.

Perhaps postmodern theory offers the best source for finding conceptual terms to articulate the ideas that follow in this book. While there are many versions of postmodern theory, if there is a unifying factor, it involves rewriting. This leads to a whole generation of postmodern theorists who conceive of every form of writing as a rewriting. For example, in *The Illusion of the End* (1994 [1992]), Jean Baudrillard discusses culture as experiencing the ever-increasing process of "agonizing revision," "reviewing everything," and "rewriting everything" (Baudrillard 1994 [1992]: 12). Further, in *Simulacres et simulation/Simulacra and Simulation* (Baudrillard 1994 [1981]: 12–15), Baudrillard suggested that all forms of writing create images, or better said, images of previous images—all regenerating upon each other to the point that the "original" disappears. While I do not agree with much of Baudrillard's pessimistic view of the future, on the matter of rewriting he and I find consensus. Images of images, copies of copies, and although he does not mention translation specifically, translations of translations, build upon and inform each other not in a linear, but in a continual and mutually informing process. His theories challenge translation theories that posit sources and targets or senders and receivers. Texts, according to Baudrillard, *circulate* rather than originate; fixed target cultures or fixed receivers can never be located as such. Perhaps because we spend more time on the Internet and electronic texts have become easier to copy and paste, never before have art, music, film, and translations been easier to search, scan, reproduce, and send. There can be no doubt that taking an existing text and copying, pasting, tweaking, tweeting, cropping, and recaptioning have taken translation and rewriting to a new level. Future translation studies scholars are going to have to deal with such issues.

Derrida, Freud, and Baudrillard tend toward theoretical extremes. Translation and rewriting tend to be about making choices and stopping that endless chain of semiosis. While the *mise en abyme* may be attractive to poststructural thinkers, translators and rewriters work in more concrete situations. All translation is a decision-making process and generates results that can be studied about selection, foregrounding, highlighting, and emphasizing. In this book, I argue that *both* the awareness of that unlimited semiotic chain *and* the act of choosing certain terms and forms of expression, despite awareness of their limitations, are the characteristics of translation in the twenty-first century. More in tune with my thinking about translation and rewriting, and indeed forming a basis for this book, is Susan Bassnett and André Lefevere's work on translation and rewriting. For example, in "Proust's Grandmother and the Thousand and One Nights: The 'Cultural Turn' in Translation Studies" (1990), which serves as the introduction to their historical volume *Translation, History and Culture*, Bassnett and Lefevere wonder if anyone today actually reads *À la recherche du temps perdu*, either the French, which is seven volumes long and thousands of pages, or in translation, most of which are shortened or partial versions. Rather, they suggest, people are *more* familiar with abridged versions, excerpts in anthologies, and summaries. Non-professional contemporary readers are much more likely to have seen the movie *Swann in Love*, a mere excerpt of the first volume, and to think about the main character as looking more like the British actor Jeremy Irons, who played Swann in the 1984 Franco-German movie directed by Volker Schlöndorff. For Bassnett and Lefevere, this new form of translation—interlingual and intersemiotic; adapted and rewritten—is increasingly the trend, and they were more willing to branch out to consider adaptations in film, music, television, and theater. Bassnett and Lefevere felt that translation studies scholars needed to include rewriting in their corpora and consider both written translations as well as the circulating rewritings of those same texts. Narrow definitions of what constitutes a translation have hindered the field from following Bassnett and Lefevere, and it is time to begin that endeavor.

While translation studies scholars have not come up with a discourse with which to analyze such an expanded corpus, scholars in literary and cultural theory certainly have. I mention two in the Introduction who frequently resurface throughout this book. In *Palimpsests* (1997 [1982]), Gérald Genette discussed a variety of forms of rewriting and coined the term "hypertext" to refer to rewritings, which has assumed resonance for a new generation of scholars. In the introduction, Gerald Prince cites Genette as arguing that "any writing is rewriting" and that literature is always "in the second degree" (1997 [1982]: ix). Genette studied a variety of types of rewriting—from imitation, parody, pastiche, caricature, to even plagiarism—and various strategies employed—from translation, prosification, and versification, to transtylization, reduction, and augmentation. Every act of reading, of writing, of translation, involves acts of choosing certain elements, privileging certain ideas and forms of expression. He writes that even in a complete edition, many readers "pass (over)" certain parts, and this "spontaneous infidelity" alters the conception of the work. Genette, too, asks, "How many scrupulously read the *Recherche du temps perdu* from beginning to end?" (1997 [1982]: 230). He adds, "To read means to *choose*, for better or worse, and to choose means to *leave out*" (1997 [1982]: 230, emphasis in original). Genette was remarkably well read in major and minor works of World Literature in French translation, citing illuminating examples from translations of Homer, Virgil, Cervantes, Jules Verne, Walter Scott, and James Fenimore Cooper by both great and lesser-known French translators.

Some have called Genette an "open structuralist" (1997 [1982]: ix), bridging the gap between poststructuralism and translation, always on the lookout for the relationships between the texts, how both writers and translators read and rewrite one another. Rather than focus on the "text itself" and its self-contained unity, he instead looked at "relations between texts" and "the ways they reread and rewrite one another" (1997 [1982]: ix) in a perpetual transtextual performance, how rewriters play with previous texts and reshape them into new images of their own. Unfortunately, Genette had little to say about translation itself, merely one short chapter of four pages out of a 490-page book. The chapter itself is not that informative, oscillating as it does between Maurice Blanchot's concepts of untranslatability in "La Poésie de Mallarmé est-elle obscure?" (1943) and Eugene Nida's concept of everything is translatable in his and Charles Taber's *The Theory and Practice of Translation* (1969). Ironically, in subsequent chapters on other forms of rewriting, Genette comes closer to Bassnett and Lefevere's definition. Further, in the process, he also provides a critical vocabulary for analysis for the multiple techniques of rewriting, which include transposition, transmetrification, transtylation, reduction, augmentation, abridgement, summary, commentary, continuation, and intervention, most of which are supported by examples drawn from translation.

Finally, in this book I often refer to the Canadian theorist Linda Hutcheon, who in *A Theory of Adaptation* (2006) discusses the new age of translation and rewriting. No longer content with a simple comparative analysis of a source text into target text or of a novel into a film, Hutcheon allows for TV, radio, music, opera, ballet, websites, video games, theme parks, YouTube and other forms of new media. She argues that *all* writing is a form of storytelling and that the storytellers are multiplying and finding new forms of outlet. Hutcheon explodes traditional definitions of and loyalties to fidelity and instead turns to forms of intertextuality to make her points. She even uses "adapted text" instead of "source text," as all "originals" have already been adapted as well. In today's world, viewers often *see* a production before they *read* the book. At some point, the two become indistinguishable. She becomes very interested in the different modes and how they interact, and in the *specific* processes of rewriting. She is also quite open to the collaborative and creative processes involved in rewriting and adaptation, as frequently original writers, translators, adapters, rewriters, and directors work in a more ensemble process.

In the second edition of *A Theory of Adaptation* (2012), rewritten and now co-authored with Siobhan O'Flynn, even more platforms and media are introduced, including iPads, iPhones, YouTube, fan culture, and social networking sites. Hutcheon and O'Flynn ask if the changes are one of *degree* or of *kind*, coming down in favor of something *new* happening in many instances, such as in the art world where installations have become increasingly interactive. In "The Work of Art in the Age of Mechanical Reproduction" (1968b [1955]), Walter Benjamin suggested that the aura of original had changed in the age of printing and mass reproduction. So too, do I argue, that the aura of translation has changed in the era of electronic reproduction. The new media not only alters how authors and translators write, translate, and rewrite stories, but also alters how readers and viewers navigate the rewritten text. Close-ups, cross-tracking, and links to tangential texts now allow readers to enter the text and to manipulate the reading process, turning receivers into authors or, better said, rewriters themselves. Questions of control, authorship, and authority are raised. Copying becomes a new form of creativity; modifying a text becomes a new form of authorship. New terms are needed, and Hutcheon and O'Flynn begin the process, such as introducing terms such as "transmedia producers" for what has hitherto been referred to as "authors" or even "adapters" (2012: 181–82). These are all matters with which translators are well familiar, but are also issues translation studies scholars have been slow to discern. I hope to begin such an engagement in the chapters that follow.

In the first chapter, *"A Midsummer Night's Dream* in Germany," I look at Shakespeare's *A Midsummer Night's Dream*, suggesting that Shakespeare, too, was a rewriter from the beginning. Drawing material from Chaucer's "A Knight's Tale," Theseus's *Plutarch's Lives*, Ovid's *Metamorphoses*, Spenser's *Fairie Queene,* and King James's *Daemonology*, among other sources, Shakespeare crafted a play that is all about translation and transformation. Again, I look at the translational culture of Elizabethan England, a great age of translation there that served as a platform for Shakespeare's work. I next look at translational elements within the play, of which there are many. Then I turn to the play's first translations, some of which were co-terminus with the first productions in London, as the play traveled early and often to Holland, Germany, and Scandinavia, led by a group of traveling English players. The reception in northern Europe was crucial, as the play may have been performed more often abroad than in England. I suggest that the play, sometimes deemed unperformable by British critics, was kept alive via translation. Finally, I look at the post-translation rewritings of the play, which are considerable, including Mendelssohn's *Overture*, Max Reinhardt's theater productions in Germany and subsequent Hollywood film in the United States, and George Balanchine's ballet, using Mendelssohn's music, for the New York City Ballet.

In the second chapter "Postcolonial *Faust*," I discuss all the creative neologisms for rewriting developed by the creative writers and translators in Brazil, suggesting that their various forms of cannibalizations of European texts serve as a kind of a model for new world and postcolonial translators, who were often more open and creative in their approach. First I look at the translation culture of the *Sturm und Drang* and later classical periods in

Germany, a prolific age of translation that preceded and/or was coterminous with Goethe's writing of *Faust*. Moreover, the German cultural inheritance was being formed by translation from Greek and Roman classics and from Central and Eastern European folklore, upon which Goethe drew heavily. Goethe himself constantly rewrote, making changes, additions, and deletions to the Faust legend, beginning with his *Urfaust* as early as 1772 and ending with *Faust II* in 1832, 60 years later. I then turn to the translation history of *Faust* into English, where there were dozens of translators. Finally, I discuss the post-translation repercussions, which again are multiple: the number of silent films during the early part of the twentieth century is astounding alone. Novel adaptations, music versions, and theater productions proliferate.

In the third chapter "Proust for everyday readers," I review Susan Bassnett and André Lefevere's work on translation and rewriting, which I argue has held up very well. Then I look at one of their chosen examples, Proust's *À la recherche du temps perdu*, which offers not only two superb translations into English, but also a marvelous series of rewritings in novels, films, theater, comics, and even art, including the Volker Schlöndorff film, through Harold Pinter's film script, and up to a series of paintings by Andy Warhol. In this chapter, I talk about pre-original culture and the international nature of the Belle Époque in Paris, which provided the cultural conditions for the emergence of a writer such as Proust, and the post-translation repercussions of the translations of Proust that have impacted any number of fields, including film, art, and especially creative writing. Finally, I look at the translational aspect of the original text, as Proust was constantly rewriting the text, cutting and pasting passages, adding new material, rephrasing old material, and circling from the end back to the beginning in terms of his aesthetic perspective. Proust was still revising right up until his death in 1922 and never had a chance to look at the proofs of the final three volumes, leaving it to his editors and heirs to put the last books in final form. As scholars issue new "final" versions of the originals, translators have to scramble to get the revised translations to capture a portion of the ever-growing market.

In the fourth chapter "*Hamlet* in China," I look at the two-way flow of ideas and prevalence of rewritings over translations in the contemporary world. *Hamlet* traveled to China first in 1904 with Lin Shu's "translations," which were characterized by two forms of rewriting: first, Lin Shu did not speak English, so a bilingual colleague read to him a sight translation of *Hamlet*, and then Lin Shu rewrote the story with Chinese characters, settings, beliefs, and prose style. Second, the version read out loud was not a translation of Shakespeare, but a translation of Charles and Mary Lamb's abridged version, primarily aimed at children. Thus, *Hamlet* arrived in China via a rewriting of a rewriting of an oral translation. Lin's translations were very popular, produced on the stage many times and issued in several editions, indeed, for many years being the only version available in China.

With the May Fourth Movement during the 1920s, new translations were issued, but the precedent of rewriting remained strong. Traditional Chinese predominates, and allusions to Chinese classics prevailed. Newer versions of *Hamlet* in China included multimedia versions such as *Hamlet, Hamlet*, performed in Hong Kong, reflecting both the classic image of English actors on video, and live Chinese actors interpreting the text on stage; and *Who Kills the King*, with three different styles—puppet show, Chinese opera, Western opera—and three different versions of the "To be, or not to be" soliloquy.

Let me now turn to the first chapter on the travels of Shakespeare's *A Midsummer Night's Dream*, which took a long journey through Germany and across northern Europe and into Russia, before returning to Western cultural capitals such as Paris, New York, and eventually London. The play's transformations were many, into vaudevillesque theater, a musical overture, a Russian ballet, and a German film, many of which became better known than the Shakespeare play itself. The analysis that follows includes sections on (a) the translational culture *preceding* the original; (b) the translational elements and themes *within* the text; (c) traditional translations; and (d) a post-translation analysis of rewritings and adaptations, some derived from the translations, but others based on intermediary forms of rewriting. This pattern of focusing on not just the translations of the text, but of the pre-translational culture giving rise to the original, the translational elements within a so-called monolingual text, translation proper, and the post-translation after-effects of translation continues in subsequent chapters on *Faust*, *À la recherche du temps perdu*, and *Hamlet* in China. The chapters are loosely organized around a chronological order, beginning with Elizabethan-Age British, followed by German romanticism, Belle Époque French, and twentieth-century Chinese modernization. While the texts themselves are "canonical," the translations and rewritings are of every variety—from translations of "great books" editions, to counter-culture, cannibalized, postcolonial, and feminist contemporary versions.

Bibliography

Barthes, Roland. 1968. "La mort de l'auteur." *Manteia 5*. "The Death of the Author" (1977), trans. Stephen Heath, in Stephen Heath, ed. *Image-Music-Text*. London: Fontana, 42–48.

Bassnett, Susan. 1980. *Translation Studies*. London: Methuen.

Bassnett, Susan and André Lefevere. 1990a. "Proust's Grandmother and the Thousand and One Nights: The 'Cultural Turn' in Translation Studies." In Susan Bassnett and André Lefevere, eds. *Translation, History and Culture*. London: Pinter.

Bassnett, Susan and André Lefevere, eds. 1990b. *Translation, History and Culture*. London: Pinter.

Baudrillard, Jean. 1994 [1981]. *Simulacres et simulation*. Paris: Éditions Galilée. *Simulacra and Simulation*, trans. Sheila Glaser. Ann Arbor: University of Michigan Press.

Baudrillard, Jean. 1994 [1992]. *L'illusion de la fin*. Paris: Galilee. *The Illusion of the End*, trans. Chris Turner. Stanford: Stanford University Press.

Benjamin, Walter. 1968a [1955]. "The Task of the Translator," trans. Harry Zohn. *Illuminations*. New York: Schocken, 83–110.

Benjamin, Walter. 1968b [1955]. "The Work of Art in the Age of Mechanical Reproduction," trans. Harry Zohn, ed. Hannah Arendt. *Illuminations*. New York: Harcourt, Brace and World, 217–52.

Blanchot, Maurice. 1943. "La Poésie de Mallarmé est-elle obscure?" In *Faux Pas*. Paris: Gallimard, 125–39.

Bloom, Harold. 1997 [1973]. *The Anxiety of Influence: A Theory of Poetry*. Oxford: Oxford University Press.

Campos, Haroldo de. 1981. *Deus e o Diabo no Fausto de Goethe*. São Paulo: Perspective.

Campos, Haroldo de. 1986. "The Rule of Anthropophagy: Europe under the Sign of Devoration," trans. María Tai Wolff. *Latin American Literary Review* 14(27): 48–60.

Derrida, Jacques. 1985. "Des tours de Babel." In Joseph Graham, ed. *Difference and Translation*. Ithaca: Cornell University Press.

Derrida, Jacques. 1992. *Acts of Literature*, ed. Derek Attridge. London: Routledge.

Derrida, Jacques. 1998 [1996]. *Le Monolinguisme de l'autre: ou la prothèse d'origine*. Paris: Galilée. *Monolingualism of the Other: or the Prosthesis of Origin*, trans. Patrick Mensah. Stanford: Stanford University Press.

Freud, Sigmund. 1913 [1899]. *The Interpretation of Dreams*, trans. James Strachey and Anna Freud. London: Hogarth Press.

Genette, Gérald. 1997 [1982]. *Palimpsests: Literature in the Second Degree*, trans. Channa Newman and Claude Doubinsky. Lincoln: University of Nebraska Press.

Gentzler, Edwin. 1993. *Contemporary Translation Theories*. London: Routledge.

Gentzler, Edwin. 2008. *Translation and Identity in the Americas*. London: Routledge.

Hutcheon, Linda. 2006. *A Theory of Adaptation*. London: Routledge.

Hutcheon, Linda and Siobhan O'Flynn. 2012. *A Theory of Adaptation*, revised edn. London: Routledge.

Jakobson, Roman. 1959. "On Linguistic Aspects of Translation." In Reuben A. Brower, ed. *On Translation*. Cambridge: Harvard University Press, 232–39.

Kristal, Efraín. 2002. *Invisible Work: Borges and Translation*. Nashville: Vanderbilt University Press.

Lecercle, Jean-Jacques. 1990. *The Violence of Language* London: Routledge.

Lefevere, André. 1992. *Translation, Rewriting, and the Manipulation of Literary Fame*. London: Routledge.

Nergaard, Siri and Stephano Arduini. 2011. "Translation: A New Paradigm." *Translation: A Transdisciplinary Journal*, Inaugural Issue: 8–17.

Nida, Eugene and Charles Taber. 1969. *The Theory and Practice of Translation*. Leiden: Brill.

Nouss, Alexis. 2010. *Paul Celan, les lieux d'un deplacement*. Paris: Le Bord de l'eau.

Piaget, Jean. 1967 [1953]. *The Origin of Intelligence in the Child*, trans. Margaret Cook. London: Routledge.

Proust, Marcel. 1989 [1871–1922]. *À la recherche du temps perdu*, ed. Jean-Yves Tadié. Paris: Gallimard, Pléiade Editions.

Raw, Laurence, ed. 2012. *Translation, Adaptation, and Transformation*. London: Continuum.

Shakespeare, William. 1978. *A Midsummer Night's Dream*, ed. Harold F. Brooks. London: Methuen.

Simon, Sherry. 2006. *Translating Montreal: Episodes in the Life of a Divided City*. Montreal: McGill Queens University Press.

Simon, Sherry. 2012. *Cities in Translation: Intersections of Language and Memory*. London: Routledge.

Spivak, Gayatri Chakravorty. 2003. *Death of a Discipline*. New York: Columbia University Press.

1 *A Midsummer Night's Dream* in Germany

The most widely traveled production of Shakespeare has been Peter Brook's 1970 *A Midsummer Night's Dream*, which went on a world tour, played in dozens of countries, and was performed more than 80 times. This was, of course, Brook's famous Shakespeare-in-a-white-box production, the largest and longest international tour ever attempted by a British theater company. This production served to export Shakespeare to the world, and it remains one of the most famous. Yet, other than a review from Zagreb by a British journalist (Beauman 1973), an acting edition of the script by Glen Looney (1974), and a few photographs, no further record exists of Brook's production. There is no video or audio recording, and reviews are scant. Brook's play broke with all performance traditions—no pageants, no castles, no woods, and no Elizabethan or Athenian costumes. Brook also deviated from the performance tradition by leaving the language of the play intact. Most innovative was the set, designed by Sally Jacobs, a plain white box with two doors and ladders along the walls leading to a catwalk above the stage.

Historically, the main problem in staging *A Midsummer Night's Dream* has been how to portray the fairies and stage the magic. Brook's solution was to drop trapezes from above upon which the fairies, to illustrate flight, could swing. To show the magic, the actors practiced juggling and acrobatics, techniques derived from Western circuses and Chinese acrobats. The character Puck was particularly adept at the acrobatics, lending a swift and energetic nature to the magic world, one less constrained by human corporeal limitations. With this production, Brook transformed Shakespeare from a historical play to a contemporary one, from a national tradition, with its Anglo-Germanic and Greek-Latin roots, to an international one, and from an Elizabethan play to a postmodern one, full of parody and self-reflexivity. For Brook, Shakespeare had relevance and meaning in an increasingly complex and global world.

The *Midsummer* world tour poses many questions for translation and interpreting scholars, including in what language were the programs and press releases? Were prologues, epilogues, summaries provided? How many in the respective audiences knew English and how well? Was *chuchotage*

Figure 1.1 Midsummer in a white box, set design by Sally Jacobs. Scene: Bottom
     "translated" with Titania, (III.i.122) Peter Brook, dir. *A Midsummer
     Night's Dream*, RSC, 1970, © Reg Wilson.

available? Surtitles? Puck claimed to be able to say his famous last lines of
"If we shadows have offended,/Think but this, and all is mended" (V.i.423–
4) in 13 different languages. Were local interpreters hired to facilitate communication? I suspect that involved behind the scenes were many translators
and interpreters.

   Theater is of necessity ephemeral, and it was Peter Brook's intention
not to leave a video or audio record. There was a Japanese recording, but
Brook requested the tape be destroyed because he felt that a film could
never reproduce the theater experience, especially with a play as imaginative as *A Midsummer Night's Dream* and with a set as minimal as Sally
Jacobs' (Brook 2013). How much or little of the performances were
adapted to the local languages and cultures will forever remain a mystery,
but Brook was keen on inventing *new* ways to communicate with audiences, creating an international form of semiotics and taking advantage of
international theater conventions. Although born in London, Brook had an
international background; his parents were both Jewish immigrants from
Latvia. In addition, the acting theories of Antonin Artaud (French), Jerzy
Grotowski (Polish), Vsevolod Meyerhold (Russian-German), and Bertolt
Brecht (German) served as strong influences. How the play evolved from its
initial tour of central Europe through its final stages also remains unknown,
but how could it *not* change as the actors developed skills while performing for non-English speaking audiences? Comedy is, after all, very cultural.

Bottom's bawdiness might be hysterical to some and offensive to others. How literary texts are adapted, translated, and performed is one of the main concerns of this book. This chapter looks at the ways in which *A Midsummer Night's Dream* travels, initially to Germany by the traveling English players, later to Russia via intersemiotic translations in music and ballet, and finally back to the English-speaking world through film and other rewritings.

The discussion of how texts travel has become one of the leading topics of a new generation of scholars studying World Literature, including David Damrosch (2003), Theo D'haen (2012; D'haen et al. 2012), and Franco Moretti (2000, 2003); not unsurprisingly, translation and rewriting figure heavily in those considerations. The study of World Literature is not new; it dates back to the age of Goethe in Germany. There, creative writers, scholars, and translators intended to build the repertoire of German-language literature by importing classical and contemporary forms to try to raise German-language literature to the standards of the best writing in the world. Many countries, especially new and emerging nations, have gone through a similar process, using translation to import new forms and genres, and rewriting those forms into "original" writing of their own. The German model is worth looking at more carefully.

Compared to other countries in Europe, Germany was late to nationalization, late to establishing colonies around the world, and late to industrialization and economic development. While the country today seems entrenched in the strength of its industrial expertise, strong economy, and great literature, in many ways Germany of the eighteenth century was adrift, often looking to French, Greek, or Latin texts for inspiration, creating via translation an imported cultural heritage. All of the canonical writers of the period also translated: Gottsched from French; Voss from Greek; Herder from Central European languages; Schiller from English; Goethe from Italian; and Schlegel from English. The first group of scholars/writers to coin the term *Weltliteratur* were Germans: August Ludwig von Schlözer wrote a history of World Literature (Schlözer 1792–1801), and Christoph Martin Wieland, an early translator of *A Midsummer Night's Dream*, used the concept in a note to his translations of Horace (D'haen 2012: 5). But it was Johann Wolfgang von Goethe who took the term and made it into an international concept, fueled by his lifelong obsession with the writing and rewriting of the *Faust* legend (see Chapter 2).

In his conversations with Johann Peter Eckermann, Goethe first referred to his concept of *Weltliteratur* in a similar vein, aware that a changing world with its new printing and shipping technologies allowed for a wider international circulation of texts. In his *Gespräche mit Goethe*, Johann Peter Eckermann reports Goethe as saying: "I therefore like to look about me in foreign nations, and advise everyone to do the same. National literature is now a rather unmeaning term; the epoch of World literature is at hand, and every one must strive to hasten its approach" (Eckermann 1982

[1835]: January 31, 1827). According to his biographer John Williams, Goethe read authors in Greek, Latin, Italian, French, and English, plus a variety of folk literature in German, Nordic, Central European, and pre-Hellenic traditions (Williams 1998: 6–7). However, Goethe's conception of World Literature was not just of classical and European origin; particularly later in his life, he developed an expanded understanding of World Literature while reading Chinese, Indian, and Persian literature, albeit in French translation.

In *What is World Literature?* (2003), David Damrosch takes up this definition of World Literature derived from Goethe and revises it in the following manner: "I take world literature to encompass all literary works that *circulate* beyond their culture of origin, either in translation or in their original language" (Damrosch 2003: 5, emphasis added). For Damrosch, World Literature is less a sum game and more of a *movement* activity: World Literature is literature that circulates, that travels. His idea of circulation has a postmodern twist to it, recalling the definition posited by Jean Baudrillard above (see Introduction) that texts today circulate rather than originate. Unlike some scholars of World Literature today, Damrosch is open to translation as one of those vehicles for circulation. In the conclusion to *What is World Literature?* Damrosch talks about certain patterns emerging from his research: "World literature is an elliptical *refraction* of national literatures" and "World literature is writing that *gains* in translation" (Damrosch 2003: 281, emphasis added).

The term "refraction" recalls Lefevere's usage when speaking about translation. He uses the word in the articles "Mother Courage's Cucumbers: Text, System and Refraction in a Theory of Literature" (1982); "On the Refraction of Texts" (1984); or "Shakespeare Refracted: Writer, Audience and Rewriter in French and German Romantic Translations" (1993). Damrosch's positive view of the contribution of translation to the definition of World Literature is insightful, particularly his definition of literature that *gains* in translation, which calls to mind Walter Benjamin's concept of literature that lives on [*fortleben*] in translation. Damrosch argues:

> As it moves into the sphere of world literature, far from inevitably suffering a loss of authenticity or essence, a work can *gain* in many ways. To follow this process, it is necessary to look closely at the *transformations* a work undergoes in particular circumstances, which is why this book highlights the issues of *circulation* and *translation*.
>
> (Damrosch 2003: 6, emphasis added)

Accordingly, this chapter does not just focus on how texts travel, but also how they go *back*, for translation is a multidirectional activity, and increasingly international translations and rewritings are having reciprocal effects on the source cultures. In this chapter, I look at how *A Midsummer Night's Dream* travels both to Germany and then back to the English-speaking world.

The path leading up to Brook's production of *A Midsummer Night's Dream* is a long and varied one. But before turning to translations and rewritings of the play, I examine the foundations upon which the play is built. The first two sections of this chapter discuss (1) translational culture in Elizabethan England and (2) Shakespeare as a translating author. Section (3) turns to *A Midsummer Night's Dream* in seventeenth-century Germany; (4) to *A Midsummer Night's Dream* in eighteenth-century Germany; and (5) nineteenth- and twentieth-century rewritings as the play begins to circle back to English-language cultures. Finally, (6) I return to Peter Brook, international theater, and twenty-first-century rewritings.

Translational culture in Elizabethan England

Post-translation studies does not just look at the translated texts, but also looks at the translational culture that serves as a foundation for an emerging work of World Literature. Many claim that Shakespeare was a genius, but during the age of Shakespeare and the English Renaissance, the concept of authorship was different than it is today. Most of Shakespeare's plays have earlier sources from which he borrowed heavily. Indeed, during this period, much of the Italian Renaissance was being "translated" into the backwater English culture—not just Dante, Ovid, Boccaccio, Tasso, and others, but Italian theater, music, art, architecture, gardens, cooking, wines, dress, movement, and manners. As Marjorie Garber says in *Shakespeare After All*, "In the Renaissance, the notion of *inventio*, with its etymological root in 'finding,' referred to the discovery, by search or endeavor, of ideas or images that could be used in rhetoric" (2004: 19). "Inventio" derives from *invenire*, or "to come upon," "to discover," or "to find."

In *A Midsummer Night's Dream*, Shakespeare made use of many sources, drawing upon the opening lines of Chaucer's "The Knight's Tale" in *The Canterbury Tales*, the "Life of Theseus" from *Plutarch's Lives*, and Ovid's *Metamorphoses*, most likely from Arthur Golding's 1567 translation. The fairies are inspired by Celtic and Germanic folklore, popular culture, previous plays in London, Spenser's *Faerie Queene*, and from King James VI of Scotland's musings summed up in *Daemonology* (1597). This is not to diminish Shakespeare's originality; it is just to say that the concept of authorship was *different* at the time. Borrowing, rewriting, adaptation, even plagiarism, were more permissible (cf. Chaucer's rewriting, borrowing from Boccaccio and others in "The Knight's Tale"), and Shakespeare as a rewriter was the most brilliant of the age, changing the very definitions of both rewriting and authorship. Indeed, *A Midsummer Night's Dream* thematizes those very translations/transformation/metamorphoses. Reality is translated into dreams and dreams back to reality. Which comes first? In terms of creative writing, I suggest, discoveries during the Elizabethan Age were less inspired and more *imported*, translated from antiquity, Italy, France, Holland, Germany, and other countries.

Thus to fully understand the emergence of Shakespeare's *A Midsummer Night's Dream*, one needs to come to terms with the fundamental role translation played in the culture of the Elizabethan period. Shakespeare did not travel much nor was he particularly well versed in foreign languages. Nevertheless, the foreign languages came to him: the histories that he consulted, the cultures on which the tragedies, and the stories on which many romantic comedies are based, invariably were imported from abroad. Up until the fifteenth century, England ruled portions of northern France, a fact well documented by Shakespeare's history plays about the medieval kings, such as *Henry IV*, Parts I and II, and *Henry V*. In these dramas, many of the English rulers speak several languages, including French, or married into the continental aristocracy; Henry VII (r. 1485–1509), for example, spoke Welsh, French, Latin, and English. James V of Scotland (r. 1513–42) married a French woman, and their daughter Mary Stuart (r. 1542–67) signed her name the French way, "Marie." Latin remained very strong in government, university, and aristocratic circles. In the early sixteenth century, English, or better said, Anglian dialects of English, were used primarily by the uneducated, and the language lacked the breadth and diversity needed to sustain a World Literature. Early Modern Britain was multilingual from within: the northern English dialect was different from the southern; people in Cornwall spoke their own brand; Scots English and Irish English differed, not to mention the Irish Gaelic, Scottish Gaelic, and Welsh languages. Language unification began to coalesce during the sixteenth century, and with Elizabeth's reign, which started in 1558, the English language, while still in flux, became better established.

In terms of her efforts to unite England, Elizabeth is well known for many qualities, including her foreign policies such as defeating the Spanish Armada, and domestic policies such as securing the Church of England, but underestimated is her role of advocating *translation*, which contributed both to her foreign and domestic policies, and helped establish an identifiable British literature. In *Translation: An Elizabethan Art* (1931), F.O. Matthiessen opens his book with the following:

> A study of Elizabethan translations is a study of means by which the Renaissance came to England. The nation had grown conscious of its cultural inferiority to the Continent, and suddenly burned with the desire to excel its rivals in letters, as well as in ships and gold. The translator's work was an act of patriotism.
>
> (Matthiessen 1931: 3)

Matthiessen writes insightfully about the fundamental importance of translation in the development of English literature, finding translation, rather than a footnote, *just as important* as trade, exploration, science, politics, or war. By comparing the British translations to the original sources, Matthiessen highlights the aspects of the source texts most valued in British culture. He pertinently asks, who the translators were, which texts were selected and why; who read those texts and what repercussions those translations had on larger cultural development. The questions Matthiessen addressed, are all questions I raise in this book. In one passage Matthiessen writes:

> [The Elizabethan translator] had an extraordinary eye for specific detail. Whenever possible he substituted a *concrete image* for an abstraction ... The result was an increased liveliness, a heightened dramatic pitch that often carried the words into a realm of imagination and feeling unsuggested by the original. Theoretically there may be no defense for such a method of translating, but in practice, it succeeded as no other method could. For it made the foreign classics rich with English associations; it took Plutarch and Montaigne deep into the national consciousness.
>
> (Matthiessen 1931: 4, emphasis added)

Matthiessen covered four translators in his book: Sir Thomas Hoby, translator of Castiglione's *The Courtier* (1561); Sir Thomas North, translator of Plutarch's *Lives* (1579); John Florio, translator of Montaigne's *Essays* (1603); and Philemon Holland, translator of many classical writers, including, Livy (1600), Pliny (1601), and Plutarch (1603). While Holland was the most distinguished translator of the age, Matthiessen could have picked from a dozen other translators, since during this period, nearly everything from Latin and Greek became available in English; much of the Italian literature, stories, and art came across; plus many works by non-British European explorers were translated. The Bible together with Protestant theology also arrived, and humanist ideas from abroad flourished. Even more popular forms such as French romances, Spanish picaresque, and Nordic folklore appeared (see Table 1.1).

Among the talents of Queen Elizabeth I (1533–1603), was her proficiency in multiple languages: she often spoke with her ambassadors in foreign languages and spoke Latin when visiting Oxford or Cambridge. She also translated texts from and into Latin, French, and Italian, including epistles by Cicero and Seneca, religious works by Calvin and Marguerite de Navarre, and Horace's *Ars poetica*. Her translation expertise played a formidable role in her domestic and foreign policies and lent her confidence and command of many complex discussions and negotiations. While critics of previous generations have denigrated her translation work, recent scholars are taking her work more seriously, as well they should. Certainly discourses on translation formed a large part of her identity, and she, in turn, greatly influenced the age. Janel Mueller and Joshua Scodel have collected Elizabeth's translations in an impressive two-volume set of more than 500 pages in *Elizabeth I: Translations 1592–1598* (2009).

Elizabeth's education in translation was typical for the period. In rhetoric and classical languages, she was required to translate from Latin and

Table 1.1 Translations during the Elizabethan Age (1558–1603)

Date	Translator	Original
1557	Sir Thomas North, *Diall of Princes*	*Reloj de Principes* (1529) by Antonio de Guevara (Spanish; North trans. from the French).
1561	Sir Thomas Hoby, *The Courtier*	*Il Cortegiano* (1528) by Count Baldessare Castiglione (Italian).
1566	William Painter, *Palace of Pleasure*	60 stories from Herodotus, Boccaccio, Plutarch, Livy, Tacitus, Giraldi, Mandello, De Navarre, and others (Italian, French, and Latin).
1566	Richard Addington, *The XI Bookes of the Golden Asse*	*Asinus Aureus* (late second century) by Lucius Apuleius Madaurensis (Latin).
1567	Arthur Golding, *Metamorphoses* (new editions in 1575, 1587, and 1603)	*Metamorphōseōn librī* (8 AD) by Publius Ovidius Naso (Latin).
1568	Various translators under supervision of the Church of England, *The Bishop's Bible*	Βιβλία (*Bishop's Bible* based on Hebrew, Aramaic, and Greek).
1570	Sir Thomas North, *The Morall Philosophie of Doni*	*The Fables of Bidpai* (Italian) of *Panchatantra* [पञ्चतन्त्र], (third century BC), Sanskrit collection of animal fables.
1577	Raphael Holinshed et al., *Chronicles of England, Scotland, and Ireland*. Second edition issued 1587 (the version used by Shakespeare)	Holinshed worked as a translator for Reyner Wolfe (Netherlands), who was working on a universal history of the world, but died before completion. Holinshed, translating from Latin, French, and Scots, worked in England, Ireland, and Scotland. Sources were many (mostly from Latin and French, but also Greek, Irish, Welsh, and Scots).
1578	John Florio, *Firste Fruites*	A collection of hundreds of proverbs from Italian, including a translation of Guevara into both Italian and English (Italian and Spanish).
1579	Sir Thomas North, *Lives of Noble Grecians and Romans* (with 2nd and 3rd editions in 1595 and 1603)	Βίοι Παράλληλοι (100–155 AD) by Lucius Mestrius Plutarchus (Greek, via Jacques Amyot's French *Vies des hommes illustres* (1470)).
1580	John Florio, *A Shorte and Briefe Narration of the Two Nauigations and Discoueries to the North-weast Partes called Newe Fraunce*	*Brief recit* (1545) by Jacques Cartier (French translated into Italian as *Navigationi et viaggi* by G.B. Ramusio and into English by John Florio).
1584	James VI of Scotland (later King James I of England), *Urania* into Scots	*L'Uranie* (1574) by Guillaume de Salluste Du Bartas (French).
1588	Thomas Kyd, *The Householder's Philosophy*	*Il padre di famiglia* (1580) by Torquato Tasso (Italian).

(*continued*)

Table 1.1 (cont.)

Date	Translator	Original
1590	Mary Sidney, Countess of Pembroke (Sir Philip Sidney's sister), *Antonius*	*Marc Antcine* (1578), play by Robert Garnier (French).
1591	John Florio, *Second Frutes*	Thousands of Italian proverbs (Italian and Latin).
1595	Thomas Kyd, *Pompey the Great, his faire Cornelia's Tragedie*	*Cornélie* (1574) by Robert Garnier (French).
1598	John Florio, *Worlde of Words*	An Italian–English dictionary with 46,000 words.
1598	George Chapman, *Iliad*	Ἰλιάς (1194–84 BC) by Homer (Greek).
1600	John Florio, *The Essais of Michell Lord of Montaigne*	*Les Essais* (1580) by Michel de Mongaigne (French).
1600	Philemon Holland, *The Romane Historie*, with outline of lost books by Livy and guide to topography of Rome	*Ab Urbe Condita* (25–27 BC) by Titus Livy (Latin).
1603	Philemon Holland, *The Philosophie, commonly called, the Morals*	Ἠθικά [*Ethika*] [Moralia] (100 AD) by Plutarch (Greek via Latin translation).
1603	James VI of Scotland becomes James I, King of England. He appoints 54 translators to work on the new *King James Bible*. In 1611, 47 translators complete the Old Testament and in 1612 the New Testament.	Based on the *Bishop's Bible* (1568), plus selected translations from Tyndale's, Coverdale's, Matthew's [Rogers'], Witchchurch's, Kramer's, and the Geneva Bible (Hebrew, Latin, Greek, and rewritings of earlier English translations).

Greek into English, and then back-translate her work into the original. Translation served as a way not just to import texts and ideas, but also to polish modes of expression and manners. The exposure to translation in education thus helped serve as a unifying force within Tudor England. It also served to enlarge the British lexicon, especially in the humanities, as new words were imported from other European languages. The evolution of sixteenth-century England from its early provincial, divided, and fragmented state to a unified and powerful nation under Elizabeth was thus very much tied to the practice of translation. I argue that the translational culture of Elizabethan England serves as a *precondition* for the emergence of a writer such as Shakespeare.

This culture was exemplified by one of Shakespeare's primary sources, Arthur Golding (1536–1606), who translated more than 30 works from Latin into English. Shakespeare, of course, consulted Golding's translation of Ovid's *Metamorphoses*, which appeared in 1567, and was published in four further editions. Other Ovid translators followed, but Golding's

remained popular. Golding translated *Metamorphoses* faithfully but flu-
ently into verse, with a rhyming iambic heptameter, which might seem
awkward, but which reads easily, a bit like a 4-3-4-3 ballad. Other translations by Golding included Caesar's *Commentaries* (1563), the geography
of *Pomponius Mela* (1585), *Aesop's Fables* (1590), and a host of works by
sixteenth-century Protestant leaders, including John Calvin's commentaries
on the Psalms (1571). Golding's influence upon the evolution of England,
thus, was not just literary, but also religious and political as Elizabethan
culture evolved from a Catholic country to a Protestant one (Head 2006:
444–45; Birch 2009: 424).

Another influential translator upon Shakespeare was Sir Thomas North
(1535–1604), best known for his translations in English of *Plutarch's Lives
of Noble Greeks and Romans* (1910 [1579]), which he translated from the
French edition, the first volume of which, dedicated to Queen Elizabeth,
was published in 1579. Further editions, with additional entries, came
out in 1595 and 1603, right during Shakespeare's writing of *Midsummer*.
North not only provided the historical background for plays such as *Julius
Caesar*, *Coriolanus*, and *Antony and Cleopatra*, but also characters for the
plays and, in some cases, such as in *Antony and Cleopatra*, some of the very
speeches themselves. Illustrative of the age, North did not translate from
original texts; rather he translated from Jacques Amyot's French translation
of Plutarch's *Lives*, rewriting Amyot's work to heighten the emotional force.
Shakespeare does much the same to North's rewriting. North's work was
tremendously influential on all writers of the period, not only for the content but also for his literary style, which helped raise the register and import
many Renaissance French expressions.

Perhaps the most influential translator upon Shakespeare was John
[Giovanni] Florio (1553–1625), an Italian who moved to London and
served as a tutor to James I. Florio considered the English language barbaric
and English manners lacking; one of his goals via his translations was to
teach the British better manners and a more sophisticated form of speaking. He spent much time tutoring the British royalty and clergy in Italian
and French as well as developing bilingual teaching materials, including an
Italian–English dictionary published in 1598. He was well known for his
translations of a series of Italian proverbs, collected in two editions called
First Fruits (1578) and *Second Fruits* (1591) and translations of works such
as Jacques Cartier's *Navigations and Discoveries* (1580) and Boccaccio's
Decameron (1620). Florio's most influential work on the period, and on
Shakespeare himself, was his translation of Michel de Montaigne's *Essays*
(1892–93 [1603]), published in three volumes. Gonzalo's speech from *The
Tempest* (II.i.856–74), for example, is very close to a passage in Montaigne's
"Of Cannibals." In *Shakespeare's Debt to Montaigne* (1925), the scholar
G.C. Taylor lists more than 750 words and phrases from Shakespeare not
used previously, but that *first* appeared in Florio (Taylor 1925: 49–51,
58–66). Matthiessen (1931: 161) sees "striking similarities" in the speech

and thought of Montaigne and Shakespeare, suggesting that Shakespeare was influenced by Montaigne in much the same way readers today are by Shakespeare. Florio and Shakespeare also were contemporaries; they read the same books, knew the same people, and witnessed the same events.

Sixteen of Shakespeare's plays have Italian plots and demonstrate an intimate knowledge of the Italian, language, culture, and geography. Florio and Shakespeare shared translation strategies. In "Translata Proficit: Revisiting John Florio's translation of Michel de Montaigne's Les Essais," Oana-Alis Zaharia tells us that "casting himself in the role of a 'foster-father,' Florio foregrounded the idea of translation as *rewriting of the original text into a new creation*" (Zaharia 2012: 115, emphasis added). Florio felt free to make additions, summarize, expand, and add rhetorical flourishes. One of his goals was to introduce humanist thought, which was picked up in Shakespeare in his depiction of natural man. The title of Zaharia's article is drawn from Florio's quoting the Latin proverb *Translata, proficit arbos*, or "a tree makes progress when transplanted," but he deliberately shortens it to *translata proficit*, or "what is translated increases/augments/advances" (2012: 120–21), a common understanding of the role of translation in Elizabethan England, and a theme developed in this book.

For Shakespeare as well as most Elizabethans, the most significant translated text was the Bible. Elizabeth I was not only Queen of England but also head of the Church of England. When England was Catholic, the head of the Church was the Pope, and Bible translation into English was banned. Translation studies scholars well know the case of the Bible translator William Tyndale (1494–1536), a pre-Elizabethan era translator of the New Testament into English. When the British aristocracy found out about Tyndale's project, he had to flee to Germany. In 1526, Tyndale published the New Testament in Cologne, and these Bibles, issued in pocket-sized editions, were smuggled back into England. While many were intercepted and burnt, some copies got through. In 1534, a second pocket-sized edition was printed, this time with Tyndale's name on the title page. In 1536, he was caught in Brussels, imprisoned, strangled, and burned at the stake. One year later, Henry VIII converted and licensed the first official English Bible, called "Matthew's Bible" (1537) mainly based on Tyndale's translation. The Geneva Bible, drawing heavily upon Tyndale, followed, and with the ascension of Elizabeth, the Geneva Bible became the most accepted version.

Shakespeare referred to both Tyndale and the Geneva Bible in his plays; there are thousands of references and even direct quotations in Shakespeare's work (Shaheen 1999). In *The Bible in Shakespeare* (2013), Hannibal Hamlin offers a full-length study of Shakespeare's Biblical allusions, finding, for example, that the Adam and Eve story of the fall of man as depicted in Genesis 1–3, is threaded through *Love's Labours Lost*, *Richard II*, *Hamlet*, and *The Winter's Tale*. The history plays are replete with references to the Crucifixion (Hamlin 2013: 4). Perhaps more pertinent to the argument of this book, the comedic characters frequently misquote or manipulate Bible passages. Falstaff, for example, in a brilliantly awkward fashion, alludes to Bible passages, and, as we shall see below, in *A Midsummer Night's Dream*, Bottom rewrites a passage from 1 Corinthians.

In 1568, Elizabeth commissioned a new official version of the Bible, which became known as the Bishop's Bible, because it was the bishops of the Church of England who did not want the Calvinists, who were proposing lay elders, to take over, and because many bishops were commissioned to work on the translation. But its lifespan was short-lived: while it became the version used in Anglican services, it did not displace the Geneva Bible in popular culture. In 1603, when James VI of Scotland, himself a published translator of French, became King James I of England, one of his first acts was to commission a new translation, which became the King James Bible. James hired 54 translators and scholars to work on the new Bible, which they based on the Bishop's Bible, Tyndale's Bible, and several other earlier versions. The process for the King James Bible was less of translating from an original and more a *rewriting* from existing translations. The goal, as stated in a "Translator's Preface to the Reader," was *not* to produce a new translation, but to produce from the many competing translations "one principal good one" (*Bible* 2008: lxv). Thus Bible translation was one of rewriting, a method completely consistent with the approach to translation in the Elizabethan Age. The King James Bible, sometimes referred to as the Authorized Version (AV), quickly became the standard for the field and was the preferred text in both Anglican and Protestant churches.

Furthermore, the Elizabethan Age was also the age of trade and discovery and thus oral translation was prevalent, a natural result of the news spread by explorers returning from their voyages. Situated on the docks of the River Thames, the Globe Theater and its actors, including Shakespeare, were surrounded by Spanish, French, German, Dutch, Swedish, Portuguese, Welsh, Irish, Scots, and other languages in the boats, bars, hostels, bull-baiting rings, and streets. Readers well know Elizabeth's role in setting up the East India Company in 1600. She also started several other trading companies, including the Eastland Company (1579), the Spanish Company (1577), the Turkey Company (1581), the Venice Company (1583), the Barbary Company (1585), and the Africa Company (1588) (Davies 1999: 471–72). All of these companies needed travelers, traders, and translators. Elizabeth was very immigrant-friendly, especially to those in the Netherlands and France who were persecuted religiously. As many Catholics left London, fearing British hostility, they also abandoned their houses and businesses; the Elizabethan government welcomed new Protestant immigrants from France, the Low Countries, and Germany.

English ships ventured as far as the New World. Sir Francis Drake (1540–1596), serves as one example. From 1577 to 1580, Drake became the first explorer to circumnavigate the world after Ferdinand Magellan's voyage for the Portuguese in 1519–22. Stories from such voyages naturally made exciting hearing and reading. Richard Hakluyt is best known for *Divers Voyages Touching the Discoverie of America* (1582) and *The Principal Navigations, Voiages, Traffiques and Discoueries of the English Nation* (1589–1600), which contains the first published narrative of Francis Drake's travels. Hakluyt's work is based on texts authored in English, French, and other languages, included first-hand material from other sailors and traders, and was well known to Shakespeare.

Given the number of sailing allusions in his work, some speculate that Shakespeare spent time with sailors, and perhaps even served aboard a ship. Moreover, sailors between jobs served as actors and stagehands. In addition to devouring Richard Hakluyt's translations and tales of Drake and other English explorers, Shakespeare was familiar with and fascinated by depictions of abroad from explorers such as Giovanni [John] Cabot, an Italian who sailed for Henry VII, and the Breton Jacques Cartier who sailed for France. In this chapter, I suggest that Shakespeare *reflected* the age of translation, or better, that Shakespeare's original work is a *post-translation* aftereffect that would have been impossible without the preceding translational foundation. Ben Jonson's claim that Shakespeare knew "small Latin and less Greek," may be indicative that Shakespeare relied heavily upon translation to write. During Shakespeare's time, the English language was being *formed in translation*, as was English literature and, I would argue, English identity. Without this translational basis for his work, much of Shakespeare's *oeuvre* would have been impossible: Shakespeare's knowledge of foreign languages was not only limited, but the English language itself lacked the number of words, verse forms, and genres.

Shakespeare as a translating author

When turning to Shakespeare, most translation studies scholars focus on translations of Shakespeare's plays, and seldom consider Shakespeare himself as a translator or rewriter. Shakespeare was continuously rewriting and updating his *own* work. There are no copies of the original *A Midsummer Night's Dream*, and attempts to date the first performance to 1594 or 1596 are speculative at best: early scholars base their opinion on weather almanacs stating that there was a rainy summer in 1594, or that in 1594 King James VI of Scotland was baptizing a son in Edinburgh. The play was entered into the Stationers' Register in 1600, published in the first quarto in 1600, a second quarto in 1619, and compiled in the First Folio in 1623. Thus *A Midsummer Night's Dream* had several incarnations, and there can be no doubt that Shakespeare changed many passages. The Shakespeare critic Dover Wilson points out that in the first part of Act V of *Midsummer*, many endings to the lines are changed, and inconsistencies occur where the rhythm of the verse is freer than in other parts of the play. Wilson attributes these changes to later additions, perhaps written in the margins of the manuscript (Harrison 1952: 511–12). Indeed, before the "final" version of the play was set down, in this chapter, I suggest that the performance and reception in Germany by the traveling English Comedians may have had some influence on the version staged in London in the early seventeenth century.

Marjorie Garber argues that in many ways *A Midsummer Night's Dream* was a rewriting of *Romeo and Juliet*, which Shakespeare had just completed, transformed into a comedy. Both plays have strong figures of authority, fathers who want to choose husbands for their daughters, and women who refuse to marry their chosen-for-them husbands and make plans to run away with "true" lovers. Both plays figure daylight as rigid and related to law and order, and the night as open and transformative, associated with dreams and fantasy. Key images reoccur in both *Romeo and Juliet* and *A Midsummer Night's Dream*—nightingales' evening songs, larks' morning songs, passionate speeches by strong women, talk of star-crossed lovers, and images of celestial lightning. It could very well be that Shakespeare was rewriting for an audience that wanted a comedy, a romance with Romeo and Juliet that does *not* take a late tragic turn, particularly Juliet's death. There are records of performed versions in which Juliet lives. Certainly the material was fresh in Shakespeare's mind, and many scholars suggest that *A Midsummer Night's Dream* was written very shortly after, or even concurrently with, *Romeo and Juliet*. And certainly the play-within-the-play of the "tragic-comedy" of *Pyramus and Thisbe* has this very sense of parodying, metamorphosing, translating the tragedy of Romeo and Juliet into a "tragical-mirth" (V.i.57).

In Shakespeare's *A Midsummer Night's Dream*, the story of Pyramus and Thisbe comes from Ovid, perhaps Shakespeare's most revered Latin writer, or even more likely, from Golding's translation of the *Metamorphoses* (1567), which was very popular at the time. Here is a sample from Golding's translation:

> Now as at one side Pyramus and Thisbe on the other
> Stood often drawing one of them the pleasant breath from other
> "O thou envious wall," they said, "why let'st thou lovers thus?
> What matter were it if that thou permitted both of us
> In arms each other to embrace?"
>
> (quoted by Harrison 1968: 512)

Shakespeare was probably parodying the bad translation by Golding, including the simplified and mechanical language, further mimicking Golding's English in the play-within-the-play by the "rude mechanicals" (III.ii.9). Here is Shakespeare's rewriting:

> And thou, O wall, O sweet, O lovely wall,
> That stand'st between her father's ground and mine;
> Thou wall, O wall, O sweet and lovely wall,
> Show me thy chink, to blink, through with mine eyne

[WALL *stretches out his fingers*]
Thanks, courteous wall; Jove shield thee well for this!

(V.i.172–77)

Not only does Pyramus address the wall, but also, in Shakespeare's case, the wall answers back. The similarities in the personification of inanimate objects, tone and register, of forced and awkward rhymes, and of padding to keep the meter are striking. I suggest Shakespeare was well-aware of both Ovid's Latin and the existing English translations, including Caxton's prose translation in 1480, and perhaps even earlier French translations.

While Shakespeare was not averse to commenting upon the London literary scene through his plays, in this case I see it as a comment on translation itself, where a translation can be a mere shadow of the original, just as actors are but shadows of real life. When later in the same scene Hippolyta says, "This is the silliest stuff that ever I heard," Theseus answers, "the best in this kind are but shadows, and the worst are no worse if imagination amend them" (V.i.213–15). Many critics take these lines as self-referential comments on acting. However, bad acting has at its root bad translation, and so perhaps Shakespeare is commenting on both the mechanicals' acting skills and Golding's translation, or other poor translations during the period. Theseus, who well knows the story from Ovid, as does the audience, can use his memory of the play, an image of the original itself to amend the poor performance. Moreover, amends are restored: the mechanicals' performance provides a heart-warming ending, the lovers unite, and peace reigns in the palace. Returning to the shadow metaphor of translation and performance, Puck delivers his final speech, "If we shadows have offended…" (V.i.409).

One of the most famous uses of the term "translate" in all of Shakespeare's works comes during the mechanicals' rehearsal of *Pyramus and Thisbe*. As Thisbe, played by Flute, rehearses her Ninus's tomb speech, Pyramus, played by Bottom, leaves the stage and returns with his head turned into an ass's head. Quince comments, "Bless thee, Bottom, bless thee! Thou art *translated*" (III.i.114, emphasis added). This scene may have been derived from a different text also called *Metamorphoses*, this time, a novel in Latin by Lucius Apuleius, translated as *The Golden Asse* by William Adlington in 1566. In the seventeenth chapter, Apuleius writes about being rubbed with ointment and thinking himself turned into a bird, discovers that he instead is transformed into an ass. In Adlington's translation, the passage reads:

> After that I had well rubbed every part and member of my body, I hovered with myne armes, and moved my selfe, looking still when I should bee changed into a Bird as Pamphiles was, and behold neither feathers nor appearance of feathers did burgen out, but verily my haire did turne in ruggednesse, and my tender skin waxed tough and hard, my

fingers and toes losing the number of five, changed into hoofes, and out of myne arse grew a great taile, now my face became monstrous, my nosthrils wide, my lips hanging downe, and myne eares rugged with haire: neither could I see any comfort of my transformation, for my members encreased likewise, and so without all helpe (viewing every part of my poore body) I perceived that I was no bird, but a plaine Asse.

(Apuleius 2013)

Etymologically, during Shakespeare's time, a translation could either mean a linguistic translation of a text from one language to another, or a conversion from one medium to another, often used in a more religious sense such as being translated from earth to heaven. Here Bottom is translated from human to animal form, perfectly in keeping with the metamorphoses and translation theme that runs throughout the play. The *Pyramus and Thisbe* play is already a translation of a translation; Bottom's conversion, then, produces a translation *within* a translation. If the mechanicals were making fools of themselves by their attempting such a play for a royal audience, as Bottom indicates, this new state of affairs does "make an ass of me" (III.i.115). The transformation is both physical and metaphorical. Shakespeare compounds the buffoonery when Titania awakes and falls in love with Bottom.

When reporting back to Oberon, in his "My mistress with a monster is in love" speech, Puck relates:

I led them on in this distracted fear,
And left sweet Pyramus *translated* there;
When in that moment, so it came to pass,
Titania wak'd, and straightway lov'd an ass.

(III.i.31–34, emphasis added)

Some of Bottom's transformation is derived from translation, in this case, Apuleius, translated by William Adlington as *The XI Bookes of the Golden Asse* (1566), which provided Shakespeare with some aspects of Bottom's transformation with an ass's head, and Titania's infatuation with him. Apuleius's ass also lies with several women, including those from the aristocracy, some of whom show not only erotic fascination but also, surprisingly, loving affection, similar to Shakespeare's depiction of Bottom and Titania.

Apuleius is more sexually explicit than Shakespeare, as he includes passages wondering how a woman might physically accommodate an ass whereas Shakespeare leaves this much more open to the imagination of the audience. In Shakespeare's retelling, the viewer is encouraged to think less physically and more metaphorically: in the woods, forms are distorted; shapes change and the imagination is let loose. Multiple midsummer night's dreams occur. Distinctions between dreams and reality blur and language is shown to be woefully inadequate to describe events. Translations are needed: from dreams to reality, from night to day, from animals to humans, and from figurative speech to everyday language. The distorting and disfiguring translation in the forest, both of Bottom and of the play as a whole, in fact comes *closer* to the "truth" than the ordered, rational discourse of Theseus in his palace in the city. For it is in the woods that the romances are sorted out, the mismatches corrected, and harmony restored.

The master translator of the play is, of course, Puck, who serves as a go-between for Oberon, delivering his wishes, performing his magic, and reporting back on the results. Puck is often invisible, but still watches the action, describes events, and at times intervenes. Puck is willing to translate himself into any shape or form to get the intended results. In the same scene in which he translates Bottom, he gives his transformation speech:

> I'll follow you, I'll lead you about a round!
> Through bog, through bush, through brake, through brier;
> Sometime a horse I'll be, sometime a hound,
> A hog, a headless bear, sometime a fire;
> And neigh, and bark, and grunt, and roar, and burn,
> Like a horse, hound, hog, bear, fire, at every turn.
>
> (III.i.101–7)

The neighing, barking, grunting, and roaring are, of course, the different languages spoken in the multilingual forest, and Puck speaks them all. He talks to the fairies, to animals and humans, and serves as master of ceremonies to the audience. Puck also makes mistakes, such as putting the love potion inadvertently in Lysander's eyes, but he can correct them. Puck is also a world traveler, not just well aware of events in India where Oberon first met Titania and the two fought over the changeling boy, but also when Oberon charges Puck to fetch the love-in-idleness herb (English pansy, derived from French *pensées* or "thoughts") that will make Titania fall in love with the first creature she sees upon waking. Puck travels around the world: "I'll put a girdle round about the earth" (II.i.175). Puck is both a good and bad fairy, doing and undoing his tricks and magic, usually obeying his master Oberon, but also more than capable of, and often taking delight in, his mistakes and disobediences. He thus is a perfect amalgamation of both the Germanic woodlands folklore magician and the British domestic prankster.

From where did Shakespeare gain his knowledge of fairies? While belief in spirits was in the process of slowly dying out in England during the Elizabethan Age, it was by no means eliminated; a great many people still believed in fairies and elves, and magic spells remained very popular in British folk culture. As possible sources, Edmund Spenser, in *The Shepheardes Calender* (1579) and later *The Fairie Queene*, the first installment published in 1590, influenced Shakespeare's language and his depiction of friendly rather than evil fairies. Also, I suggest, that another origin comes from indirect translations: the primary proposed source for Shakespeare's Puck is attributed to

Reginald Scot, author of *The Discouerie of Witchcraft* (1584). While Scot is not a translator per se, translation and summarization figure heavily in his work. Of the 240 authors he consulted on and about witchcraft, 212 wrote in Latin, with the few remaining in English. Much of the material for his study of witchcraft derived from cases in courts of law, where witches, often from rural villages, were still hunted, accused, and severely punished.

While Scot came out *against* the belief in witchcraft, citing religious as well as scientific reasons, there was no shortage of books published at the time *defending* witchcraft and those who still believed, including one by King James VI of Scotland called *Daemonology* (1597). King James believed in witches, sorcery, and magic, but as a good Christian, found them to be Devil-induced. He advocated that judges in courts of law trying such cases not be fooled by a little sorcery. *A Midsummer Night's Dream* was probably written before James VI published his *Daemonology*, but what Shakespeare was doing was writing down oral beliefs from a broad range of sources. The writing down of oral beliefs *is* a form of translation, and the fact that many of the sources, including stories and songs, were in Latin, Celtic, Anglo-Saxon, Norse, and Germanic further attests to the translational nature of the project. Furthermore, the play is set in Athenian woods; not only classical Greek but also pre-Platonic Greek beliefs enter into the mythology.

No wonder the fairies in *A Midsummer Night's Dream* are an odd assortment, often hybrid spirits. "Puck," according to the *Oxford English Dictionary*, is an import from Norse mythology: "puki" in Old Norse: "puke" in Old Swedish: and "puki" in Icelandic, which refers to a semi-wild spirit of the woods who often lead people astray. In *The Anatomy of Puck* (2007 [1959]), Katharine Mary Briggs looks at the origin and post-Shakespeare uses. The word "pixie," for example, a diminutive of "puck," also derived from Germanic languages, and has lasted into present-day usage, but it is a domesticated usage and less threatening (Briggs 2007; Schleiner 1985: 65). There were plenty of English, Celtic, and Welsh terms for fairies that could have served Shakespeare well, but in *A Midsummer Night's Dream* he settles on "Robin Goodfellow," more of a trickster domestic fairy, to whom Shakespeare restores many of the Germanic traits. Shakespeare's description of Puck, often attributed to Scot, is as follows:

> Either I mistake your shape and making quite,
> Or else you are that shrewd and knavish sprite
> Call'd Robin Goodfellow. Are not you he
> That frights the maidens of the villagery,
> Skim milk, and sometimes labour in the quern,
> And bootless make the breathless housewife churn,
> And sometime make the drink to bear no barm,
> Mislead night-wanderers, laughing at their harm?

(II.i.32–39)

A very similar description of Robin Goodfellow is to be found in Scot, in which "Robin God-fellow" visits the "God-wife" of the house, skims her milk and grinds her malt or mustard, and the woman, showing sympathy for his nakedness, lays out clothes for him (Scot 1964 [1584]: 85). These domestic chores and sexual innuendos do not seem to fit the Puck of *Midsummer*; Shakespeare domesticates as he translates so that his audiences can find more in common with this particular fairy.

Midsummer's Eve refers to a pre-Christian northern European pagan cele-bration, often centered on the summer solstice. During this holiday, spir-its roamed freely, witches held meetings, bonfires were lit, and dances held, songs sung, wine or beer consumed, maidens sought romance, and couplings occurred under the obscurity of darkness. In some places, such as Sweden, during the evening, flowers and herbs are picked, their magic properties being thought to be particularly potent, and references to the flora remain visible in Shakespeare's fairies. Rites of fertility are a significant part of the celebration. The largest gathering of witches is thought to have taken place at Broken Mountain in the Harz region of Germany (see section on Goethe in Chapter 2). In Shakespeare's time, the celebrations of this sort were going strong, especially in wooded and rural regions, and a pagan association with these rites remained. The fairies that attend Bottom are not satanic, for example, but kind and courteous, feeding him apricots, grapes, and figs. They prepare him a bed of flowers, put honey bags on his eyes, scratch his head, and fan him with the wings of butterflies. In fact, Oberon says when commanding Puck, "But we are spirits of another sort" (III.ii.388), ones who may play tricks at night but who have goodness at heart in the light of day.

The Bible figures prominently in *A Midsummer Night's Dream*, albeit in an ironic fashion. After his magical night with Titania, Bottom awakes and thinks that he has been dreaming. His speech begins by citing 1 Corinthians 2:9, but he ends up elaborating in a more prosodic fashion far more reveal-ing of his character:

> The eye of man hath not heard, the ear of man hath not seen, man's hand is not able to taste, his tongue to conceive, nor his heart to report what my dream was. I will get Peter Quince to write a ballad of this dream. It shall be called "Bottom's Dream" because it hath no bottom.
>
> (IV.i.209–15)

In *The Bible in Shakespeare* (2013), Hannibal Hamlin reviews the evidence of the Tyndale, the Geneva Bible, and the Bishop's Bible as a possible source for Bottom's ecstatic version. He then cites the next verse of an early Geneva Bible (1557), 1 Corinthians 2:10, which refers to "the *bottom* of Goddes secretes," a phrase derived from Tyndale's Bible, as a convincing argument that Shakespeare was again punning on a Biblical reference and appealing to a popular version that most of the theater-goers would know (Hamlin 2013: 109, emphasis added).

Sir Thomas North's translations from the *Lives of Plutarch* also appear in *A Midsummer Night's Dream*. Many details of the description of Theseus and Hippolyta are drawn directly from North, not only depictions of Theseus as the wise ruler of the city, but also the accusations made against him by Hippolyta for his previous philandering with other women, including Perigenia, Aegles, and Ariadne (II.i.77–80). In "Antique Fables, Fairy Toys: Elisions, Allusion, and Translation in *A Midsummer Night's Dream*" (1998), Thomas Moisan makes a strong case that Shakespeare translations from Plutarch are curious rather than faithful translations. Shakespeare *disassociates* himself from North as he rewrites, defining his play and version of Theseus *against* that of his source, just as he did with his rewriting of Pyramus and Thisbe against that of Golding's version. Theseus, of course, represents the law and order of the city, and his order that Hermia marry Demetrius sends the lovers into the forest in the first place. But to assume this role of strict Athenian law when it comes to love and marriage, Theseus has much to hide, and Shakespeare provides several hints of what is being covered up, i.e., Theseus's infidelities, to establish an autocratic rule. North's "translation" or "biography" of Plutarch's *The Life of Theseus* (1579) is notoriously incomplete. It is derived from, as Moisan relates, "a patchwork of what 'some say' and what 'others write,' ultimately offering a biography of Theseus definitive in all details save those concerning his parentage, his death, and the major events, achievements, and *faux pas* of his life" (Mowat 1989: 337, quoted by Moisan 1998: 286). Theseus attempts to rule his court, marry his captured bride, and assert his authority over women in general and Hermia in particular, by deciding what needs to be suppressed or allowed. Theseus also tries to distance himself from a disturbing and contradictory past. Hippolyta was not wooed and won in a process of traditional courtship; rather she is to become Theseus's wife as a spoil of war. Furthermore, Theseus has a history of infidelities, including his couplings with many earlier Greek women and mythological figures. Despite the appearances of happy resolution at the end of the play, with all the lovers united, questions about Theseus linger. Indeterminacy of translation, then, is one of the points of the play.

Moison claims that Shakespeare was well aware of these vagaries through translation, and that he was playing with, exploiting, and thematizing them throughout *Midsummer*. Fidelity in translation is related to fidelity in marriage, or better said, infidelity in translation is linked to infidelity in love and marriage. In the mechanicals' rewriting and simplification of Golding's translation of Ovid and in Theseus's rewriting and reversioning of Plutarch's *Lives*, more sophisticated versions peek through. In the character of Theseus, Titania and Hippolyta both know of Theseus's previous lives and indiscretions and are not easily fooled by the façade of strength and consistency constructed for public performances. Moisan suggests that there is a *palimpsestic* quality to Shakespeare's use of translations that the past is not easily recoverable, and, in Moisan's words, "In the process of allusive retrieval and translation...the 'discord' of the past remains audible" (1998: 292). Moisan summarizes his views on Shakespeare's translation strategy in a uniquely postmodern sense:

> As Walter Benjamin observes, "translation is only a somewhat provisional way of coming to terms with the foreignness of languages," and "translation" in the *Dream* seems persistently "provisional," wreaking change that bears with it traces of its original, producing hybrids of the foreign and the domestic that at times render metamorphosis as something akin to transmogrification, with the products thereof rather misshapen, but not totally unrecognizable.
>
> (Moisan 1998: 278, quoting Benjamin 1969: 75)

It can be inferred that Shakespeare, as a translating author, was well aware of the unreliability of his sources and of the provisional nature of those translations. As a playwright he is doing more than a translation; he is crafting a new work out of multiple sources and adding his own unique insights. However, the translational quality of the writing remains visible, and Shakespeare may well have been aware of the hybrid nature of his writing as both translational and original.

The other aspect related to Shakespeare's rewriting of earlier sources is his translation and rewritings *within* the single play itself, manifested through doublings of the characters, a form of meta-commentary on or meta-translation in the play itself. Doublings of actors were common in Elizabethan England, and in this play the obvious pairings would be Oberon and Theseus and Titania and Hippolyta. The couples' tensions and resolutions, in fact, parallel one another. So, too, does the play *Pyramus and Thisbe* offer a meta-commentary on the use of the Ovidian source for both Shakespeare's play and the play-within-the-play. The wooers Demetrius and Lysander and the wooed Hermia and Helena appear interchangeable, and in the latter case, their names are phonetically intertwined. Indeed, the structure of the play *A Midsummer Night's Dream* is highly patterned with such doublings, characters and themes translating each other, providing multiple perspectives on the same character or plot.

While Bottom's "translation" may be Shakespeare's most famous use of the term, the word itself surfaces early in the initial act when Helena wishes that she might be "translated" into Hermia (I.i.191). Jealous that Hermia has captured the love of Demetrius, Helena's opening speech when she first enters the palace runs as follows:

> O were favour so,
> Yours would I catch, fair Hermia, ere I go:
> My ear should catch your voice, my eye your eye,
> My tongue should catch your tongue's sweet melody.

> Were the world mine, Demetrius being bated,
> The rest I'd give to be to you *translated*.
> Oh teach me how you look, and with what art
> Your sway the motion of Demetrius' heart!
>
> (I.i.185–93, emphasis added)

Here the use of the term "translated" is similar to the usage in the case of Bottom, referring to a sense of "transformation," but in this instance, the translation suggests less physical change and more a personality trait. While Helena is thought to be fairer than Hermia, what she lacks is the look in the "eye," the "melody" of the voice, and the "sway" in the motion, i.e., behavior that supposedly attracts men.

Ironically, Hermia and Helena were once very much the same. In the forest scene, Puck mistakenly caused both Demetrius and Lysander to fall in love with Helena. Cursing her fate, Helena thinks that all three, Hermia included, are in a conspiracy to make fun of her lovelorn condition. In her well-known "double cherry" speech, Helena thinks back on her close friendship with Hermia when they were young:

> O, is all forgot?
> All school-days' friendship, childhood innocence?
> We, Hermia, like two artificial gods,
> Have with our needles created both one flower,
> Both on one sampler, sitting on one cushion,
> Both warbling of one song, both in one key,
> As if our hands, our sides, voices and minds,
> Had been incorporate. So we grew together,
> Like to a double cherry, seeming parted
> But yet an union in partition,
> Two lovely berries moulded on one stem.
>
> (III.ii.201–12)

The sexual innuendos of this passage have been much analyzed, but here I want to suggest that translation metaphors abound—two voices but one song; two creators making one creation; an union in partition. In this case, the one who is translated is not Helena but Hermia, who, taking on a new disposition, has abandoned her love and friendship for Helena for another goal.

The further irony of Helena's wish to be translated into Hermia is that the desire is fulfilled. First Puck mistakes Lysander for Demetrius, further illustrating the two men's similar identities; then Oberon attempts to correct Puck's error by putting the magic love potion in Demetrius's eyes; the result is that both men fall now in love with Helena. Shakespeare turns the scene into a comic one by having Helena believe neither of the two lovers' overtures, but her increasing desperation manifests itself, and the scene turns increasingly cruel. The translation of love has a dangerous, transformative aspect, which I suggest is one of the main themes of the play. In this case, old friendships dissolve, love turns to spite, trust is broken, invectives flow, and fighting breaks out, proving a sport for Puck, but one with tragic undertones, or, dare I say, of tragic mirth? If the fairies were truly demonic, one could not have wished for a more distressing outcome with the fulfillment of Helena's wish to be translated. Fortunately, these fairies, despite their bumbling, are of a different sort, and the living nightmare is turned into an awkward dream as Puck makes his amends.

Pyramus and Thisbe provides the final replication and serves as Shakespeare's best example of doubling from within: a play-within-the-play or, more accurately, a translation-within-a-translation. Ironically, as we shall see in the sections to follow, the *Pyramus and Thisbe* play enjoyed a life of its own, primarily in Germany, but also in England, and for many years was separated from the first four acts. Audiences were not only familiar with the Ovid version but also expected the bumbling mechanicals to exaggerate and add vaudevillian effects. Many of Shakespeare's ideas about translation and performance, about Shakespeare as a translational author, can be seen in the play: the rehearsals, additions to the play, and the audience's comments. The *Pyramus and Thisbe* production in *Midsummer* highlights the degrees translation travels from its source, in this case a story in Latin told by Ovid, translated into elevated English verse by Golding, parodied by Shakespeare with the mechanicals, and performed before, and in dialogue with, the aristocracy. The rewritings, abridgements, masks, disguises, subjective interpretations, imaginative inventions, and even mistakes all are emphasized in Shakespeare's depiction of the play-within-the-play. The truth in jest here may reveal more about translation than a more accurate performance might have been able to depict, and may illustrate more about Shakespeare's views of translation in particular.

The adaptation of *Pyramus and Thisbe* begins in Act III when Quince and his troupe meet in the woods and start rehearsal. Here the ensemble makes cuts, alters scenes, adds stage directions, and adds a prologue, only to be interrupted when Bottom is translated into an ass and most of the mechanicals flee. Later, Theseus calls for "an abridgement" for the evening's entertainment, which, in Lefevere's approach, represents another form of translation, followed by the famous two-line synopsis in which the genre is transposed from a tragedy to a "tragical-mirth" (V.i.57).

As the mechanicals begin their play, the performance is rude indeed, with Quince mixing up syntax, Snout as the wall conducting the opening lines, Bottom exaggerating, and Thisbe mixing up proper nouns. However, in the middle of the play, something turns, with the lion's roaring, Thisbe's fright, the lion ripping her cloak, and Pyramus finding the bloody mantle.

The commentary by the royalty in the audience consists now of merely "Well roared, Lion" and "Well run, Thisbe." (V.i.254–55). Even Hippolyta claims, "Beshrew my heart, but I pity the man" (V.i.279). The scene in which Pyramus dramatically kills himself, repeating the word "die" five times, is frequently played as a farce, but could also be performed quite slow and painful. It certainly causes Demetrius pause, who makes a sad pun with "No die, but an ace for him, for he is but one" (V.i.296), followed by Lysander's stilling "Less than an ace, man, for he is dead, he is nothing" (V.i.297), which is about as tragic a line as might be uttered. So too, after Thisbe's death, all Theseus can muster is "Moonshine and Lion are left to bury the dead" (V.i.335). Only when Bottom bounces up saying, "No, I assure you; the wall is down that parted their fathers" (V.i.337) does the mood improve, the comedy restored, and the Bergomask ensues.

Regarding translation, there are many markers. The wall dividing the two families serves as a metaphor for border crossing. In *Pyramus and Thisbe*, the lovers need to flee Babylon and meet at the mulberry tree by Ninus's tomb, paralleling the action of *A Midsummer Night's Dream*, with the lovers fleeing the confines of Athens to meet in the woods, ostensibly at Lysander's aunt's house. In some ways, the play *Midsummer* is a translation and rewriting of the *Pyramus and Thisbe* story into Elizabethan England. Further, the fact that the mechanicals perform so poorly speaks to the general state of translation in Elizabethan England, when many of the early translations from Greek and Latin were hastily performed. The palimpsest quality to Shakespeare's sources leaves us to wonder what the original might be, or if any "faithful" version will ever be produced.

Shakespeare's *A Midsummer Night's Dream* is one of the few plays for which no known single source text can be identified. I suggest that the sources are so multiple and so disparately translated and rewritten in Elizabethan England that Shakespeare could free himself from a single retelling to create anew. In "Antique Fables, Fairy Toys: Elision, Illusions, and Translation in *A Midsummer Night's Dream*," Thomas Moisan writes, "there is a curious sense in which the *Dream* seems at times to 'enjoy' an adversarial relationship with its sources, seeking parasitically, to dissociate itself from and define itself as dramatic entity against the various textual shreds and patches that it cannibalizes" (1998: 282; more on the cannibalistic metaphor follows in Chapter 2). I conclude by suggesting that this freedom in recreating *within* translation is one of the primary purposes of the *Pyramus and Thisbe* play and thus fits well into the play as a whole. Despite its abridgements, infelicities, misappropriations, subjective interpretations, and plethora of "mistakes," the working-class version of *Pyramus and Thisbe* returns Ovid to the everyday theater-goers, provides entertainment for the wealthy, and retains a form of translation *vérité* in and of itself, one created by Shakespeare as a translational author. It also prefigures further dramatic translations and rewritings of the play, to which I now turn.

A Midsummer Night's Dream in seventeenth-century Germany

England was not just importing narratives and discoveries from around the world, but it was also *exporting* to other countries, and one of its exports was theater. While Shakespeare's fame in London rose during the early 1600s, not all of his plays were successful, and one with mixed and even negative reviews was *A Midsummer Night's Dream*. While no eyewitness accounts exist to the play during the English Renaissance, there are references to seeing plays with Thisbe or Robin Goodfellow; the few other accounts only mention the mechanicals (Griffiths 1996: 9). The erotics of the play, the general disregard for authority, and, especially, Titania's relationship with the "translated" Bottom suggest it would not be presented without heavy editing. Beginning in the 1620s, the Puritan Reformation eventually led to an outright ban on *all* theater in London from 1640 to 1660. Even after 1660, in Restoration England, *A Midsummer Night's Dream* did not make a comeback. In a diary entry from 26 September 1662, Samuel Pepys writes, "We saw 'Midsummer Night's Dream,' which I had never seen before, nor shall ever again, for it is the most insipid ridiculous play that ever I saw in my life" (Pepys 1970–82 [1605–18], vol. 3: 208, quoted by Griffiths, 1996: 10). In his introduction to *A Midsummer Night's Dream*, part of the Shakespeare in Production Series for Cambridge, Trevor R. Griffiths tells us that its subsequent stage career was very limited until the *nineteenth* century: "There are only two known performances of the play under its own name between 1660 and the 1816 production of a comic-opera adaptation by the journeyman dramatist Frederic Reynolds" (Griffiths 1996: 1).

While less than popular in England, *A Midsummer Night's Dream* survived in translation and adaptation in Germany, Holland, and other North European countries. The turn of the century was the age of the traveling English players, which began as early as 1596 in Nürnberg, continued in the early 1600s, when Shakespeare was still writing his early plays, and lasted throughout the Puritan period, when Shakespeare's plays were limited or banned outright in London. Performing *before* copyright law, which was not adopted in England until the early eighteenth century, these actors felt like they "owned" the plays and could treat them as they wished. In Germany, Peter Quince became Peter Squentz; Bully Bottom became Meister Bulla-Butain; Theseus and Hippolyta became German dukes and duchesses. The mechanicals became blacksmiths, cabinetmakers, linen-weavers, and spool-makers. Scatological references were added and burlesque aspects were exaggerated, as the artisans got into staged fights when they disagree. There is one eyewitness account by Johannes von Rist, written in 1666, recounting a version he saw "in his youth," probably in Hamburg.

In *Shakespeare in Germany 1590–1700*, Ernest Brennecke offers a translation of Rist's account of the *Pyramus and Thisbe* performance by the English traveling players (Brennecke 1964: 56–68). Rist recounts the story of a king trying to marry his son to the daughter of another king, multiple wedding celebrations, a group of rude mechanicals, a list of plays that the artisans could perform, including the offer to play *Pyramus and Thisbe*. The king and his party go off on a hunt, and the mechanicals, which include a rat-catcher, chimney sweep, ropedancer, and broom-maker, begin to decide which play to perform and, after much bumbling, finally select *Pyramus and Thisbe*. The parts get divided up, again with much slapstick, and rehearsals begin. Soon, the king returns, and the play begins, first with music that includes six Jew's harps, a fiddle, and an out-of-tune lute, and then a prologue with very nonsensical rhymes. Monsieur Pickleherring—the fat, stout, and most famous comedian in German vaudeville—who plays Thisbe by wearing women's clothing, disguising his large beard, and using a tiny little-girl voice receives the biggest laughs. Pyramus is played by the chimney sweep, the moon by the ropedancer and the lion by the broom-maker. The lion roars, Thisbe runs off, and the lion, having just given birth, pours blood onto the stage. Pyramus enters, sees the blood, and fears that Thisbe has been killed. According to Rist, Pyramus says:

> There, there it lies; I've spied it out:
> My Thisbe's robe, beyond all doubt.
> A lion's rent her, bit by bit;
> In terror do I almost shit.

(Brennecke 1964: 66)

Pyramus beats his breast with a cudgel and proceeds to die. Thisbe returns and in grief falls upon the chimney-sweep, seizes his cudgel, and beats herself on her bottom, again to the delight of the audience, and dies moaning, "Now I am dead." Pyramus springs up, announcing, "but see, I am not dead" (Brennecke 1964: 67) and merriment ensues, including dancers with candles parading around the corpses.

The English Comedians were soon performing less in English and more in German as German actors translated, rewrote, and performed Shakespeare's plays in German, with no mention of Shakespeare as the author. For example, in 1663, Andreas Gryphius's *Absurda Comica oder Herr Peter Squentz* (Brennecke 1964: 72–104) appears in German, but by this time the school-master and master of ceremonies Squentz and the main counselor and clown Pickleherring, among others, were deeply ingrained in the German psyche. Gryphius's play includes Pickleherring, who again plays Pyramus; Master Bulla-Butin, a bellows-maker who plays the wall; a blacksmith who plays the moon; a cabinet-maker as the lion; a linen-weaver as the fountain; and a spool-maker as Thisbe. The royal party includes King Theodorus, Queen Cassandra, a Prince Serenus, and a Princess Violandra. The play has three acts: the first has the mechanicals deciding upon *Pyramus and Thisbe* and rehearsing the play; the second has Squentz presenting possible selections to the king and carefully steering him toward choosing the play they have prepared; and the third contains the play itself, and includes the comments by members of the royal court. The play-within-the-play is longer than Shakespeare's, including the prologue by Squentz, a lengthy monologue by the wall, who actually has no lines in the play, and songs by the moon and the fountain. The play is full of mistakes and burlesque moments, such as Bulla-Butain smashing the wall over Pickleherring's head or Thisbe striking the lion over the head before she runs away. In one scene, the moon and the lion begin calling each other names for lingering on the stage once their lines are over:

KRIX [THE MOON]: You've got the kind of mug that I'd like to stuff with hogshit and make pretty with donkey-farts. Get the hell inside, or I'll speed up your legs!

KLIPPERLING [THE LION]: You crippled frenchified smith! You'll speed up my legs? I've as good a right to see the comedy as anybody else.

(Brennecke 1964: 97)

The name-calling, naturally, is followed by a burlesque fight, which involves the moon hitting the lion over the head with the lantern and the two falling into and destroying the fountain. In another example, when Pyramus discovers Thisbe's bloody mantle, he exclaims: "Ein grimmes Thier hat sie erbissen,/Mir ist als hätt' ich in die Hosen gesch. [By grisly beast has she been bitten,/Into my pants I feel I've shi–ten!]" (Brennecke 1964: 99). The lovers both die, the spring comes back to life, and Pyramus carries Thisbe off the stage.

These two plays, one an account of the English players, and the second a summary of a very similar German version, are given as an example of the *Midsummer Night's Dream* performances by the English players in Germany during the seventeenth century and the great success they enjoyed there. The Internet site "Shakespeare in Europe" compiled by the University of Basel, Switzerland, lists all the Shakespeare translations into European languages. Remarkably, during the seventeenth century, the *only* translations, except one Portuguese version that was performed aboard a ship, are into German or Dutch (see Table 1.2).

Only after nearly two dozen Shakespeare translations and rewritings published in Germany over the course of the seventeenth century, and what must have been many more performances, do we again see a new British publication: the 1709 Nicholas Rowe edition. This too was a form of rewriting, since it was the first edition to modernize the spellings and divide the plays into acts and scenes. The next English edition was Alexander Pope's in 1723, which also corrects spellings and punctuation, deletes some lines thought not to be by Shakespeare, and makes cuts—especially lines thought to be in poor taste—and adds footnotes. Many of these changes survive in current English editions, reinforcing the argument that editing is also a form of rewriting.

Table 1.2 Seventeenth-century translations of Shakespeare into German and Dutch. (Based on 'Shakespeare Translations: A Chronology' (online))

Shakespeare translations: a chronology

1604	German	Anon. *Von Romeo und Julitha*, performed at Nördlingen (Creizenach, S. XLI)
1607	Portuguese	*Hamlet*, performed by Captain Keeling's crew on board of the *Red Dragon*, running translation by Lucas Fernandez in Sera Lyoa (Sierra Leone) on board of a European ship
1611	German	Anon. *Teutsche Komedia der Jud von Venedig, auss dem engelländischen* (Creizenach, S.XL) (*Merchant of Veni*ce)
1620	German	Frederick Menius: *Englische Comoedien 2. Theil*
1621	Dutch	Adriaen Van den Bergh (Utrecht): *Titus Andronicus* (lost)
1623	**English**	**John Hemminge and Henry Condell:** *The First Folio*
1624	German	2nd edition of Frederick Menius's *Englische Comoedien*
1626	German	Anon. *Tragoedia von Romeo und Juliette*, (Dresden, 2. Juni, 29. Sept.) (Cr. XLI) Anon. *Tragoedia von Julio Cesare* (aufgeführt in Dresden, 8. Juni 1626) Anon. *Tragoedia von Lear, König in Engelandt* (aufgeführt in Dresden, 26. Sept.) Anon. *Tragoedia von Hamlet einen Printzen in Dennemarck* (Dresden)
1627	German	Anon. *Tragikomödie von Julio Caesar*e (aufgeführt in Torgau 1627)
1631	German	Anon. *Julius Caesar* (Dresden, 1631)
1638	Dutch	Jan Vos: *Aran en Titus of Wraak en Weerwrak* (more than 30 editions till 1726)
1641	Dutch	First performance of *Aran en Titus of Wraak en Weerwrak* in Amsterdam
1646	German	Anon. *Tragoedie von Romeo und Julia* performed in Dresden (15th Oct.)
1650	Dutch	Matthus Gramsbergen: *Kluchtige Tragedie of den Hartoog van Pierlepon* (Pyramus and Thisbe episode from *Midsummer Night's Dream*)
1651	German	Anon. *vom julio Caesare, dem ersten erwählten römischen Kaiser* (performed in Prag)
1654	Dutch	A. Sybant: *De dolle Bruyloft, Bley-eyndend-Spel*, (*Taming of the Shrew*)
1656	German	*Aran und Titus, Oder Tragödia von Raach und Gegen-Raach* (Translation of Vos' *Aran*)
1658	German	Andreas Gryphius: *Absurda Comedia oder Herr Peter Squenz* (influenced by Gramsbergen, see 1650)
1660	German	Anon. *die Tragoedia von Cajo julio Caesare* performed at Güstrow *vom Römischen Kayser Julio Caeesare, wie er auf dem Rathhause zu Rom erstochen wirt*
1661	German	Anon. *Tragicomoedia vom Mohren zu Venedig* performed in Dresden Hieronymus Thomae: second German translation of Jan Vos' *Aran en Titus*
1665	German	Salomon Adler (shoemaker) lists "*Comedie vom König Lier auss Engellandt*"

(continued)

Table 1.2 (cont.)

Shakespeare translations: a chronology

1666	German	Anon. *von dem Könnich Liar auss Engelandt, ist eine materien worin die ungehorsamkeit der Kinder gegen Ihre Elder wirt gestraffet, die Gehorsamkeit aber belohne Lueneburg*; Drey: *Von Tito Andronicuo*
1676	German	Anon. *König Lear aus Engellandt* (performed in Dresden, July 22)
1677	German	Anon. *Tugend- und Liebesstreit* (*Twelfth Night*) in print
1693	German	Christian Weise, *Kömödie von der bösen Catherina* (*Taming of the Shrew*)
1699	German	Anon. *Tragoedia genannt Raache gegen Raache. Oder der streitbare Römer Titus Andronicus...* performed in Breslau

In this section, I argue that Shakespeare was *kept alive* through translation in Germany and the Low Countries or, better said, through the efforts of itinerant English actors performing first in English and later in translation. By the 1640s the "English Comedians" were increasingly being referred to as "English-German Comedians." In the early years, much of the "translation" was done through intersemiotic means, via miming and gestures, costumes and songs. Later, the English actors began employing German actors, and the "texts," more often than not oral adaptations, shifted into German. Thus, the actors are the translators, similar to the mechanicals performing Ovid in English in England. Without the traveling troupes, and their oral translations, the later *published* translations may not have appeared. The *Midsummer Night's Dream* version performed in Germany was heavily edited, usually including the fairies, a scene from the King and Queen, plus the rude mechanicals, including their version of *Pyramus and Thisbe*.

My point is twofold: first, Shakespeare plays that traveled abroad, including *A Midsummer Night's Dream*, were performed *more frequently* with a *more receptive audience* in Germany than in England; second, the traveling players initiate the cultural dialogue that opened the path to the later translations of Shakespeare in Germany and the rest of Europe. In the case of this particular play, the productions and adaptations in Germany kept the play alive during a period of censorship and restrictions governed by Elizabethan, Jacobean, and Puritan taste. While there are no first-hand reports of *A Midsummer Night's Dream* in England during the seventeenth century, some parts of the play, very similar to the selections performed in Germany and Holland, were performed in England. For example, a play called *Bottom the Weaver* was published in 1661 and republished in 1673 (Halio 2003: 14), with significant portions of the roles for Titania, Oberon, and Puck cut. The fairies were also popular, and in 1692, Elkanah Settle rewrote Shakespeare into an opera called *The Fairy Queen*, with music by

Henry Purcell, first produced in 1692. The text, spoken or sung, however, was *not* Shakespeare's. And while some of Shakespeare's characters were included, many new ones were added, not just fawns, nymphs, and wood-men, but also a chorus of Chinese men and women, and a dance of six monkeys. Thus, during the seventeenth century, the rewriting process was well underway.

A Midsummer Night's Dream in eighteenth-century Germany

In the eighteenth century, Shakespeare translations increased, with the French getting into the act: during the middle part of the eighteenth century, Voltaire, Pierre-Simon La Place, and Jean-François Ducis led the way, although these translations, too, were heavily adapted to conform to French literary taste at the time. The first Italian, Russian, and Spanish translations emerged during this period. Ironically, in early eighteenth-century Germany there were fewer translations and performances of Shakespeare. Influenced by the Gottsched School, Germans showed a stronger preference for French rather than English literary and theatrical conventions. But in the latter part of the century, the Germans again dominated the world of Shakespeare translations, this time not in productions intended for the town halls and market squares, but in intellectual circles and theaters. This period forms the great age of German translation, with the most important scholars— Lessing, Herder, Wieland, Goethe, Schiller, Tieck, and the Schlegel brothers— translating, editing, or staging Shakespeare. Shakespeare translation became critical to the development of original writing, the *development of a German literary tradition* as separate and independent from the French, and the emergence of Germany as a unified nation. Shakespeare offered a model to *resist* French pseudo-classicism; Shakespeare was viewed as a more natural, realistic writer than the conventional, artificial playwrights preferred in France. *A Midsummer Night's Dream*, with its forested setting, disorder and chaos, folklore, and magic, held a strong appeal and became the preferred dramatic vehicle during this period. In 1761, the *first* Shakespeare play translated by Christoph Martin Wieland was *A Midsummer Night's Dream*; in 1773 (although the manuscript has been lost), the *first* play translated by Johann Gottfried Herder was *Midsummer*; in 1773, the *only* play translated by Joseph Von Pauersback was *Midsummer*; and in 1788, the *first* play translated by August Wilhelm von Schlegel in 1788 was *Midsummer*.

In *Shakespeare in Germany 1740–1815* (1937), Roy Pascal discusses Lessing's *Literaturbrief* of 1759, in which Lessing proclaims his preference for Shakespeare over other writers and issues a call for more excitement, passion, and emotion in the German theater, which he was not feeling from the French imports. As opposed to Corneille, Voltaire, and other French neo-classical dramatists, Shakespeare came as "a bolt from the blue" (Pascal 1937: 5), yet the ground had been well cultivated during the previous century. The French influence was comparatively short-lived; and thus the turn to Shakespeare allowed the Germans to return to their roots. Using Alexander Pope's edition of *A Midsummer Night's Dream* as the original (1725), which already contained some changes regularizing the meter and eliminating some lesser-quality lines, Wieland's first of 22 translations of Shakespeare's plays was *Ein St. Johannis Nachts-Traum* (1762). Wieland translated *Midsummer* into verse, whereas the latter plays, except a few short lyrics, were translated into prose. Wieland had trouble with Shakespeare's coarse language, eccentric characters, and what he called bad taste, echoing Voltaire's criticism of Shakespeare and supporting Pope's urge to sanitize. However, Wieland was attracted to the fantasies of Shakespeare, the new morality, and Shakespeare's individualism. Wieland also published a long epic poem called *Oberon* (1780), a post-translation product, showing how his translation work infiltrated his creative work as well.

In the 1770s, the German love of Shakespeare accelerated, with Johann Gottfried Herder, Johann Wolfgang von Goethe, and Jakob Michael Reinhold Lenz leading the charge, all publishing essays on Shakespeare, translating Shakespeare, and, in the case of Goethe, producing Shakespeare on the stage. *Midsummer*, with its emphasis on the lovers' escape into the woods and flights of the imagination, became a perfect vehicle. To a degree, these intellectuals were rebelling against German bureaucracy and authority, and there was a romantic, even revolutionary spirit in the air. Leading this generation of *Sturm und Drang*, the first heave, was not an original text, but an author imported via translation. Using Shakespeare as an inspiration, these writers all called for a new form of theater, a new form of literary criticism and a new license to let their imaginations roam freely. Great men of action and women of passion were preferred; the woods and scenes in nature revered. Fairies and ghosts appeared, and even the depiction of madness becomes permissible.

This great age of translations of and essays about Shakespeare, of highly intellectual assessments of the artistry and innovations in Shakespeare, was soon followed by a wave of new Shakespeare productions on stages in many German cities, including Hamburg, Berlin, Vienna, Dresden, and Weimar. Plays were often freely translated and adapted, up until Eschenburg's revision of Wieland's translations, which came out in an accessible prose version in 1775. Actor-producers such as F.L. Schröder began producing and performing, overdramatizing the main characters at the expense of the minor characters. In some cases, happy endings were preferred, such as Schröder's first *Hamlet* that offered a different ending and in which the prince lives, or *Romeo and Juliet*, in which Juliet survives. Goethe experimented with Eschenburg's translations as well, and he also staged a version in which Hamlet stays alive. Still, performances were purified of puns and vulgar language. Indeed, in the latter part of the century, Shakespeare moved from the intellectual realm with its high aesthetics to become more amenable to the middle and lower classes. By the end of the century, Goethe found himself restoring minor characters such as Laertes, including vulgar scenes such as the gravediggers and allowing the whole tragedy to unfold. Schiller staged his translation of *Macbeth* in 1800 in Weimar, and the play was nearly fully restored, although Goethe insisted on the witches being beautiful. As the translations improved, Goethe became increasingly interested in *hearing* the lines, including the minor characters, and producing the *whole* play, which was precisely the interest of Shakespeare's greatest German translator August Wilhelm von Schlegel. After 1800, Goethe switched from using Eschenbach's to Schlegel's translations for his productions.

Germany's most famous translator, August Wilhelm von Schlegel saw a consistency, balance, and artistry throughout Shakespeare's plays, and to him all the characters and their lines became important. Even the comic characters, jesters and nurses, mechanicals and soldiers, while they may not drive the plot forward, served, in his mind, to echo, reflect, and enhance upon the main characters. These echoes, doublings, redoubling, reversals reinforce, as I pointed out above, the translational themes of *A Midsummer Night's Dream*. The processes of folding and unfolding, doubling, quadrupling images as they undergo translation and transformation, complicate and distort the ideas on the stage until the "truth" becomes very elusive. Indeed, the wealth of reflections, mirrorings, rewritings, and refractions multiplies. This too, I suggest, is the movement of *translation*, of creating a perspective of the same but not the same, ideas and myths drawn from a different language and belief system, performed on the stage in England, then doubling back across the continent from which they arose. The content, literary traditions, and allusions all have multilingual roots. I argue that the Germans, particularly the late eighteenth-century generation, saw something in Shakespeare *in translation* and well understood Shakespeare as a translating author. Late eighteenth-century Germany was simultaneously finding itself in translation and searching for a national language and identity, in a similar fashion to England's use of translation to form its identity in Elizabethan England.

In eighteenth-century England, there was little emphasis on restoring Shakespeare to its original, and no record of a full version. Rather, excerpts, abridgements, rewritings, and adaptations continued. Examples include the *Comick Masque of Pyramus and Thisbe* by Richard Leveridge, a comic version of an Italian opera of the *Pyramus and Thisbe* play-within-the-play and an opera titled *The Fairies* (1755) written by David Garrick and John Christopher Smith.

Rewritings of *A Midsummer Night's Dream* in the nineteenth and twentieth centuries

August Wilhelm von Schlegel's translation of *A Midsummer Night's Dream* not only had a revolutionary impact on the literary scene in Germany, but it also influenced other artistic fields, including music. The most famous *A Midsummer Night's Dream* performance in the nineteenth century in

Table 1.3 Were Schlegel's translations better than Shakespeare?

Some argue that Schlegel's translations of Shakespeare are *better* than the original. They are, in many ways, brilliant, retaining much fidelity and passion. Schlegel's translations did not happen overnight; instead they followed upon a generation of German translations, rewritings, essays, and performances, all improving upon each other. I illustrate my point with one example of Wieland's translation of *Midsummer*, and two from Schlegel's translations.

Shakespeare (1594)

HELENA ... Fie, Demetrius!
Your wrongs do set a scandal on my sex.
We cannot fight for love, as men may do;
We should be woo'd, and were not made to woo.
(Exit Demetrius)
I'll follow thee, and make a heaven of hell,
To die upon the hand I love so well. (II.i.239–44)

From Shakespeare's *Midsummer*, Act II, scene 1: Demetrius rejects Helena, but she will not take no as an answer, and curses him as he departs. But she follows him anyway.

Wieland (1772)

HELENA. O! schame dich, Demetrius, deine Härte
Entehret mein Geschlecht. Wir können nicht
Für Liebe fechten, wie die Männer mögen;
Gesucht zu werden, und nicht selbst zu suchen,
Sind wir gemacht! –Jedoch ich folge dir;
Und selbst der Tod von dieser werten Hand
Wird eine Hölle mir zum Himmel machen. (Sie gehen ab) (II.i.19–26)

Six lines expanded into seven. Rhyming couplets gone; Fye replaced by O; shame added. Moral wrongs changed into "dishonor." Wooing changed into seeking. Death by this "worthy" hand added.

Schlegel I (1789)

HELENA ... Pfui, Demetrius!
Du schändest mein Geschlecht, und seine heil'gen Rechte:
Wie ziemt sich, dass ein Weib um Liebe männlich fechte?
Ihr Männer seyd gemacht, um uns euch zu bemühn,
Nicht wir, voll Leidenschaft euch buhlend nachzuziehen,
(Demetrius ab)
Ich folge dir, und raubt nur deine Hand mein Leben,
So soll die Höllenqual mir Himmelswonne geben. (ab)
(II.i.271–77)

Alexandrines used instead of iambic pentameter; rhymes preserved. Wordy. "Holy right" added to men; "courting" instead of "wooing." Passion heightened. Demetrius leaves early. Compound nouns for heaven and hell.

Schlegel II (1797)

HELENA ... Pfui Demetrius!
Dein Unglimpf würdigt mein Geschlecht herab.
Um Liebe kämpft ein Mann wohl mit den Waffen;
Wir sind, um Euch zu werden, nicht geschaffen.
Ich folge dir und finde Wonn' in Not,
Gibt die geliebte Hand mir nur den Tod. (beide ab)
(II.i.295–301)

Iambic pentameter restored; rhyming couplets, tight: no added adjectives or compound nouns. "Wrongs" changed to "insult." "Scandal" changed to "dishonor." Men fighting with "weapons" added (for rhyme sake). A bit chivalric. Heaven and hell turned into passion in distress. Is "Wonn' in Not, ... nur den Tod" not better than Shakespeare?

Germany and England alike was the Felix Mendelssohn *Overture in E major*, Opus 21, titled *Ein Sommernachtstraum*, which to this day may be better-known than the play because of the famous Wedding March. What makes this *Overture* remarkable is that Mendelssohn composed it when he was 17 years old, showing how deeply ingrained *Midsummer* was in German culture. In 1826, Mendelssohn read Schlegel's translation, which inspired him to write his overture. Similar to Mozart before him, Mendelssohn was a child prodigy, writing chamber pieces by the age of 12, publishing his work by the age of 13, and by 15 writing his first full symphony. But his best-known early work, the one showing his greatest talent, was his *Overture* to *A Midsummer Night's Dream*.

Although not widely acknowledged, Mendelssohn was a translator himself. In 1826, the same year as the *Overture*, he published a translation of Terence's Roman comedy *Andria* (already an adaptation of a Greek play). Mendelssohn's translation work, not his music, qualified him for entry into Humboldt University. Further, translation ran in the family: his aunt, Dorothea Veit Schlegel, translated many works from French as well, including *Corinne* by Madame de Staël in 1807; and her husband, the philosopher Friedrich Schlegel, brother of August, was a distinguished translator of classical languages, including work by Plato. Friedrich Schlegel even provided a prose translation of *Midsummer* that Mendelssohn incorporated into his music.

Mendelssohn wrote two pieces of music for *A Midsummer's Night's Dream*. The first was the *Overture in E major*, Opus 21, romantic in nature but with certain classical forms, harmonies, and transitions. The piece is best known for its instrumental effects, such as the translation of the play's action into music, especially the strings emulating the dancing fairies, the low tones of the horns signaling tricks and mischief caused by Puck, right down to the voice of Bottom when turned into an ass. Regarding intersemiotic translation, the instrumentation is innovative, the music imitating the characters' movements and emotions. In addition, the orchestra includes a new instrument, the ophicleide (a precursor to the tuba), to better imitate Bottom's braying. Since German audiences knew the story well, they could easily imagine the light and fleeting dance of fairies or Bottom's astonishment at his transformation. The woodland scenes dominate the music: that which had stumped theater directors—how to portray the fairies by large and clumsy human beings—is easily and successfully translated into music, and further serves to keep the play alive. In 1827, the *Overture* premiered in Stettin (now Szczecin in Poland), Mendelssohn's first public appearance, but traveled quickly back to England, being performed in London as early as 1829, conducted by Mendelssohn himself, now 20 years old. Mendelssohn's music soon became very popular in England; indeed, a Mendelssohn mania hit England, with the composer returning up to eight times to conduct pieces.

In 1842, Mendelssohn wrote the second composition of *A Midsummer Night's Dream*, this time called *Incidental Music*, Opus 61. The earlier

Overture is incorporated, but in this second version Mendelssohn adds vocal songs, voiceovers, and new instrumental sections. A scherzo is added when the lovers enter the forest, and the song "Over Hill Over Dale" narrates their sleep. Oberon enters via a march, and a nocturne shadows the resolution and the couples finding their suitable partners. The Wedding March becomes an intermezzo between the fourth and fifth acts and the four chords that famously begin the first overture accompany Puck's famous speech "If we shadows have offended…"

The earlier *Overture* was simply too short to accompany a production of the entire play, and productions at the time were adding pieces from other composers to flesh out the score. The expanded rewriting allows for a full-scale production and has been frequently used in Shakespeare performances in music, ballet, theater, and film since. The composition was first played in Potsdam in 1843, with Ludwig Tieck, the famous poet, translator, and later editor of August Wilhelm von Schlegel's Shakespeare translations, including *A Midsummer Night's Dream*, as producer. Tieck was also the co-translator, rewriting and scoring Friedrich Schlegel's prose translation. They planned to publish the work simultaneously in German and in English in 1844, as Mendelssohn wanted to control the copyright of the English translation and thus prevent substandard versions from circulating. But the translation proved tricky into English, as the words had to fit the German music.

In "For You See I am the Eternal Objector" (2008), John Michael Cooper talks of the difficulties faced by Mendelssohn's translator Edward Buxton, who had to back-translate from the German into a Shakespearean English. Even though Buxton was a friend of—and in correspondence with—Mendelssohn throughout the process, he encountered many problems, especially in the final act. In the last section, Mendelssohn, who was meticulous in his review of the English translation, *changed* the music to adapt to Buxton's English version to resolve the problems (Cooper 2008: 220–21). Mendelssohn traveled to perform in England selections from the *Incidental Music* in 1844 but did not live to see the 1848 premier. After his death, Mendelssohn's popularity in England grew, and in 1858 Princess Victoria married the Crown Prince of Prussia at St. James's Palace to the music of Mendelssohn's Wedding March.

Mendelssohn's *Sommernachtstraum* music serves as a structural and aesthetic basis for many directors' productions of *A Midsummer Night's Dream* all over the world, including England. The translational background of Mendelssohn's music shows the circularity of translation: not just a one-way move from English to German, but instead a complex interplay of English to German translation, which is then rewritten as an overture, expanded into a full production, then back-translated into English made to sound like Shakespeare. An entire milieu of translational culture serves as an underlying condition for such a free-flow of language, theater, and music across multiple borders. Mendelssohn's music remains popular to this day, played by nearly all the most famous conductors, and some, such as Eugene

Ormandy with the Philadelphia Orchestra, prefer to use the *German* translation of Shakespeare's text, rather than the English. In fact, Mendelssohn's music helped *revive* Shakespeare's *A Midsummer Night's Dream* in England during the nineteenth century.

As mentioned above, productions of *A Midsummer Night's Dream* had all but disappeared from the stage in England for nearly 200 years. The only production running in England during the first part of the nineteenth century reflected the perceived problems of the play. Frederic Reynolds staged it in 1816 and again in 1833 (Halio 2003: 22–23). Yet his version could hardly be called Shakespeare's, as Reynolds rewrote the play by moving scenes around, placing the performance of *Pyramus and Thisbe* in the middle, adding many new scenes, and incorporating scenes from traveling productions, such as the mechanicals' bumblings or the fairies' dances. In Reynolds' version, the structure of Shakespeare's play and the language are difficult to discern. Audiences did not like the play. The reviewer in the *Examiner*, for example, wrote, "All that was fine in the play was lost in the representation. The spirit was evaporated; the genius was fled" (January 21, 1816, quoted by Griffiths 1996: 18). The *Times* critic went even further, "Story there is none ... There is no interest to excite the passions ... Shakespeare's words have been superseded by more foolish words" (January 17, 1816, quoted by Griffiths 1996: 19). The play quickly disappeared from the repertoire. Revived once again in the 1833 season, it appeared as a mere two-act afterpiece, again with disastrous results. The reviewer for the *Literary Gazette* this time wrote, "tawdry as a country barn and mutilated with barbarian recklessness" (December 7, 1833, quoted by Griffiths 1996: 19–20). Nevertheless, Reynolds' 1833 version was the first in England to use Mendelssohn's *Overture* (Halio 2003: 24).

The most successful and influential nineteenth-century production of *A Midsummer Night's Dream* was Madam Lucia Elizabeth Vestris's 1840 production. In contrast to Reynolds' and other productions over the past two centuries in England, Vestris returned to the language of Shakespeare, kept many scenes intact, and did not add new material. She did make some cuts; for example, some of the lines of the lovers were omitted or toned down, mostly to conform to Victorian tastes. However, she did turn the play into a spectacle, not shying away from the large number of characters or the complexity of scenery and costume. The final scene, for example, while using Shakespeare's lines, also involved more than 50 fairies flying or dancing while carrying tiny blue or yellow lanterns. She also used Mendelssohn's music, supplemented by other songs by the composer Thomas Simpson Cooke. Notably, Madam Vestris played Oberon and sang nine of the 14 songs. She felt that a woman could better portray the idea of a fairy; a woman, too, played Puck, a tradition often continued today.

Madam Vestris's production of *A Midsummer Night's Dream* that premiered in Covent Garden in London in 1840 was innovative. The reviewer for *The Spectator* talks about the "sylvan and visionary" nature of the woodlands (November 21, 1840, quoted by Halio 2003: 26). The *Theatrical Journal* reviewer finds the palace "sparkling with the countless hues of light" (May 1, 1841, quoted by Griffiths 1996: 23). With floating gauze-portrayed mists, moonlight reflecting off of watery surfaces, and lovers chasing shadowy figures, the scenes do not change but flow into each other, as in a dream. Bottom is less a mechanical clumsy buffoon and more a refined, ephemeral figure from a dream. For the first time, critics judged the play a success: the *Times* reviewer wrote: "As far as theatrical representation of this ethereal drama is possible, it was achieved last night" (November 17, 1840, quoted by Halio 2003: 24). Mendelssohn's 1826 *Overture* had a significant role in the play's success, and for the next hundred years it became hard to find a production that did not use the music. The German vision of the play finally returned to England.

I should mention one more nineteenth-century intersemiotic translation of *Midsummer*, this time into ballet. In addition to Holland and Germany, Shakespeare's *A Midsummer Night's Dream* continued its travel through northern Europe, including Denmark, Sweden, Poland, and Russia, where audiences were often more familiar with German translations than the English original. In 1876, Marius Petipa adapted Mendelssohn's music to a ballet, first performed by the St. Petersburg Ballet in Russia. Marius Ivanovic Petipa was born in France, and danced in Bordeaux, Nantes, and Paris, but moved to St. Petersburg in 1847, where he began producing ballets almost immediately. Instrumental in the construction of the golden age of Russian ballet, some consider him the most influential choreographer in ballet history. Of all of Shakespeare's comedies, *A Midsummer Night's Dream* attracts the most interest from choreographers, and Petipa's version has been revived, revised, and repeatedly staged ever since. Ballet adaptations of the play, invariably using Mendelssohn's music, continued throughout the nineteenth and twentieth centuries. Some of the more famous include Mikhail Fokine's *A Midsummer Night's Dream*, premiering in St. Petersburg in 1906; David Lichine's *A Midsummer Night's Dream* opening in Paris in 1933; and Jean-Jacques Etcheverry's *Songe d'une nuit d'été* staged in Brussels in 1955 (Ick 2011).

The most famous ballet version of *A Midsummer Night's Dream* must be George Balanchine's 1962 adaptation for the New York City Ballet. Born in 1904 in St. Petersburg, Giogi Balanchivadze learned his techniques at the Imperial Ballet School, where Pepita had served as lead choreographer. When he was eight years old, Balanchine performed in *Midsummer* as an elf in a ballet in St. Petersburg, and he could recite many lines of the play in Russian by heart. Because of the Russian Revolution, he was forced to flee, landing in Paris where there was a large Russian exile community. He soon was working for the Ballets Russes with many composers, including Prokofiev and Stravinsky, and artists such as Picasso and Matisse. In 1933, he moved again, this time to the United States, where he founded the School of American Ballet in New York. *A Midsummer Night's Dream* traveled with him. The play became his first full-length production in the United States.

Based on Mendelssohn's *Sommernachtstraum*, Balanchine added other works by Mendelssohn, including his String Symphony No. 9, *Die erste Walpurgisnacht*, and *Der schöne Melusine*, to produce a full version of *A Midsummer Night's Dream*. As with Mendelssohn's music, Balanchine's ballet glosses the first act and begins in earnest with the second. The fairies, danced by children, enter with adult elves and Puck. The lovers wander through the forest, Oberon and Titania quarrel, and the mechanicals rehearse. The plot continues to move rapidly, following the pace of the music, with the dancers miming the action. Bottom is bewitched, but is more tender than animalistic, and dances smoothly with Titania to the nocturne as the lovers go to sleep. The ballet is more sensual and elegant than burlesque and comedic. The mechanical's play is omitted, and the ballet ends in the forest, with the reconciled couples dancing (Brissenden 2011: 102).

In the ballet, Balanchine rewrites less the language of Shakespeare and instead translates Mendelssohn's music to the medium of ballet. Balanchine facilitates a full circulation of the play from England to Germany, through Russia, and then via France, back to the English-speaking world, where the play's meaning can only be viewed as enhanced. Ballet adaptations continue during the late twentieth century, including John Neuimeier's *A Midsummer Night's Dream* in Hamburg in 1977; Uwe Scholz's *Ein Sommernachstraum* in Zurich in 1989; and Amedeo Amodio's *Sogno di una notte di mezz'estate* in Italy in 1993, all choreographed to Mendelssohn's music (Ick 2011).

As Balanchine's ballet emphasized the surreal, perhaps influenced by the modernist artists he worked with in Paris, another form of artistic experimentation known as expressionism was going on in Germany. Probably the most radical theater director pioneering new effects was Max Reinhardt, who from 1905 to 1933 managed more than 30 theaters in Germany and directed up to 500 plays, before immigrating to the United States in 1933. Not only one of the most popular plays at the time in Germany but also Reinhardt's favorite play, *A Midsummer Night's Dream* was produced 29 different times in Germany, with more than 2,527 performances (Styan 1982: 51, 54). The first performance, in 1905 at the Neues Theater in Berlin, was a huge success, running for more than 500 performances. One later performance at the *Grosses Schauspielhaus* in Berlin was attended by more than 3,000 people (McQueen 2007 [1935]). At the end of his stay in Europe, Reinhardt produced an outdoor version in the Boboli Gardens in Florence, Italy, in 1933, and later in that same year in England in a park outside of Oxford. However, the most famous of his productions was not in Germany, Italy, or England; rather it was at the Hollywood Bowl in Los Angeles, staged in 1934, for which he brought in live trees to replicate the forest. A year later, in 1935, the Hollywood Bowl version was turned into a film also titled *A Midsummer Night's Dream*, directed by Reinhardt together with William [Wilhelm] Dieterle, and starring the unlikely cast of Mickey Rooney, James Cagney, Olivia de Havilland, and Joe E. Brown.

Not only is Reinhardt's *A Midsummer Night's Dream* a translation of a play into a film, but it is also a translation of a successful *German* production of Shakespeare back into English, or better said, into American-English. The Warner Brothers studio, which produced the film, was most famous for its gangster films, westerns, and comedies, and had little or no experience with classical texts or Shakespeare. It seemed strange that Warner Brothers would take a chance on a German director for a Shakespeare play. In addition, at the time of its production, Max Reinhardt could only speak German. His communication with the actors had to be translated either by his co-director William Dieterle, who had worked with Reinhardt for years in Germany, or his producer Henry [Heinz] Blanke, who had worked with Ernst Lubitsch and Fritz Lang before joining Warner Brothers. Reinhardt also hired Eric Wolfgang Korngold, an Austro-Hungarian composer who had collaborated with Reinhardt on several plays in Germany, to adapt Mendelssohn's music for the film. Korngold "rewrote" and modernized Mendelssohn's *Incidental Music*, sometimes playing whole sections, repeating parts, pulling out small portions and playing them with different instrumentation, speeding up sections, and syncopating other parts. Korngold also added new pieces from Mendelssohn's *Symphony No. 3 in A minor*, known as the Scottish Symphony, and *Symphony No. 4 in A major*, known as the Italian Symphony, as well as songs from *Songs Without Words* [*Lieder ohne Worte*], plus a few of his own short compositions. Definitions of source and target, original and translation, tend to blur under such circumstances. Just as in the play, acting merges into the music, music into a dream, dream into reality, and then back into the action, all delivered in the new medium of film.

The language of the film is the most striking. Shakespeare's text is used throughout, with only a few minor changes: updating archaisms, simplifying an occasional expression, or moving a line to another part of the dialogue. However, all the lines are Shakespeare's, with the metrics and rhyming couplets preserved. Still, given the time constraints of a feature film, plus the directors' emphasis on cinematic imagery, the play had to be shortened. As usual, Helena's lines are drastically reduced and she becomes a minor character to Hermia's lead; also, the royalty's comments on the mechanicals' performance of *Pyramus and Thisbe* are much shortened. The most striking aspect of the language is not that Shakespeare's lines were restored, but that the American-English spoken is an amalgamation of colloquial, working-class dialects, including Brooklyn gangster, southern drawl, and Midwestern twang. One London reviewer likens the language to truck drivers talking (McQueen 2007). Additionally, the actors' lack of Shakespearian training plus the American accents served Reinhardt's expressionistic purposes well.

The set for Reinhardt and Dieterle's film is exceptionally dark; in fact, many of the trees had to be highlighted in silver to be captured on film.

Figure 1.2 Oberon in the Reinhardt & Dieterle film *A Midsummer Night's Dream* (1935).

While Reinhardt's film includes Mendelssohn's music and dancing fairies, mimicking ballets prevalent in Europe, it also retains a dark side. The hybrid result combines (1) the spectacle and celebration favored by Madam Vestris; (2) a realistic side that included trees and animals; and (3) a darker, more threatening version with the cloud of twentieth-century politics lurking behind the scenes. Oberon, for example, enters riding a black horse, dressed in a villainesque black with antlers growing out of his head.

The dark palette and the branch-like antlers lend Oberon a sinister aura, and special effects are not needed to make him appear or disappear into the landscape. His bewitching of Titania to fall in love with an ass is vengeful, and it allows him to abduct the changeling Indian child. Bottom's translation into an ass seems less out of place with such an emphasis. Dark, bat-like fairies accompany Oberon, and in one dream sequence, he is shown wearing a large billowing black cape, similar to F.W. Murnau's depiction of Mephisto in his 1926 film of *Faust* (see Chapter 2). At the end of the scene, Oberon's cape envelopes dozens of white fairies, with one of the main fairies abducted and carried off by an anonymous black figure.

In the same production, Puck works for Oberon, and he too has a dark side, more goblin than Robin. His role is startling; not only does he keep most of his lines, but he also repeats and mimics those of the foolish mortals.

His laughter, while sometimes playful, more often retains a mocking or even sinister edge. His repetitions serve to provide a new angle on lines often perceived as innocent or romantic. Puck's imitations are particularly effective with the lovers in the woods, as the lovers' discomfort, alienation, and anger, already much present, are enhanced. Mickey Rooney, just 14 years old while playing Puck, received wonderful reviews from the American press, and even begrudgingly positive mention by the British papers (Halio 1995: 94–95).

The other lauded performance is that of James Cagney as Bottom. In the film, the mechanicals' roles are enhanced, as they are laced through many of the early scenes. Reinhardt well understands the seminal role of the play-within-the-play in which the mechanicals represent (and mock) the larger play. In this case, the actors' *in*experience and working-class accents prove an asset. While Cagney, de Havilland, and Brown were famous Hollywood actors, they had never been cast in Shakespearean roles. Joe E. Brown as Flute, and later as Thisbe, serves as one example. Brown grew up poor in Ohio, played professional baseball, worked in the circus, and later performed in vaudeville before turning to theater and film. Not a Shakespearean actor, Brown's face is impressionable: his large mouth is caught in a perpetual smile, his hair is slicked-down and parted in the middle, and his voice is expressively high. When cast as a woman, the burlesque traits are only enhanced, thus his role as Thisbe suits him well. Under Reinhardt and Dieterle's direction, a grotesque element in both Cagney's Pyramus and Brown's Thisbe can also be discerned from their faces, accents, and unfamiliarity with Shakespeare (or Ovid). Close-ups only enhanced the expressionistic effect.

Transparent representation is not Reinhardt's goal; this is a twentieth-century American depiction in a quasi-Victorian garb of an Elizabethan play set in Athens and directed by two Germans. The distortions are many. Reinhardt painted trees orange and silver; lighting is often from the side or the back, creating shadows across even the most innocent faces; the woods has a distinct Black Forest air; most of the fairies are Germanic. The mechanicals, while stumbling through lines and making mistake after mistake, further expose their characters. The actors do not have to play being rude; they are rude. Theseus's words "The best of this kind are but shadows" (V.i.211) take on new meaning in the Reinhardt-Dieterle production. The directors take the mechanicals and their production seriously; the working-class actors—farmers, truck drivers, ball players, and gang members with barbaric American accents—provide Reinhardt with an expressionistic bent on the long-neglected British play, giving it new life.

Reinhardt and Dieterle's film *A Midsummer Night's Dream* opened in New York and London simultaneously, plus 25 other cities in the USA and 13 other cities from around the world, making it truly an international release. The film broke the Victorian reign of light romantic music and ballet-influenced productions and opened the way for darker interpretations. It also set the stage for future film productions of Shakespeare and many of the techniques, including translating the text into visual images, adapting the music to the action, providing close-ups to enhance the intimacy of the speeches, and rewriting the language to make it more accessible.

Unlike Balanchine's ballet of *A Midsummer Night's Dream*, which spawned numerous other ballets of the play, Reinhardt's film did not generate any more films of the performance until Peter Hall's 1968 film. Still, Reinhardt's influence can be seen here. Hall first staged the play in Stratford with the newly emerging Royal Shakespeare Company in 1959 and then revived it again in 1962 with substantial changes. Restoring many previous cuts and adding a new cast, including Ian Richardson as Oberon, Judi Dench as Titania, Helen Mirren as Hermia, and Diana Rigg as Helena, this was the version translated into film. In contrast to the many fairy-laden productions played to Mendelssohn's score, Hall's production marks a break with preceding performances: no Mendelssohn, no ballet-like fairies, and no direct moonlight. Instead, a new score is heard, clouds cover the moon, and only a handful of forest spirits suffice. The setting of the forest does follow upon Reinhardt: Hall's dark green lush woods also are wet and rainy. Most importantly, instead of relying on spectacle and music to carry the play, Hall restores *all* of Shakespeare's language. Actors, not magic, drive the film, all the lines are spoken, not to the audience, but to each of the performers. Compared to Reinhardt, the diction is superb; the Shakespearean actors know not only their lines, but also their meaning and purpose, and deliver them with insight. Indeed, in Hall, translational elements and foreign influences are minimal. Most importantly, this production may be the first to deliver the *complete* Shakespeare play *A Midsummer Night's Dream* to the stage in England.

Ironically, by letting Shakespeare's language speak for itself, Hall introduces foreignizing effects. The mechanicals are less burlesque and more credible English working-class men. While their accents are not Oxonian, their diction is clear, and they set up an alternative to the heightened discourse of Shakespearean theater. The landscape is also very British, but ironically, by restoring the original Shakespeare language, Hall achieves an alienating effect. For example, the woods are not just dark green, but also drenched by rain and dripping water. Shakespeare's play does call for dark and damp: Titania's opening speech in the woods emphasizes the bad weather, including whistling wind, incessant rain, pelting rivers, contagious fogs, drowned fields, and rotting crops (II.i.81–121). The setting is one of distemper, which contributes to the confusion and dissension. Frequently, past romantic versions portray the woods as a lovers' playground, with warm summer nights, full moons, and happy dancing fairies. The woods in Elizabethan England were in fact scary places, dark, unkempt, inhabited by renegades and robbers. The fairies are very natural, too, clothed with leaves and vines, or cobwebs and flowers, as dictated by the script. Titania is alluring and Oberon sinister. The naturalism extends to Titania's bower, where her fairies, really quite natural and endearing, dote on Bottom. Even the love scene between Bottom as an ass and Titania when bewitched is affectionate and not burlesque: his eyes gleam lovingly; she kisses him full on the lips; and the two lie intimately together, caressing each other. However, the estranging effect of Shakespeare's having the Fairy Queen lie with an animal speaks for itself. Some jump cuts, camera tricks, and sound effects are employed for the fairy world, but not many are needed as more often than not the fairies seamlessly appear or disappear into the foliage. Puck has a reptilian quality with his quick movements and tongue darting in and out. The dominant alienation effect is the quickness with which the fairies speak as if they might be in an accelerated time zone.

In the final *Pyramus and Thisbe* play-within-the-play, Hall again prefers naturalism. The rude mechanicals bumble rustically as they might. Again, the cuts are remarkably few, and royal commentary on the play has been restored, but many are delivered with a sympathetic rather than patronizing tone. There is enough comedy and slapstick to keep the scene humorous and still serve as a comment on the play as a whole. Moreover, as the performance is an adaptation of Ovid's story, the awkwardness and outright mistakes by the mechanicals could be attributed to translation. The overall impression, however, is of the amateur actors' sincerity, which in this portrayal, is indulgently appreciated by the royal audience, coming closer to Shakespeare's purpose all along. Certainly it is the naturalism, as opposed to the conventions and elitism characteristic of French theater of the early eighteenth century that drew the Germans to *A Midsummer Night's Dream* in the first place. That Hall's film seems so experimental and unconventional is what makes the return of a naturalistic production to England all the more remarkable.

Return to Brook: Toward an international theater

I began this chapter with a discussion of Peter Brook's 1970 production of *A Midsummer Night's Dream* in a white box, which in many ways is the very *opposite* of Peter Hall's 1968 outdoor, naturalistic, dark, and rainy film version. Brook's interest in *A Midsummer Night's Dream* derives from his view of theater as an imaginative space that *transports* the audiences from their everyday world to the new realm of art; another form of translation. *A Midsummer Night's Dream*, with all its transformations from the real world to the dream world and from dreams back into reality, becomes a perfect vehicle. The actors serve as the translators or the mediators between the dream and actual worlds. The play-within-the-play of *Pyramus and Thisbe* illustrates Brook's aesthetic approach. According to Halio, "The key to the production, Brook announced at the first rehearsal, was the play-within-the-play" (Halio 1995: 56; Selbourne 1982: 3), further reinforcing the theme of acting as a bridge to the realm of the imagination. For Brook, it is important to take the mechanicals' performance seriously, as it serves as a metaphor for the entire play, and, according to Brook, for theater in general. While the quality of the acting may have been inconsistent, the quality of the *imagination* of the tradesmen is ever so rich. Despite the poor diction, missed lines, and awkward performance, the mechanicals still create magic on the stage, sometimes mocked but often appreciated by the royals in the audience of Theseus's court. Acting in the theater is likened to translation, as in the translation of fictional Ovidian characters into local names and places, however rustic.

Whereas many scholars see the play-within-the-play *Pyramus and Thisbe* as mirroring the play *A Midsummer Night's Dream*, for Brook, the direction goes both ways, i.e., *A Midsummer Night's Dream* also serves as a reflection of *Pyramus and Thisbe*. Ovid turned into Shakespeare turned into Ovid. Such a path of re-reflection also supports Baudrillard's thesis that texts circulate rather than originate. Indeed, there is a Borgesian postmodern element to the self-reflexivity of *A Midsummer Night's Dream*, with the two plays serving as a comment upon and parody of each other. As this chapter has shown, regarding *A Midsummer Night's Dream*, the multiple rewritings by artists, directors, and performers from many fields, including theater, music, dance, and film, have contributed to the international movement and global understanding of the play.

Just after his success with *A Midsummer Night's Dream* with the Royal Shakespeare Company, Peter Brook left England and, with Micheline Rozan, founded the Centre International de Recherche Théâtrale (CIRT), a multicultural research and production company based at the Bouffes du Nord Theater, near the Gare du Nord in Paris. The company was made up of actors from Iran, Mali, France, Greece, the United States, Spain, Portugal, and Morocco; directors from England, Romania, Armenia, and Germany. Brook stayed on until he was 83 years old, finally retiring in 2008. The Centre was primarily a training laboratory for actors, singers, acrobats, and clowns; the general goal being to develop a universal international theater.

For Brook, the boundaries between the world of experience and the world of the imagination are fluid. While no public performances are held at the Centre, the company sometimes performs in workers' districts of Paris. They also take their work on international tours to Iran, Africa, and New York. Indeed, performances are unannounced so as to attract not just a theater-going audience, but everyday people as well. There is no common language, and many of the experiments have to do with speech in a variety of ways, always looking for a direct and immediate way of communicating. While French and English predominate, the company's members also study Greek, Latin, Malinese, and Japanese. In his search for an international semiotics of theater, Brook went so far as to *invent* new, artificial languages. For example, the play *Orghast*, performed in Iran, is based on Zoroastrian and Greek myths. Ted Hughes, who worked as a writer for the Centre, created the new language from words and sounds drawn from Sanskrit, Persian, Greek, Latin and Avesta, an ancient Zoroastrian ceremonial language (Kramer 2011).

While some say Brook's experiments have failed or were a product of the times, his interest of exporting Shakespeare, of finding alternative theatrical sign systems with which to communicate, greatly expanded the boundaries of theater. In many ways, it is the image, or better said, the imagination, that lies at the root of *A Midsummer Night's Dream*, and Brook's definition of a universal theater may be more intersemiotic, even Freudian, in nature than traditional definitions dependent upon the written text. As Theseus suggests at the end of *A Midsummer Night's Dream*:

> Lovers and madmen have such seething brains,
> Such shaping fantasies, that apprehend
> More than cool reason ever comprehends.
>
> (V.i.4–6)

In this chapter, I suggest that while Shakespeare was one of the first to break down the distinction between translation and rewriting, he could not have envisioned the extent to which artists—from traveling British actors to Schlegel, from Mendelssohn to Balanchine, from Max Reinhardt to Peter Brook—adapt, add local references and idioms, change sign systems, import alternative acting techniques, and integrate the English language into entirely different paradigms. I argue that the voyage of *A Midsummer Night's Dream* to Germany, through northern Europe, and around the world has at long last returned to England. Today, its international reception and cross-cultural links play just as important a role, maybe *more* important, in contemporary productions in English. Indeed, many writers today might claim that all writing is a form of rewriting, or better said, a rewriting of a rewriting of a rewriting. Post-translation studies, if broadly conceived, has much to tell us about those re-visioning and re-versioning processes that are reshaping cultures worldwide today.

The journey of *A Midsummer Night's Dream* has not ended. Indeed, one could argue that it has entered a more international and imaginative phase. The play is now one of the most popular of Shakespeare's works and one of the most performed on college campuses in the United States. While today's audiences have little sense of its difficult past, *Midsummer*'s magical properties seem to be fueling the imagination of a new generation. Peter Brook would be proud to see how this new wave of rewriters and their readers are transported into the imaginative realm of *Midsummer*. Late twentieth- and early twenty-first-century translations and rewritings well demonstrate the exponential growth of the play's popularity. From British graphic novelist Neil Gaiman's comic book series *The Sandman: Dream Country, A Midsummer Night's Dream* (1991) in which Shakespeare and Company perform for a "real" Oberon and Titania; through gender reversals in feminist productions such as New Zealand playwright Jean Bett's *Revenge of the Amazons* (1996); to the musical *Midsummer*, directed by Gregory Wolfe for the New York theater company Moonwork (1999) with Pyramus and

Thisbe as part of the band, the forms in which *Midsummer* appears are multiplying. From adolescent fiction writers such as Venezuelan-American Tui Sutherland's *This Must Be Love* (2004) told from the point of view of Hermia and Helena in diaries, emails, and instant messages; through fictional sequels such as Orson Scott Card's *Magic Street* (2005) set in Los Angeles with a black hero Mack Street as Oberon; to children's fantasy fiction in works such as the American Michael Buckley's series *The Sisters Grimm*, especially book four titled *Once Upon a Crime* (2008) featuring two girl detectives teaming with the trickster fairy Puck, *Midsummer* has fueled the imagination of a new generation of audiences. Finally, *Midsummer* proliferations are spreading via a variety of fan fiction furtherings on numerous sites, 66 by my last count. The post-translation reverberations seem endless, and the 80 performances by Peter Brook's 1970 *Midsummer* world tour seem dwarfed in comparison. Translation studies scholars must take the post-translation turn to keep up not just with the changing nature of translation, but with the changing definition of texts themselves and the media through which they travel.

Bibliography

Apuleius, Lucius. 2013 [1566 (2nd century AD)]. *Metamorphoses or The XI Bookes of the Golden Asse*, trans. William Adlington. Ware: Wordsworth. Online at *The Golden Asse*, ed. Donal O'Danachair and David Widger. Online at the Project Gutenburg Ebook at www.gutenberg.org/files/1666/1666-h/1666-h.htm.

Ashcroft, Bill, Gareth Griffiths, and Helen Tiffin. 1989. *The Empire Writes Back: Theory and Practice in Post-Colonial Literature*. London: Routledge.

Balanchine, George. 2015 [1962]. *A Midsummer Night's Dream*. New York: New York City Ballet.

Bassnett, Susan and André Lefevere, eds. 2000. *Translation, History and Culture*. London: Routledge.

Baudrillard, Jean. 1988. *America*, trans. Chris Turner. New York: Verso.

Baudrillard, Jean. 1994. *The Illusion of the End*, trans. Chris Turner. Stanford: Stanford University Press.

Beauman, Sally. 1973. "The Revels are in Hand—and Touring." *Sunday Telegraph Colour Supplement*. March 9. Online at www.alanhoward.org.uk/revels.htm, accessed March 2, 2014.

Benjamin, Walter. 1969 [1955]. "The Task of the Translator." *Illuminations*, trans. Harry Zohn. New York: Schocken, 69–82.

Bett, Jean. 1996. *Revenge of the Amazons*. Wellington: The Women's Play Press.

The Bible: Authorized King James Version. 2008 [1611–12]. Ed. Robert Carroll and Stephen Prickett. Oxford: Oxford University Press.

Birch, Dinah, ed. 2009. *The Oxford Companion to English Literature*. Oxford: Oxford University Press.

Brayley, Edward Wedlake, James Norris Brewer, and Joseph Nightingale. 1810. *London and Middlesex: or An Historical, Commercial, and Descriptive Survey of the Metropolis of Great-Britain*, Vol. 1. London: W. Wilson for Vernon, Hood, and Sharpe.

Brennecke, Ernest. 1964. *Shakespeare in Germany 1590–1700*. Chicago: University of Chicago Press.

Briggs, Katharine Mary. 2007 [1959]. *The Anatomy of Puck: An Examination of Fairy Beliefs among Shakespeare's Contemporaries and Successors*. London: Routledge.

Brissenden, Alan. 2011. "Shakespeare and Dance: Dissolving Boundaries." In Christa Jansohn, Lena Cowen Orlin, and Stanley Wells, eds. *Shakespeare Without Boundaries: Essays in Honor of Dieter Mehl*. Lanham: University of Delaware Press, 92–106.

Brook, Peter. 1996 [1968]. *The Empty Space*. New York: Touchstone.

Brook, Peter. 2013. "Peter Brook on A Midsummer Night's Dream: A Cook and a Concept." *The Guardian*. 15 April. Online at www.theguardian.com/stage/2013/apr/15/peter-brook-midsummer-nights-dream, accessed May 10, 2015.

Buckley, Michael. 2008. *Once upon a Crime*. Book 4. Sisters Grimm Series. New York: Amulet Paperbacks.

Card, Oscar Scott. 2006. *Magic Street*. New York: Del Ray.

Cooper, John Michael. 2008. "For You See I am the Eternal Objector." In Siegwart Reichwald, ed. *Mendelssohn in Performance*. Bloomington: Indiana University Press, 207–49.

Damrosch, David. 2003. *What is World Literature?* Princeton: Princeton University Press.

Davies, Norman. 1999. *The Isles: A History*. Oxford: Oxford University Press.

Delabastita, Dirk. 2004. "'If I Know the Letters and the Language.' Translation as a Dramatic Device in Shakespeare's Plays." In Ton Hoenselaars, ed. *Shakespeare and the Language of Translation*. London: Thomson Learning, 31–52.

D'haen, Theo. 2012. *The Routledge Concise History of World Literature*. London: Routledge.

D'haen, Theo, César Domínguez, and Mads Rosendahl Thomsen, eds. 2012. *World Literature: A Reader*. London: Routledge.

Eckermann, Johann Peter. 1982 [1835]. *Gespräche mit Goethe in den letzten Jahren seines Lebens*, ed. Regine Otto. Berlin: Aufbau Verlag. *Conversations with Eckermann* (1823–1832), trans. John Oxenford. San Francisco: North Point.

Gaiman, Neil. 1991. *The Sandman: Dream Country, A Midsummer Night's Dream, #19*. Burbank: DC Comics.

Garber, Marjorie. 2004. *Shakespeare After All*. New York: Anchor.

Gentzler, Edwin. 2008. *Translation and Identity in the Americas: New Directions in Translation Theory*. New York: Routledge.

Griffiths, Trevor R., ed. 1996. *A Midsummer Night's Dream*. Shakespeare in Production Series. Cambridge: Cambridge University Press.

Gryphius, Andreas. 1964 [1663]. *Absurda Comica oder Herr Peter Squentz*, trans. Ernest Brennecke. In Ernest Brennecke. *Shakespeare in Germany 1590–1700*. Chicago: University of Chicago Press, 72–104.

Halio, Jay L. 2003 [1995]. *Shakespeare in Performance: A Midsummer Night's Dream*, 2nd edn. Manchester: Manchester University Press.

Hall, Peter, dir. 1968. *A Midsummer Night's Dream*. Stratford-upon-Avon: Royal Shakespeare Enterprises and Filmways.

Hamlin, Hannibal. 2013. *The Bible in Shakespeare*. Oxford: Oxford University Press.

Harrison, George Bagshaw, ed. 1952. *Shakespeare: The Complete Works*. New York: Heinle and Heinle.

Harrison, G.B. 1968. "Introduction: *A Midsummer Night's Dream*." In G.B. Harrison, ed. *Shakespeare, The Complete Works*. New York: Heinle and Heinle, 511–15.

Hawkes, Terrance. 1992. *Meaning by Shakespeare*. London: Routledge.

Head, Dominic, ed. 2006. *The Cambridge Guide to Literature in English*, 3rd edn. Cambridge: Cambridge University Press.

Hutcheon, Linda. 2006. *A Theory of Adaptation*. London: Routledge.

Hutcheon, Linda and Siobhan O'Flynn. 2013. *A Theory of Adaptation*, 2nd edn. London: Routledge.

Ick, Judy. 2011. "A Survey of Ballet Performances for William Shakespeare's *A Midsummer Night's Dream* in the 19th and 20th Centuries." *Transmedial Shakespeare*. Online at https://transmedialshakespeare.wordpress.com/2011/01/16/a-survey-of-ballet-performances-for-william-shakespeare's-a-midsummer-night's-dream-in-the-19th-and-20th-centuries, accessed July 15, 2015.

James VI. 2012 [1597]. *Daemonology*, ed. Donald Tyson. Woodbury: Llewellyn.

Kramer, Richard E. 2011. "Peter Brook's International Centre of Theater Research." *Rick On Theater*. August 23. Online at http://rickontheater.blogspot.com/2011/08/peter-brooks-international-centre-of.html, accessed July 15, 2015.

Lefevere, André. 1977. *Translating Literature: The German Tradition: From Luther to Rosenzweig*. Assen: Van Gorcum and Co.

Lefevere, André. 1982. "Mother Courage's Cucumbers: Text, System and Refraction in a Theory of Literature." *Modern Language Studies* 12(4): 3–20.

Lefevere, André. 1984. "On the Refraction of Texts." In Mihai Spariosu, ed. *Mimesis in Contemporary Theory*. Amsterdam: John Benjamin, 217–37.

Lefevere, André. 1992. *Translation, Rewriting, and the Manipulation of Literary Fame*. London: Routledge.

Lefevere, André. 1993. "Shakespeare Refracted: Writer, Audience and Rewriter in French and German Romantic Translations." In Gerald Gillespie, ed. *Romantic Drama*. Amsterdam: John Benjamins, 101–13.

Lefevere, André and Susan Bassnett. 2000. "Introduction: Proust's Grandmother and the Thousand and One Nights: The 'Cultural Turn' in Translation Studies." In Susan Bassnett and André Lefevere, eds. *Translation, History and Culture*. London: Routledge, 1–13.

Littau, Karin. 1997. "Translation in the Age of Postmodern Production: From Text to Intertext to Hypertext." *Forum for Modern Language Studies* 32(1): 81–96.

Littau, Karin. 2011. "First Steps Towards a Media History of Translation." *Translation Studies* 4(3): 261–281.

Looney, Glen. 1974. *Peter Brook's Production of William Shakespeare's "A Midsummer Night's Dream" for the Royal Shakespeare Company: The Complete and Authorized Acting Edition*. Stratford-upon-Avon: Royal Shakespeare Company.

Matthiessen, Francis Otto. 1931. *Translation: An Elizabethan Art*. Cambridge: Harvard University Press.

McQueen, Scott. 2007 [1935]. "Commentary" to Max Reinhardt and William Dieterle's film *A Midsummer Night's Dream*. Burbank: Warner Home Video.

Mendelssohn, Felix. 1990 [1842]. *Incidental Music*, Opus 61 (includes *Overture*). London Symphony Orchestra, dir. André Previn. London: EMI

Mendelssohn, Felix. 1997 [1826]. *Overture*, Opus 21, *Ein Sommernachtstraum*. Gewandhausorchester Leipzig, dir. Kurt Mazur. LGO.

Moisan, Thomas. 1998. "Antique Fables, Fairy Toys: Elisions, Allusion, and Translation in *A Midsummer Night's Dream.*" In Dorothea Kehler, ed. *A Midsummer Night's Dream: Critical Essays.* New York: Garland.

Montaigne, Michel de. 1892–93 [1603]. *The Essays of Montaigne: Done into English by John Florio.* London: D. Nutt.

Moraru, Christian. 2001. *Rewriting: Postmodern Narrative and Cultural Critique in the Age of Cloning.* Albany: Repressed Publishing.

Moraru, Christian. 2011. *Cosmodernism: American Narrative, Late Globalization, and the New Cultural Imaginary.* Ann Arbor: University of Michigan Press.

Moretti, Franco. 2000. "Conjectures on World Literature." *New Left Review* 1: 54–68.

Moretti, Franco. 2003. "More Conjectures." *New Left Review* 20: 73–81.

Mowat, Barbara. 1989. "A Local Habitation and a Name: Shakespeare's Text as Construct." *Style* 23: 335–51.

Mueller, Janel and Joshua Scodel. 2009. *Elizabeth I: Translations 1592–1598.* Chicago: University of Chicago Press.

Neilson, William Allan and Ashley Horace Thorndike, eds. 1837. *The Tudor Shakespeare.* New York: Macmillan.

North, Sir Thomas, trans. 1910 [1579]. *Plutarch's Lives, Englished by Sir Thomas North*, 10 vols. London: J.M. Dent.

Ovid. 2000 [1567]. *Metamorphoses*, trans. Arthur Golding, ed. John Frederick Nims. Philadelphia: Paul Dry Books.

Pascal, Roy. 1937. *Shakespeare in Germany 1740–1815.* Cambridge: Cambridge University Press.

Pepys, Samuel. 1970–82 [1605–18]. *The Diary of Samuel Pepys*, eds. Robert Latham and William Matthews, 11 vols. London: G. Bell and Sons.

Plutarch, Lucius Mestrius. 1579. *The Life of Theseus*, trans. Thomas North, ed. J.W. Skeat. Online at http://perseus.mpiwg-berlin.mpg.de/JC/plutarch.north.html, accessed February 15, 2015.

Proust, Marcel. 1987 [1913–27]. *À la recherche du temps perdu*, 7 vols. Paris: Gallimard.

Reinhardt, Max and William Dieterle, dirs. 1935. *A Midsummer Night's Dream.* Burbank: Warner Brothers.

Schleiner, Winifried. 1985. "Imaginative Sources for Shakespeare's Puck." *Shakespeare Quarterly* 36(1): 65–68.

Schlözer, August Ludwig von. 1792–1801. *Weltgeschichte nach ihren Haupttheilen im Auszug und Zusammenhange*, 2 vols. Göttingen: Vandenhoef und Ruprechtigchen Verlage.

Scot, Reginald. 1964 [1584]. *The Discoverie of Witchcraft*, intro. Hugh Ross Williamson. Carbondale: Southern Illinois University Press.

Selbourne, David. 1982. *The Making of "A Midsummer Night's Dream": An Eye-Witness Account of Peter Brook's Production from First Rehearsal to First Night.* London: Methuen.

Seneca, Lucius Annaeus. 1927 [1581]. *Seneca: His Tenne Tragedies Translated into English*, 2 vols, ed. Thomas Newton, trans. Jasper Heywood, John Studley, Thomas Newton, Alexander Neville, and Thomas Nuce. London: Constable and Sons.

Settle, Elkanah and Henry Purcell. 1969 [1692]. *The Fairy Queen.* London: J. Tonson.

Shaheen, Naseeb. 1999. *Biblical References in Shakespeare's Plays*. Newark: University of Delaware Press.

"Shakespeare in Europe/Shakespeare Translations: A Chronology." University of Basel. Online at http://shine.unibas.ch/translators.htm, accessed February 2, 2014.

"Shakespeare Translations: A Chronology." Online at https://shine.unibas.ch/translators.htm, accessed January 15, 2015.

Shakespeare, William. 1800 [1797]. "Ein Sommernachtstraum." In *Shakespeares Dramatische Werke*, Bd. 7, trans. A.W. von Schlegel. Leipzig und Wein: Bibliographisches Institut, 263–346.

Shakespeare, William. 1967 [1788] *Sommernachtstraum*, trans. A.W. Schlegel. In Frank Jolle, ed. *A.W. Schlegels Sommernachtstraum in der ersten Fassung vom Jahre 1789*. Göttingen: Vandenhoeck und Ruprecht, 55–135.

Shakespeare, William. 1968 [1772]. *Ein St. Johannis Nacht's-Traum*, trans. Christoph Martin Wieland. In *Werke*, Bd. 5. Munich: Carl Hanser, 517–85.

Shakespeare, William. 1979 [1600]. *A Midsummer's Night's Dream*. Arden Edition. London: Methuen.

Siskind, Mariano. 2010. "The Globalization of the Novel and the Novelization of the Global: A Critique of World Literature." *Comparative Literature* 62(4): 336–60.

Straznicky, Marta. 2009. *Privacy, Playreading, and Women's Closet Drama, 1550–1700*. Cambridge: Cambridge University Press.

Stow, John, and Edmund Howes. 1631. *Annales, Or a General Chronicle of England*. London: Richardi Meighen.

Styan, John L. 1982. *Max Reinhardt*. Cambridge: Cambridge University Press.

Sutherland, Tui. 2004. *This Must be Love*. New York: HarperTeen.

Taylor, G.C. 1925. *Shakespere's Debt to Montaigne*. Boston: Harvard University Press.

Tymoczko, Maria, and Edwin Gentzler, eds. 2002. *Translation and Power*. Amherst: University of Massachusetts Press.

Williams, John R. 1998. *The Life of Goethe: A Critical Biography*. Malden, MA: Blackwell.

Wolfe, Gregory, dir. 1999. *A Midsummer Night's Dream*. New York: Moonwork Theater Company.

Zaharia, Oana-Alis. 2012. "Translata Proficit: Revisiting John Florio's translation of Michel de Montaigne's Les Essais." *Sederi Yearbook* 22: 115–36.

2 Postcolonial *Faust*

As we have seen in the new wave of translations and rewritings of Shakespeare's *A Midsummer Night's Dream*, the new age of new media and digital communication has ushered in a new era of not just translation studies but of World Literature as well. Certainly the movement of *A Midsummer Night's Dream* to Germany through Russia, then back to the English-speaking world via music, ballet, and film helps illustrate the manner in which texts circulate. While I am heartened by the place of importance accorded to translation in the new discussions of World Literature by scholars such as David Damrosch (2003, 2009), Theo D'haen (2012, D'haen et al. 2013), and Emily Apter (2005, 2013), despite redefinitions and the broad range of languages being considered, cultural biases and imperialistic aspects to the new definitions remain. For example, in "The Globalization of the Novel and the Novelization of the Global: A Critique of World Literature" (2010), Mariano Siskind talks about the Modern Language Association's (MLA) goal of publishing 100 texts in their Teaching World Literature Series. Through 1997, however, out of the 95 titles published, 65 were in English, 14 in French, three each in Italian, German, and Spanish, three in classical Greek and Latin, and one each in Russian, Norwegian, Japanese, and Hebrew (2010: 343): all European with merely *two* exceptions. In this chapter, I would like to push the boundaries of such definitions and add translation, rewritings, and the multidirectional circulation of texts in both postmodern and postcolonial terms. In addition to a synergy and cross-fertilization process involved in translation and rewriting that is very invigorating, there are also ideological considerations with regards to the texts included in the World Literature paradigm. Translation, retranslation, and rewriting have been used to critique the criteria establishing such a canon.

In this book I build upon literary theories advocated by translators, rewriters, and creative writers associated with Brazilian cannibalist movement, or *movimento antropofágico*, expanding it to include cannibalizations that extend beyond Brazilian borders. The emphasis of *antropofagia* on the creative and transformative nature of translation, or, in Haroldo de Campos's creative neologisms, "*transcriação*," "*transluminação*," "*transfusão*," and in terms of my arguments in this chapter on international *Faust "translu-ciferação mefistofáustica"* (Campos 1981: 180, 208–9) have challenged definitions of static texts and forced scholars to rethink the very definition of translation. The translation/rewriting approach for the *antropofagis-tas* is not a domesticating or foreignizing one, but *both*: importing ideas and expressions via translation *plus* rewriting those ideas and texts in the vein of the receiving culture. A radical political reversal takes place in the process: the translator/rewriter appropriates the language of the European original and reverses it, using it as one's own *against* the source culture, redefining those very texts that comprise World Literature. The cannibalistic approach to translation has become one of the leading postcolonial theories of translation (Bassnett and Trivedi 1999: 1–5). Every translation is a form of double writing: domesticated and resistant, Eurocentric and indigenous, global and local, appropriating and expropriating, elite and popular.

On the one hand, cannibalistic translators select primarily European and North American texts to introduce into their respective countries, and in many ways, the translations are remarkably *faithful* to their sources, espe-cially regarding literary devices such as tone, the play of language, and metaphor. On the other hand, the cannibalistic translators are remarkably inventive, reorganizing European ideas in a new context, playing with signs, sights, and images in a way that allows for alternative insights. The move-ment is always bidirectional. For example, when Haroldo de Campos dis-cusses Bible translation, he argues that he "Portuguizes" the Hebrew with Brazilian sounds and connotations, and, at the same time, "Hebrewizes" the Portuguese with historical Hebrew terms and metaphors. Radical forms of "indigenizing" classical European texts follow, transfiguring the very defi-nition of translation: think in terms of Oswald de Andrade cannibalizing Hamlet's soliloquy into "Tupi or not Tupi" (1928: 38–39). By changing just one phoneme, de Andrade relocates it in a paradigm of Brazilian history and the Tupinamba Indians (Gentzler 2008: 80–82)

The cannibalistic form of double writing focuses less on the one-directional flow of ideas, such as from Europe to Brazil, and more on the *circulation* of texts or, better said, the *spiraling* flow of ideas, often beyond the control of those Western literary institutions who tend to govern trans-lational taste. In this chapter, I suggest that international productions of *Faust*, often because of their postcolonial or postmodern interpretations, are just now beginning to influence cyclically the reception of *Faust* as it returns to Germany. Translation invariably operates in multiple directions, not just from source to target cultures, but also in a much wider sense, often crossing multiple linguistic and cultural borders as the translations travel. For example, Latin American translations of Caliban in Shakespeare's *The Tempest* have reshaped how many countries around the world now think of both Prospero and Caliban, to the point that British producers cannot help but consider the Latin American readings and worldwide reception when staging the "original" (see Conclusion in this volume). I argued above that the reception of Shakespeare's *A Midsummer Night's Dream* in Germany influenced productions all across northern Europe, and eventually circled back to London. I suggest that World Literature itself is taking a rewriting turn, fueled by translation and transcreation.

In *Deus e o Diabo no Fausto de Goethe* (1981), Haroldo de Campos provides a fine example of a cannibalistic approach to translating/rewriting Goethe's *Faust*. De Campos's book contains three sections, each one representing a different kind of translation or rewriting: the first part is a literary translation; the second offers criticism; and a third articulates cannibalistic theories of translation. In the opening section, de Campos translates the final scenes of Goethe's *Faust II*, beginning just after the death of Faust and carrying on until the end. The plot concerns the battle between Mephistopheles and the angels for the spirit of Faust. While Faust had agreed to sell his soul to the Devil, there still appears to be a final chance at redemption, calling into question the pacts made not just between Mephistopheles and Faust, but, more significantly, between God and Mephistopheles. The second section includes the essays "A escritura mefistofélica" and "Bufoneria transcendental," in which de Campos first traces the multiple versions of Faust versions *before* Goethe and then discusses the carnivalesque nature of the final scene, incorporating both German beliefs and the carnival tradition in Brazil. The third section recapitulates antropofagist theories of translation and recreation, including de Campos's famous neologisms mentioned above.

Just as Goethe rewrote and recreated the Faust legend in Germany, de Campos rewrites and recreates in a different time and place in contemporary Brazil. Goethe was very open about his borrowings. For example, Goethe plagiarized a song from Ophelia from Shakespeare's *Hamlet* for one of the early Gretchen scenes, providing an excellent example of de Campos's later theory for what he calls "plagiatropy" (Vieira 1999: 107). In *Aus meinem Leben. Dichtung und Wahrheit* (1811), Goethe admitted that he borrowed heavily from other writers. He wrote, "Das Erfinden aus der Luft war nie meine Sache" [Inventing things out of the air was never my approach] (Goethe 2013 [1811], quoted and translated in Mason 1967: 15). Further, when discussing his borrowings from other sources, Goethe said:

> The World remains always the same; situations are repeated ... why should not one poet write like another ... Walter Scott used a scene from my Egmont. He also copies the character of my Mignon in one of his romances... Lord Byron's transformed Devil is a continuation of Mephistopheles, and quite right too... Thus, my Mephistopheles sings a song from Shakespeare (see lines 3682–97), and why should he not?
> (Goethe 1901 [1836–48], January 18, 1825,
> cited in Hamlin 1976: 412–13)

Thus, Goethe cannibalized work from other writers in his creations, too. As creative writers draw upon and incorporate the best writers in their work, so too do translators incorporate the best material at their disposal, drawing from and rewriting into both source and target cultures. Concerning *Faust*, connotations of "plagiarism" arise frequently; the word's etymological roots such as "kidnapping," "seducing," "blood consumption," and the "plague," closely connect to de Campos's definition of *antropofagia*.

The third section of *Deus e o Diabo no Fausto de Goethe* is called *"Transluciferação mefistofáustica"* and includes some of de Campos's key theoretical, and I would argue most postcolonial and postmodern concepts. Whereas most translation theories tend toward the faithful, the angelic, or minimally the least invasive, de Campos's accepts and even embraces the "satanic" in translation. He does not want the translator to be passive, submissive, faithful, or angelic. Translation, de Campos argues, is always a *transgressive* activity, playing with the limits of signs and signifying in multiple directions, languages, and cultures. In addition to the diabolical, however, there is also a reverential, spiritual dimension to transcreation: diabolic and angelic, rebellious and respectful, faithful and free all at the same time. Remember, Christ died for the sins of others; at the Last Supper, his disciples, at least metaphorically, "ate" of his body and "drank" of his blood. In the Brazilian tradition of cannibalism, the Tupinamba Indians picked only the *best* warriors to devour, often marrying them to, or breeding them with, their strongest women before devouring them.

Surprisingly, what strikes me about Haroldo de Campos's translation of *Faust II* is its remarkable *faithfulness* to Goethe, in some ways more faithful than any translation I have read. I first read the play in English as an undergraduate at Kenyon College, where Faust's striving for knowledge was viewed as his redeeming quality. I next read the play in German as a graduate student at the Free University of Berlin, where I felt that many readers underestimated the ironies of Faust's striving. In Berlin, the leading *Faust* scholar was Wilhelm Emrich, who emphasized Faust's final Christian redemption offered at the end of both Parts I and II, with the saving of Gretchen in *Faust I*, and Faust being forgiven and whisked off to "heaven" by the good angels in *Faust II* (Emrich 1943, 1965). In his critical work, Emrich attempts to find a coherent, unified whole, with all symbols pointing to Christian salvation. Adjectives describing Faust seem exaggerated. For example, in "The Enigma of Faust, Part II: A Tentative Solution," Emrich writes, "Faust of Part II was a man more pure, objective, superior, noble, and dignified" (Emrich 1976 [1971]: 587). Even when there is clearly a hybrid union, such as Helena as a classical Greek woman united with the Faust of sixteenth-century Germany, Emrich stresses Christian assimilation: "Helena is taken into the modern, Christian world ... She is introduced to the more profound, more heartfelt depths of Christian poetry ... Greek polytheism is left behind, Nordic tribes take possession of Greece" (1976 [1971]: 599–600). Finally, for Emrich, the end of the play is Christian and angelic: "Christian and humanistic elements are inextricably interwoven ... Man cannot be redeemed by his own effort. He needs grace and love from above. This is Christian" (1976 [1971]: 601). As the pre-eminent Goethe scholar and a former student of and later friend to Theodore Adorno, Emrich influenced a generation of critics. Yet today his influence is in decline. In the second edition of *Faust: A Norton Critical Edition* (1998), for example, the 1976 Emrich essay "The Enigma of Faust," included in the first edition, has disappeared.

My most recent rereading of *Faust*, this time in Portuguese in the de Campos version, which underlies this chapter, provokes a rethinking of Faust in more international terms. De Campos's translation preserves the carnival aspect of the final scene, emphasizing not only Mephistopheles's irony—he is tiring of Faust's "striving" and is disappointed that Faust does not seem to learn from his mistakes. Also, Mephistopheles questions God's going back on His word. Mephistopheles feels that he has won the bet for Faust's soul, yet he still loses in the end. Irony, as we know from Linda Hutcheon's work, is one of the hardest elements to translate. In *Irony's Edge: The Theory and Politics of Irony* (1994), for example, Hutcheon talks about irony as a kind of double writing that combines what is said on the surface of the text with a certain unsaid critique below (Hutcheon 1994: 89). I have found that de Campos not only keeps the irony of Mephistopheles's loss, but he also enhances it.

De Campos also kept the erotics of the play, especially Mephistopheles's homosexual feelings toward his former fellow angels. The reason Mephistopheles loses Faust's soul is that he is distracted for just a moment by the attractive qualities of the good angels. Those homoerotic connotations are present in Goethe's play, but are almost uniformly deleted from the English versions and seldom mentioned in Anglo-German scholarship. With the emergence of queer studies in the past two decades, those homoerotic passages have been productively analyzed (Kuzniar 1996; Tobin 1996; Lorey and Plews 1998). For Goethe, depicting Mephistopheles as multisexual, interested in men and women, old and young, witches and humans, and good and bad angels was essential to the play, and especially to the ending, which calls into questions dichotomies such as good and evil, and saved or condemned. In his translation, de Campos keeps, if not adds to, the many double metaphors present in the original.

These doubled readings lend much insight to Goethe's play, for he, as the author, was clearly conflicted, which may explain why he continually rewrote and revised right up to his death. Goethe had real doubts about Christianity, especially Catholicism, and struggled to find an alternative ending. In most pre-Goethe versions of *Faust*, Mephistopheles *wins* the bet and Faust is either killed onstage or taken away by the Devil, which can also be interpreted as Christian: Faust being condemned for his sins. Goethe may well have been aware of the double bind, that his play would be Christianized whether he condemned or saved Faust. However, de Campos chose a third way, this time emphasizing the feminine, poetic, multisexual, polytheistic, by using phonetic and metaphoric associations to suggest

Table 2.1 Last lines of *Faust* translated by Walter Kaufmann and Haroldo de Campos

Chorus mysticus	Chorus mysticus	Chorus Mysticus
Alles Vergängliche	What is destructible	O perecível
Ist nur ein Gleichnis;	Is but a parable	É apenas simile.
Das Unzulängliche,	What fails ineluctably,	O imperfectível
Hier wird's Ereignis;	The undeclarable,	Perfaz-se enfim.
Das Unbeschreibliche,	Here it was seen,	O não-dizível
Hier ist's getan;	Here it was action;	Culmina aqui.
Das Ewig-Weibliche	The Eternal-Feminine	O Eterno-Feminino
Zieht uns hinan.	Lures to perfection.	Acena, céu-acima.
– Goethe, *Faust II*, lines 12104–11	– trans. Kaufmann 1961: 503	– trans. de Campos 1981: 65

alternative interpretations—in short, a form that allows a "translational" other to arise (see Table 2.1).

The endings of both Parts I and II are at most ambiguous: if anything Faust is transported *not* to heaven, but to a kind of in-between space, dare I say a *translational* space. Neither is it a humanistic space; rather a magical/spiritual realm above the earth but not yet in heaven, perhaps a transitional space with further judgment yet to come. It may be a pre-Christian space (Northern Gothic or Neolithic European), for it is not God the Father, but the Ewig-Weibliche [Eternal Feminine], an Ur-Goddess/Mother/Queen figure, who grants Faust's final freedom. Faust's sins have been enormous: blasphemer, murderer, negligent father, colonizer, militarist, thief, imperialist, and slave-owner. His thirst for knowledge might keep him from Dante's lowest circle, but his best hope is to land in a middle stage, which is probably Goethe's point after all. The twentieth-century reception of the Faust figure in Germany may preclude insight into the repercussions of his sins. It may take a series of translations and rewritings from *outside* the culture to make headway to that reified image, first undertaken by de Campos with his Brazilian transluciferations. To make my argument, this chapter has four sections (1) the translational culture of eighteenth-century Germany; (2) Goethe as a rewriter; (3) translations of *Faust* into English; and finally (4) rewritings of *Faust* in a variety of media, including theater, cinema, and music.

The translational culture of eighteenth-century Germany

Unlike the late sixteenth-century teeming harbor of London, with the trade, exploration, traveling merchants and artists coming and going, the Germany of Goethe's youth was splintered and isolated, not offering an attractive hub for immigration. There was a German culture and language, but the region at large was just an amalgamation of many small dukedoms, a few free cities, and a handful of religious enclaves. Any number of German dialects were spoken, some barely comprehensible to people from other districts. Five hundred little *Fürstentumern* [Fiefdoms], existed, all with petty aristocratic rulers. While Berlin may have headed a loose confederation of principalities, they were hardly centralized, and certainly not international. Travel was difficult: while there were exchanges through the mail, no trains or telegraphs existed; horse-drawn carriages could travel at the most 50 miles a day. Goethe, who worked in Weimar most of his life, had much trouble even traveling back to Frankfurt to see his mother. As a famous author with a plum patronage job in Weimar, even Goethe seldom traveled outside of "Germany": a few trips to Switzerland, an occasional visit to spas in Bohemia, and two longer trips to Italy.

Over his lifetime, Goethe lived under the fragmented conditions of the late Holy Roman Empire, and the Maximilian referred to in *Faust*, as "King" of the Germans was the Holy Roman Emperor during the early sixteenth century, although the Pope never crowned him as travel to Rome was too difficult. In *The Life of Goethe* (1998), John Williams tells us that Goethe, born in 1749, would have first experienced international troops in Frankfurt during the Seven Years' War (1756–63), known in the USA as the French and Indian War. The war was particularly horrific, characterized by open battles and whole towns being burned; nearly one million people died. Goethe was well aware of the consequences in Germany. Goethe also saw Napoleon conquer most of Europe, including Germany. Even after the coalition of German forces in 1813 that defeated Napoleon, and the Congress of Vienna that re-established a new system of monarchies, Germany remained very weak. At the Congress of Vienna in 1815, when Europe restored boundaries after Napoleon, a "German Confederation," of 39 "states" was established. The "nation" at the time, was referred to as "The Germanies." German unification only came in 1871, nearly 40 years after Goethe's death in 1832. During his lifetime, Goethe showed more allegiance to the French, especially to Napoleon, than to the emerging German nation: the bloodshed and social disruption caused by the French Revolution bothered him, and Goethe's sympathies for Napoleonic order can be easily discerned.

Many translation studies scholars, including Toury, Even-Zohar, Bassnett, and Lefevere, posit a strong period of translation under weaker regimes, and the Germany of this period certainly qualifies. The most powerful leader at the time was Frederick the Great, who spoke more French in his court than German and self-translated many of his works in French. Frederick was also well known for his *dislike* of the German language and literature. During the early 1800s, the "German" language, as one might imagine from a loose collection of little states, was still a loose collection of dialects; *Hochdeutsch* at the time was still only a written language. The teaching of languages in Germany also fluctuated; standard German, more often than not, was taught as a foreign language. The Grimm brothers' dictionary, the first German dictionary, for example, was only published in 1852, 20 years after Goethe's death. Further, Frederick seemed unimpressed with Goethe's early work, or

Figure 2.1 Map of "The Germanies" during the eighteenth century (Höckmann online).

the *Sturm und Drang* movement with which he was associated. The fact that Goethe found a patron in Karl August, Duke of Saxe-Weimar, then loosely affiliated with the Prussian Kingdom, was fortuitous indeed.

Despite its splintered political and linguistic landscape, or perhaps because of its lack of a national culture and language, Goethe's era was a great age for translation, providing a translational environment that served as a precondition for the emergence of a work of the stature of Goethe's *Faust*. Germany's very weakness as a nation-state allowed a handful of creative writers and translators to initiate profound changes, paving the way for the later German unification. In *Translating Literature: The German Tradition* (1977), André Lefevere provides insight into this period with sections on Gottsched, Lessing, Herder, Goethe, Von Humboldt, and the Schlegel brothers. So too, in *Shakespeare in Germany 1740–1815* (1937), does Roy Pascal give a good overview of Gottsched and his School, plus the post-Gottsched reaction by the great generation of German translators/writers.

Goethe would have become well familiar with the translation work of Johann Christoph Gottsched (1700–66), the leading German critic during the early part of the eighteenth century, when Goethe, at 16 years old, went to the town of Leipzig to study law. Gottsched, a professor at Leipzig, edited a number of important literary journals and authored several important eighteenth-century texts defining the art of poetry for the Germans. Gottsched translated (and adapted) French and British theater and opera and his wife Luise Gottsched translated Alexander Pope, Horace, Voltaire, and Molière. The two worked together by importing French theater, poetry, and literary criticisms, thereby shaping the future of German letters.

Over time, several Germans writers, including Goethe, began to distance themselves from the Gottsched School. More influential upon Goethe's development was a writer such as Gotthold Ephraim Lessing (1729–81), who also translated French plays for his actress wife Caroline Neuber and served as a dramaturge in Hamburg. He too translated and adapted French plays for the stage, but not the same type of plays as the Gottscheds. For example, Lessing translated anti-Aristotelian plays by Nivelle de la Chaussée, or more naturalistic plays by Jean-Jacques Rousseau and Philippe Néricault Destouches. Lessing was primarily known for editing the journal *Hamburgishe Dramaturgie* (1767–69), which developed theories of drama that *opposed* Gottsched and his disciples. Lessing, as mentioned in Chapter 1, was instrumental in introducing Shakespeare to the German public. In his "Letter of Literature XVII" (1759), Lessing speaks admirably of Shakespeare's plays, suggesting that if they were to be translated, they would have a larger impact than French playwrights such as Corneille and Racine (Lessing 2014 [1759]: 391). In the same letter, Lessing also suggests that the old German play *Doctor Faust* contains many scenes that only a Shakespearean devotee could produce (Lessing 2014 [1759]: 391). At the end of that same letter, Lessing offers a scene of *Faust and the Seven Spirits of the Devil*, the transition from good to evil, and states his hope to one day see a full play with such scenes. Goethe took Lessing at his word and worked to produce a new German play and theatrical form.

Another prolific translator who proved influential to Goethe's work was Christoph Martin Wieland (1733–1813), who in addition to being the first translator of *A Midsummer Night's Dream* also translated Horace's *Satires*, Lucien's *Works*, Cicero's *Letters*, and 22 plays of Shakespeare. The most famous translator from Greek during this forerunner period to Goethe was Johann Heinrich Voss (1751–1826), who translated Homer's *Odyssey* (1781), *Iliad* (1793), and Virgil's *Eclogues* and *Georgics* (1789). Voss lived for several years in Jena, a town neighboring Weimar, and knew Goethe well. The language philosopher Johann Georg Hamann (1730–88), translator of David Hume, offered a critique of Enlightenment and emphasized *gaps* in human understanding. In his theology as laid out in, for example, "Essay of a Sibyl on Marriage," Hamann seems open to a sexual and erotic theology, thinking in terms of a Woman-Man-God Trinity that shows up at the end of *Faust*. Hamann favored expression, communication, and even passion over intellectual analysis. Goethe held Hamann as one of the leading intellectuals of his time.

However, it was Hamann's student Johann Gottfried Herder (1744–1803) who was the most influential in positing the idea that translators are fundamental to the construction of culture. He told Goethe to read the Old Testament and Homer in order to gain insight on the ancient languages of the Middle East, and to read German and Norse folktales to build a more multilingual and multicultural heritage. Herder lent Germans new pride in their origins, helped German writers better value their previously marginalized language, and served as an inspiration, not just to Goethe for his complex understanding of German heritage, but also later to the Grimm brothers and their collection of German fairytales. Herder translated works as diverse as Homer, Shakespeare, Hebrew poetry, Cervantes, Norse poetry and mythology, always looking to ancient peoples and folk traditions. He also translated James Macpherson's Scottish-Gaelic *Ossian* (1760), a supposed collection of ancient oral tales, well known in translation studies circles as a pseudo-translation, but in part based on old folk tales heard by Macpherson in Scotland. Herder's influence can be easily seen in one of Goethe's first translations, which was *The Songs of Selma* (1771) from Ossian. It is during this period that Goethe began planning his version of *Faust*.

This generation of precursors to and contemporaries of Goethe thus began the process of using translation in their search for a German language, culture, and identity. They started with the French aristocratic and classical language and forms, added to them canonic Latin and Greek authors, and finally turned to English theater and Norse histories and folklore to round out the German repertoire. These writers and translators changed the cultural landscape, lending Germans a new pride in their language, cultural history, and art forms. Gothic, Norse folk art, and culture gained the status of Greek and Roman literature. By the end of his lifetime, Goethe could talk about German literature as *Weltliteratur*, something merely dreamed about in his early days. Only from such a wide range of verse forms, a passion for German history and folklore, and the elevation of the German language to a status equal to its European counterparts could a text such as *Faust* emerge. Post-translation studies scholars argue that without the *translational* culture preceding Goethe, no *Faust* could emerge.

The pre-*Faust* translational culture was not just a generational phenomenon, but in the case of the Faust legend, also extended back historically. Of all the ironies that characterized this quintessential German tale, the most unusual is that Goethe seems to have arrived at the Faust story *not* from the German originals, but via translation. The history of the Faust saga dates back to the *Historia von D. Johann Fausten* first published in Frankfurt in 1587 by Johann Spies (Baron 1992: 95). Several scholars also point out that Faust was a "real" person who lived in the Württemberg area in the 1480s and died in the town of Staufen in southwest Germany, a full generation before the Spies publication. This living character seems to have mastered several arts of astrology and alchemy, frequently traveled around Germany, and was embraced by the masses but derided by scholars and theologians (Mason 1967: 2).

The story about a Devil making a pact with a man of learning goes back to both German folklore and the oral traditions of many Central and Eastern European countries. Witchcraft was common in the Middle Ages, and figures such as Merlin, and men of learning interested in the occult and alchemy go back well into the Medieval period. Belief in the occult continued in emerging Lutheran and Catholic Germanies during the eighteenth and nineteenth centuries, and Goethe himself may have believed more in the so-called "dark" sciences than the established secular sciences or Christian theology. Witch-burnings took place in Europe throughout the sixteenth and seventeenth centuries, and while banned in England by the Witchcraft Act of 1735, they continued in Germany well into the eighteenth century. Almanacs, horoscopes, and astrological charts were widely available, and belief in ghosts, supernatural beings, and alchemy was not uncommon.

Although it includes examples of occult behavior, the Spies *Historia von D. Johann Fausten* primarily serves as a warning *against* those who follow such practices. Faust's adventures with the occult did not serve him well, and in the end, in this first written tale of Faust, he does not achieve salvation. After the appearance of the Spies *Faustbuch*, which seems to be less original and more a collection and reframing of oral versions, many other rewritings followed. These other versions, including *Das Wagnerbuch* (1593), *Das Widmann'sche Faustbuch* (1599), *Dr. Fausts großer und gewaltiger Höllenzwang* (1609), *Dr. Johannes Faust, Magia naturalis et innaturalis* (1612), *Dr. Fausts großer und gewaltiger Meergeist* (Dutch 1692), and *Das Faustbuch des Christlich Meynender* (1725), all tell more or less the same story, some copying sections from the original, and others adding and deleting liberally ("Faust" online). The Widmann version, for example, is particularly unwieldy, expanding the Spies text to some 671 pages. The reverse is true of the 1725 *Faustbuch*, shortened to 41 pages by the anonymous "Christlich Meynender" [a "man with a Christian view"] (Mason 1967: 10). In all these early versions, Gretchen is condemned, Faust is damned, and the end is often quite brutal, dismemberment not uncommon, after which Faust's body is carted off to hell. While set in a Christian context, Faust and Mephisto play irreverently, often vulgarly; pagan elements are incorporated and magical acts occur frequently.

Despite this wealth of oral and written versions of the Faust legend in German culture, Goethe actually may have first encountered the story in translation. A "P.F., Gent[leman]" translated the 1587 Frankfort *Faustbuch* into English as early as 1592 in *The Histoire of the Damnable Life, and Deserved Death of Doctor John Faustus*. This translation served as the basis for Christopher Marlowe's *The Tragical History of Dr. Faustus*, which

Table 2.2 Precursors to Goethe's *Faust* in German and English

German versions of *Faust* during the sixteenth to eighteenth centuries:	Early translations into English:
Historia von D. Johann Fausten (1587) by Johann Spies	*The Historie of the Damnable Life, and Deserved Death of Doctor Iohn Faustus* (1592), trans "P.F., Gent[leman]"
Rewritings of *Historia*:	
Das Wagnerbuch (1593)	*The Tragical History of Doctor Faustus* (1604), rewritten by Christopher Marlowe
Das Widmann'sche Faustbuch (1599)	
Dr. Fausts großer und gewaltiger Höllenzwang (1609)	
Dr. Johannes Faust, Magia naturalis et innaturalis (1612)	**English to German translations:**
Das Pfitzer'sche Faustbuch (1674)	*Die Sage vom Faust*, trans. Wilhelm Müller (1818)
Dr. Fausts großer und gewaltiger Meergeist (Dutch 1692)	
Das Wagnerbuch (1714)	
Faustbuch des Christlich Meynenden (1725)	

was performed in the mid-1590s in London, but not published until 1604, 11 years after Marlowe's death. Marlowe's rewriting of the translation was the first dramatization of the story. In Marlowe, the Faust character displays more admirable qualities than the German comic figure, but the conclusion, given the Protestant and Calvinistic climate in Britain during the period, was never in doubt: forgiveness was not an option. This play was performed in London by the Admiral's Men several times from 1594 to 1597 and revived again in 1602 to much acclaim, with some spectators in the audience believing the Devil himself appeared on stage.

In the *A Midsummer Night's Dream* chapter above, the English players— or, in this case, the English-German players—took the British play abroad, more often than not to Germany, with records of its performance in Graz in 1608, and Dresden in 1626 (Mason 1967: 3). The English-German actors, performing a rough version of Marlowe's play, actually *served as the basis* for the German dramatic versions. This version—translated and adapted into English, then translated and adapted *back* into German—became the core of subsequent German productions, serving as the "source" for Goethe's further dramatic rewriting. I should add a further translational stage for this "original," as Goethe seems to have first encountered Marlowe's text *not* by the German-English human actors, but in a puppet-show, which was the play's main performance genre from the late eighteenth century. No single authorized text exists for this oft-performed puppet play, which was reportedly cruder and more farcical than its human counterpart.

Goethe probably did not read Spies's original *Faustbuch*, as it seems to have largely disappeared from circulation during Goethe's lifetime, and he may not have read Marlowe's play until 1818, when he appears to have read it in Wilhelm Müller's translation. Nevertheless, Goethe's initial encounter with the Faust story seems to be in translation, or better said in multiple translations—both of language and genre: from German to English and back to German, from oral to prose to puppet-plays to drama. Thus I argue that the "original" for Goethe's *Faust* was already *in translation* by the time he began to work on his version. Goethe restores Faust to his intellectual stature as well as offers the possibility of an alternative ending.

Goethe as a rewriter

Not only was the source text for Goethe's *Faust* already in translation, Goethe himself rewrote his composition frequently, beginning with the so-called *Urfaust* in 1772 and ending with the completion of *Faust II* right before his death in 1832. Thus Goethe worked on this text on and off for some 60 years—his entire literary career. The first installment, now known as the *Urfaust* (1887), was discovered in the nineteenth century, allowing scholars to work backward to see the origins of the Goethe version and revealing a kind of palimpsest of earlier versions beneath the polished sheen of the "original." In *Urfaust*, most of the scenes of the later *Faust I* are already present, although in a much-changed form. *Urfaust* contains some 30 pages of poetry and 20 scenes, many concerning Faust's love for Gretchen, a character Goethe added to the Faust legend. Gretchen's tragedy is entirely present: her love for Faust, his leaving her after murdering her brother, her becoming pregnant, her killing the child for fear of being socially ostracized, the death of her mother via poisoning, her incarceration, and her refusing rescue at the end.

The play is Gretchen's tragedy. Faust is depicted first as in despair but intellectually greedy, and then enamored but emotionally reckless. Mephistopheles has little to do other than to encourage Faust to follow his urges. *Urfaust* also has an opening monologue, as did Marlowe's. However, still missing from the *Urfaust* is the pact scene between Mephistopheles and Faust. Theatrically, the break with the French is complete, and the influence of Lessing, Herder, Marlowe, and Shakespeare is everywhere to be seen, including folk songs, Middle-Age German theatrical forms, Germanic verse and meter, tavern songs, and religious skepticism. In the end, Gretchen refuses to be rescued by Faust and is executed, and Faust disappears with Mephistopheles.

In 1790, 15 years after *Urfaust*, the next version called *Faust: A Fragment* appeared, well after Goethe had moved to Weimar. Much of *Urfaust* is still present, although several scenes are rewritten, including an addition to the Faust's Study scene; a new Forest Cavern Scene in which Faust seems to increasingly value nature; a revision of the Auerbach's Cellar scene with Mephistopheles more active and, significantly, a new ending. Questions about the ending, about whether or not Faust will return to Gretchen, about who will be condemned and who will be saved, are all left hanging.

Table 2.3 Goethe's own writings and rewritings of *Faust* (Boyle 1987: xi–xvi)

1772–75	*Urfaust*
1790	*Faust: A Fragment* published
1797	Dedication, Prelude, Prologue to *Faust* written
1800	Draft of Helena scene
1806	Draft of Walpurgis Night scene
1808	*Faust: Der Tragödie erster Teil* published
1816	Outline for *Faust II*, unpublished
1827	*Helena, a classical-romantic phantasmagoria; Interlude for Faust II* published
1828	Part of Act One, Part II published
1830	Acts One and Two, *Faust II* finished
1831	Acts Five and then Four, *Faust II* finished
1832	Goethe dies (March, 22 1832)
1832	*Faust: Der Tragödie zweiter Teil* published posthumously

Mephistopheles assumes a larger role; Faust's faith in natural man is growing, and uncertainty about God's role, heaven, and the afterlife continues (Bucchianeri 2008: 209–10).

When he returned to *Faust* in 1797, Goethe was nearly 50 years old and had made the decision to add a second part to the story. Also at this time, Goethe was thinking of a *written* play rather than a performable script. Over the next decade, this decision became increasingly apparent: the first Walpurgis Night was drafted, Goethe's interest in Germanic, Gothic, and Norse history and folklore was further displayed, and Mephistopheles reigns more heroically. Helena, who appeared in Marlowe's version, was drafted but tabled until Part II. The ending, however, was still in limbo. A new Dedication reveals Goethe's interest in those in-between spheres: those "schwankende Gestalten" [wavering shapes] (line 1) that are neither past nor present, flesh nor spirit, arising out of the mists of the high mountains above the earth but not yet in heaven. The new Prelude reveals a conflicted purpose, with the poet, director, and a clown (writer, director, performer) all offering their perspectives. Goethe, at this stage in his life, was in contact with Schiller and was shifting from a *Sturm und Drang* to a more classical vision of German theater, but Schiller was wise enough to encourage Goethe to keep the Devil and witches, which he found more creatively vibrant (Williams 1998: 189–90). The Prologue helps frame the drama from Mephistopheles's and God's perspective, setting up the competition for Faust's soul, but also revealing that Mephistopheles and the Lord may not be that adversarial after all. One wonders if Goethe was unsure, or if the religious climate of the time gave him pause. Faust's striving indicates a desire to escape the limited intellectual world as well as to discover a new spiritual path between heaven and earth; it is a very modern vision with, I would argue, post-Christian inclinations.

By the time Goethe published *Faust I*, the material was for the most part settled. Gaps are filled in, the primary addition being the pact between

Mephistopheles and Faust; the bet ends up being a bit different than many imagine it, initiated not by Mephistopheles but by *Faust* (line 1414), and the wager is less for Faust's soul and more that Mephistopheles would not be able to relieve Faust's incessant striving (lines 1690–98). Faust initiates the wager because he has no interest in living beyond death or going to heaven or, as Goethe called it, "das Drüben" ["the beyond"] (line 1660). At this point, Goethe was demonstrably not a Christian. Ironically, the text of what Faust eventually signs in blood is omitted in the play, allowing Goethe to incorporate the pactless material previously written and to keep the ending open, thereby deferring the ending for *Faust II* until later. As we shall see, it is more the power of love (or of sex), the care of Gretchen, and *her* connection to a very mysterious Eternal Feminine that eventually leads to Faust's "salvation." Mephistopheles's role, although expanded in *Faust I*, is still more of a companion or guide than a satanic figure attempting to corrupt Faust; our hero needs no extra encouragement for his erotic or criminal actions. Yes, Mephistopheles has his bag of tricks—magic jewels, sleeping potions, carnal pursuits, and magic rides—but as Faust needs little persuasion, the tricks are complementary.

The most significant addition to *Faust I* are the Walpurgis Night and the Walpurgis Night's Dream scenes, which allowed Goethe to demonstrate his attraction to German folklore, his familiarity with the rituals of the Brocken [Blocksberg] in the Harz mountains, and certain pre-Christian, pantheistic beliefs. In many ways, Goethe is translating earlier oral and underground traditions into the more academic High German language, and he proved very knowledgeable in the subtleties of demonology, witchcraft, and Gothic art. He also added homage to Shakespeare's *A Midsummer Night's Dream* with his interlude of the wedding of Oberon and Titania. The additions certainly retain folk and comic elements dear to the theater-going audience and made the ensuing Gretchen tragedy, which is horrific, more palatable. Unlike previous versions of *Faust*, Goethe saves Gretchen by adding an ambiguous secular/religious "Stimme (von oben)" ["Voice (from above)"] by simply saying "Ist gerettet" [Is saved] (line 4612), but not saying by whom. Instead of Gretchen sweeping Faust up with her, Mephistopheles snatches Faust away, and the two disappear while Gretchen, in the last line of the *Faust I*, is left meekly calling his name. The ending, for the time being, remains open; the sequel foreshadowed.

Although many themes from *Faust I* are carried forward, *Faust II* seems an entirely new play. Faust is still striving, now less for individual gain and more for national or even international recognition. He still has sexual conquests to pursue. In his outline for *Faust II*, composed in 1816, Goethe sketched a plan for Helen of Troy to be incorporated into his play, but they were very vague. The plan unites Faust not with a female peasant figure from the German past, but a reified beauty of Homeric origin. The 1816 outline has Helen being magically conjured up from Hades and transported to the Germany of Maximilian I, the Holy Roman Emperor from 1508 to 1519. The two have a son, representing the union of Germany with its Greek cultural heritage, classical with romantic, and pantheism with monotheism. Unfortunately the son dies, after which Helen disappears into a mist, presumably back to Hades. Faust, however, in avenging his son's death, is rewarded with increased land holdings, which will figure prominently in the *Faust II* conclusion.

A decade later, Goethe takes up the tale again, a continuation of the first part. Faust continues his aspirations, which are increasingly megalomaniacal: sleeping with the most beautiful woman in antiquity; winning military battles for and returning riches to the Holy Roman Emperor; using slaves to build great dikes, reclaiming land from the sea; and founding utopian communities. Mephistopheles clearly wins his bet multiple times, as Faust appears more than content with Helen and their son, his military successes, his imperialistic pursuits and, especially, his attempt to create harmonious communities where everyone will be "free." Faust even claims that he "Im Vorgefühl von solchem hohen Glück/Geniess ich jetzt den Höchsten Augenblick" [As I presage a happiness so high, I now enjoy the highest moment] (lines 11585–86, trans. Kaufmann). Mephistopheles does help Faust with more magic tricks, such as conjuring up armies to help Faust with his military efforts or supplying ships to bring back the "products of foreign countries" gained maybe by trade, but more likely by looting and piracy (line 11187). At times, Mephistopheles turns away in disgust, such as during Faust's venture to reclaim land from the sea, doomed to failure. Faust is so greedy, so at ease with displacing innocent people to build his utopian commune, that he does not see any problem with using slaves and servants, nor desiring ownership of the land as far as the eye can see. Mephistopheles views the highest moment of pleasure for Faust as "den letzten, schlechten, leeren Augenblick" [The final wretched, empty moment] (line 11589, trans. Kaufmann), and Mephistopheles is sure that he has won: "Er fällt, es ist vollbracht" [He is fallen, it is finished] (line 11594, translation mine). De Campos, as well as most postcolonial translators, are more than alert to such depictions.

It is arguable that Faust in Part II is still striving for increased knowledge, that his military and social conquests are aimed at constructing a larger good, but in retrospect, and in light of contemporary literary criticism, Faust's conquests seem very limited in worldview, highly subjective, and nationalistic in nature. The Germans, of course, came late to national identity and very late to the colonization of Third World countries. In many ways, Goethe is trying to catch Germany up with his fellow Europeans, pursuing riches derived from colonization, establishing utopian New World settlements, and investing in large infrastructure national projects. Goethe and Faust seem blind to the consequences of such actions and to the enormous costs to the lives and livelihoods of those displaced through such projects. Goethe is magnificent in translating Ur-Germanic tales and oral forms into verse, and of translating Greek, Roman, and Italian culture into German theater and art. During the early 1800s, Germany is still a loose confederation of independent princedoms; Goethe's vision is more Napoleonic, or Maximilianic than revolutionary. As great as the *Faust* plays are, as visionary as Goethe's conception of *Weltliteratur* is, Goethe's vision is flawed by a yet unrealized German pride, a distorted view of European social and economic progress, and, especially, an indifference to the poor and indigenous peoples' lives disrupted by such "striving." As shall be seen in the section on international theater productions and contemporary interdisciplinary rewritings of *Faust*, the dominant humanistic and Christian interpretations of Faust are less frequent.

The ending of *Faust II* is still controversial. After Faust gives his speech regarding the construction of a utopian community, Faust encounters lemurs digging a grave, recalling Shakespeare's gravedigger's scene in *Hamlet*. Mephistopheles approaches with the pact signed in blood, ready to claim his deserved prize, and the jaws of hell open on the side. Phosphorus glows. The lemurs, Roman spirits of the dead, often vengeful, lend the scene a comic quality, as do the gravediggers in *Hamlet*, which, given the gravity of what is to come, can confuse viewers and critics. I suggest the lemurs represent more than just a comic interlude, but another in a long list of spirits in an in-between state, not in either heaven or hell. Next, angels from both the Devil and the heavens appear and begin to compete for "Faust's immortal part" [Faustens Unsterbliches] as Goethe would have it, and not necessarily his "soul," as many translators interpret it (stage direction, line 11825). After being bombarded by roses thrown down by the good angels, the Devil's angels blink first, and although Mephistopheles urges them to fight back, many flee. Even Mephistopheles is charmed, homoerotically drawn to the heavenly angels, and, while distracted for just a moment, he loses his hold on Faust. Again, the comic, even carnival elements dominate: the whole scene casts an aura of the occult—apparitions, magicians, witches seducing other angels, and Mephistopheles, out of character, erotically distracted.

Unlike all previous versions of *Faust*, in Goethe's rewriting the heavenly angels win and "kidnap" or "abduct" Faust's spirit. The verb "entführen" (line 11824) is quite clear in German, but it is often smoothed over—"carried off" or "bourne away"—in English translations of *Faust*. De Campos is unafraid to call a kidnapping for what it is, using the word "arrebatando," which connotes a sudden and almost violent capturing or snatching away. Mephistopheles, this time, is left calling, wondering to what power he might turn to claim his right: "Wer schafft mir mein erworbnes Recht" [Who will enforce the rights that I possess?] (11834, trans. Kaufmann). De Campos strongly emphasizes this sense of injustice in the final scenes, with Mephistopheles as the victim. Everything happens very quickly, in a state of confusion. Although good angels abduct Faust, Faust does *not repent* in any way and shows no change. He also does *not* go to heaven, but to in-between spaces no longer on earth but not yet in heaven, consistent with Goethe's exploration throughout the two plays. The first stop is at Mountain Gorge where Faust meets three obscure figures: religious hermits who bear Latin names: Pater Ecstaticus, Pater Profundus, and Pater Seraphicus. The symbolic connotations are vague, Ecstaticus, for example, may be a Dionysian rather than Christian term; Pater Profundus is perhaps also a veiled reference to something deep below. A chorus of blessed boys and younger angels appear and sing, but most are not yet fully developed spiritual beings, in varying stages of transition. Something transformative is brewing, but God or gods are yet to be seen in the picture.

Finally, another mysterious character enters, a Doctor Marianus, a medieval philosopher and theologian, perhaps based on Duns Scotus, and devotee of the Ur-Feminine. Heidegger, for example, was interested in Duns Scotus's thought for both its onto-ontological exploration and for its emphasis on movement. Marianus introduces the "Himmelskönigen" [Queen of Heaven], the "Höchsete Herrscherin der Welt" [The highest ruler of the world]. It is not God the Father who appears to judge or save Faust, but rather this Female Queen, Ur-Mother, Eternal Feminine, accompanied by a chorus of penitent women. Again, the depiction is very mystical, goddess-driven and non-patriarchal; Faust's striving for knowledge, lovemaking with Helen, imperial conquests, and socially progressive projects all seem for naught. The primary redeeming character seems to be Gretchen, who also appears as one of the repentant women, and who forgives Faust for abandoning her. It is Gretchen who takes Faust and asks for time "ihn zu belehren" [to teach him] (line 12092). Faust is set to go on *another* journey. The Mater Gloriosa, Virgin Mary, Mary *before* the conception of Jesus, grants Gretchen the right to take him to "höhern Sphären" [higher spheres] (line 12094), leaving ambiguous just how high those spheres might be. The last line of the play is "Das Ewig-Weibliche/Zieht uns hinan" [The Eternal Feminine/Draws us on high] (line 12210–11, trans. Kaufmann). The final line implies movement not stasis, transition not finality. Whether or not Faust goes to heaven is still to be determined. The final scene strikes me as magical, transitional, and translational, and thus in keeping with the translational theme of the two plays. The end is very positive and life-affirming, not necessarily in a Christian way, but in a process-oriented and non-judgmental fashion.

Faust's "immortal parts" thus are translated in the sense of moving from one place to another by good angels to higher spheres, but these angels seem to be part of *another* spiritual discourse, one characterized by a Mother Goddess, an Eternal Feminine Figure, who could very well be pre-Christian, even pre-Hellenic. She offers a substantial alternative to the secular striving for knowledge, the masculine physical and obsessive action that has characterized Faust's behavior throughout. Faust has always been depicted as a translator/traveler; he first meets Mephistopheles in his study while he is translating the first verse of the Gospel According to John. Here he is struggling, trying at first, "In the Beginning was the *Word*," then changing it to "In the beginning was the *Mind*," and to "In the beginning was the *Force*" before deciding on "In the beginning was the *Act*" (lines 1224–1237). Indeed, the whole play might be viewed as an attempt to figure out how to best translate these lines; certainly the choice of "act" appears to be subjective, based on Faust's frustration with scientific learning and desire to experience the world. The translation motif continues in his constant movement: he travels back in time to the Sparta in Greece, the Crusades, medieval German kingdoms, Holy Roman Empires, the tops of the Harz mountains, and to windswept spheres higher above. In the end, I suggest that he is about to embark on a new voyage, equally distant, mystical, and unknown, but completely in keeping with his desire for new discoveries, his restlessness with the present, and his openness to spiritual alternatives.

Translations of *Faust* into English

The translations of *Faust* are too numerous to count—many texts and films disappeared from the record before they could be catalogued. During the later part of the nineteenth and the early twentieth century, there were upward of 50 translations into English, many self-published or with very small presses (Heinemann 2012 [1884]); it seems as if every German-American writer or German teacher in the United States had translated *Faust* at some point. More astonishing, in the early days of cinema, dozens of silent films of Goethe's *Faust* were made, most lost to the historical record. With the two world wars and the fear of a powerful German nation in Europe and the Americas, the steady flow of *Faust* translations slowed. However, today a regular stream of new versions appear on the market, some scholarly, some poetic, and some performance-oriented.

The earliest *Faust* translations happened during Goethe's lifetime, before the publication of *Faust II*. One of the most discussed is the 1821 *Faustus: From the German of Goethe*, whose translator is unknown, but based on a stylistic comparison; some attribute it to Samuel Taylor Coleridge (Burwick and McKusick 2007). This is an illustrated *Faust*, with the publisher seeking an English translation to accompany the engravings by the German illustrator Moritz Retzsch in *Faust: Eine Tradödie* (1808). Boosey and Sons, the publisher, did contact Coleridge in May 1820, asking for texts for his edition, but it is unclear how Coleridge replied. It appears that Coleridge did begin a *Faust* translation in 1814 for another publisher, and that he had already successfully translated plays by Schiller, including *Wallenstein*. While Coleridge may not have been the translator of this particular *Faust*, in the early 1800s in England a substantial interest in Goethe's work existed as well as a lively exchange between writers and publishers in the two countries.

In 1831, Abraham Hayward published *Faust: A Dramatic Poem by Goethe* to high acclaim in the United Kingdom. The literal prose translation conveyed the depth and breadth of Goethe's thought, if not the poetry. Hayward included a 100-page introduction, comparing his translation

Table 2.4 Selected translations of Goethe's *Faust* (Frantz 1949; Classe 2000; Heinemann 2012 [1884])

1821	Verse translation of *Faust* (Part I) trans. attributed to Samuel Taylor Coleridge
1822	Scenes from *Faust*, trans. P.B. Shelley
1828	French trans. by Gérard de Nerval, *J.W. von Goethe's Faust*
1838	Abraham Hayward, prose, 3rd edition, London
1870–71	Bayard Taylor, Chicago
1880	J.S. Blackie, 2nd edition revised, London
1880	Thomas E. Webb, LL.D., Dublin/London
1887	Loosely adapted by William Gorman Wills for Lyceum Theatre London, production starring Henry Irving as Mephistopheles
1932	George Madison Priest NY: Covici Friede
1941	C.F. MacIntyre, Norfolk, Conn.
1949	Philip Wayne, Penguin Books, Harmondsworth
1950	Russian, trans. by Boris Pasternak
1952	Louis MacNeice, London
1957	C.F. MacIntyre, New Directions
1961	Walter Kaufmann, Doubleday
1962	Peter Salm, Bantam, rev. 1985
1965	Charles Passage, Bobbs Merrill
1970	Barker Fairley, University of Toronto Press
1976	Walter Arndt, Norton Critical Edition
1987	David Luke, Oxford World's Classics, Part II 1994
1992	Martin Greenberg, Yale University Press
1994	Stuart Atkins, Princeton University Press

to earlier English versions available, mostly to abridgements or excerpts appearing in literary journals. His arguments are forceful, setting up a new genre of *Faust* introductions. Hayward points out flaws of earlier versions and praises the depth and quality of the original. Hayward subsequently travels to Germany and talks with German writers such as Ludwick Tieck, Jacob Grimm, and August Wilhelm von Schlegel, making corrections and new contextualizations for the 1833 second edition. Interest in Goethe's *Faust* was high in the English-speaking world.

In Olive Classe's *Encyclopedia of Literary Translations into English* (2000), Julie Mercer Carroll starts a comparative analysis of significant *Faust* translations. Carroll begins with some of the nineteenth- and early twentieth-century translations, generally praising the verse translations over the prose. Bayard Taylor's 1870 verse translation serves as a case in point. Taylor reproduces the feminine rhymes, and, while admitting that he could not find rhymes for all the lines, he made up for it by adding rhymes to unrhymed passages (Carroll 2000: 544). While Carroll discusses the verse forms, often more Victorian than Germanic, she is not averse to the politics, citing George Madison Priest's 1932 translation of *Faust* as sympathetic to the Nazis, with the Faust depiction becoming a kind of hero-worship.

When Carroll turns to more contemporary versions, from Philip Wayne's Penguin edition in 1949–50, up to David Luke's Oxford version in 1994, the emphasis is on the innovative translation strategies. In the more recent translations, there seems to be again a continued emphasis on the poetics, but also an indication that some are breaking away from smooth Victorian British verse and open to more estranging Germanic forms, particularly the folk-literature forms that make *Faust* so popular in Germany. Wayne varies the quality of the verse, from the Earth Spirit's high verse forms to more colloquial forms for Mephistopheles and the Devil. Walter Kaufmann (1961), Charles Passage (1965), and Walter Arndt (1976) all receive praise for their formally rhymed and metered translations. This trend is then followed by a period with increased emphasis on readability, with Peter Salm's free-verse translation of 1962 allowing for greater prosodic freedom and more focus on the meaning; Barker Fairley's prose version of 1970, which is very easy for a reader with little or no knowledge of German literature to understand, and David Luke's translation (Part I 1987; Part II 1994), which lowers the register, reflects the German style, modernizes the language, and makes the translation more readable.

These later translations served a generation of college students perhaps better versed in German philosophy than literature. In his 1961 translation, Walter Kaufmann, a philosopher well known for his Nietzsche translations, retains a dialectic and suggests that what at first may appear Christian could be the *antithesis* of traditional Christianity. Kaufmann suggests that the interpretation of Goethe's treatment of Christian salvation is more ironic than literal. Kaufmann retains much "buffoonery," which he sees not as interludes, but an important aspect of *every* scene, from the Prologue through the final graveyard scene. Thus, Mephistopheles's lines are invariably comic, cutting, and satiric; they dialectically inform Faust's characterization. Kaufmann also well understands Goethe's borrowings, especially from British writers, and sees the overt as well as covert Hamlet, Laertes, and Ophelia connections throughout. Kaufmann is also not adverse to the vulgarity of the original, restoring some obscenities deleted from German editions, such as for "Es f—t die Hexe," Kaufmann fleshes out "The witches fart" (line 3961), often omitted in English. This emphasis on retaining the buffoonery helps Kaufmann shine in the Walpurgis Night Scenes, particularly giving insight into the dynamic and fiery role Mephistopheles plays. Kaufmann's Nietzschean impulses occasionally creep in, such as a reference to the "herd" (line 1640), or a female *Göttin* in the German turned into a masculine "God" (line 1084) on another, but it helps him portray Goethe's skepticism and not shy away from what might be considered blasphemous. One of the particularly enjoyable features of the Kaufmann version is that his more existential outlook allowed him to see better Faust's multiple intellectual interests and to better understand his overall frustration with the science, philosophy, and religion of the time. Kaufmann lets readers make up their minds by leaving the ending ambiguous. Faust does not recant, nor is he condemned.

In his 1976 translation for the Norton Critical Edition, Walter W. Arndt, the Russian and German translator famous for his verse translations, paid particular attention to the varied poetic forms employed by Goethe—everything from *ottava rima* to Germanic medieval couplets, from iambics and trochaics to prose, and from any number of musical and choral forms and Latin hymns to folk ballads. Arndt achieves a nice balance between high verse forms and colloquial expressions. The metrics are precise and fluid; the rhymes are readable, even quotable, and closer to the German than many earlier attempts at keeping the meter and rhyme in translation. Other advantages of the Arndt edition are the paratextual elements, including footnotes of the obscure sources, especially from Germanic, Greek, and Latin mythology. In addition, the editor Cyrus Hamlin, perhaps together with Arndt, offers many insights from Faust scholarship in an appendix, including references to major German critics—Schelling, Hegel, and Eckermann. One of the earlier attempts to make World Literature available to the English-language readers, came via the Norton Critical Edition Series. The *Faust* edition included information on sources, excerpts from Goethe's letters, essays by eighteenth- and nineteenth-century critics, such as the Schlegel brothers and Madame de Stael, plus twentieth-century essays by critics such as Herman Meyer, Wilhelm Emrich, Emil Staiger, and Georg Lukács.

Although Arndt's *Faust* translation has been well received, it nevertheless smoothes over the sardonic, satiric, and demonic elements. The scholars' essays in the paratextual portion are for the most part early twentieth-century German and British critics, and the largely structural or symbolic interpretations skirt more problematic and controversial issues. Kaufmann may be rougher on the rhymes but is more open to the irony. Moreover, the critical essays offered at the end represent a kind of scholarly consensus rather than a range of alternative readings. However, in the "Rewritings of *Faust*" section below, reinterpretations by feminists, queer theorists, minorities, ethnic groups, pantheistic, Wiccan, and postcolonial studies scholars, many from non-British-Germanic traditions, serve to reinvigorate the text, and, as I argue in this book, may shed *more* light on the original than the Anglo-Germanic reception.

The final translation I wish to discuss is the 1987/1994 Oxford World Classic translation of *Faust I and II* by David Luke, well known for his translations of Goethe's poetry, Thomas Mann's novels, and the Grimm brothers' parables. Luke's version combines Arndt's poetic qualities and Kaufmann's philosophic aspects. Luke has a very sensitive ear for Goethe's poetics, capturing the meter and rhyme, but demonstrates more poetic flexibility than Kaufmann and Arndt, not always insisting on line-ending stop rhymes, thereby adding fluidity. Despite his adherence to the verse forms, Luke also makes the text readable, avoiding syntactical inversions forcing rhymed words to the end of lines and shying away from archaisms. Using contemporary English and a lower register than Arndt makes the reading smoother. More important than the poetics is the content: Luke is careful *not* to impose his worldview on the text and instead allows Goethe's complex and varied meanings to emerge, including his philosophic and religious skepticism.

To his translation of *Faust I*, Luke offers a very thoughtful introduction explaining his poetic and philosophical goals. About God and Mephistopheles, he suggests, the two are less divinely opposed and instead share attributes. He also sees them in a stream of spiritual characters drawn from pre-classical, Hellenic, Nordic, and romantic sources. Luke writes, "The classical Goethe's Mephistopheles is even further than the young Goethe's from being the Satan of Christian tradition … He is neither Milton's nor Marlowe's Devil, he is de-theologized" (Luke 1987: xxx). About Goethe's depiction of God, Luke takes a more open approach. He suggests, "Equally, the Lord himself is not so much the Christian or even the Old Testament God as the impressive spokesman of the mature Goethe's positive and life-affirming view of things" (Luke 1987: xxx). Luke does not see Faust without spiritual qualities, but they are closer to the translational, transitional aesthetics I foreground in this book. Luke argues that Goethe celebrates the "cyclic Nature and the process of eternal Becoming" (1987: xxx). Goethe's Earth Spirit is not necessarily diabolical, but also retains a life-affirming aspect. Luke's depiction of the Lord thus represents less a Christian deity and more a "third voice" and "higher perspective" (1987: xxxi), which allows Goethe to maintain a religious distance in the final scenes and permits him to show a certain amount of irony.

Indeed, this middle path is indicated throughout, as in many scenes God and Mephistopheles are portrayed as similar to each other rather than diametrically opposed. Mephistopheles's role in the salvation process is contradictory as he leads Faust to his final destination. When Faust first encounters this unknown intruder in his study and asks him "who are you?" Mephistopheles replies that he is "part of the power which would/Do evil constantly, and constantly does good" (lines 1335–37, quoted by Luke 1987: xxxiii). Thus the dichotomies—good/evil, saved/condemned, moral/immoral, God/Devil—are less distinct, and another philosophy/theology needs to be applied when translating: a middle way, more integrative, open, and multi-theological. While some may look for universal meanings or religious resolutions, *Faust* has always been translational and performative, constantly revised and rewritten over its lifetime, and then released to the world as *Weltliteratur*, translated scores of times into English alone. Perhaps the instability of the text facilitates its frequent translation. Luke's edition strikes me as being more open to the conflicts and contradictions, theological and secular, virtues and vices, and idealism and cynicism than many translations into English. He also offers a "translatable" translation, one that stimulates critical thinking and serves the source text as well as teachers, students, non-professional reader, rewriters, and performers.

Rewritings of *Faust*

The first set of rewritings to be looked at are the theater versions of *Faust*. While *Faust* is ostensibly written as a play (or as two plays), most directors agree that the plays are unperformable: they are too long, too fragmented, with too many characters and too many foreign and classical references. While *Faust I* has been attempted for the stage, *Faust II*, with all its references to classical antiquity, multiple characters, and the use of Greek and Latin verse forms, is nearly impossible to perform. There have been, however, a few efforts. In 2000, Peter Stein, director at the *Schaubühne* in Berlin for many years, staged a full version of *Faust* in conjunction with the Hanover Expo 2000, calling it a "world premier." The play had 35 actors and ran 21 hours. Expo 2000's theme was "Humankind-Nature-Technology" and was intended to be Germany's coming-out party for the new century, underscoring its economic and technological accomplishments during the previous decades. The play contains *all* of Goethe's lines and follows *all* of Goethe's stage directions. Staged over two days, the play was so demanding that two actors were needed to play the main role, with Christian Nickel as a younger, and Bruno Ganz as an older Faust. The sets, as might be imagined, were elaborate, with spiral staircases leading up to heaven, fortresses on mountaintops, magical witches, and sea gods swimming. According to a *New York Times Review*, the "literalness" approached "caricature" (Midgette 2000), many serious passages became comic, and the play was hard to follow. Most other reviewers agreed that the play was less than successful, underscoring the argument that the play as written is unstageable. However, as Midgette points out, the German public was overjoyed; reviews in *Die Welt am Sonntag*, for example, were "ecstatic," perhaps demonstrating more national pride than aesthetic pleasure.

As was the case with the Hanover production, Goethe's *Faust* has been viewed by a series of different German governments as an heroic model. The Weimar Republic held their native son dear, especially for his German spirit and humanist ideas, and so too did the fascists who claimed Faust as one of their own, particularly emphasizing the German Volk, the global striving, and heroic action. Indeed, Thomas Mann's novel *Doktor Faustus* served as Mann's attempt, while in exile, to take back the Faustian heritage assumed by the Nazis (Hedges 2009: 44–45). So too did the socialist government of the German Democratic Republic (GDR) hold *Faust* up as a model for the construction of a socialist culture. Goethe's *Faust* was viewed as important as Marx's *Communist Manifesto*; Walter Ulbricht, First Secretary of the GDR Communist Party, writes "Ich denke es ist ein Symbol, daß das 'Kommunistische Manifest' von Karl Marx und der 'Faust' von Goethe die Lieblingswerke der Sozialisten sind" [I believe it is a symbol, that the *Communist Manifesto* by Karl Marx and *Faust* by Goethe are the favorite works of the socialists] (John 2012: 74–75). East German officials were proud to point to line 11580 at the end of

Table 2.5 Theater productions and novel adaptations of *Faust*

Selected theater productions:

1828	Christian Dietrich Grabbe, *Don Juan and Faust*
1887	William Gorman Wills, *Faust*, starring Henry Irving, Lyceum Theatre, London
1946	Carl Zuckmayer, *The Devil's General*
1952	Bertolt Brecht and Egon Monk, *Urfaust*
1965–81	Fritz Bennewitz, three versions of *Faust* in the GDR, later staged in New York, Manila, and Mumbai
1968	Volker Braun, *Hans Faust*; later rewritten as *Hinze und Kunze* in 1973
1976	Kottayam Kaliyarangu, *Dr. Faust – Kathakali*, Kerala, India
1982	Richard Nieoczym, *Faust I*, Actor's Lab, Toronto, Canada
1985	Václav Havel, *Pokoušení* [Temptation]
1995	W. Kentridge and L. Rampolokeng, *Faustus in Africa*, Cape Town, S. Africa
1997	Mark Ravenhill, *Faust is Dead*
1999	Eimuntas Nekrošius, *Faust*, Menos Fortas, Lithuania
1999	Márcio Meirelles, *Fausto#Zero*, Bahia, Brazil
2000	Peter Stein, *Faust*, full versions, starring Bruno Ganz, Expo 2000 Hanover, 21 hours
2014	Sharon Ann Fogerty, *Faust 2.0*, Barnard Center for Translation Studies and Mabou Mines

Selected novel adaptations:

1791	Friedrich Maximilian Klinger, *Faustus* [*Faust's Life and Death and Journey Through Hell*]
1855	Ivan Turgenev, *Faust*
1877	Louisa May Alcott, *A Modern Mephistopheles*
1891	Joaquim Maria Machado de Assis, *Quincas Borba*
1898	Alfred Jarry, *Exploits and Opinions of Dr. Faustroll, pataphysician*
1929–40	Mikhail Bulgakov, *The Master and Margarita*
1947	Thomas Mann, *Doktor Faustus*
1955	William Gaddis, *The Recognitions*
1969	Philip Dick, *Galactic Pot-Healer*
1978	William Hjortsburd, *Falling Angel*
1980	Robert Nye, *Faust*
1986	John Banville, *Mefisto*
1990	Terry Pratchett, ~~Faust~~ *Eric*
1994	Tom Holt, *Faust Among Equals*
2003	Susanne Alberti, *Fausts Gretchen. Roman einer Verführung*

Faust II when the dying Faust claims "Auf wahrhaft freiem Grund und Boden stehen" [With free men on free ground their freedom share] (trans. Kaufmann), a line that Goethe rewrote several times. East German cultural officials would often say that if a *Faust III* were to be written, it would have been written in the GDR (John 2012: 49). In the early years of the new and optimistic socialist state, GDR productions depicted Faust heroically as a progressive figure pushing forward, tackling problems, and offering new initiatives.

Officially endorsed versions of *Faust* were not the only rewritings to appear in East Germany during its formative stages. In fact, a critique of the orthodox German line begins in the GDR, as many of the leading East German writers approached *Faust* in a different fashion. Bertolt Brecht and Egon Monk staged an *Urfaust* (1952–53) at the *Schiffbauerdamm* (later the Berliner Ensemble); Hans Eisler wrote a libretto called *Johann Faustus* (1952); and the poet Volker Braun wrote a play titled *Hans Faust* (1968), which he later rewrote as *Hinze und Kunze* (1973); Adolf Dresen and Wolfgang Heinz staged a *Faust I* (1968) in the Deutsches Theater Berlin; and Christoph Schroth wrote a new version of *Faust* (1979) for the Mecklenburgishes Staatstheater Schwerin. Many of these adaptations were experimental in nature, as writers committed to socialism tried to figure out what they could derive from the classical theater, as well as what might be allowed in the new communist state.

In many ways, the international rewriting paradigm began with Brecht's *Urfaust* (1986 [1952–53]), which was particularly threatening to the new regime: too experimental, too fragmentary, and too radical. Brecht considered the play as a way to stage a critique of the canon from a socialist if not postcolonial perspective. Brecht's vision was more pessimistic than traditional German interpretations, using the play to highlight past German exploitation of the masses and pointing out contradictions in Faust's behavior, whereas both the new West and East German governments preferred a more dynamic, striving Faust with few contradictions. It is not surprising that Brecht chose *Urfaust*, with its increased humor, populism, pre-classical epic themes, and lack of resolution. An ensuing debate between artists and government officials over the role of art, the use of the German cultural heritage, the incorporation of the classics, ensued unabated in the German Democratic Republic for the next 40 years, with varying periods of freezes and thaws. Certainly the Marxists could see the contradictions contained within the work, and party officials were not about to *ban* Goethe from its theater repertoire. Thus, for East German writers, the play provided a perfect means to smuggle in alternative ideas and forms, claim literalism while performing contradictions, and support the regime but also pose probing questions.

In his book *Bennewitz, Goethe, "Faust": German and Intercultural Stagings* (2012), the Canadian scholar David G. John talks about Fritz Bennewitz, director of the Weimar National Theater, who produced several different versions of Goethe's *Faust* during the years of the German Democratic Republic. The first production staged in 1965/67 was grand, conforming in many ways to the GDR vision: large orchestra, period costumes, with a towering multitiered structure portraying Faust's office. Faust is very heroic, intellectually insatiable. The language was kept intact and the play ran for more than six hours. But in other ways, it stands in opposition to earlier versions. Bennewitz toned down the emphasis on magical associations: saints are faceless, choruses muted, Mephistopheles's tricks are minimal, and sexual connotations omitted. The ending is changed, too, as Faust comes back to life, escapes from the lemurs and fallen angels, and speaks the lines normally played by the Chorus about the Ewig-Weibliche. Faust is portrayed as free from his self-centered obsessions and now focused on the secular and material possibilities that may contribute to shaping the new social order (John 2012: 86–87).

In the second Bennewitz version in 1975, the vision is more tragic. By this time the Prague Spring has come and gone, and disappointment in the politics of the GDR is growing. Perhaps influenced by international theater, Bennewitz, a member of the Communist Party who had permission to travel internationally, displayed a kind of split personality, at home in the GDR, but also looking abroad. In the 1975 version, the set is less grand, set instead in villages and rural areas; the backdrop is a Pieter Bruegel the Elder painting of fallen angels. The musicians are few, and the large choruses are gone. Faust, an angry young man, exhibits doubts in the progress of human knowledge. Faust's conflicts and guilt are displayed, and the ironies of the capitalism and imperialism of *Faust II* revealed. In Faust's last speech, while stating that he is enjoying this "höchsten Augenblick" [highest moment], the lines are delivered with irony and disillusion, implying that the reality he sees does not measure up to the grandiose goals (John 2012: 117).

Bennewitz's third version, staged in 1981, goes even further in emphasizing the irony and disillusionment. The play is cut to three hours; full scenes are omitted; jump cuts fragment the text; and the costumes are modernized but eclectic. The grandeur of the set is gone: the stage is in shadows, decorations are sparse; the tower in the study is dilapidated; and Gretchen comes from a derelict boardinghouse. Faust is no longer heroic; instead, he is now depicted as uncertain of his identity or direction. The music includes decadent Western rock; farcical elements are added such as scientists dancing a can-can. The aura of the language has been destabilized. In the final scene, Faust does not walk past death to envision a glorious future; rather, he delivers his speech and remains standing, frozen on the stage. The lemurs never return (John 2012: 147–48). My sense is that Brecht's *Urfaust* influenced Bennewitz's second and third versions, as Bennewitz staged several Brecht plays, as well as Shakespeare, during this period. East German productions were among the first to offer an alternative to Western interpretations and begin a critique of the humanist, capitalist, colonial, and Christian versions that dominate Western reception.

While the East German playwrights began the process of questioning earlier German interpretations of Faust, the power of the GDR Ministry of Culture was strong, and there were limitations on how far they could go. The real break occurs in international productions. In "Contemporary African and Brazilian Adaptations of Goethe's *Faust* in Postcolonial Context" (2008), Katharina Keim discusses two such examples: the first is *Fausto#Zero, de Goethe* (1999), a production by Márcio Meirelles at Teatro Vila Velha in Bahia, Brazil; and the second is *Faustus in Africa* (1995) by

William Kentridge at the Handspring Puppet Company in Cape Town, South Africa. The Brazilian play is particularly illuminating in light of Haroldo de Campos's theories of transculturation. Bahia was one of the main centers of the slave trade, and its population today is predominantly black or *pardo* [mixed race], with whites making up less than 20 percent of the population. Bahia also has the largest carnival in the world and the biggest population following the *Candomblé* religion, an originally Yoruban religion preserved in parts of Bahia despite attempts by colonial governments and Christian religions to ban it. Meirelles is well known in Brazil for his work with the Bando de Teatro Olodum, which started out as a carnival organization for the working-class Afro-Brazilian population before turning to theater.

Meirelles chose *Urfaust* initially as a basis for his play *Fausto#Zero* because of its folk-tale elements (Keim 2008: 250). While the *Fausto#Zero* adheres closely to Goethe's text, other connotations are specifically directed to an Afro-Brazilian audience. Whereas Faust appears as an outsider, cut off from the people, Mephistopheles is a black actor strongly connected to the receiving culture, well versed in *Candomblé* practices and its worship of multiple gods. For example, Mephistopheles takes on characteristics of the Exú, a Yoruban messenger god and trickster deity, often associated with the Devil by Christian believers. In that role, Mephistopheles is better able to fulfill Faust's intellectual, material, and sexual desires. The Earth Spirit is also represented by a ritual *Candomblé* dance performed by Exú. A black actress, a lower-class woman largely attracted to Faust because of her desire for social advancement, plays Gretchen. In many ways, the Gretchen tragedy translates well to Brazil, as white intellectuals have seduced and abandoned black women for centuries, murdered brothers trying to protect them, and separated girls from their mothers. In one of the more moving scenes from the play, Keim cites Gretchen, when weeping at her mother's grave, being haunted by an *evil* spirit, this time in the form of the crucified Christ, wearing his crown of thorns, symbolizing the Jesus figure as both a perpetrator of European colonial injustices and a victim of earlier Roman imperial powers: good and evil here appearing in the same figure (Keim 2008: 252). This creation of characters neither good nor bad, connecting a Christian Devil character to a positive *Candomblé* god, and hinting that the Christian Savior may not be infallible, provides a good illustration of de Campos's *transluciferation mefistofáustica* translation approach and may explain *Fausto#Zero*'s appeal to contemporary Bahian audiences.

In *Faustus in Africa*, William Kentridge, a South African director, uses much from Goethe's two plays, including parts of *Faust I* and fragments of *Faust II*, but he also adds *new* material written by Lesego Rampolokeng, a well-known black poet, and playwright from Johannesburg. The approach of combining the old material with the new serves to cannibalize the play, creating a version that is not just another European import, but both, part European and part South African. *Faustus in Africa* uses large puppets derived from the Bunraku tradition, a Japanese theater form adapted to

Figure 2.2 Faustus in Africa, Handspring Puppet Theater (1995).

South Africa, as the actors. In a certain fashion, the play exhibits a return to a pre-Goethean traveling *Faust* when it was performed for local villagers as a puppet play in marketplaces and town squares in sixteenth-century Germany. Additionally, Rampolokeng's contributions are composed in traditional *dithoko*, an oral Bantu South African form, and then blended with contemporary rap. These adaptations unveil the degrees of hybridization taking place in such a form of translation/rewriting.

Similar to the Bahian Faust, *Faustus in Africa* shows Faust as a light-skinned puppet from the period of German colonization (1884–1915) with humanitarian goals, but his pursuit of economic gain and sexual conquests undermine such strivings. Wagner, his servant, renamed Johnston, is black, and so too is Mephistopheles, cast as a clerk in a telegraph office, yet with magical powers, including the ability to converse with God on his telephone. God is always offstage, and, although characterized as male, is performed by a female voice. Faust and Mephistopheles soon sign their pact, and the two go off, this time on a tour of the entire continent of Africa, shown by black and white animation film sequences interwoven into the action. Gretchen is a nurse in a hospital taking care of lepers, and a black actress plays her as well. After the seduction, Faust goes off on a safari, where he shoots African wild animals, buys Ife heads, and eats African meals, devouring Africa as he goes. The end portrays the servant Johnston as part of the ruling class, Gretchen seduced and abandoned, and Gretchen's family murdered, all of which serve as a reflection of the early post-apartheid nation. The scene recalls the trials of the Truth Commission, dealing with numerous deaths and injustice, and trying to find a way to bind, forgive, and move on. Unlike Goethe's *Faust*, in the South African version, Faust realizes his guilt and asks for redemption. Faust's former servant, who is now in charge, offers Faust amnesty. God's voice then intervenes as he/she asks for Mephistopheles to return to his "rightful" place in hell, but this command is ignored, and God's voice is simply turned off. Mephistopheles is released from the European constraints of power and religion, and the final scene shows him laughing and free.

These two productions show just how de Campos's theories of *antropofagia* continue to be relevant in the world of translation studies and of World Literature. In former colonies and new and emerging nations, such a cannibalistic form of rewriting is not the exception, but the norm. Genres are repeatedly hybridized, old material is reinterpreted in light of the local culture, and new elements are added. Theatrical presentations tend toward the innovative and creative. Old definitions of white and black, good and evil, source and target, and faithful and unfaithful are called into question. The very act of relocating a European classical play in the space of postcolonial culture modifies how it is interpreted and performed. Taking a written text and performing it in an oral tradition produces different effects. Changing the race of the actors alters the audience's impressions. Translation studies must expand its methodological repertoire. Much can be learned from intersemiotic approaches and transformational processes in translation and rewriting. Issues of power and context continually arise in such postcolonial productions, and Bassnett and Lefevere's focus on issues of cultural studies and ideology are more relevant today than ever.

I suggest that a black Mephistopheles with both good and bad qualities is not absent from Goethe's *Faust*; certainly Goethe saw the negative qualities with Faust's striving for material gain and sexual promiscuity, hence such postcolonial interpretations are not necessarily unfaithful. De Campos's transculturation theories threatened translation studies scholars at the time, as his metaphors for the translation process were deliberately provocative. I suggest that as scholars consider additional international translations and productions of *Faust*, they will find de Campos's theories increasingly relevant. I also suggest that such international interpretations are already circling back to Germany and, in turn, influencing the German reception as well. The Handspring Puppet Theater production *Faustus in Africa*, for example, has been staged not only in France, Spain, Italy, Israel, the United Kingdom, and the United States, but also performed throughout Germanic-language cultures, including Germany, Switzerland, and Denmark, as well as the Czech Republic and Belgium.

Faust *adaptations in cinema*

While theatrical productions of *Faust* have been relatively few, film adaptations of *Faust* are many. In this section, I discuss F.W. Murnau's silent version *Faust: Ein deutsche Volksage* (1926), René Clair's *La Beauté du diable* [Beauty of the Devil] (1950), and Alexander Sokurov's *Faust* (2011). The image of Faust and the Devil are captivating; viewers know the story and have their interpretations, consequently, filmmakers have to manage audience expectations all the while aiming to leave their marks. It can be argued that not only film influenced *Faust* productions, but also that *Faust* influenced the very development of the emerging genre of film. While some argue that *Faust* is unstageable in theatrical productions, F.W. Murnau shows the expanded capabilities of film; its ability to play with light, characterization, costumes, make-up, jump cuts, close-ups, time sequences, and special effects, such as Faust and Mephistopheles flying through the sky with the earth passing below. The play *Faust* could very well have dictated some of these techniques. Additionally, the filmmaker creates images that provoke the audience's imaginations, allowing them to participate in the experience, similar to Peter Brook's call to transport viewers into the imaginative realm of the play (see Chapter 1 in this volume).

F.W. Murnau was German-born but immigrated to the United States in 1926. He was skillful at adapting novels to film, such as *Nosferatu* (1922), his version of Bram Stoker's *Dracula*, one of the most famous horror films ever made. Murnau was a student of Max Reinhardt (see Chapter 1 in this volume). His film draws upon Goethe's *Faust* plus earlier versions ingrained in the German psyche. Certainly influenced by German culture and expressionism, the film sets up a paradigm of visuals for both Faust and Mephistopheles. The film is fairly faithful to Goethe's version, particularly with the Gretchen episode at its center, with Faust sleeping with her, getting her pregnant, murdering her brother, and fleeing with Mephistopheles; Faust returns when Gretchen has been condemned and is being burned to death. In Murnau's film, Faust throws himself into the fire, and as the fire consumes them, they rise together to heaven. Murnau makes some changes, especially at the beginning: Mephisto's bet is with an archangel, not with God or with Faust; Faust is less an academic scholar and more an elderly alchemist who becomes frustrated with both alchemy and religion, burning his books, including the Bible, as Mephistopheles appears. The two first make a 24-hour pact, which is then extended as Faust is making love to an Italian duchess and needs more time to finish. Faust and Gretchen's love affair begins when he grows tired of lust.

German audiences tended to dislike the Murnau's film, claiming that it took too many liberties with their beloved Faust and trivialized the conflict between good and evil. However, audiences abroad loved the film, and critics list it among the greatest movies ever made. Murnau was also astute enough to create *different* versions for various countries. Some included just additions or cuts to the many scenes, but in other cases actors wore different costumes and the cinematographer used different camera angles. While many of the different versions of the film are lost, German, French, American, and bilingual German-English copies still exist. Most scenes seem to be shot at least twice, setting up a precedent for the localization of

Figure 2.3 Mephistopheles from Murnau's *Faust* (1926).

international film; cuts or changes appear dictated by the audience's familiarity with German culture and the Faust legend. Still other changes are more aesthetic and interpretive, as, for example, in the USA version, where the final ascent into heaven is quite explicit. Other language versions allow for a less redemptive and more speculative interpretation of the ending. The subtitles for the German version are good, written and adapted by Gerhardt Hauptmann, a famous German playwright, and novelist, winner of the 1912 Nobel Prize for Literature, and the other films use translated versions of Hauptmann's script. It is the *images* that stay with the viewer and influence nearly all-subsequent translations, written or cinematic. Figure 2.3 represents Mephistopheles with his wings/cape blocking out the sky and entirely enveloping a German village.

While the international versions of Murnau's film may lack in linguistic equivalence and metaphysical philosophic insight, they certainly provide an astonishing cinematic experience and offer visual images that are lasting, all of which support Bassnett and Lefevere's claims that in this day and age, images of texts may be stronger than the written texts themselves (see Chapter 3 in this volume). With the exception of German language students and scholars, for the next generation of "readers," the film versions are perhaps more influential and lasting.

Table 2.6 Film adaptations of *Faust*

Selected film productions/adaptations:
1897	*Faust: apparition de Méphistophélès*, August and Louis Lumière
1897	*Faust and Mephistopheles*, dir. George Albert Smith (English)
1897	*Faust et Marguerite*, Georges Méliès
1910	*Faust*, dir. Oskar Messter, starring Franz Porten as Faust
1895–1926	More than 100 *Faust* films made in era of silent films. Most have been lost to history
1926	*Faust*, dir. F.W. Murnau, starring Gösta Ekman (Murnau's last German film)
1949	*La Beauté du diable*, dir. René Claire (French)
1952	*Ikiru*, dir. Akira Kurosawa (Japan)
1960	*Faust*, dir. Peter Gorski, starring Gustaf Gründgens as Mephisto (German)
1967	*Bedazzled*, dir. Stanley Donen (UK)
1967	*Doctor Faustus*, dir. Richard Burton, Nevill Coghill (UK)
1981	*Mephisto*, dir. István Szabó (German, Hungarian, Austrian)
1986	*Crossroads*, dir. Walter Hill (USA)
1994	*Lekce Faust* [The Legend of Faust], dir. Jan Švankmajr (Czech). Animation
1995	*O Convento*, dir. Manoel de Oliveira (Portugal/France)
1997	*The Devil's Advocate*, dir. Taylor Hackford (USA)
2000	*Faust*, dir. Thomas Grimm and Peter Stein, based on Hanover theater production (Germany)
2001	*Fausto 5.0*, dir. Alex Ollé (Spain)
2002	*I was a Teenage Faust*, dir. Thom Eberhardt (Canada)
2009	*The Imaginarium of Doctor Parnassus*, dir. Terry Gilliam (USA)
2011	*Faust*, dir. Alexander Sokurov (Russian director; German language film)

The tendency toward international productions intended for a global audience continues with the French filmmaker René Clair, director of *La Beauté du diable* [Beauty of the Devil] (1950). A post-World War II adaptation, the movie was filmed in Italy and is a French-Italian production, with the French actor Gérard Philipe as Faust and the Swiss actor Michel Simon as Mephistopheles. Clair himself spent much of World War II in Hollywood, and the film also comments on the United States and its nuclear legacy. In the movie, the filmmaker questions human striving and "progress" as often seen in Faust, at least in its reception in Germany. Indeed, while set in the nineteenth century, with aristocratic palaces, ornate costumes, and horse-drawn carriages, the film also connects to the post-World War II present, making a strong commentary not only on Nazism and its industrial/technological "progress," but also on the "advance" of both science and religion, not just in Germany, but internationally as well. The most interesting part of the film consists of its foreshadowing of the future of alchemy/science, i.e., the ability to create energy out of physical matter. The projected horror of a nuclear holocaust is perhaps *more* present than the atrocities committed by Nazi Germany. The final scene is quite pessimistic, even apocalyptic: Clair presents the viewer with bombed-out towns, accompanied by fire and smoke, emblematic not only of contemporary representations of hell and post-World War II Germany but also post-Hiroshima and its worldwide implications. After Faust turns sand into gold during his scientific advances, the gold at the end reverts to sand, thereby ruining the economy. As the scholar/alchemist Faust, with Mephisto's help, figures out how to manufacture nuclear energy out of dust, in its own way connecting contemporary science to the alchemy of the eighteenth and nineteenth centuries, the sense is that all cannot end well.

In an interesting twist, in René Clair's *La Beauté du diable*, Mephistopheles and Faust swap identities. The older Faust turns into the younger Mephistopheles for much of the film, and the younger and quite handsome Mephistopheles becomes Faust, thus the title of the film. While at times confusing to the viewer, the doubling of the characters locates good and evil in the *same* character, resulting in a split personality. Regarding the pact with the Devil, Faust resists for much of the film, maintaining a distant belief in the possibility of Christian salvation; thus, Faust has to trick Mephistopheles into granting him eternal youth. Gretchen is portrayed as Marguerite, a circus/gypsy performer, and Helen of Troy is rewritten as a French princess. Only when Mephistopheles threatens to relieve Faust of his magical powers and youthful vitality does Faust finally sign the pact in blood. Marguerite, however, resists to the end, holding out for the promise of eternal life with Faust. When the gold reverts to sand, the people of the kingdom blame Faust and demand revenge; Mephistopheles is only too happy to comply, assuming the license to enact the final destruction. At the end, true to Goethe's version, Mephistopheles is stripped of all his powers. Faust and Marguerite live on, young and in love, and both join the circus/gypsy players and travel on to their next production.

While Clair changes *La Beauté du diable*, a large amount is also retained, such as the negative consequences of the military/industrial striving, the triumph of love, and the open ending as Faust and Gretchen go off on a new journey. Viewers also cannot help but note how some of the imagery of Murnau's film is furthered in Clair's *La Beauté*. An intersemiotic paradigm emerges for images of Faust and Mephistopheles in the new genre of film, creating another kind of palimpsest, as the film images are layered over linguistic representations.

The final motion picture to be discussed is the 2011 film *Faust* directed by the Russian filmmaker Alexander Sokurov. It was an international production, filmed in the Czech Republic, Iceland, and Germany, with German and Russian actors, a Russian production team, and a French cinematographer. According to Condee (2012), 38 countries contributed to the film's $9.3 million budget. Johannes Zeiler, a relatively unknown German actor, plays Faust; the Russian actor Anton Adasinsky plays Mephistopheles (a moneylender named Mauritius); the Russian-German actress Isolda Dychauk plays Margarete, and the famous German actress Hanna Schygulla plays the moneylender's wife. The supporting cast includes actors from Germany, Russia, and Iceland. Despite the Russian production, financing, and directing, the language of the film is German. Sokurov's *Faust* continues the theme of the powers of corruption previously explored in his series: first on Adolf Hitler in *Moloch* (1999), next on Vladimir Lenin in *Taurus* (2001), and finally on Hirohito in *The Sun* (2005). It may strike the reader as strange that *Faust* should be included in this series of films about the most vicious dictators of the twentieth century. While set in the nineteenth century, the themes explored are contemporary to Germany and Russia, and, as Sokurov would have viewers to believe, the whole world.

The film explores the psychology of Faust and how his quest for scientific and alchemic knowledge parallels the quest for political and military power by these brutal dictators. What Sokurov shows is that middle and lower classes have the same set of desires as the great dictators (or vice versa): most people want to gain knowledge, have new ideas, create new products, seek pleasure, and find love, as does this Faust figure. Thus, Sokurov taps into a kind of populism to which viewers can relate. The Faust of this film is a doctor who begins to examine people's entrails for their souls, conducting autopsies to see what lies *inside* the body. What is different about this film from Goethe's *Faust* is that instead of seeking knowledge in the *higher* spheres, this Faust, with Mephistopheles's help, searches both into the bowels of human cadavers and into the figurative *bowels of the earth*. The film is very earthy: poor people, crowded streets, animals running free, filthy interiors, with scatological references, all leaving Faust increasingly pessimistic about the existing human condition. Faust is also poor and hungry and thus seeks out the moneylender Mephistopheles, a very strange character who, in the famous nude scene in the bath, where Faust first encounters Margarete, reveals strange folds of fat on his belly and appears to have no genitals.

Mephistopheles and Faust get along very well, much like Faust and Mephisto in the puppet shows. They go on a labyrinthine tour of the village and surrounding countryside, fueled by curiosity. First discussing the translation of the Gospel According to John—in this encounter, Mephistopheles is the one who comes up with "in the beginning was the 'deed.'" Later, when talking about the nature of good and evil, Mephistopheles wonders whether anything such as good even exists. During their exploration of the town, their conversations are underscored by the visual imagery: the dirty streets, corrupt priests, rats in the corners, dogs sniffing around graves, war-weary soldiers stumbling through the streets, and, especially, hungry and poor people everywhere. Many scenes are so base they are shocking, such as the Virgin's statue in a church being sexually groped. However, that is the point: Mephistopheles is showing Faust a kind of hell on earth; heaven and salvation are absent; philosophic or scientific inquiries useless; and even love is called into question. Both characters are comic and ironic, portrayed more as anti-heroes than heroes, which destabilizes versions portraying Faust as a hero.

While the pact is slow to come in Sokurov's *Faust*, much of the plot of the earlier versions remains: Mephistopheles eventually leads Faust to Margarete, who retains her peasant beauty and innocence. Lust is Faust's first emotion toward Margarete—he lifts her skirt in the bath scene—that morphs into love toward her in a later scene. Faust, upon Mephistopheles's urging, murders the protective brother Valentine, in a similar way to the German version. The end of the film is shot in Iceland first at a geyser and then at a glacier. Sokurov leaves it ambiguous as to whether Faust and Mephistopheles are going to hell or heaven, as their orientation becomes confused—perhaps, in fact, there is no difference. In this version, Faust breaks the pact by stoning Mephistopheles to death and going off on his own, claiming he no longer needs this diabolic guide. Where he is headed is *not* heaven or a higher sphere, rather it is to a desolate landscape of volcanic rock and ice, with no vegetation or indication of life. As with René Clair's apocalyptic ending, Sokurov grants no resolution; the viewer is left with no answers. Neither religion, human knowledge, or love provides an answer; Faust's efforts are futile.

I suggest post-translation studies can help better analyze such cinematic translations and rewritings. A consultation of both the original and previously translated or rewritten texts becomes valuable, while directors deviate from those scripts, they still, consciously or subconsciously, draw upon earlier versions. Reviewers suggest, for example, that the Sokurov film is more Dutch Brueghelian, showing everyday lower and middle-class life than High German intellectual. It also becomes necessary to know the Germanic tradition *before* Goethe by consulting Marlowe and other pre-Goethe versions in which Gretchen is condemned to death for her infanticide and Faust is condemned to hell for his blasphemy and murder. Post-translation studies encompasses the *intersemiotic* transfers as well as the linguistic and literary: in Sokurov's case, detectable is the influence of Murnau's visuals, especially depictions of the village, as well as the influence of Clair's post-World War II apocalyptic ending. Cultural studies must take local reception into account, which, in Sokurov's case, would be Russian, but also a much wider international view, as Sokurov is clearly intending to make *global* cinema appealing to international audiences. New questions arise, such as what is the influence of Sokurov's film beyond Germany and Russia, but in Latin America, Asia, or, especially, Africa?

International translations provide new insights and viewpoints for the *source* culture as well as the target culture. Translations flow in multiple directions and often slip over unintended borders. Mere source/target comparisons are insufficient. Murnau, Clair, and Sokurov are creating new strands as I write, thereby creating a new paradigm, one that literary translators or translation studies scholars can no longer ignore. Cinema, perhaps *more* than literary translation, has turned *Faust* into World Literature. Post-translation studies also looks at how translations aid in the creation of whole new *genres*: for example, *Faust* translations have helped create a new genre of cinema. One of the first films ever shot was *Faust: apparition de Méphistophélès* (1897) by Auguste and Louis Lumière, inventors of the Cinematograph, the first motion picture camera, and the first filmmakers in history. While producing *Faust* onstage is nearly impossible because of the fragments, jump cuts, time lapses, plethora of characters, magic tricks, and celestial perspectives, *all* of those obstacles can be circumvented through cinema, and I would argue that the experiments producing *Faust* for film *helped establish the genre* of cinema for what it is.

Finally, the postmodern "meaninglessness" of the conclusion of Sokurov's *Faust*, the Icelandic volcanic wasteland at the end, is one of the possibilities suggested by the play, perhaps more appropriate for post-World War II productions. Sokurov plainly inculpates all of those politicians, military officials, industrialists, and even religious figures who committed atrocities in Germany, Russia, and the rest of Europe during the past century, as well as incriminates emerging dictators and despots around the world in the present. Goethe is perhaps more prophetic than the best critics of German literature have imagined. Mephistopheles's ironic musings must be taken more seriously, which is what Hutcheon calls for, and which is what Sokurov does.

Faust *rewritings in music*

Musical adaptations of *Faust* began early and have continued to grow, especially in popular culture. Franz Schubert wrote, "Gretchen am Spinrade" [Gretchen at the Spinning Wheel] during Goethe's lifetime and after the French composer Hector Berlioz read Gérard de Nerval's translation of *Faust I* as early as 1828, he wrote "Eight Scenes from Faust" (1829), which Goethe seems to have heard and enjoyed. Berlioz returned to the Faust theme in 1845, rewriting the earlier piece as part of a larger work entitled *La damnation de Faust* (1846), which he first called a "concert opera," as it included voice solos and a chorus in addition to the orchestral portion. Berlioz later called it a "dramatic legend," which seems an appropriate name for the new genre. The "dramatic legend" has been performed worldwide, from the Opéra Comique in Paris (1846) through the Metropolitan Opera in New York (first performance 1896), to an innovative production directed by the Canadian Robert Lepage in 2008 at the Met. Lepage's full opera included multimedia images of fields, water, sky, and fire, created by computers and infrared cameras linked to the singers' voices, which triggered the projected images onto the stage. Thus, no two performances were ever the same, as the images changed every night. Lepage is well known in translation circles, participating in the Québécois and post-Québéccis theater and translation movements in Canada, Scotland, and more recently producing multilingual and multicultural theater pieces worldwide (Donohue and Koustas 2000; Simon 1998).

The most famous opera production of *Faust* is Charles Gounod's *Faust et Marguerite* (1856–59), which has been staged all over the world and translated into more than 25 languages. First performed at the Paris Opéra in 1862, it became an enormous hit, the most frequently played opera throughout the nineteenth century and well into the twentieth. Shortly afterward, the opera was rewritten again, with a ballet inserted for the Walpurgis Night scene. Gounod significantly domesticated the play, it is set in nineteenth-century France with full period costumes. Mephistopheles is dark, mysterious, and evil; Marguerite is innocent, Catholic, and nun-like; and Faust is in-between, mighty, and tragically heroic. Much of the dialogue is from Goethe, although there are many additions, such as several extended wooing scenes as Faust professes his love for Marguerite. There are also deletions, such as the Germanic material, which is probably why the Walpurgis Night scene was added as a ballet in 1869. In addition to the love scenes, the most moving scene is Marguerite's infanticide, which takes place offstage in Goethe's *Faust*, but is very present and quite dramatic in the opera. In the end, however, Gounod reverts more to Marlowe's than to Goethe's *Faust*, as Gretchen is condemned and guillotined in the version I saw, and Mephistopheles gets his prize, enveloping Faust in smoke and fire as the two descend into hell.

Just as cinema has dominated the *Faust* international landscape in the twentieth century, Gounod's opera dominated the nineteenth. Theater-goers in Paris and Monte Carlo, Munich and Vienna, Milan and Rome, and New York were more likely to have heard the *musical* version than to have *read* the play in German or in translation. Although the opera has been translated into many languages, in Europe it is often performed in French, therefore many viewers receive the story in translation. First carried out at the Metropolitan Opera in New York in 1883, even today it is the *eighth* most performed opera there, with 747 performances through the 2011–12 season. For many years, it was the *most* popular opera in New York, and for decades, the Met opened its season with Gounod's *Faust*. Indeed, there are many post-Gounod rewritings of *Faust*, from the Argentine writer Estanislao del Campo's satirical poem *Fausto* (1866), to its serving as the opera portrayed in the French writer Gaston Leroux's *The Phantom of the Opera*, a novel written in 1909–10. Leroux's novel was then adapted to the screen in the well-known 1925 film directed by Rupert Julian and starring Lon Chaney; and rewritten again for the stage in Andrew Lloyd Webber's 1986 musical. The ballet portion of Gounod's opera has been performed separately by many companies, including one in 1975 by the famous Russian choreographer George Balanchine for the Paris Opéra Ballet, and it continues to be performed worldwide. Extracts from Gounod's opera are even referred to in the comic *The Adventures of Tintin* by the Belgian cartoonist Georges Remi, including *Les bijoux de la Castafiore* (1963). The *Tintin* series has been translated into more than 70 languages. Thus, one can easily see how rewritings quickly turn into rewritings of rewritings and translations of rewritings,

Table 2.7 Music versions of *Faust*

Selected music versions of *Faust*:	
1814	Franz Schubert, "Gretchen am Spinrade"
1844	Robert Schumann, "Scenes from Goethe's *Faust*"
1846	Hector Berlioz, "Legende dramatique" *La damnation de Faust*
1857	Ferenc Liszt, *A Faust Symphony in Three Sketches after Goethe*
1859	Charles Gounod, opera *Faust et Marguerite*
1868	Arrigo Boito, opera *Mefistofele*
1906	Gustav Mahler, Symphony No. 8, a cantata for the last scene in part II of Goethe's *Faust*
	Hans Eisler, opera libretto *Johann Faustus*
1974	Brian de Palma, *The Phantom of Paradise*, music by Paul Williams
1983	Randall Paris Dark, *Starboy*
1993	Randy Newman, musical *Faust*
2003	Little Tragedes (Russian) "New Faust," symphonic rock
2003 & 2005	Kamelot (heavy metal band, USA), *Epica* and *The Black Halo*, two album rock opera inspired by Goethe's *Faust*
2006	Switchfoot (alternative rock band, USA) "Faust, Midas, and Myself" song
2007	Radiohead (English rock band), "Faust Arp," song/mash-up of Faust
2012	Agalloch (metal band, USA), "Faustian Echoes," two-part song based on Goethe's work

creating an intersemiotic and transnational network of connections and paradigms characteristic of the postmodern and post-translation age.

Turning to more contemporary and popular rewritings of *Faust*, let me begin with the American singer-songwriter Randy Newman's musical *Faust*, first written in 1993 and released as an album in 1995. It caused a sensation among rock musicians and their fans alike when performed at the New York City Center in July 2014. This show was a collection of singles woven into a musical. The original production in 1995 in San Diego was praised for its music but criticized for its script, after which the US playwright David Mamet agreed to help Newman rewrite the play. The second production in Chicago fared much better and was turned into an album. The musical features a group of famous North American rock stars: Newman as Mephistopheles, James Taylor as the Lord, and Don Henley as Henry Faust, the lead character. Other cast members include Linda Ronstadt as Margaret, and Elton John as an Angel. Tracks include "Glory Train" and "Can't Keep a Good Man Down."

The 2014 New York performance emphasized the music more than the story, but with Newman orchestrating as the Devil from his seat at the piano, the storyline, and Newman's take on it, was clear to be seen. Known for his acerbic wit and critical attitude, as well as a kind of playfulness and self-irony, Newman seems appropriate for the role. In "Randy Newman's Faust: The Devil Laughs and Cries" (2014), a review in *Time Magazine*, Richard Corliss connects the musical to vaudeville, although of an "acerbic sort." He writes, "In tone and viewpoint, this is the anti-Faust, an atheist's Faust." Both God and the Devil are bored, humanity is committing more sins than Mephistopheles could ever imagine, and the bet between the Lord and the Devil is that the Devil can convince *any* human to sell his soul to the Devil. They pick the poorly performing student named Henry Faust, a lazy sophomore at Notre Dame, the leading Catholic school in the United States. Henry does not need much convincing when promised pleasure and glory for his soul. Mephistopheles soon introduces Henry to Margaret, and the story unfolds. Along the way, the cynical Mephistopheles relates unforgivable tales of violence, crime, racism, and imperialism that go unpunished and are in fact often *rewarded* in the jaded American society. As the Devil, Newman points out that he has little to do, as the world is already corrupt, and that the real orchestrator of such as state of affairs is God. With black and telling humor, Newman seems to be representing the outsiders, the renegades, and the misfits. According to Corliss, the audience was pleased despite the dour outlook; they demonstrated an "exuberant mood throughout" and "erupted into cheers" at the end.

In "They Sold their Soul for Rock 'n Roll: Faustian Rock Musicals" (2008), Paul Malone talks about several other rock productions in addition to Newman's musical. The first was a type of double rewriting, as Paul Williams wrote the music to Brian de Palma's film *The Phantom of the Paradise* (1974), a retelling of *The Phantom of the Opera*, which was a rewriting of the Gaston Leroux novel, and a rewriting of the Gounod opera, which was an adaptation of Goethe's *Faust*. This process of rewriting winds the text through a postmodern labyrinth, and Genette's concept of palimpsest is useful in this context. The Faust character in de Palma's film is a rock songwriter named William Leach, who writes a song titled "Faust," which he plays at a local club to much acclaim. There, Leach meets an evil producer who tries to get him to sell the rights to the song, but Leach resists. An associate of the producer then steals the music and has Leach framed for a drug deal, which results in Leach's incarceration. When he hears his song on the radio, Leach becomes enraged, breaks out of prison, and then into the recording studio to destroy the records. In the process, he falls and is scarred horribly, thereby becoming a phantom (Malone 2008: 217–18). In addition to the song "Faust," other Williams's songs include "The Hell of It." The songs consist of rhythm and blues and rock and roll with a harder edge than the soft rock for which Williams is normally associated. According to Malone, Williams apparently wanted to play the phantom, perhaps revealing a rebellious side repressed in much of his music (2008: 219).

The second rock opera treated by Malone was the Canadian Randall Paris Dark's *Starboy* (1983), with lyrics by Cary Dark and music by Ian Crowley. Mephisto, in this case, is Mephista, a woman named Satina. An aspiring rock musician named Jimmy Paul Bradley plays the Faust character, and when asked if he would sell his soul to become a rock star, he agrees. Satina, who only collects women's souls, tricks Jimmy into signing away himself and his girlfriend, a Gretchen figure named Christine. To do so, he must seal the deal by burning a lock of her hair. The end deviates from the Faust legend, as Jimmy tricks Satina back by burning the lock of another person's hair. Jimmy gets to keep his girlfriend and star in a rock show, rock and roll triumphing in the end (Malone 2008: 220–21).

Malone cites other rock musicals that include the Austrian *Fäustling: Spiel in G* (1973), written by Josef Prokopetz with music by Wolfgang Ambros, inventor of "Austropop." This music is a hybrid of American rock and French chansons, creating an "indigenous" German/Austrian rock form to fight against the importation of American music. The opera uses a Viennese dialect; in line 1338, when Mephistopheles enters Faust's study and says "Ich bin der Geist der stets vermeint" [I am the spirit that denies forever], Ambos has the Devil in *Fäustling* sing, "I bin da Teife und I sog, 'Na!'" [I'm the devil and I say, "no"]. Malone cites a fourth rock opera Rudolf Volz's 1999 *Faust: Die Rockoper*, which remains the most faithful to Goethe's text, although, as is always the case with literal versions, it is much abridged. Volz's purpose of the rock medium is to introduce Faust to a new generation of listeners, those who follow variants of death metal. Faust and Mephistopheles sing heavy metal rock, but Gretchen sings more pop and slower rhythm and blues. The action blends the classical with the modern and postmodern: for example, when Faust and Mephistopheles interact with the witches, they use computers, electric violins, cell phones, and space shuttles. Volz's music is dynamic in the Germanic scenes: the songs for the Erdgeist or Walpurgis Night are particularly haunting. Volz stages a regular show on the Brocken/Blocksberg mountain peak in the Harz, the location for Goethe's Walpurgis Night scene. Malone also tells us that the work is constantly undergoing revision, offering new versions of Spanish and English performances. A single CD, double CDs, DVDs, now even quadruple CDs (2007) of performances are available, as the works seem to grow with offshoots, expanded originals, and newly added material (Malone 2008: 226).

While Newman plays down the translational aspect of his rock musical, saying in an interview that he first read *Faust* in a comic version (Corliss 2014), and Volz says that he wants to make the play "easily digestible" (Malone 2008: 224), my sense is that Newman, Volz, and other rock musicians were subconsciously well versed in the Faust history via textual, musical, and cinematic versions. As with Newman and Ambos, most musicians insist on playing Mephistopheles themselves, which locates their position. For a generation of rock musicians, a rebellion has been the main motif, and Mephistopheles has held a great attraction. The story, of course, is that the great blues musician Robert Johnson went down to the crossroads and sold his soul to the devil in exchange for improving his ability to play guitar. Since then, blues has been called the devil's music, banned from churches, radio, and television during its early period, and today serving as the roots for later rock and roll. It is not unsurprising then that these rock musicians turn to Faust, offering an atheistic interpretation, sympathizing with the devil (Jagger and Richards 1968), and successfully staging concerts worldwide.

There are heavy metal bands named Mephisto in Cuba and Austria, a German psychedelic krautrock group named Faust whose first album was also named *Faust* (1971), a film and production company named Mephisto Productions, and an alternative press named Mephisto. Many individual songs are devoted to the Faust theme, including the Russian rock band Little Tragedies "New Faust" (2003), the USA alternative rock band Switchfoot's "Faust, Midas, and Myself" (2006), and the heavy metal band Agalloch's "Faustian Echoes" (2012). Many rock revolutionaries and alternative cultural musicians have turned to Faust for inspiration. For example, the British band Radiohead pays homage to this Faust tradition in rock music with their song "Faust-Arp" (2007), whose central character is "dead from the head up" and asks the question when "is enough is enough is enough?" In the 1990s, one of Bono's alter egos onstage during U2 concerts is the Mr. MacPhisto character, the devil as an older rock star losing fame, "Satan as a mixture of Elvis Presley, Frank Sinatra, and a 1930s Berlin cabaret stage" (Cogan 2008: 35). The Portland, Oregon band Agalloch's 21-minute "Faustian Echoes" (2012), heavy metal with meditative pauses, is their most ambitious work: to date the video contains dramatic readings (with some shouting) of Goethe's texts plus clips from the Czech filmmaker Jan Švankmajr's film *Lekce Faust* [The Legend of Faust] (1994), which uses live action combined with puppetry and claymation, creating another new hybrid genre.

While rock and roll embraces Faust for the demonic associations of the legend, other popular forms such as comics and video games have pursued the theme of the competition between God and the Devil for Faust's soul. DC Comics first introduced Felix Faust, a sorcerer/supervillian as early as 1962 as an adversary for their Justice League of American heroes; the ancient villain Felix Faust begins losing his superpowers and makes a deal with Mephisto to get them back. Beginning in 1987, Avatar/Rebel Press began issuing several series of comic books/graphic novels written by David Quinn all around the theme of "Faust," the main series being *Faust: Love of the Dammed*, which came out in 15 installments, ending in 2012. In 2001, a film by Brian Yuzna with the same title was made out of the first book. The famous German graphic artist Felix Görman, better known as Flix, wrote two adaptations: "Who the Fuck is Faust?" (1998) and "Faust, erster Teil," set in a contemporary multicultural Berlin with Gretchen as a Turkish salesgirl. Video games of Faust are also numerous and include *Faust: Seven Games of the Soul* (2000), located in a deserted US theme park; the player of the game is the Faust character who works at the park when a strange visitor Mephisto appears and conjures a series of traps. The player must discover the seven-mysteries to obtain salvation. In the Japanese game *GrimGrimoire*, the Faust figure is a girl named Lillet Blau who comes

Table 2.8 Comics and video games of *Faust*

Selected comics of *Faust*:

1950	"Faust" by Osamu Tezuka (manga)
1962–	"Felix Faust," character in DC Comics
1972	"Devilman" by Go Nagai (anime)
1987–	"Faust" by Avatar Press, a series of comic books by Tim Vigil (art) and David Quinn (stories)
2007	"Spiderman: One More Day," Marvel
1998 and 2010	"Who the Fuck is Faust?" and "Faust, Erster Teil," by German artist Flix (Felix Görman)
2011	"Puella Magi Madoka Magica" prod. by Shant and Aniplex, dir. Akiyuki Shinbo (anime television series)

Link to Faust, Erster Teil by Flix: www.youtube.com/watch?v=Ydk0aLSjKTA

Selected video games of *Faust*:

1993	*The Seventh Guest* (Virgin Games)
1998	Guilty Gear (series of games) (Arc Systems)
2000	*Faust: The Seven Games of the Soul* (Dreamcatcher)
2004	*Animamundi: Dark Alchemist* (Game/Visual Novel, Hirameki International)
2007	*GrimGrimoire* (Nipon Ichi)
2010	*Shadow of Memories* (Konami)
2011	*Knights Contract* (Namco Bandai)

Link to *Seven Games of the Soul*: www.youtube.com/watch?v=3sLZytieiz0

---

from a disadvantaged family and wants to learn sorcery to help her brothers. She goes to a magic school where the Mephistopheles character named Advocaat teaches sorcery. My guess is that many players of such games have no idea who Faust is and have little or no connection to the German versions. However, by now the image of Faust has been planted in their brains and will serve as an original when they encounter other versions. Indeed, given the addictive nature of such games, Faust is becoming culturally ingrained at a young age.

Is this fascination of rock musicians and popular culture with Goethe's *Faust* a coincidence, a popular turn, a successful translation, or a post-translation after-effect of the importation of a foreign text? The phenomenon is hard to analyze with traditional translation studies methodologies; source texts and target texts have disappeared: the sources consulted include any number of versions, some already popularized. The new versions are not just derivatives, but instead are highly creative, often used to push the genres of rock and roll, the comic, graphic novel, and video games to new forms and modes of expression. Musicians are using Faust to combine media to allow new forms of expression to emerge. However, the inventions are not just formal; it is the *content* that speaks to the rock generation, and in a deep and profound way.

In her book *Through Other Continents* (2004), Wai Chee Dimock talks about "deep" time and translation. One of her examples circles around the notion of civil disobedience: in *Walden* (1854), Henry David Thoreau wrote about the philosophy of the *Bhagavad-Gita* (also not a single work, but a work with a long history of layers or rewriting) with its pacifist opening from which Thoreau derives his concept of civil disobedience; Mohandas Gandhi also read the *Bhagavad-Gita*, and was so impressed that he improved his Sanskrit to translate it into Gujarati. Gandhi had also read Thoreau, first in South Africa in 1906, taking the name of his movement *Satyagraha* from Thoreau's essay on "Civil Disobedience." Finally, Martin Luther King read Thoreau in college and was well familiar with Gandhi's employment of *Satyagraha* in the independence movement in India. King adapted the concepts to his form of civil disobedience characterized by sit-ins, boycotts, marches, and freedom rides; three time periods, three different continents, but one idea across cultures (Dimock 2004: 18–22). These authors read each other's work, but also, in a deep and uncanny way, the ideas contained in the texts and speeches touched each other in a profound manner, not translation from the outside but resonating from *within*. In some ways, American blues and rock have roots in pre-imperialistic African sources. The resistance to the white, racist, and capitalist culture during the years when blacks were enslaved in America forms part of the genre. So, too, do Germanic passages in Goethe extend back to a pre-Roman, pre-Christian period and place in Europe, when Germans enjoyed a different identity before being referred to as heathens, pagans, and Huns. Such characterizations may be flawed; many Germanic cultures, especially the northern ones that fascinated Goethe, were peaceful, agrarian, and harmonious. Yes, the Nordic cultures worshiped different gods, and they celebrated nature's cycles in a different fashion. However, in a deep translational sense, the Gaelic, Nordic alternative to Roman and Latin Empires bears similarities to African-American resistance to the Anglo-American slaveholders. In the sense of Wai Chee Dimock, there may be some deep translational connection that makes the Faust legend less than a foreign imported other, and more an idea or emotion contained *within* an African-American cultural heritage, an idea or emotion that expresses a deep feeling that feels just. In a remarkable fashion, this deep feeling in its new form of expression—and some critics say that blues is the only indigenous American art form—has successfully crossed-over, or I might argue, has been translated into and rewritten by an Anglo-American white rebellious youth culture, which then, of course, subsequently went global, as rock, comics, and video games have become popular worldwide.

Goethe's *Faust* has thus gone global via elaborate systems of translations and rewritings in new cinematic, musical, and popular genres. Many times the translators are *not* listed in credits, and the texts are *not called* translations, adaptations, or rewritings as such, but that is what they are. Post-translation studies looks at the complex movements of texts, not just source to target, but to target and beyond, west to east, north to south, linear to non-linear, texts to images, and forward in time and space through multiple languages, cultures, and genres. David Damrosch's definition of World Literature refers to texts that travel. In the twenty-first century, the modes of travel have never been more diverse. De Campos's point, I believe, is to use his transluciferian style of translation to allow for transgressive interpretations and new semiotic configurations. By avoiding culturally transparent equivalents and instead cannibalizing them, translators, theater directors, filmmakers, graphic novelists, rock musicians, and video-game developers allow for words and symbols to repeat the old while taking on new meanings. The goal is a re-versioning, rewriting, or reinvention of the source text material in target cultures, some yet to be determined, thereby allowing for the new movement of signs in a new multilingual and multicultural artistic environment.

Bibliography

Andrade, Oswald de. 1928. "Manifesto Antropófago." *Revista de Antropofagia* 1: 1, trans. Leslie Bary. 1991. "Oswald de Andrade's 'Canabalist Manifesto." *Latin American Literary Review* 19(38): 35–47.

Apter, Emily. 2005. *The Translation Zone: A New Comparative Literature*. Princeton: Princeton University Press.

Apter, Emily. 2013. *Against World Literature: On the Politics of Untranslatability*. London: Verso.

Ashcroft, Bill, Gareth Griffiths, and Helen Tiffin. 1989. *The Empire Writes Back: Theory and Practice in Post-Colonial Literature*. London: Routledge.

Baron, Frank. 1992. *Faustus on Trial: The Origins of Johann Spies's "Historia" in an Age of Witch Hunting*. Tübingen: Max Niemeyer.

Bassnett, Susan and André Lefevere, eds. 2000. *Translation, History and Culture*. London: Routledge.

Bassnett, Susan and Harish Trivedi, eds. 1999. *Post-Colonial Translation: Theory and Practice*. London: Routledge.

Baudrillard, Jean. 1988. *America*, trans. Chris Turner. New York: Verso.

Baudrillard, Jean. 1994. *The Illusion of the End*, trans. Chris Turner. Stanford: Stanford University Press.

Boyle, Nicholas. 1987. *Goethe, Faust. Part One*. Cambridge: Cambridge University Press.

Braun, Volker. 1968. *Hans Faust*. Weimar: Deutsches Nationaltheater. Online at http://archive.thulb.uni-jena.de/staatsarchive/receive/ThHStAW_performance_00045592, accessed January 12, 2016.

Braun, Volker. 1973. "Hinze und Kunze." *Spectaculum* 19. Also *Theatre der Zeit* 2: 46–63.

Brecht, Bertolt and Egon Monk. 1986 [1952–53]. *Urfaust-Inszenierung mit dem Berliner Ensemble*, ed. Bernd Mahl. Stuttgart: Besler Verlag.

Bucchianeri, Elizabeth Ann. 2008. *Faust: My Soul be Damned for the World*, 2 vols. Bloomington: Author House.

Burwick, Frederick and James C. McKusick. 2007. *Faustus: From the German of Goethe Translated by Samuel Taylor Coleridge*. Oxford: Oxford University Press.

Campos, Haroldo de. 1981. *Deus e o Diabo no Fausto de Goethe*. São Paulo: Perspectiva.

Carroll, Julie Mercer. 2000. "Faust." In Olive Classe, ed. *Encyclopedia of Literary Translations into English*. London: Fitzroy Dearborn, 544–45.

Clair, René, dir. 1950. *La Beauté du diable*. France and Italy: Les Films Corona and ENIC.

Classe, Olive, ed. 2000. *Encyclopedia of Literary Translation Into English*, 2 vols. London: Fitzroy Dearborn.

Cogan, Višnja. 2008. *U2: An Irish Phenomenon*. New York: Pegasus.

Condee, Nancy. 2012. "Aleksandr Sokurov: Faust." *KinoKultura* 37. Online at www .kinokultura.com/2012/37r-faust.shtml, accessed January 5, 2015.

Corliss, Richard. 2014. "Randy Newman's Faust: The Devil Laughs and Cries." *Time Magazine*. July 6. Online at http://time.com/2956937/randy-newman-faust/, accessed January 15, 2015.

Crick, Joyce. 2008. "On *Faustus from the German of Goethe* translated by S.T. Coleridge ed. F. Burwick and J. McKusick." *Coleridge Bulletin*, 32: 70–84. Online at www.friendsofcoleridge.com/MembersOnly/CB32/CB32Crick.pdf, accessed January 7, 2015.

Cunningham, John. 2014. *The Cinema of Istán Szabó*. New York: Columbia University Press.

Damrosch, David. 2003. *What is World Literature?* Princeton: Princeton University Press.

Damrosch, David. 2009. *How to Read World Literature*. Hoboken, NJ: Wiley-Blackwell.

D'haen, Theo. 2012. *The Routledge Concise History of World Literature*. London: Routledge.

D'haen, Theo, César Domínguez, and Mads Rosendahl Thomsen, eds. 2013. *World Literature: A Reader*. London: Routledge.

Dimock, Wai Chee. 2006. *Through Other Continents: American Literature Across Deep Time*. Princeton: Princeton University Press.

Donohue, Joseph and Jane Koustas, eds. 2000. *Theater sans frontièrs: Essays on the Dramatic University of Robert Lepage*. East Lansing: Michigan State University Press.

Dresen, Adolf and Wolfgang Heinz, dir. 1968. *Faust I*. Berlin: Deutsches Theater.

Eckermann, Johann Peter. 1981 [1836–1848]. *Gespräche mit Goethe in dem letzten Jahren seines Lebens*. Frankfurt am Main: Insel Verlag.

Eisler, Hanns. 1952. *Johann Faustus. Oper*. Berlin: Aufbau Verlag.

Emrich, Wilhelm. 1943. *Die Symbolik von Faust II. Sinn und Vorformen*. Berlin: Verlag Junker & Dünnhaupt.

Emrich, Wilhelm. 1965. "Das Rätsel der 'Faust-II' Dichtung; Versuch Einer Lösung." In *Geist und Widergeist. Wahrheit und Lüge der Literatur Studien*. Frankfurt am Main: Athenäum, 211–35.

Emrich, Wilhelm. 1976 [1971]. "The Enigma of Faust, Part II: A Tentative Solution." In Cyrus Hamlin, ed. *Faust: A Tragedy*. New York: W.W. Norton and Co., 585–603.

"Faust." *New World Encyclopedia*. St Paul: Paragon House Publishers. Online at www.newworldencyclopedia.org/entry/Faust, accessed January 6, 2015.

Fitzsimmons, Lorna, ed. 2008. *International Faust Studies: Adaptation, Reception, Translation*. London: Continuum.

Frantz, Adolf Ingram. 1949. *Half a Hundred Thralls to Faust: A Study Based on the British and American Translators of Goethe's Faust 1823–1949*. Chapel Hill: University of North Carolina Press.

Gentzler, Edwin. 2008. *Translation and Identity in the Americas: New Directions in Translation Theory*. New York: Routledge.

Goethe, Johann Wolfgang von. 2010 [1808]. *Faust. Eine Tragödie*. Online at www.gutenberg.org/ebooks/2229, accessed August 12, 2013.

Goethe, Johann Wolfgang von. 2010 [1831]. *Der Tragödie Zweiter Theil*. Online at www.gutenberg.org/ebooks/2230, accessed August 12, 2013.

Goethe, Johann Wolfgang von. Editions of *Faust* prepared by Goethe:

Goethe, Johann Wolfgang von. 1790. *Faust. Ein Fragment*. In *Schriften*, vol. 7. Leipzig: Georg Joachim Göschen, 1–168.

Goethe, Johann Wolfgang von. 1808. *Faust, der Tragödie I. Teil*. *Werke*, vol. 8. Tübingen, 1–234.

Goethe, Johann Wolfgang von. 1827. *Helena. Klassisch-romantische Phantasmagorie. Zwischenspiet zu Faust II. Teil*. *Werke. Ausgabe letzter Hand*, vol. 12. Stuttgart, 1–247 and 249–313.

Goethe, Johann Wolfgang von. 1832. *Faust, der Tragödie zweiter Teil. Nachgelassene Werke*, vol 1. Stuttgart.

Goethe, Johann Wolfgang von. 1887. *Ur-Faust. Goethe's Faust in ursprünglicher Gestalt, nach der Göchhausenschen Abschrift*, ed. Erich Schmidt. Weimar.

Goethe, Johann Wolfgang von. Selected editions of *Faust* in English translation:

Goethe, Johann Wolfgang von. 1821. *Faustus: From the German of Goethe*, trans. anonymous, sometimes attributed to Samuel Taylor Coleridge. London: Boosey and Sons.

Goethe, Johann Wolfgang von. 1831. *Faust: A Dramatic Poem by Goethe*, trans. Abraham Hayward. London: Privately Printed.

Goethe, Johann Wolfgang von. 1871. *Faust: A Tragedy. The First Part and The Second Part*, trans. Bayard Taylor. Boston: James Osgood.

Goethe, Johann Wolfgang von. 1879. *Goethe's Faust in Two Parts*, trans. Anna Swanwick. London: G. Bell and Sons.

Goethe, Johann Wolfgang von. 1930. *Faust: A Tragedy. The First Part*, trans. Alice Raphael. New York: Rinehart and Co.

Goethe, Johann Wolfgang von. 1932. *Faust Parts I and II*, trans. George Madison Priest. New York: Covici Friede.

Goethe, Johann Wolfgang von. 1949. *Faust Part One and Part Two*, trans. Philip Wayne. Middlesex: Penguin.

Goethe, Johann Wolfgang von. 1961. *Goethe's Faust, Part One and Selections from Part Two*, trans. Walter Kaufmann. Garden City.

Goethe, Johann Wolfgang von. 1965. *Faust*, trans. and ed. Charles E. Passage. Indianapolis: Bobbs-Merrill.

Goethe, Johann Wolfgang von. 1970. *Goethe's Faust*, trans. Barker Fairley. Toronto: University of Toronto Press.

Goethe, Johann Wolfgang von. 1976. *Faust: A Tragedy*, trans. Walter Arndt, ed. Cyrus Hamlin. A Norton Critical Edition, first edition. New York: WW Norton.

Goethe, Johann Wolfgang von. 1987. *Goethe Faust: Part One*, trans. Nicholas Boyle. Cambridge: Cambridge University Press.

Goethe, Johann Wolfgang von. 1901 [1836–48]. *Conversations with Eckermann*, trans. anon. New York: M. Walter Dunne.

Goethe, Johann Wolfgang von. 1998. *Faust: A Tragedy*, trans. Walter Arndt, ed. Cyrus Hamlin. A Norton Critical Edition, second edition. New York: WW Norton.

Goethe, Johann Wolfgang von. 1999 [1773–75]. *Urfaust*, trans. C. Röhrig. *Fausto#Zero*. Bahia: Companhia Teatro dos Novos.

Goethe, Johann Wolfgang von. 2013 [1811]. *Aus meinem Leben. Dichtung und Wahrheit*. Berlin: Holzinger.

Goethe, Johann Wolfgang von, Henry Moses, illus. and M. Retsch, illus., Percy Bysshe Shelly, trans. 1832. *Faustus: From the German of Goethe. An Appendix Containing the May-Day Night Scene; Schiller's Fight with the Dragon, With the Poem in English*. London: Edward Lumley.

Görman, Felix (Flix). 1998. *Who the Fuck is Faust?* Frankfurt am Main: Eichborn.

Görman, Felix (Flix). 2010. *Faust. Der Tragödie erster Teil*. Hamburg: Carlsen Verlag.

Gounod, Charles, composer. 1856–59. *Faust et Marguerite: Opéra en cinq actes*. Sheet music and recordings online at http://imslp.org/wiki/Faust_(Gounod,_Charles), accessed January 5, 2015.

Hamlin, Cyrus, ed. 1976. *Faust: A Tragedy*. A Norton Critical Edition. New York: W.W. Norton;

Hamlin, Cyrus, ed. 2001. *Faust: A Tragedy*. A Norton Critical Edition, 2nd edition. New York: W.W. Norton.

Hedges, Inez. 2009. *Framing Faust: Twentieth-century Cultural Struggles*. Carbondale: Southern Illinois University Press.

Heinemann, William. 2012 [1884]. "An Essay Towards a Bibliography of Marlowe's Tragical History of Doctor Faustus." *The Bibliographer* 5–6: 40–46. Online at https://books.google.com/books?id=hSADAAAAYAAJ&pg=RA1-PA43&lpg=RA1-PA43&dq=translations+of+Goethe%27s+Faust+list+archive&source=bl&ots=rl5ZtBhFSP&sig=1xPovzp8eveqV2q8oGbeQvDgxpU&hl=en&sa=X&ei=nCmsVMieK47asASNp4LIDQ&ved=0CEAQ6AEwBQ#v=onepage&q=translations%20of%20Goethe's%20Faust%20list%20archive&f=false, accessed January 5, 2015.

Höckmann, Thomas. "Map of 'The Germanies.' " Online at www.hoeckmann.de/germany, accessed January 21, 2016.

Hutcheon, Linda. 1994. *Irony's Edge: The Theory and Politics of Irony*. London: Routledge.

Jagger, Mick and Keith Richards, composers. 1968. "Sympathy for the Devil" on the album *Beggars Banquet*. London: Decca.

John, David G. 2012. *Bennewitz, Goethe, "Faust": German and Intercultural Stagings*. Toronto: University of Toronto Press.

Keim, Katharina. 2008. "Contemporary African and Brazilian Adaptations of Goethe's *Faust* in Postcolonial Context." In Lorna Fitzsimmons, ed. *International Faust Studies: Adaptation, Reception, Translation*. London: Continuum, 244–58

Kentridge, William, dir. 1995. *Faustus in Africa*. Cape Town: Handspring Puppet Theater.

Klee, Ernst. 2007 [2003]. *Das Kulturlexikon zum Dritten Reich: Wer war was vor und nach 1945*. Frankfurt am Main: S. Fischer Verlag.

Kuzniar, Alice A., ed. 1996. *Outing Goethe & His Age*. Stanford: Stanford University Press

Lefevere, André. 1977. *Translating Literature: The German Tradition: From Luther to Rosenzweig*. Assen: Van Gorcum and Co.

Lefevere, André. 1982. "Mother Courage's Cucumbers: Text, System and Refraction in a Theory of Literature." *Modern Language Studies* 12(4): 3–20.

Lefevere, André. 1984. "On the Refraction of Texts." In Mihai Spariosu, ed. *Mimesis in Contemporary Theory*. Amsterdam: John Benjamin, 217–37.

Lefevere, André. 1992. *Translation, Rewriting, and the Manipulation of Literary Fame*. London: Routledge.

Lefevere, André. 1993. "Shakespeare Refracted: Writer, Audience and Rewriter in French and German Romantic Translations." In Gerald Gillespie, ed. *Romantic Drama*. Amsterdam: John Benjamins, 101–13.

Lefevere, André and Susan Bassnett. 2000. "Introduction: Proust's Grandmother and the Thousand and One Nights: The 'Cultural Turn' in Translation Studies." In Susan Bassnett and André Lefevere, eds. *Translation, History and Culture*. London: Routledge, 1–13.

Lessing, Gotthold Ephraim. 2014 [1759]. *Briefe, die neueste Literatur betreffend*. Berlin: Holzinger.

Littau, Karin. 1997. "Translation in the Age of Postmodern Production: From Text to Intertext to Hypertext." *Forum for Modern Language Studies* 32(1): 81–96.

Littau, Karin. 2011. "First Steps Towards a Media History of Translation." *Translation Studies* 4(3): 261–281.

Lorey, Christoph and John L. Plews. 1998. *Queering the Canon: Defying Sights in German Literature and Culture*. Columbia: Camden House.

Luke, David. 1987. "Introduction." In *Goethe Faust, Part I*. Oxford: Oxford University Press, ix–lv.

Malone, Paul. 2008. "They Sold their Soul for Rock 'n Roll: Faustian Rock Musicals." In Lorna Fitzsimmons, ed. *International Faust Studies: Adaptation, Reception, Translation*. London: Continuum, 216–30.

Mason, Eudo C. 1967. *Goethe's Faust: Its Genesis and Purport*. Berkeley: University of California Press.

Mautz, Kurt. 1996. *Der Urfreund*. Paderborn: Insel Verlag.

Meirelles, Márcio, dir. 1999. *Fausto#Zero, de Goethe*. Bahia: Teatro Vila Velha.

Meirelles, Marcio. 2004. *Teatro de cabo a rabo: do Vila para o interior e vice versa*. Bahia: Teatro Vila Vela.

Midgette, Anne. 2000. "Germany's Classic of Classics, All 21 Hours." Theater Section, *New York Times*. August 6. Online at www.nytimes.com/2000/08/06/theater/germany-s-classic-of-classics-all-21-hours.html, accessed February 5, 2015.

Moraru, Christian. 2001. *Rewriting: Postmodern Narrative and Cultural Critique in the Age of Cloning*. Albany: SUNY Press.

Moraru, Christian. 2011. *Cosmodernism: American Narrative, Late Globalization, and the New Cultural Imaginary*. Ann Arbor: University of Michigan Press.

Murnau, F.W., dir. 1926. *Faust: Eine deutsche Volksage*. Babelsburg: Universum Film AG.

Newman, Randy, composer. 1995. *Faust*. Burbank: Reprise/Warner Bros.

Pascal, Roy. 1937. *Shakespeare in Germany 1740–1815*. Cambridge: Cambridge University Press.

Retzsch, Friedrich August Moritz. 1820. *Goethe's Tragedy of Faust in Illustrations of Retzsch*. London: Bosey and Sons.

Schlözer, August Ludwig von. 1792–1801. *Weltgeschichte nach ihren Hauptheilen im Auszug und Zusammenhange*, 2 vols. Göttingen: Ruprechtischem Verlag.

Schroth, Christoph, dir. 1979. *Faust*. Schwerin: Mecklenburgishes Staatstheater.

Simon, Sherry. 1998. "Robert Lepage and Intercultural Theater." In Steven Tötösy de Zepetnek and Yiu-nam Leung, eds. *Canadian Culture and Literature and a Taiwan*

Perspective. Edmonton: Research Institute for Comparative Literature, University of Alberta, 123–43.

Siskind, Mariano. 2010. "The Globalization of the Novel and the Novelization of the Global: A Critique of World Literature." *Comparative Literature* 62(4): 336–60.

Sokurov, Alexander, dir. 2011. *Faust*. St. Petersburg: Proline Film.

Spies, Johann. 1965 [1587]. *Historia von D. Johann Fausten*, trans. H.G. Haile. Champaign: University of Illinois Press.

Stein, Peter, dir. 2000. *Faust I und II*. Hamburg: Expo 2000.

Stephanides, Stephanides. 2003. "The Translation of Heritage: Multiculturalism in the 'New' Europe." In Robert Shannan Peckham ed. *Rethinking Heritage: Culture and Politics in Europe*. London: I.B. Tauris, 45–60.

Thoreau, Henry David. 1854. *Walden*. Boston: Tickner and Sons.

Tobin, Robert D. 1996. "In and Against Nature: Goethe on Homosexuality and Heterosexuality." In Alice A. Kuzniar, ed. *Outing Goethe & His Age*. Stanford: Stanford University Press, 94–110.

Tymoczko, Maria and Edwin Gentzler, eds. 2002. *Translation and Power*. Amherst: University of Massachusetts Press.

Vieira, Else Ribeiro Pires.1999. "Liberating Calibans: Readings of Antropofagia and Harold de Campos' Poetics of Transcreation." In Susan Bassnett and Harish Trivedi, eds. *Postcolonial Translation: Theory and Practice*. London: Routledge, 95–113.

Williams, John R. 1998. *The Life of Goethe: A Critical Biography*. Malden: Blackwell.

3   Proust for everyday readers

For those who have been thinking in terms of post-translation or transdisciplinary translation studies, older definitions of translation do not hold, and the first and most important distinction to be broken down is the separation among originals, translations, and rewritings. Books such as Homer's *Odyssey*, Virgil's *Iliad*, Dante's *Divine Comedy*, Shakespeare's *Hamlet* or *A Midsummer Night's Dream*, or Goethe's *Faust* are texts often imbued with a great deal of aura, as if the authors of these texts were divinely inspired with access to original ideas and expressions. Yes, maybe these authors are geniuses, but postmodern literary critics and post-translation scholars suggest that they are geniuses of a different sort—of construction, form, composition, importing new ways of expression, and, especially, translation. Homer (if indeed he were the author) transcribed and rewrote from a history of oral tales passed down over centuries. Goethe rewrote *Faust* from a series of plays and oral performances deeply embedded in Germany literary history. In *A Midsummer Night's Dream*, Shakespeare rewrote many texts—Chaucer, Ovid, Plutarch, Apuleius, Golding, various almanacs, as well as a miscellany that are written and oral depictions of Celtic and Germanic folklore. For example, the primary theme of *A Midsummer Night's Dream* is *transformation*, including translation and metamorphosis, and as Shakespeare rewrote, he transformed (see Chapter 1 in this volume). No, the source texts for many of the classics, as Jorge Luis Borges has cleverly argued, are already rewritings. As Bassnett and Lefevere have shown over the past 30 years, it is impossible to analyze textual matters without looking at the poetics and ideology of the cultures into which they are being rewritten. A few translation studies scholars, such as Lawrence Venuti (2007) and John Milton (2009), have begun the dialogue with academics who study rewritings, but most investigations of rewritings are conducted by scholars in the fields of film studies, children's literature, reception theory, and the new field of adaptation studies.

In the age of telecommunications, mass media, the Internet and the emergence of a variety of new forms: film, games, blogs, music videos, cartoons, and fan fiction, the prevalent use of rewriting/adapting/translation is growing at an unprecedented pace. Indeed, it is hard to conceive of a study of "original" writing in the contemporary age *without* considering translation and rewriting. Even the conservative Shakespearean critic Harold Bloom talks about the pervasiveness of influence and all original writing as cast under the weight of the writer's predecessors. In his 1997 revision of *The Anxiety of Influence*, he adds sections on Shakespeare's debt to Ovid, Chaucer, and Christopher Marlowe. If we look at the major contemporary creative writers of the world involved in rewriting—James Joyce, Italo Calvino, Jorge Luis Borges, Haroldo de Campos, Toni Morrison, Christa Wolf, Paul Auster, Nicole Brossard to mention a few—translation and rewriting have taken center stage.

This chapter is divided into six sections: the first emphasizes the influence of the work of Susan Bassnett and André Lefevere on translation, rewriting, and cultural studies; the second looks at the pre-translation culture of turn-of-the-century France; the third examines the translational nature of Proust's *À la recherche du temps perdu*; the fourth discusses Proust as a reviser/rewriter himself; the fifth looks at the translation history of *Recherche* into English; and finally the sixth discuss a selection of post-translation and post-modern rewritings in a variety of media.

Rethinking Bassnett and Lefevere

As mentioned above, much work has gone into trying to set up distinctions between and among translations, versions, adaptations, and rewritings. For example, in the introduction to *Translation, Adaptation and Transformation* (2012) Laurence Raw summarizes some of the objections by translation scholars to adaptations. In "Translation and Comparable Transfer Operations," Hendrik van Gorp, one of the leading members of the Leuven Group, argues that adaptations should *not* be thought of as translations, even if they "represent a primary text with comparable form and volume" (van Gorp 2004 [1985]: 66; quoted by Raw 2012: 1). Van Gorp went on to suggest that the reference to adaptation implied a negative connotation, as opposed to translation, which in his mind remained positive. While scholars in the Low Countries attempted to distance themselves from theories of equivalence, they could never quite escape the allure of the faithful implicit criterion. While translations were considered faithful, positing an "invariant for comparison," adaptation tended to remain outside such parameters, with too many subjective factors involved that steered such texts toward the disloyal. The new and emerging field of adaptation studies also retains such distinctions, although their prejudices are reversed, neglecting advances made in translation studies. For example, a new journal called *Adaptation* with Oxford University Press, founded in 2008 and reissued seven times during its publication, tends to omit references to that mundane field of translation. Most of the articles are on theater and film adaptation of novels and scripts or remakes of the previous film and TV shows; very few articles mention translation. An International Association of Adaptation Studies has been holding annual meetings since 2006, with its first conference in Leicester, UK. The theme of the 2010 conference was "Rewriting, Remixing, and Reloading: Adaptations Across the Globe," which logically should have included translation, but sadly the notion of "universal access" ghosted many of the papers and arguments, with the openness of linguistic borders uncritically assumed. In 2007, the *Journal of Adaptation in Film and Performance* was founded, with the editors hoping to bridge the gap between translation and adaptation. However, as Katja Krebs states in "Translation and Adaptation—Two Sides of an Ideological Coin" (2012: 43), the majority of submissions maintain the same divisions that have continued to keep the fields apart. Theoretically, much of the discussion in adaptation studies still revolves around issues of equivalence and fidelity, terms from which translation studies scholars have long since distanced themselves.

While the barriers between translation and adaptation continue to remain strong, I suggest that it is time to break them down. I wholeheartedly agree with Susan Bassnett, who had little patience for those who tried to discriminate too closely among translation, rewriting, and adaptation. As early as her pioneering volume *Translation Studies*, she wrote: "Much time and ink has been wasted in attempting to differentiate between *translations, versions, adaptations* and the establishment of a hierarchy of 'correctness' between the categories" (1980: 78–9, emphasis in original, quoted by Raw 2012: 1). How prophetic those words have become. I suggest that the two fields not only overlap, but also have much to learn from each other.

Susan Bassnett and André Lefevere's pioneering work on rewriting has held up very well. Lefevere's *Translation, Rewriting, and the Manipulation of Literary Fame* (1992) remains the book most often cited by scholars on the topic. The volume contains extended sections on the criteria by which Lefevere measures shifts in rewritings: patronage, poetics, and ideology, categories that informed cultural studies research on translation in the subsequent decades. "Patronage" refers to those who hire and pay translators—from kings and queens to governments, churches, and large publishing houses, and today one cannot analyze translators' "subjective" choices without an awareness of the institutional forces that play a role in their decisions. "Poetics" refers to the literary devices, genres, motifs, and characteristics prominent in the receiving culture. Translators can play with these devices, but straying too far from the local literary conventions and the translators run the risk of estranging the audience. Finally, "ideology" points to constraints upon the translator because of the political climate in which the translator lives. All of these factors are useful to keep in mind while describing the pre-translation context in which the translation occurs. The cases Lefevere looked at were often extreme—Anne Frank's *Diary* in Germany; Bertolt Brecht's *Mother Courage* in the United States; or Catullus's homoerotic translations in Victorian England—but they nevertheless illustrated processes of censorship and self-censorship because of social-political ideas or literary preferences in the receiving culture. According to Lefevere, all three categories—patronage, poetics, and ideology—are intertwined so that the translator never produces "true" translations, but rather "images" of the original that were often more powerful than the originals themselves. As a strong proponent of the cultural turn in translation studies, I do not stray far from many of Lefevere's fundamental ideas, especially his contention that translators and rewriters, because of aesthetic and ideological constraints, produce what might be better termed an "image" of an original text than a faithful translation. But as fundamental as Lefevere's book remains, it was primarily focused upon *professional* rewriters: after his work on patronage, poetics, and ideology, the book contains chapters on historiography, anthologies, criticism, and editing, all of which are important forms of translation and rewriting and served to expand the field, but did not consider the myriad of forms of rewriting today by professionals and non-professionals alike.

In this chapter, I wish to turn to the essay, "Proust's Grandmother and the Thousand and One Nights: The 'Cultural Turn' in Translation Studies" (1990), the introduction to Susan Bassnett and André Lefevere's *Translation, History and Culture* (1990). In translation studies, this famous article contains two frequently quoted sections. First, it offers the first official pronouncement of the term "cultural turn" in translation studies. Lefevere and Bassnett wrote:

> At the end of her contribution, Mary Snell-Hornby exhorts linguists to abandon their "scientistic" attitude and to move from "text" as a putative "translation unit" to culture—a momentous step that would go far beyond the move from the word as a "unit" to the text. The contributions in this volume have all taken the "cultural turn" advocated by Snell-Hornby.
>
> (Lefevere and Bassnett 1990: 4)

The second famous line from the essay is the suggestion that comparative literature, which at the time marginalized the study of translation, had had its day, and it was time for comparative literature to be subsumed under the new and emerging field of translation studies. They wrote:

> We have both suggested on occasion, with the deliberate intention of subverting the status quo and drawing attention to the importance of Translation Studies, that perhaps we should rethink our notions of Comparative Literature and redefine it as a subcategory of Translation Studies instead of vice versa.
>
> (Lefevere and Bassnett 1990: 12)

This assertion, i.e., that comparative literature needs to take the translation turn itself, is similar to my claim in this book that adaptation studies needs to take the translation turn as well. Indeed, Lefevere and Bassnett anticipate one of the tenets of post-translation studies, i.e., that other fields in which translation plays a crucial role need to make a similar disciplinary re-evaluation, from philosophy, political science, and economics, to all language departments, including English and World Literature.

The aspects that concern me in this chapter are Bassnett and Lefevere's insights on translation and rewriting, not for professors, critics, and editors, but for everyday readers. In the same essay, Bassnett and Lefevere talked about rewritings for *non-professional readers*, in this case, exemplified by Proust's grandmother. Standards and norms for translation are not universal, nor can they be discerned as national traits, as many system theorists contend. Rather, translation norms are *relative* to different groups of readers even within the *same* culture; everyday readers view translation differently than the critics. Micro-cultures exist within larger cultures—young versus old, men versus women, gay versus straight, of color versus white, multilingual versus monolingual—and all have different criteria and preferences. This is *the cultural turn in its formative stage*: the move from scholarly judgments, scientific attitudes, and generalizations/norms/laws as juxtaposed to more common-sense popular cultural observations in all their diversity and allegiances.

Proust's grandmother serves as an example. She reads work in translation, such as *The Odyssey* or *The Thousand and One Nights*, but when she looks at new translations, she finds them, while maybe more scholarly, also more foreignizing and off-putting. She cannot seem to find her familiar "Ulysses" or "Sheherazade," "Caliph" has become "Khalifat," and "Genies" are transformed into the unfamiliar "Gennis." Proust's grandmother's editorial decisions, if she were to have a say, may have been quite different from the professional translators/editors in charge of the newer versions.

> Something, indeed, has changed between the two translations, but that something was not any expert's mind. Rather, the experts who gave us the translations familiar to Proust's grandmother a favorable recommendation have, most likely, passed on and been replaced by other experts. But surely we are entitled to ask, together with Proust's grandmother, that should not matter, because are the standards themselves not for ever beyond any conceivable change?
>
> (Lefevere and Bassnett 1990: 2–3)

In short, this new generation of scholars found that different translations could co-exist in the same culture and fulfill *different* functions for *different* audiences. Traditional measuring devices held dearly by critics such as equivalence and faithfulness were viewed by Bassnett and Lefevere with skepticism, who showed how such assumptions were clouded by aesthetic and political favoritism. Texts ceased to be examined in isolation, and critics were required to delve into additional factors to analyze reception—factors that included history, religion, politics, economics, class, gender, and power. The authors selected to be published in the volume *Translation, History and Culture* well represented such factors: Mary Snell-Hornby discussed function and translation; Barbara Godard and Mahasweta Sengupta talked about power and translation; Dirk Delabastita analyzed mass media and translation.

In the same article, Lefevere and Bassnett distinguish between "intracultural" and "intercultural" translation. They seem acutely aware that both processes are always ongoing. To return to the Proust example, they wrote:

> Histories of French literature, published in Paris, Quebec or Dakar, are likely to include at least some attempt at a summary of *À la recherche*, and there are professors busily writing almost line-by-line commentaries, designed to elucidate nearly every word. But the French-speaking man or woman in the street is likely to think of Jeremy Irons when asked about Swann if s/he thinks of anything or anybody at all ... This then would be "intracultural" translation, which we propose to call "rewriting."
>
> (Lefevere and Bassnett 1990: 9)

Lefevere and Bassnett concluded their article by arguing that in this day and age, translation operates more by its "image" as constructed not by the original text or scholarly articles about that text, but rather the images created by translations and rewritings, more often than not in the cinema, television, and popular culture. They concluded:

> What impacts most on members of a culture, we suggest, is the "image" of a work of literature, not its "reality" ... It is therefore extremely important that the "image" of a literature and the works that constitute it be studied alongside its reality. This, we submit, is where the future of "translation studies" lies.
>
> (Lefevere and Bassnett 1990: 9–10)

Lefevere and Bassnett could not have been more prophetic. Their proposal for the future of translation studies submitted as early as 1990 marked the advent of the cultural turn in translation studies, and marked the beginning of a postmodern analysis of translational phenomena, not restricted to translations alone, but also including post-translation rewritings in any number of media. Unfortunately, while the field has increased its analysis of cultural factors involved in translation, it has not followed through on the "image" of a text created through and by translation in subsequent rewritings. In this book, I hope to begin some of that post-translation research and illustrate the many linkages among translation, rewriting, and adaptation to show how they might work synergistically to explain better how cross-cultural communication works in the new electronic age.

However, first let me turn to what I call the pre-translation culture just before Proust began his mammoth project of *In Search of Lost Time*: i.e., late nineteenth- and early twentieth-century France. Because of advances in industrialization, new modes of transportation, and innovations in art, music, and film, the culture in which Proust lived and wrote was predisposed to translational evolution.

Translational culture in late nineteenth-century France

In *Cities in Translation* (2012), Sherry Simon is particularly astute in talking about bilingual cities and how not only the language dynamics but also the geographic and spatial landscapes serve to encourage and promote translation. For example, during the 1940s and 1950s in Montreal, certain translators served to break down the divide, physically demarcated by the Boulevard Saint-Laurent, that separated the French and English sectors of the city, and crossed over to the other side, meeting writers, musicians, filmmakers, playwrights, and visual artists. Gaining an understanding of the movements and imaginative communities, they brought ideas and new forms back to the other side (Simon 2012: 124–25). The bilingual city, the various modernist movements, and the institutions that supported such movements, created the dynamic conditions for a new generation of translation; the translators served as mediators connecting groups and facilitating discussions. At first, the translations marked the distance between and among different groups and languages. Later, in the 1960s and 1970s, with translators such as Michel Garneau, the lines separating language communities began to break down, exchanges were more frequent, commonalities were discovered, and a kind of third space emerged, a culture of not one or the other but in-between, modifying earlier polarities. Ideas and languages began to mingle, and a new wave of translation resulted: translation as a creative, enabling genre in and of itself. New concepts related to translation also emerged at this time as well, self-translation, transmigration, overlapping, doublings, playful neologisms, bilingual codes, hybrid forms, and, not insignificantly, jokes. Translation became a shaping presence, not just in the literature, but also for the geographical, the spatial construction, of the city itself (Simon 2012: 149–50). Simon makes similar cases for Prague, Calcutta, and Trieste, and her evidence is compelling.

In this section, I wish to discuss the translational culture of Paris. On the one hand, Proust was not very international at all. He lived his whole life in France, most of it in Paris. He seldom traveled, except for a trip to Venice, and, as a semi-invalid for much of his adult life, he spent many days in his room writing. He slept much of the day and wrote at night, sometimes all night long. How might he be characterized as a translational writer? On the other hand, the city of Paris was alive and changing, filled with international visitors, art exhibitions, theater performances, industrial and technological innovations, visiting aristocracy, and immigrant laborers. Proust was a keen observer, and the translational aspect of the culture did not escape him. Some of these translational aspects were interlingual, but many others were intercultural. In many ways, he did not have to travel internationally to experience the foreign; the foreign came to him. Paris at the turn of the century was alive with international arrivals—many aristocrats in exile, especially from Russia and central Europe; industrialists, including German, English, and Americans; artists from all over the major European capitals and several Latin American ones, including painters, musicians, and dancers; and immigrant workers, most from Italy, Poland, and central Europe, as Proust documents only too well in *À la recherche du temps perdu*.

The technological changes came rapidly in late nineteenth- and early twentieth-century France, improving the means of travel and communication so that one did not have to go abroad to experience new ideas and modes of expression. In 1886, the German Karl Benz invented the automobile, and within a few years, France was leading the world in auto-technology, with Peugeot offering the four-wheeled car with a German/French Daimler petrol engine. Proust, of course, was thrilled with the automobile, as it made him much more mobile, and he also loved the drivers, chauffeurs, and mechanics who worked on them. In 1889, the Eiffel Tower was constructed to celebrate the Exposition Universelle, which included a large *Gallerie des machines*, a colonial exhibition, and visiting international artists such as James Whistler, Edvard Munch, Vincent van Gogh, Henry James, and Thomas Edison. In the 1890s, the first telephone line was laid between France and England, and the first radio transmissions, based on the Italian Guglielmo Marconi's wireless telegraph, were carried out. The Lumière brothers invented cinematography in 1895.

By the first decade of the new century, Parisians could attend films in public cinemas, make international telephone calls, send wireless telegrams, drive around in horseless carriages, and even fly in airplanes during certain exhibitions. In 1900, Paris held its second World's Fair, this time coinciding with the launch of the Paris Metro, with the stations designed in an Art Nouveau style by the French architect Hector Guimard. The fair, which served to import new technology and accelerate development of recent inventions, included the famous Grande Roue de Paris Ferris Wheel, an exhibition of diesel engines, a display of talking films, innovations such as escalators, and the first audio recording. More than 50 million people, many from abroad, attended the fair. The new mobility led to a new way of *seeing* the world, one impacted by speed, multiple perspectives, and variable viewpoints. While the French did not call this new movement "modernism," the rest of the world was beginning to see it that way.

Proust's infatuation with technology in *Recherche du temps perdu* is obvious, with extended passages on trains, automobiles, airplanes, and even elevators. Proust also seemed to have an infatuation with those who operated the new machinery—mechanics, chauffeurs, conductors, and pilots. One of his lovers was an Italian from Monaco named Alfred Agostinelli, who worked first as his chauffeur and then later as a secretary during the early 1900s. In one of the automobile trips with Agostinelli, Proust first saw the steeples of Caen, which became so moving in Proust's recollection. When described in *Recherche*, the Martinville steeples seem to change places and alter their appearance as the car accelerated along winding roads, varying the distance and the clarity of their appearance. While this relative perspective may seem obvious to readers today, at the time it was quite new and exciting, and many artists were trying to capture the phenomenon in different media. In *Proust and his World* (1973), William Sansom makes the connection to *The Church at Eragny,* a landscape painted by the Danish-French artist Camille Pissarro in 1895, which depicted steeples of a small village in a pointillist style, creating the illusion of movement when viewed from the distance (Sansom 1973: 76).

While Proust was fascinated by the new technologies, he tended to be fairly traditional in his taste in art. In *Recherche*, most of Proust's artistic references are to fairly classical artists, such as the Italian artists Tintoretto, Ghirlandaio, Botticelli, Carpaccio, or Mantegna, or Dutch artists, such as Vermeer, Rembrandt, Hals, or de Hooch. But Proust also demonstrated interest in artists with innovative ways of dealing with light and perspective, both premodern and modern. On occasion, newer artists appear in his fiction, such as Gustave Moreau, with his fantasy and sensuality; William Turner, with his play with light and landscape; or Claude Monet, with his impressionistic depictions and variations upon a single structure, such as the Rouen Cathedral, in different kinds of light. Other more modernist painters, such as Maurice Denis, whose triple portraits in works such as Mlle Yvonne Lerolle, with its *mise en abyme*, fascinated Proust, as the newer artists seemed to mirror Proust's aesthetic approach.

To return to the topic of Proust's romantic inclinations, in addition to his affair with Agostinelli, it seems as if several of Proust's relationships were with international residents of Paris. While still in his late teens, Proust courted Laure Hayman, a South American descendant of the English painter Francis Hayman. Laure Hayman, who is depicted as the elegant lady in pink who visits his uncle Adolphe in *Swann's Way*, was more than 20 years older than Proust and had many lovers in Paris, including the King of Greece, the Duc d'Orléans, and, as some speculate, Proust's father (White 1999: 36–37). One of Proust's first gay lovers was the composer Reynaldo Hahn, who was from Venezuela, but who had a German-Jewish father. Proust met him when he was 22 years old while Hahn, then only 19, was already a successful performer at high society dinner parties. After the period with Agostinelli, Proust spent time with Ernest Forssgren, a Swedish man who served as a valet to Proust toward the end of his life and who has written a memoire of those final days, in some ways the first biography of Proust (Forssgren 2006).

In addition to an international milieu of painters, musicians, aristocracy, and high society in general, Paris was also full of immigrant laborers. The second International Labor Congress was held in Paris in 1889, and workers, who had to manufacture and repair all the new technologies, were also flooding into Paris. In the 50 years between 1851 and 1901, the population of Paris grew 220 percent, from 1.2 million to more than 2.7 million (Evenson 1979: 363). Because of the loss of population due to the 1870–71 war, France needed workers and established labor agreements with Italy, Belgium, and Poland, among other countries. German peasants and Central European Jews were also arriving. During this period, after the United States, France had the largest percentage of international immigration of any country in the world. While much concerned with the decay of high culture, Proust was observant of all levels of society, and the dynamism brought in by international artists, industrialists, and workers formed a large part of the narrative.

When younger, Proust, of course, attended the theater, the opera, and art galleries, all of which were alive with international performances. He went to soirees and salons and met many painters, musicians, and artists. The art world in Paris was changing faster than perhaps anywhere in the world, but modernist art was a worldwide phenomenon. Most of his depictions of high society events were based on real life experiences. Proust also attended school, receiving a law degree in 1893 and a philosophy degree in 1895. Moreover, while Proust did not socialize much with the new wave of artists, he did socialize with the elite, who could not help but gossip about the sensationalist new exhibitions and productions. He also knew his share of writers and publishers, as he was trying to publish his work at the time, he was thus well aware of the new trends. The art and architecture surrounded him, and his aesthetic was changing with the time.

As Sherry Simon before me, I call these changes in the design of the city, the new architecture, the international clientele at hotels, the international cuisine, and, especially, the international exhibitions demonstrate the signs of the translational/transformational aspects of the city. I also argue that without this translational culture preceding the work, Proust would have never been able to discover such a new and innovative form for his novel. In other words, without the translational culture of Paris at the time, the writing of Proust's *À la recherche du temps perdu* would not have been possible.

I mentioned above that Proust knew few languages and spoke only French; that is a bit deceptive. According to Anka Muhlstein in *Monsieur Proust's Library*, as all who were educated in the French lycée at the time, he would have studied Latin, Greek and, at least, one modern language, which for Proust was German (Muhlstein 2012: 29). His mother Jeanne Weil was born into a wealthy Parisian Jewish family and was well educated in literature and the arts, fluent in several languages, including Latin and Greek, but also German, English, and probably Yiddish. Proust also translated from Italian, probably self-taught from his interests in Venetian art and culture, in the *Fugitive* when he reports the conversation of two boys talking in Italian in one of the restaurants of a hotel along the Grand Canal in Venice. As a child, Proust was an avid reader. Because of his illness, he read much more

Table 3.1 Innovations preceding the publication of *Recherche* (Belle Époque 2015)

1903	Wright brothers (USA) stage first flight of an airplane
	First Bicycle Tour de France
	Louis Lumière (French) invents color photography
	Pablo Picasso (Spanish) paints *Le Repasseuse* and *Guitariste*
	Arnold Schönberg (Austrian) composes *Pelleas und Melisande*
	Gertrude Stein (USA) moves to Paris
	Salon d'Automne founded, created by Franz Jourdain (Belgian) and
	Hector Guimard (French) as an alternative to the official Paris Salon
1904	Agreement with England to allow France to freely colonize Morocco and
	French West Africa
	Completions of Trans-Siberian Railroad
	Giacomo Puccini (Italian) composes *Madam Butterfly*
	Anton Chekhov (Russian) writes *The Cherry Orchard*
	Auguste Rodin (French) sculpts *Le penseur*
1905	Albert Einstein (German) publishes theory of relativity
	Sigmund Freud (Austrian) publishes three essays on the *Theory of Sexuality*
	Claude Debussy (French) composes *La Mer*
	Richard Strauss (German) composes *Salome*
	Salon d'Automne exhibits work by Matisse, Derain, and Marquet, called *fauves* (wild beasts) by critics
	Gertrude Stein acquires work by Cézanne, Delacroix, Matisse, and Picasso and shows them at her home on *rue de Fleurus*
1906	Salon d'Automne shows work by Courbet, Carrière, and Gauguin
	Picasso meets Matisse through Gertrude Stein
	Max Reinhardt (Austrian) founds Berliner Kammerspiele (see Chapter 2 in this volume)
	Edvard Munch (Norwegian) paints *Tauwetter*
	Maxim Gorky (Russian) writes *Die Mutter*
	Paul Cézanne (French) dies
1907	Early Cubism exposition, mostly work by Braque (French), in Salon d'Automne
	Retrospective of the work of Paul Cézanne
	Pablo Picasso (Spanish) paints *Les demoiselles d'Avignon*, influenced by African Art
	Henri Matisse (French) paints *Asphodèles*
	Henri Bergson (French) publishes *L'Evolution créatrice*
1908	Georges Braque (French) paints *Maisons à l'Estaque*
	Gustav Klimt (Austrian) paints *Der Kuss*
	Rainer Maria Rilke (Bohemia-Austrian) publishes *Neue Gedichte*
	Claude Monet (French) paints *Vues de Venise*
	Arnold Schönberg (Austrian) composes *Second String Quartet*
	Béla Bartók (Hungarian) composes *String Quartet No. 1*
	Vassily Kandinsky (Russian) paints *Herbst in Bayern*
1909	Louis Blériot (French) becomes the first man to cross the English Channel in an airplane
	Sergei Rachmaninoff (Russian) composes *Concerto for Piano No. 3 in D minor*
	André Gide (French) publishes *La Porte étroite*
	T.S. Eliot (American) publishes *Poems*
	Gustav Mahler (Bohemian-Austrian) composes Symphony No. 9 in D major

(*continued*)

Table 3.1 (cont.)

1910	Jean Metzinger (French) paints *Nu à la cheminée* exhibited at the Salon d'Automne
	Picasso (French) paints *Figure dans un Fauteuil*
	Igor Stravinsky (Russian) composes *Fire Bird*
	Kandinsky (Russian) paints *Improvisations*
	Rainer Maria Rilke (Bohemian-Austrian) publishes *The Notebooks of Malte Laurids Brigge*
1911	Marie Curie-Sklodowska (Polish-French) wins second Nobel Prize (first Nobel in 1903) for discovery of radium and polonium
	First group exhibition of Cubist work at Salon des Indépendants
	Walter Gropius (German) designs Neubau Fagus Works
	Thomas Mann (German) writes *Tod in Venedig*
	Igor Stravinsky (Russian) composes *Petruschka*
	Georges Braque (French) paints *Le Violon*
	Expressionist Blue Rider group exhibits in Munich
1912	First modern Olympic Games held in Sweden
	Carl Jung (Swiss) publishes *Wandlungen und Symbole der Libido*
	Franz Kafka (Bohemia-German) writes *Die Verwandlung* and *Das Urteil*
	George Bernard Shaw (Irish) writes *Pygmalion*
	Henri Matisse (French) paints *La danse*
1913	Guillaume Apollinaire (French) publishes *Alcools*
	Igor Stravinsky (Russian) composes *The Rite of Spring*
	Oskar Kokoschka (Austrian) paints *Self Portrait*
	D.H. Lawrence (English) publishes *Sons and Lovers*
	Marcel Proust (French) publishes *Du côte de chez Swann*

than his peers, and his reading included French and international literature, including work by Dostoyevsky, Tolstoy, Dickens, George Eliot, and Goethe. Ironically, other than Goethe, Proust showed little interest in German writers. Most of his readings were done in translation, as when in 1921, when asked to write a review of Dostoyevsky for the *Nouvelle Revue Française*, he refused, citing a bad translation that he read as his reason (Muhlstein 2012: 45).

Despite a prevailing tendency of many nineteenth-century French literary translators to adapt the style of international writers, playwrights, and poets to existing French literary norms, translations in France during La Belle Époque were rapidly on the rise. The historical survey *Histoire des traductions en langue française: XIXᵉ siècle 1815–1914* (2012), edited by Yves Chevrel, Lieven D'hulst, and Christine Lombez, documents the state of translation in France during the nineteenth century up until World War I. Chevrel, D'hulst, and Lombez show a significant increase in the publication of translations beginning about 1890. For example, based on figures drawn from the *Bibliographie de la France* and *Catalogue general de la librairie française*, initially there was a steady growth in fiction translations from 1840 to 1855, rising from 10–15 titles per year in the 1840s to as many as 50 per year in the late 1850s, and then leveling off and even declining a bit over the next two decades (Chevrel et al. 2012: 286). By the 1890s, however, the numbers begin to rise again, moving from the 40–50 per year level in 1885–90 to 60–70 per year by 1900. If one includes poetry, theater, and children's books, that number increases to nearly 100 literary texts in translation, well over 10 percent of the books published in the country (Chevrel et al. 2012: 304–7).

Industrialization and capitalism were also on the rise, and it made good economic sense to publish translations, with as many as 20 publishing firms entering the business and lists growing longer every year. Further, the end of the nineteenth century was a significant period for the great literary revues such as *La Revue de Paris*, *Nouvelle Revue*, or *La Revue politique et litté-raire*, which increased the publication of translations, and even small presses such as *Le Décadent*, *La Revue contemporaine*, or *La Revue blanche*, which were more experimental and willing to publish younger and more avant-garde international writers, while at the same time introducing new forms and ideas. Sales figures were surprisingly high: an edition issued by *La Revue blanche* of the Polish writer Henryk Sienkiewicz's *Quo Vadis?* sold more than 170,000 copies (Chevrel et al. 2012: 317). Some of the little revues were short-lived, but others continued well into the twentieth century. Further, there was a lively debate going on in intellectual circles about the role of foreign literature in the construction of national culture, maybe for the first time in French history. Many modern writers came into French during this period—Tolstoy, Dostoyevsky, Ibsen, Strindberg, D'Annunzio, Dickens, and Hardy—and most texts were readily available. With maybe the exception of some German writers, Proust seemed to be reading them all.

The translational original

Marcel Proust is invariably viewed as a quintessential French writer who lived most of his life in either Paris or the nearby town of Illiers-Combray and was an astute observer of French places, language, and behavior. Some might therefore ask how the original *À la recherche du temps perdu* might be considered as a "translational" text. Just before he embarked on writing the novel, Proust participated in the translational fervor of the times; in fact, at the turn of the century, he was best known as a successful translator of English to French. This translation work came at the very time that he began to rethink his own fiction writing and change his aesthetic approach to *À la recherche du temps perdu*. In the late 1890s, Proust began reading the work of Thomas Carlyle, Ralph Waldo Emerson, and John Ruskin. Proust worked on the translation of two of Ruskin's works. Apparently his mother made a first draft, which was then revised and rewritten by Proust, then proofed by an English cousin of his close friend Reynaldo Hahn, and finally polished by Proust a second time (Tadié 2000: 326). In 1904, Proust's translation *La Bible d'Amiens*, with a long introduction, of Ruskin's *The Bible of Amiens* (1880–85), a book about the architecture of the Cathedral of Amiens, appeared to good reviews. In 1906, Proust's translation *Sésame et les Lys*, with an even longer introduction, of Ruskin's *Sesame and Lilies* (1872), a book about the strange power of literature and art, was equally successfully published. As might be clear from the team translation approach and Proust's role as editor, these translations were less than literal; rather they were a combination of translation and adaptation. In *Marcel Proust*, Edmund White suggests that "Proust adapted their literal translations into beautiful, idiomatic French" (White 1999: 78), characteristic of much literary translation in France at the time.

Ruskin, who was a prolific poet, essayist, art critic, and architecture student, had a broad range of literary, artistic, social, and educational interests, all of which he combined in his essays. What seems to have attracted Proust to his work was the range of Ruskin's mind and his all-inclusive writing style, which roamed freely over everyday experiences, landscapes, literary and artistic references, digressions on architecture, and, especially, espousing a kind of philosophy of romanticism or transcendentalism, sometimes all in the same text or even paragraph. One cannot underestimate the importance of this translation work preceding Proust's masterpiece. At the time, Proust was pretty much stuck as a creative writer, having published merely a group of prose poems and stories in small journals and collected in a volume called *Les Plaisirs et les jours* (1896), which was poorly reviewed. He had abandoned his first attempt at a novel titled *Jean Santeuil*, which covered many of the same topics as the subsequent *Recherche*, including the withheld kiss from the mother and the childhood experiences at Combray, but in which Proust had not yet resolved the plot, style, or aesthetic approach.

I suggest that these problems of style and aesthetics were resolved through his translation work. Again, Edmund White tells us: "The style that Proust worked out in French and retained for his later fiction with its complex syntax and long sentences (so unusual in French literature) sounds very much like Ruskin" (White 1999: 78). However, Proust reworked more than style; it was an entire aesthetic, a new theory of art, a complete rethinking of the power and potential of the form of the novel. Following and going beyond Ruskin's view of the role of the artist in culture, Proust demonstrated the power of art and the imagination to grasp one's surroundings—landscape, people, music, art, and architecture—and then to *retell* or *translate* that encounter into art, in Proust's case an autobiographical novel. In a review of Proust's *On Reading Ruskin*, Guy Davenport writes, "Proust and Ruskin are an example of pupil and teacher wherein the pupil took, with splendid comprehension, everything the teacher knew, paid the teacher the highest gratitude, and then *remade* all that he had learned in a matter wholly his own" (Davenport 1987: 64, emphasis added).

In addition to Proust's short-lived but significant life as a translator, which in terms of the aesthetic style is very much present in *À la recherche du temps perdu*, I also suggest that the text is translational in several other ways. Post-translation studies do not only consider *conventional* written translation as a topic of inquiry but other cross-cultural and intersemiotic forms of translation as well. First, the highly complex prose style has troubled translators over the years. If one thinks of Proust translating an *oral* form to a *written* form, all the long sentences, with their digressions, embedded clauses, asides, additions, and repetitions, become much more manageable. Second, Proust is translating *single images*, oftentiny epiphanies or significant moments, into larger meditations and explorations, and thus applying a Bassnett/Lefevere approach to thinking about translation more of "images" may prove valuable. Third, there is the *psychological* aspect, the translation of dreams, or better said, the translation of the space between being awake and asleep, between conscious and unconscious thought. Here translation methods of enlarging "in-between" space between two languages or cultures may prove helpful.

Regarding the translation of the oral into the written, Proust was striving to develop a prose style that resembled his speaking voice. The way Proust spoke was full of reconsiderations and digressions. Many of those who associated with Proust have mentioned that he tried to write in the same manner that he talked, with many pauses and asides. He would circle in and around a topic, meditate and reflect as he progressed, and the talking made sense to his conversation partners. In her introduction to *Swann's Way*, Lydia Davis writes:

> One friend, though surely exaggerating, reported that Proust would arrive late in the evening, wake him up, begin talking, and deliver one long sentence that did not come to an end until the middle of the night. The sentence would be full of asides, parentheses, illuminations, *reconsiderations, revisions, addenda, corrections, augmentations, digressions*, qualifications, erasures, deletions, and marginal notes.
>
> (Davis 2003: xviii, emphasis added)

Thus, Proust was rewriting, relativizing, and revitalizing as he wrote, adding new material and subtle innuendos as he thought out loud, or, in this case, writing in the same way he spoke. Associations would build on associations, metaphors would be extended, and sounds and syllables would lead to alliterations and assonance. Punctuation would vary; sometimes it was optional, leading to the non-normative use of commas and dashes, usually omitted, to allow the transmission of the thought more directly. The punctuation that did exist served as a way to measure the length of Proust's breath, no matter how long-winded it might have been. When reading his work, Proust's unorthodox punctuation made sense. When it appeared in print, however, the long sentences and unorthodox punctuation proved confusing. Even his contemporaries, who were familiar with the oral style, expressed surprise at the print versions, which seemed to carry on endlessly. The sentences seemed longer in the print version than in conversation, and, without the voice inflection, they made little sense (Davis 2003: xviii). Translators and editors have had to deal with the problem ever since, and no resolution seems satisfactory. Print does not mimic the oral very well.

Concerning the second aspect of a translational original, the translation of an image into text, if there ever was a text that lent itself to thinking less in terms of translating words and more in terms of translating as an image, it may be Proust's *Recherche du temps perdu*. Indeed, Proust himself talked about the entire text being derived from the image in his mind of the "madeleine" tea cake that his aunt served, which in turn conjured up the striking memory of his childhood in Combray and an array of positive images, senses, smells, relatives, visitors, friends, and conversations that took place while growing up there. That a seven-volume novel could emerge from just a single image is difficult to imagine, but such is the power of a little memory triggering an array of emotions over a lifetime. Here is how Proust initially describes that moment in the novel *Swann's Way*:

> [One] day in winter, as I returned home, my mother, seeing that I was cold, suggested that, contrary to my habit, I have a little tea. I refused at first and then, I do not know why, changed my mind. She sent for one of those squat, plump cakes called *petites madeleines* that look as though they have been molded in the grooved valve of a scallop shell. And soon, mechanically, oppressed by the gloomy day and the prospect of another sad day to follow, I carried to my lips a spoonful of the tea in which I had let soften a bit of madeleine. But at the very instant when the mouthful of tea mixed with cake-crumbs touched my palate, I quivered, attentive to the extraordinary thing that was happening inside me. A delicious pleasure had invaded me.
>
> (Proust, trans. Davis 2003: 45)

The scene is fictionalized. Biographies tell us that Proust did not have a madeleine, but instead a mere piece of toast, and the server seems to have been his grandfather, who lived in a different town, rather than his mother. Nevertheless, most readers of the French, English, or other languages, well know that scene *before* reading the novel, and just saying the word "Proust" triggers the "madeleine" image, that first scene from which everything else flows. Other images follow from that encounter to the mother, the infamous goodnight kiss, the house or household, the other family members, the servants, and, of course, the ensuing painful love affairs.

As is the case with such psychological realism, at a certain point those Proustian images begin to intermingle with the memories that the *reader* brings to the text. Maybe not the specific scene of dipping a madeleine tea-cake on a cold, gloomy day, but certainly adolescent love for the mother, separation anxiety, recollections of family gatherings, first loves, intense periods of loneliness, jealousy in love affairs, and other memories of joy and sadness are triggered by tangential memories. Proust's skills are many,

Table 3.2 Original and two translations of the "madeleine" episode

1954 Pléiade ed.: Proust, *Du côté de chez Swann*	1992: *Swann's Way*, trans. Moncrieff, Kilmartin, rev. Enright	2002: *The Way by Swann's*, trans. Lydia Davis
[U]n jour d'hiver, comme je rentrais à la maison, ma mère, voyant que j'avais froid, me proposa de me faire prendre, contre mon habitude, un peu de thé. Je refusai d'abord et, je ne sais pourquoi, me ravisai. Elle envoya chercher un de ces gâteaux courts et dodus appelés Petites Madeleines qui semblaient avoir été moulés dans la valve rainurée d'une coquille de Saint-Jacques. Et bientôt, machinalement, accablé par la morne journée et la perspective d'un triste lendemain, je portai à mes lèvres une cuillerée du thé où j'avais laissé s'amollir un morceau de madeleine. Mais à l'instant même où la gorgée mêlée des miettes du gâteau toucha mon palais, je tressaillis, attentif à ce qui se passait d'extraordinaire en moi. Un plaisir délicieux m'avait envahi.	[O]ne day in winter, on my return home, my mother, seeing that I was cold, offered me some tea, a thing I did not ordinarily take. I declined at first, and then, for no particular reason, changed my mind. She sent for one of those squat, plump little cakes called "petites madeleines", which look as though they had been moulded in the fluted valve of a scallop shell. And soon, mechanically, dispirited after a dreary day with the prospect of a depressing morrow, I raised to my lips a spoonful of the tea in which I had soaked a morsel of the cake. No sooner had the warm liquid mixed with the crumbs touched my palate than a shiver ran through me and I stopped, intent upon the extraordinary thing that was happening to me. An exquisite pleasure had invaded my senses.	[O]ne day in winter, as I came home, my mother, seeing that I was cold, suggested that, contrary to my habit, I have a little tea. I refused at first and then, I do not know why, changed my mind. She sent for one of those squat, plump cakes called *petites madeleines* that look as though they have been molded in the grooved valve of a scallop-shell. And soon, mechanically, oppressed by the gloomy day and the prospect of a sad future, I carried to my lips a spoonful of the tea in which I had let soften a piece of madeleine. But at the very instant when the mouthful of tea mixed with cake-crumbs touched my palate, I quivered, attentive to the extraordinary thing that was happening inside me. A delicious pleasure had invaded me.

not only writing a quasi-stream of consciousness with the bare details of the troubled adolescent mind at work but also marvelous descriptions of the French countryside and the petty concerns of the deteriorating French aristocracy in the late nineteenth century. However, most importantly, Proust has the uncanny ability to deliver subtle psychological insights that set off a range of memories and emotions and that interrupt time, bringing the past into the present, and triggering a flood of further images.

Although much of the text is autobiographical and many episodes are local, I argue that the translation elements are many. First, while drawing upon scenes from real life growing up in the French culture, the book is also fiction or, I might argue, the translation of an autobiography into fiction. The real life episodes are reimagined and reworked for aesthetic reasons. One might say that writing a biography is already a form of translation, translating real life into a narrative. By extension, writing fiction in the disguise of an autobiography might be viewed as more of a rewriting than a translation, as it uses different techniques, subtly altering experiences so that they have more impact. By combining different experiences into one symptomatic episode, the writer alters the prose to delay resolutions and to keep readers guessing, thereby falling deeper and deeper into the emotional traps. Some of Genette's categories—especially augmentation and transtylation—certainly apply to this rewriting style.

Proust himself admitted that understanding such powerful emotions is difficult and invariably involves an act of *interpreting*. In the novel *Swann's Way*, the madeleine teacake episode continues as follows:

> Where could it have come to me from—this powerful joy? I sense that it was connected to the taste of the tea and the cake, but that it went infinitely far beyond it, could not be of the same nature. Where did it come from? What did it mean? How could I grasp it? I drink a second mouthful, in which I find nothing more than in the first, a third that gives me a little less than the second. It is time for me to stop, the virtue of the drink seems to be diminishing. Clearly, the truth I am seeking is not in the drink, *but in me*. The drink has awoken it in me, but does not know this truth, and can do no more that repeat indefinitely, with less and less force, this same testimony which *I do not know how to interpret* and which I want at least to be able to ask of it again and find again, intact, available to me, soon, for a decisive clarification. I put down the cup and turn to my mind. It is up to me to find the truth. But how?
>
> (Proust, trans. Davis 2003: 45, emphasis added)

Thus, Proust's artistry is much related to interpreting, for searching for the right word or image, and to translation. It took Proust a lifetime of writing and rewriting to figure out a way to interpret those tiny but crucial scenes ingrained in his memory and to translate them into prose. Moreover, the translation or interpretation is not necessarily just finding the words with which to better describe *outside* reality, but to find the language with which to describe what was happening *inside* of himself: "The truth I am seeking is not in the drink, *but in me*." The power of Proust's prose is that he was not only skilled at describing the *external* reality in wonderfully evocative terms, but also at translating an *internal* reality, scenes, and emotions that often had never been articulated in a language before.

Critics have written about many aspects of Proust's aesthetic, and careers have been made from analyzing Proust's depiction of memory or, better said, involuntary memory, his use of time and of flashbacks, his depictions of love and loss, his codified representations of male and gay sexuality, and, especially, his reflections on the nature of art. However, few scholars discuss *the translation and interpreting* elements of Proust's writing. One critic who does discuss Proust's translational aesthetic is Roger Shattuck, author of *Proust's Binoculars* (1963), the National Book Award-winning biography *Marcel Proust* (1974), and *Proust's Way: A Field Guide to "In Search of Lost Time"* (2000). Shattuck elevates translation to the *primary* means by which Proust connects experience to art. When talking about the period in 1909, when Proust was failing as a writer but succeeding as a translator, Shattuck suggests that something *shifted* in Proust's aesthetic. While working on various ways to express the relation between memory and art, which he had failed to achieve in *Jean Santeuil* and the essay *Against Sainte-Beuve*, he stepped back from deep involvement in his own past life and its depiction and discovered a new perspective, which Shattuck argues is neither autobiography nor fiction, but something in-between, i.e., translation. He writes: "This insight in 1909 signifies a shift away from both autobiography and fiction (as a pure invention) to *translation*, a term that keeps occurring in the final section of the Search" (Shattuck 1974: 149, emphasis in original). Ironically, Shattuck quotes Borges's story "The Circular Ruins" as a comparable aesthetic, and translation studies scholars are well versed in the importance Borges gives to translation.

Shattuck further develops his theory of translation by juxtaposing it to those who argue that Proust's aesthetic depends upon depicting involuntary memory. Shattuck suggests that one must read to the end of the seven volumes of *In Search of Lost Time* to see the shift in the approach, which links involuntary memory to a process of translation. Both are necessary; Shattuck writes, "Involuntary memory links past the present into reality. 'Translation' links that reality, focused on reminiscences and impressions, to the work of art" (Shattuck 1974: 158). Shattuck supports his claim by citing a passage from the end of *In Search of Lost Time*, in which the writer discovers this new form of connecting life to art:

> If I tried to analyze for myself just what takes place in us at the moment when something makes a certain impression on us—as, for example, that day when, as I crossed the bridge over the Vivonne, the shadow of a cloud on the water made me exclaim, "Gosh, gosh," as I leaped for joy ... —I perceived that, to describe these impressions, or write that essential book, the only true book, a great writer does not need to invent it, in the current sense of the term, since it already exists in each of us, *but merely to translate it*. The duty and *the tasks of a writer are those of a translator.*
>
> (Proust 1954: vol. 3: 890, trans. and quoted by
> Shattuck 1974: 157–58, emphasis added)

Shattuck goes on to describe a very complex model of Proust's aesthetic—complete with diagrams that connect philosophic, epistemological, and aesthetic aspects—but one that essentially describes a model of communication in which translation plays a key role, especially that critical stage of translating memory into the work of art. Shattuck also connects this insight to the shift from an ambiguous narrative "I" to that complex merged narrator/protagonist "I" /"Marcel," which has so troubled critics over the years. Shattuck implies that there is at this moment a transcendence from the self as failed artist to that as a successful translator, one who has achieved enough objective distance from life experiences and memories to adequately "translate" those into prose without the narcissism or obsession characteristic of the former: autobiography once removed. Translations of Proust have had an impact on creative writing all over the world. So too might one argue that translation had an impact on Proust's *personal* creative writing. Traditional translation studies normally would not touch such an investigation, as *In Search* is deemed an "original" and not a translation; but post-translation studies would be open to studying the translational aspects of such original writing. One might also argue that a *new* genre emerges during this period, a non-autobiographical autobiography, or non-fiction fiction, or what I might call translational fiction: in Proust's words, "a great writer does not need to invent it … since it already exists … but merely to translate it" (trans. and quoted by Shattuck 2000: 146).

The third type of translational element inherent to Proust's text involves the tricky business of the translation of the psychological aspects. In the novel, the reader has the sense that Proust is psychoanalyzing himself, or minimally using writing as a form of a talking cure, and the process rehearses itself over and over. Memories rise and recede, places and people appear and disappear, images are crystal clear and then blurred, as rational voices compete with the irrational, recreating the past to fit the present, translating and transforming as the writer tries to make sense out of such impressionable episodes. This separation of the author from daily existence, this feeling of detachment that the space of translation provides, allows the writer the freedom to be inside and outside the narrative at once. The style is highly characteristic of Proust's writings, of modernist texts themselves. In the famous first paragraph, Proust refers to this state as analogous to "metempsychosis":

> For a long time, I went to bed early. Sometimes, my candle scarcely out, my eyes would close so quickly that I did not have time to say to myself: "I'm falling asleep." And, half an hour later, the thought that it was time to try to sleep would wake me; I wanted to put down the book I thought I still had in my hands and blow out my light; I had not ceased while sleeping to form reflections on what I had just read, but these reflections had taken a rather peculiar turn; it seemed to me that I myself was what the book was talking about: a church, a quartet, the

rivalry between François I and Charles V. This belief lived on for a few seconds after my waking; it did not shock my reason but lay heavy like scales on my eyes and kept them from realizing that the candlestick was no longer lit. Then it began to grow unintelligible to me, as after *metempsychosis* do the thoughts of an earlier existence; the subject of the book detached itself from me, I was free to apply myself to it or not.

(Proust 2003: 3, emphasis added)

Proust describes that liminal space in between waking and sleeping, light and dark, conscious and unconscious, the present and the past. For me, it seems quite analogous to that in-between space all translators encounter— an image, thought or reference not fully formed in one language or the other. Certainly many translation theorists, especially postcolonial theorists such as Homi Bhabha (1994) or the Québécois feminist translators such as Barbara Godard (1990), have attempted to better describe and expand that in-between space between languages and cultures. Here Proust is doing it to describe that space between waking and sleeping, the rational and irrational, the images of reality and the dream images associated with them.

I am reminded of Nicole Brossard's *Le Désert mauve* (1987), in which she also talks about those liminal spaces—the half tones of orange-red at dawn or purple-gray at dusk—as translational metaphors. Brossard also describes 15-year-old Melanie, who, while driving across the desert at night, perceives half-formed objects—blurred because of the speed of the car or her drowsiness—as translational images. Brossard's fiction led Québécois feminists to develop a theory of *réécriture au feminine*, in which writers such as Brossard encourage their translators to *rewrite in the spirit of the original*, to take such liminal images and *go further*, finding new language and metaphors to describe that space. The theory aims at breaking down those stark black and white images, and logocentric discourse that some feminists feel are characteristic of male discourse (see Gentzler 2008: 61–65). So too is Proust working to expand that in-between space between logic and illogic, familiar and unfamiliar, the conscious experience and the unconscious interpretation, thereby blurring boundaries between the present and the past, lived experiences and relived memories. This space reflects the psychological aspect of the work that is so hard to translate. My guess is that a literal translation probably would not do and would only result in confusion. Proust's translators might learn from the feminist or postcolonial translators and try to devise strategies for rewriting, going further, and inventing new metaphors. Indeed, the reference to "metempsychosis" in the passage quoted above is a metaphor, one familiar to translation studies scholars for it contains in it one of the oldest definitions of translation, that of the human body in an in-between state as it passes from earth to heaven. However, as I argued above, it might also be seen as one of the key aesthetic principles of Proust's novel: the subject detached from the text being written.

Proust as rewriter

The suggestion that the original text is already in translation tends to destabilize any fixed notion of an original text. One of the problems for translators is that *In Search of Lost Time* has always been a work in progress, undergoing multiple stages of rewriting itself, a kind of circular ruin in which the end rewrites the beginning. Proust rewrote and reinterpreted the text/s many times, to the point of creating his labyrinth. In the introduction to her 2003 translation, Lydia Davis tells us that Proust initially proposed a series of shorter works of essays, not fiction, and that only later, around 1909, did he begin telling his friends that he was working on a novel. Early excerpts published in the newspaper *Le Figaro* show that the initial form seemed more memoir, reportage, and autobiographical than fictional. From that point on, Proust wrote and rewrote many parts of the book, cutting, expanding, and revising endlessly.

In 1912 and 1913, Proust sent a manuscript now approaching three volumes to several publishers, including editors from Eugène Fasquelle, *Nouvelle Revue Française*, Gallimard, and Ollendorff, all of whom rejected the work. Some of these publishing firms were more established than others; however, Proust was receiving editorial advice and may have been rewriting, or at least, reconsidering some of his versions accordingly. He briefly changed his mind about getting published, and resubmitted his manuscript, this time for the experimental publisher Bernard Grasset. Proust offered to pay for the publishing and advertising expenses, and finally the book was accepted. However, still not finished rewriting when the proofs arrived, Proust undertook another set of extensive revisions. Davis quotes Proust from a letter to a friend as follows: "My corrections so far (I hope this won't continue) are not corrections. There remains not a single line out of 20 of the original texts … It is crossed out, corrected in every blank part I can find, and I am pasting papers at the top, at the bottom, to the right, to the left" (Davis 2003: xiv). In short, Proust was rewriting right up until the last minute. Genette's concept of palimpsest proves helpful in this context. The numerous rewritings, editorial comments, and author's revisions added to the first edition, published in late 1913, continued leading up to the second edition in 1919 by Gallimard. Proust died in 1922, but nevertheless, Gallimard brought out the final three additional volumes, with the last volume *Le Temps retrouvé* appearing in 1927, the proofs of which, of course, Proust could not revise. Figure 3.1 is a sample of the last page of the manuscript.

How the Gallimard editors made sense of Proust's handwriting is a form of rewriting itself in the professional sense anticipated by Lefevere. A third edition, a further corrected Gallimard publication, appeared in 1954, and perhaps not so finally, a fourth edition, with further corrections and additions was published in 1987. Even today, some Proust scholars suggest that the definitive edition has not yet been completed, as undiscovered manuscripts are being unearthed, all complicated by the Proust heirs, who also have a say in the process.

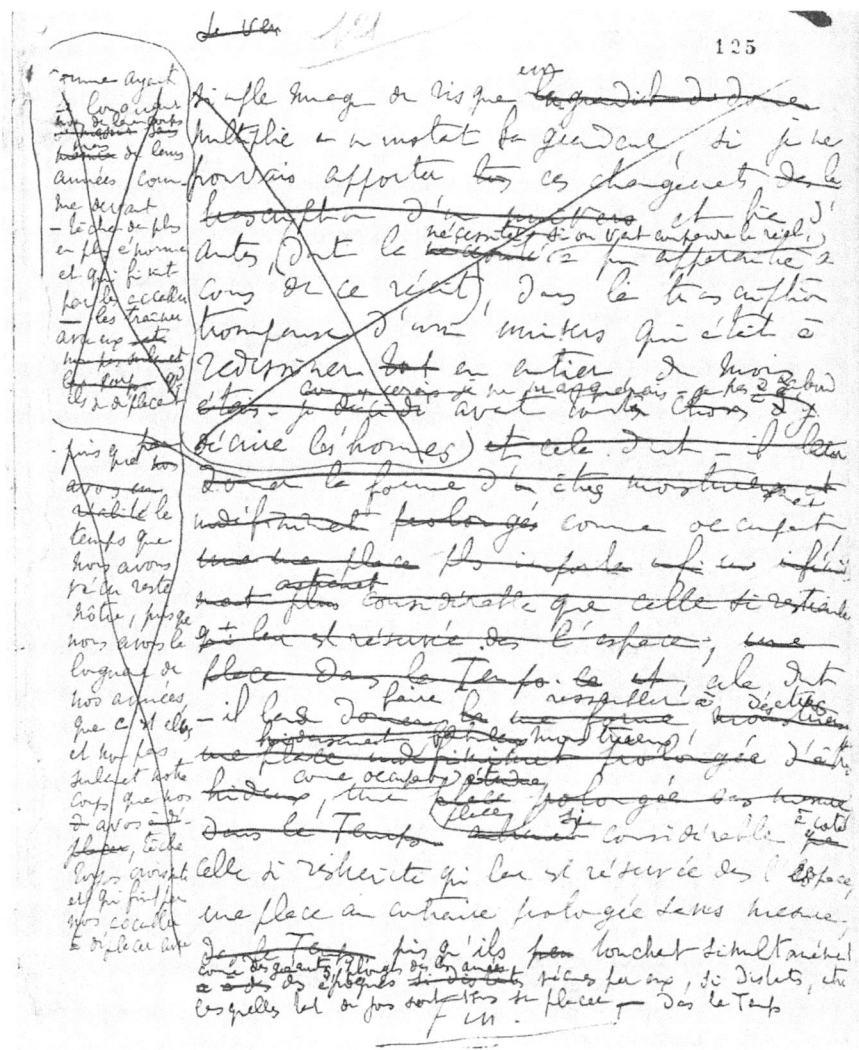

Figure 3.1 Last page of *Time Regained*, published posthumously, © Bibliothèque nationale de France.

Earlier in this chapter, I expressed my doubts about the existence of an "original" and instead argued that all originals are also in a state of rewriting. In Proust's case, the translational original is characterized less by one definitive text and more by a series of texts over the past century that are in a constant state of revision, beginning with the then-unpublished *Jean*

Table 3.3 Editions of *À la recherche du temps perdu*

Date	Edition
1912–13	Proust sent a manuscript approaching three volumes to several publishers, including Eugène Fasquelle, *Nouvelle Revue Française*, Gallimard, and Ollendorff, all of which rejected the work.
1913	The smaller and newer publishing firm Bernard Grasset accepts *Du côté de chez Swann* only after Proust agrees to pay for publication and advertising costs, thus giving him license and time to make numerous corrections in the proofs. 3,300 copies. Reviews were mixed.
1914	Grasset planned a second volume, but WWI intervenes. Proust takes the time to make more revisions.
1919–27	Gallimard, director of NRF editions, which turned down the manuscript earlier, enters into agreement with Grasset and, over the next eights years, publishes the next six volumes, including a new *Du côté de chez Swann* with minor revisions. Many volumes, especially the later versions, contain errors.
1954	Éditions Gallimard: Bibliothèque de la Pléiade published a new edition edited by university scholars Pierre Clarac and André Ferré, which becomes the definitive edition of the novel (3 volumes) for years to come.
1967	Livre de Poche publishes a pocket edition with the permission of Gallimard, exactly reproducing the 1954 Pléiade text.
1977	Gallimard issues its own pocket edition, again with the same 1954 text, which sells 1.5 million copies. Combined with other editions, over 3 million copies sold.
1985	Dispute over when the copyright reverts to public domain, largely due to the 14-year period over which the first volumes were published and a glitch in the copyright law which has different rules for publications before and after World War I. Because of a dispute with Gallimard, Flammarion brings out a new edition of *In Search* with *La Prisonnière* as their first volume, not *Du côté de chez Swann*. Gallimard has obtained permission from the Proust estate, headed by Proust's great niece Suzy Mante-Proust, which is complicated by the fact that Marcel Proust never married and had no children. The three sides reach an agreement in 1987, whereby Mme Mante receives 5% royalties from the sale of each volume.
1987	*Recherche* becomes public domain. Three new editions are published: 1. Garnier-Flammarion (GF) continues with a revised edition of the Livre de Poche editions and hires a team of university specialists to make corrections. Ed. Jean Milly. Proust specialist at Sorbonne, Director of a Center for Proust Studies, and Editor of the *Bulletin Marcel Proust*. 10 volumes. 2. Gallimard hires Jean-Yves Tadié, Professor at the Sorbonne and the most prominent Proust scholar in France, to revise the Pléiade edition, which is published and becomes a more-definitive edition (4 volumes). Tadié adds much additional material, many Proust drafts, manuscripts, letters held by the Bibliothèque Nationale. Marketed as the complete critical edition. 3. Laffont-Bouqiuns issues the complete text in a paperback edition, edited and with preface by Bernard Raffalli, and with several different scholars, including André Alain Morello, Michelle Berman, Jo Yoshida, revising original based upon Proust manuscripts and corrections by Proust held at the Bibliothéque nationale, 3 volumes.

(continued)

Table 3.3 (cont.)

Date	Edition
1988–90	Gallimard issues a Folio paperback, with minimal notes, but the same text as the Tadié Folio edition, in seven volumes. Marketed as the definitive readers edition.
1987	*Albertine disparue* Paris: Grasset, 1987, vol 6. After the death in 1986 of Proust's great niece Suzy Mante-Proust, her son-in-law discovered among her papers a typescript of volume 6 of the *Recherche*, corrected and annotated by Proust. Robert Proust prepared a posthumous publication of this volume based on an earlier handwritten manuscript, and the definitive French edition followed suit.
1992–3	Le Livre de Poche issues the complete text, ed. Bernard Brun. Seven volumes.
1999	Gallimard issues a Quarto Edition, based on the 1987 Pléiade edition, all the different texts in one volume.
2011	Omnibus (Presses de la Cité) issues the complete text in two volumes.

Santeuil (written 1896–1900; unpublished in Proust's lifetime; published posthumously in 1952 by Gallimard). The Jean-Yves Tadié edited 1987 Gallimard edition of *Recherche*, with all its notes and variations, is again thousands of pages longer than the already over 3,000-page "original." All this activity has led to many controversies about the use of all the myriad of possibilities. Roger Shattuck criticized the Tadié 1987 French edition, going so far as to call on readers to boycott it (Compagnon and Tadié 1999), which naturally drew the ire of the French.

One of the predominant forms of translation in *In Search* would be a form of interpretation as Freud might use the term in the "interpretation of dreams." Anyone who has ever undergone psychoanalysis knows how hard this task might be. Translation studies scholars have often addressed linguistic and literary problems of translation, but the study of psychological factors in translation has received little attention. The research on psychological translation that has been conducted to date exists in the form of the translation of psychological texts, such as those authored by Freud. Little work has been done on the process of translation that occurs in therapy, or, in this case, in creative writing. The translation of stream-of-consciousness modernist texts has been fraught with problems over the years. Modernist critics have suggested that readers of such texts must be psychologists to a certain degree, and the translator as reader thus must be equally insightful. Proust translators demonstrate such skills; it is to them I turn in the next section.

Translations of *Recherche*

Recently, the translation of Proust's *À la recherche du temps perdu* has become big news in many countries because of the three new French editions published in 1987–89 with all of their corrections and updates, which in turn have led to a new round of translations, or at least updates of old translations, around the world. In the English-speaking world, Penguin Modern Classics in England is the first to tackle this project. Basing their translations upon the Gallimard 1987 Pléiade edition, the editors at Penguin decided upon the slightly unusual approach of using a *team* of translators, choosing seven different translators, each one translating a different volume of the original. The decision was based in part on speed: the sooner the updated versions reached the market, the bigger the chance they would beat out the competition. The project was first directed by Paul Keegan and later by Simon Winder, with Christopher Prendergast, professor at the University of Cambridge, serving as the general editor. Translators included Lydia Davis for *The Way by Swann's*; James Grieve for *In the Shadow of Young Girls in Flower*; Mark Treharne for *The Guermantes Way*; John Sturrock for *Sodom and Gomorrah*; Carol Clark for *The Prisoner*; Peter Collier for *The Fugitive*; and Ian Patterson for *Finding Time Again*. The translators all worked at different rates in their respective parts of the world. In "A Note on the Translation" to her American version of *Swann's Way* (2003), Lydia Davis describes the process as follows:

> After a single face-to-face meeting in early 1998, which most translators attended, we communicated with one another and with Christopher Prendergast by letter and e-mail. We agreed, often after lively debate, on certain practices that needed to be consistent from one volume to the next, such as retaining French titles like Duchess de Guermantes, and leaving quotations that occur within the text—from Racine, most notably—in the original French, with translation in the notes.
>
> (Davis 2003: xxi–xxii)

What strikes any scholar of such a process for such a long and demanding book, within which the end circulates and influences the beginning, filled with such difficult aesthetic and psychological insights, is that such a process would naturally lead to inconsistencies across the volumes, which could then, in turn, serve to alienate readers. With only one meeting, which all the translators did not attend, the task by Christopher Prendergast must have been quite difficult. Indeed, in the Lydia Davis American version, despite UK editorial policies, all the French was translated into English, and the French punctuation altered to conform to US style. Six volumes have appeared to date, with the seventh volume, probably due to copyright restrictions again, due out in 2018.

The first six volumes of the 2002 Penguin edition appeared under the title *In Search of Lost Time*, effectively ending the *Remembrance of Things Past* title that reigned so poetically for more than 80 years, leaving it to older people similar to Proust's grandmother to wonder where their beloved "original" had gone. So, too, with other titles to the individual volumes: in the Penguin British edition, *Swann's Way* was changed to *The Way by Swann's*, which is also meeting opposition from those who cling to C.K. Scott Moncrieff's translation, and after much in-house debate, when the American version came out a year later, the title was changed back to *Swann's Way*. So too have the titles for subsequent volumes been controversial: for Proust's *A l'ombre des jeunes filles en fleurs*, which Moncrieff translated poetically as *Within a Budding Grove*, the Penguin edition prefers the more literal *In the Shadow of Young Girls in Flower*. The most controversial change happened in the last volume, in which Proust's *Le Temps retrouvé*, translated by Moncrieff as *Time Regained*, which endured so long in English, was rewritten as *Finding Time Again*. My guess is that the Penguin's title will be short-lived as the informal and colloquial nature of the new title strikes me as insufficient. Proust was not "finding time" in the contemporary sense, and the new title belittles the larger aesthetic and temporal search. Indeed, while the jury is still out, the literalness of the title of the new Penguin edition, up to the point of retaining the long sentences and complex syntax of the original, may be more attractive to scholars than readers, underscoring Bassnett and Lefevere's point of different readerships within cultures. In addition, all of Penguin's English volumes include guides, lists of names of characters, and notes. Many of the notes seem less aimed at explaining Proust's versions and alternatives and more directed at explicating nineteenth-century French cultural references likely lost on most modern-day readers.

Other revised editions will no doubt follow. At the time of this writing, to celebrate the 100th anniversary of its original publication, Yale University Press has announced a new revision of *À la recherche du temps perdu* by biographer William C. Carter. The first volume, *Swann's Way*, was published in November 2013, with one additional volume planned to be released in each subsequent year. The translation is not new, but an update of the *first* translation by Moncrieff, now in public domain. Carter, a professor emeritus of French at the University of Alabama at Birmingham and author of *Marcel Proust: A Life* (2002) and *Proust in Love* (2006), has added numerous notes, which appear in the margins. Spellings were Americanized, and some of Moncrieff's embellishments have been modified.

While there are copyright permissions, expediency reasons, and economic considerations for Yale going back to the early Moncrieff version, the romance with C.K. Scott Moncrieff's translation continues in the United States and the English-speaking world and the translation has held up well over time. Most translation studies scholars suggest that translations need to be updated nearly every generation, but in the case of *À la recherche du temps perdu*, other than adapting to changes in French editions, this has not been the case. Since the inception of the field of translation studies in the 1970s in Europe, most translation studies scholars hold that *target* culture factors dictate translation decisions, claiming that their data show that translators invariably conform to the literary and social norms of the receiving culture. In the United States, too, many translation studies scholars agree. In *The Translator's Invisibility: A History of Translation* (1995), Lawrence

Table 3.4 Translations of *À la recherche du temps perdu* into English

1922–30	The first six volumes translated by C.K. Scott Moncrieff (Scotland) under the title *Remembrance of Things Past*. Proust was alive during the early stage of the translation process, and Moncrieff and Proust exchanged letters. Proust seemed pleased overall. Some critics say that the Moncrieff translation is the best translation of any literary work into English. Others, Samuel Beckett for example, are more critical. C.K. Scott Moncrieff rendered the title of Proust's novel as *Remembrance of Things Past*. Many who were unaware that the phrase was taken from the second line of Shakespeare's Sonnet 30 criticized him. By the time Moncrieff died in 1930, he had translated all but the final volume.
1931–32	Stephen Hudson, a pseudonym for Sydney Schiff (UK), translates *Time Regained*, vol. 7, in 1931, followed by several translators since, including Frederick Blossom as *The Past Recaptured* (1932), Frederick Blossom (U.S.) (1932), and Andreas Mayor (U.K.) (1970).
1981	Terence Kilmartin revised the Moncrieff translation, basing his corrections on the 1954 French Pléiade edition. Some of Moncrieff's embellishments were eliminated, but the lower quality of Kilmartin's English raised additional questions. 3 Volumes.
1982	James Grieve (Australia) translates *Swann's Way*. The text is less a literal version, and more a rewriting. Grieve, a professor of French in Canberra, studied the original and rewrote hoping to preserve the meaning and philosophy of the original.
1989	Terence Kilmartin (UK) translates *Albertine Gone*, based on the 1987 Grasset version, which was based on posthumously discovered typescript corrected and annotated by Proust (see Table 3.3 above).
1992–93	D.J. Enright re-revised the Moncrieff/Kilmartin revision, based on the 1987 Pléiade revised edition. New title: *In Search of Lost Time*. Each volume includes a handful of endnotes and some contain alternative versions of some of the novel's episodes. Six volumes.
2002	Seven translators, including Lydia Davis (American), Allen Lane (Australian), and five UK translators translate the first six volumes under the title *In Search of Lost Time*, directed by Christopher Prendergast of Penguin UK. Based on the 1987 Pléiade French edition, all volumes include guides, lists of characters, and notes. The last volume is scheduled to come out in 2018.
2013–future	Yale University has announced a new translation/revision by biographer William C. Carter, the first volume due out in 2013.

Venuti, for example, suggests that translators tend to domesticate their literary translations, conforming to literary styles prevalent in the receiving culture. On the other hand, C.K. Scott Moncrieff was *not* conforming to the receiving culture's literary styles and language usage. The reason Moncrieff translated Proust's "novel" was that it was entirely new. Indeed, *no* text or style such as Proust's existed anywhere in the world. Given that Proust's first volume was published in 1913, nine years *before* James Joyce's *Ulysses*, which came out in 1922, the reason for Moncrieff's translation seems clear: the text was something new. Its aesthetic insights, circular style, long stream-of-consciousness reflections, breath-length prose units, objective/subjective narrators, and invention of a new genre of nonfictional fiction did not exist in the target culture. Moncrieff wanted to bring that newness across. In this book, I argue that this factor of introducing new ideas or forms of expression is one of the *primary* reasons motivating most translators. Some succeed more than others, but Moncrieff certainly succeeded very well.

Despite claims to the contrary by translators and editors of the new editions, Moncrieff's translation remains quite loyal to the original; at least, to how the original appeared at the time. Moncrieff was translating the first volumes as early as 1922, five years before the publication of the *last* volume in French in 1927. While Moncrieff might have taken minor liberties with lexis and tone, he largely stayed close to the original, and his liberties are few, maybe adding or embellishing an adjective here and there, and diversifying verbs. In Table 3.2 above, on translations of the madeleine episode, readers can see how *similar* the Moncrieff translation is to the Davis. There is a sound of late nineteenth-century English in Moncrieff's version that rings Victorian/Edwardian today, but that is completely compatible with the La Belle Époque tone of Proust's French. While Moncrieff's translation is a type of a performance, as the Shakespearian allusion in the title shows, it coincides with the spirit of the original and has been well received by readers. Proust himself, while he disagreed with the title, begrudgingly admitted that he was quite pleased with Moncrieff's translation overall and honored to be translated into English so quickly and well. Moncrieff's dedication to the project was heroic. Already an accomplished translator of both French and Italian, having successfully translated Stendhal's *The Red and the Black* and selected works of Pirandello, he started on Proust in 1922 and devoted himself entirely to finishing *Remembrance of Things Past*, a task he almost achieved, passing away just before completion of the final volume.

William C. Carter pays homage to Moncrieff by going back to the original translation into English, and the Yale University editions have eliminated Kilmartin and Enright from the title page. My guess is that many of the corrections made by Kilmartin and Enright are still present in their absence, as some of the changes have stayed and others have only been slightly revised. Davis, basing her work on the corrected 1987 French edition, and adhering to the Penguin guidelines, was more literal than Moncrieff while still retaining a high literary tone and feeling. I admit to being an admirer of the Davis translation, which strikes me as accurate in many ways; she retains the long sentences, but uncannily makes them readable. Maybe the breath span unconsciously works to help readers follow the argument. Davis also retains the asides, repetitions, and unfoldings, all of which tantalizingly delay outcomes and add nuanced layers of meaning and interpretation, a form of reconsideration similar to the translation process and essential to Proust's aesthetic. Despite her literalness, Davis keeps as well many tonalities, alliterations, and assonances, so important to Proust but often neglected by translators. Most importantly, perhaps as her own homage to Moncrieff, she does not modernize the English but instead leaves many nineteenth-century phrases (see Davis 2003: xvii–xix).

There has been much discussion in literary journals comparing the Moncrieff to the new Penguin translation in reviews of the two competing editions. For example, in "Reviving the Dread Deity" (2002), a review of the Penguin 2002 edition for the British newspaper *The Guardian*, Paul Davis, who teaches translation at University College London, seems to prefer the Moncrieff translation, although he hedges with favorable comments on Traherne's *The Guermantes Way* and Clark and Collier's *The Prisoner* and *The Fugitive*. On the other side, in "Style over Substance: Translating Proust" for the June 2014 issue of the *Boston Review*, Harvard professor Leland de la Durantaye reviews the Carter-edited translation and seems to come down in favor of the Penguin. In another example, in a *New York Review of Books* article titled "'Proust's Way?': An Exchange" (2006), Lydia Davis, Marcel Muller, and Christopher Prendergast state their differences with the Moncrieff translation, both in Davis's specific choices, and in Prendergast's overall approach. Davis objects to additions and intensifiers, some pronounced, but most quite subtle. And Prendergast insists that the deciding factor always bears in mind the 1987 Pléiade French edition by seeking literal solutions wherever possible. In my view, rather than judging one translation to be better or worse, readers in the English-speaking world have been fortunate to have two excellent translations, both motivated by source-text loyalties, sometimes to syntax, sometimes to meanings, but more importantly to the originality of the ideas and the inventiveness of the prose. Students in my generation grew up on Moncrieff, thus those loyalties remain strong. But the Davis translation is brilliant in another way, giving a slightly more concise Proust (if one could ever call Proust concise) and a more carefully crafted prose that reveals Proust's art in a new light. In many ways, the translations have enabled Proust to enter the English language literary tradition, and the repercussions on creative writing in English are still being felt.

Rewritings of Proust

Compared to the intense activity regarding other rewritings of internationally famous texts, such as film and theater versions of *Faust* in English, adaptations of Proust are surprisingly few. In terms of rewritings, most of what exists for *À la recherche du temps perdu* are abridgements, everything from *The 14-Minute Marcel Proust* (2014), to Proust Guide's "Summarize Proust Challenge," to Monty Python's "The All-England Summarize Proust Competition," and a variety of reading groups, as people join groups to share the reading process. Certainly the length of the original is prohibitive, trying to remake a 1,300-page novel into a two-hour film has proven daunting, and for many years was considered impossible. The action in *Recherche* is also minimal, as the interior monologues take precedence over dramatic dialogue. A history of failed attempts to turn the novel into a film exists: two important film scripts have been developed, one by Harold Pinter for Joseph Losey, and another by Suso Cecchi d'Amico and Luchino Visconti, with Visconti as the projected director, Marlon Brando proposed as Charlus, and even Greta Garbo as the Queen of Naples. Neither film got made, although there is a BBC radio play of the Pinter screenplay. Clearly, the aesthetic innovations of Proust, including multiple narrators, cyclical descriptions, and complex prose style, have hindered reproductions.

However, as Bassnett and Lefevere before me, I suggest that the imagistic nature of Proust's aesthetic, with the depiction of a single image triggering a whole series of impressions, could conceivably lend itself to film. Moreover, there have been several attempts that merit discussion. The first is Volker Schlöndorff's *Un Amour de Swann* (*Swann in Love*) (1984), which did not attempt to film the entire seven volumes, but chose only an excerpt from the first volume, one that is fairly self-standing. It also focused on an unrequited love story, one told not from a first-person point of view but with a certain amount of distance. The main character Swann is intelligent and sophisticated; and his love object, Odette, a Botticelliesque former courtesan who continues to have affairs during the relationship, drives Swann to his all-consuming jealousy. The story lends itself to film, as it is less about time and memory and more about jealousy and love.

What strikes the viewer initially about *Un Amour de Swann* (1984) is the *international* collaboration. The director Volker Schlöndorff is German; Swann is played by the British actor Jeremy Irons; Odette is played by the Italian actress Ornella Muti; the French actor Alain Delon plays the Baron de Charlus; the cinematographer is the Swedish Sven Nykvist, well known for his work with Ingmar Bergman; and the music is composed by the German Hans Werner Henze. Further, the script was co-written by British director Peter Brook (see Chapter 1 in this volume), French novelist and screenplay writer Jean-Claude Carrière, and French screenwriter and casting director Marie-Hélène Estienne. The film was shot in France and in the French language; Jeremy Irons speaks French, which is one of the reasons he was cast in the role of Swann. This internationalization of the production and the attempt to turn a revered art object into a commercially successful movie have bothered many critics, especially those most loyal to the "original," but the film has been much enjoyed by non-professional viewers.

From the Heinrich von Kleist film adaptation *Michael Kohlhaas* (1969) through the adaptation of Heinrich Böll's *The Lost Honor of Katharina Blum* (1974) (co-directed with Margarethe von Trotta), or his film of Günter Grass's *The Tin Drum* (1979), Volker Schlöndorff has demonstrated his adeptness at adapting novels to films. He has developed a knack for finding the heart of the story, showing insight concerning the historical period, and dramatically portraying it in another medium. He surrounds himself with creative and perceptive collaborators. In addition, he subtly incorporates his own literary and political perspective without disturbing too much the author's vision. Schlöndorff's co-author Peter Brook is also well known for his transnational perspective, especially his work on international theater and using international casts, and his search for intersemiotic forms of communication that lend themselves well to translation (see Chapter 1 in this volume).

Many reviewers have criticized the film *Swann in Love*, but it is often clear that the reviewers, especially in the English journals, have never read the original, either in French or translation. Jeremy Irons seems to be much-liked by the British and German viewers, especially for his portrayal of a male romantic lead; he had just successfully finished *The French Lieutenant's Woman* (1981). However, Irons was criticized by the French for his distant performance and his German-sounding accent. Anglo- and German audiences also enjoyed Ornella Muti and her coquetry in portraying Odette de Crécy, but not so French audiences, who found her naïve and clichéd. Irons performs in a restrained way, polite in high society, deferential to nobility, and servile toward women, but he can communicate his obsessions, mostly through looks and gestures. The film does have the period-piece Parisian salons and palace settings as well as the aristocratic dress that translate well to film, and the cinematography has been universally praised. But Schlöndorff does not omit the social commentary. Additionally, the flirtations and erotics play well in the adapted genre, as does the drama of the attempted pursuit and capture.

Some of the critics of the film disliked the fact that Schlöndorff turns the timeframe of the play into one day, thereby unifying the time rather than have it cyclical. That said, Schlöndorff makes liberal use of flashbacks, and there are repeated images, such as the orchid in the bosom, or the acoustic moments, including versions of the Vinteuil Sonata, which repeatedly resurface. I suggest that the use of an imagistic approach, as emphasized by Bassnett and Lefevere, holds up well. In *Schlöndorff's Cinema: Adaptation, Politics and "The Movie-Appropriate"* (2002), Bernard Moeller and George Lellis write:

> [We] assert that the whole issue of adaptation has so clouded the reception of *Swann in Love* that a number of its particular subtleties have gone unnoticed. Schlöndorff has constructed *Swann in Love* around three central, interrelated metaphors ... the movie's twenty-four hour structure, its dominant images and sounds, and the symbolic nature of its sexuality.
>
> (Moeller and Lellis 2002: 207)

The voiceovers of the elder Swann remembering events and the flashbacks of the cinematic structure clearly allow for repetition and varied perspectives. They also add layers to the linear sequence of events that complicate the time picture. The sex scenes are more than relevant: both the one with Swann at a brothel and the other in the bedroom with Charles Swann and Odette de Crécy have Swann entering the woman from behind. Given the homosexual tendencies of Charlus, the narrator, and Proust himself, this should not be too surprising.

Most importantly, the symptomatic sounds and images translate well to film. To note a few examples, Swann's tucking orchids into the bodice of Odette often recurs and becomes a coded image for their intimate relations. The erotic images of the bosom, neck, and shoulders reoccur in Swann's memory as he comes to terms with the depth of his love for Odette. This visual and even aromatic memory triggers a range of emotions—love, desire, jealousy, beauty, and even art—that serve the film well. Images of the Botticelli painting of Zephora on the Sistine Chapel also reoccur, judged by Ruskin to be one of the greatest religious paintings of all time, which is the image that Proust used to describe his powerful feelings for Odette. Schlöndorff adds images, such as the dripping of a candle snuffed out as metaphors for the relationship. The sounds of horses' hooves on the cobblestones and the image of the butler opening windows for fresh air are also added. The fresh air, in particular, might disturb Proust literalists. Many Proustian images are not present: such as the madeleine episode or the steeples of Martinville, which tend to bother purists, but which belong to other volumes of the original. A translation studies methodology that focuses on the images rather than the words could work very well in a more detailed analysis.

Perhaps the best scholar analyzing Proust images is Gilles Deleuze, who in *Proust et les Signes* (1972 [1964]) skirts the current analysis of memory and time to deal better with the *search* for meaning and *finding* a form of communication. Life experiences, he argues, are to be found in *signs*, which need to be apprehended and then *rewritten* in the art form, a bit like Shattuck above talking about Proust's aesthetic as of *translating* experience into a work of art. Proust, according to Deleuze, was searching for a way to sift through his experiences and memories, to interpret those experiences in a meaningful way, and to find a form to express them. Thus Proust is narrating a novel about an apprenticeship of a writer, and translation is a part of that formation. Deleuze talks about many different kinds of signs, the first of which are *worldly* signs that are comprised of particular signs for specific discourses, such as an aristocratic code, a diplomatic code, or a military code (1972 [1964]: 6–7). These sometimes overlap and intersect at certain points, but are well known to those within their respective circles. The second set includes signs of *love and friendship*, which are full of contradictions and even lies (1972 [1964]: 7–11). These signs tend toward the subjective and are often deceptive, concealing as much as they express; clearly the homosexual signs in the novel fall into this category. The third set of signs is what most concerns me here, which Deleuze calls *sensuous* signs that often give the reader a kind of "strange joy." The sensuous signs are different, for they are much harder to interpret, but the sensuous signs are what make Proust's novel famous: the madeleine teacake, the steeples of Martinville, or the Vinteuil musical phrase.

The translation of sensuous signs is most fraught, for it is not their source or objective meaning that is in question; rather the difficulty is in achieving a sensuous *effect* on the reader: the rise of affirmative pleasure upon the experience of them. (1972 [1964]: 13). These are the signs that are most in need of interpreting, deciphering, and explication, in short of translation and rewriting. They are what the narrator understands at the end of the novel that was not understood earlier. When analyzing these signs, Deleuze suggests that the interpreter can "go further," imbuing these signs with aesthetic meaning that extends beyond their material references. He writes: "But what now permits the interpreter to go further is that meanwhile the problem of art has been raised, and has received a solution. Now the world of art is the ultimate world of signs, and these signs, as though *dematerialized*, find their meaning in an ideal essence" (1972 [1964]: 13, emphasis in original). These sensuous signs—the images, sounds, and smells—are pregnant with meaning and have an afterlife, serving as a post-translation after-effect that the filmmakers want to capture.

Schlöndorff tries to capture both the worldly signs as well as the sensuous signs. In addition to the successful portrayal of artistic images, I would argue that much of the *history* also gets translated to the film. Proust is very subtle in his portrayal of the French aristocracy, especially its anti-Semitism and homophobia. Schlöndorff well understands the prejudices of the elite, as he did with the appeal of Nazism to working-class Germans in his film of *Tin Drum*, and as he did with the skepticism of the politics of industrial capitalism by the German youth in *Katerina Blum*. While critics praise the elegant cinematography and the costumes, what I find striking is the undercurrent of the whispered social snobbery against the lower classes; the not-so-veiled prejudices against Jewish citizens; and the secret code of associating the discrimination against Jews as a veiled metaphor for the hostility against homosexuals. There is a subtext to the film: the forbidden looks and reactions to such looks that extend beyond language but are all much present in the film. In short, Proust's subtle ironies of *fin de siècle* French culture, the residues of early nineteenth-century class identities, and the resistance to change in art, politics, and life are translated well in the film through gestures, glances, hesitations, and disguises. Schlöndorff keeps much of Proust's ironic portrayal of the hypocrisies of the aristocracy alive by way of unspoken but visual means.

While Schlöndorff begins with one of the first books of the novel, the Chilean filmmaker Raúl Ruiz takes the opposite approach and starts with the *last* volume in his film *Time Regained* (1999). Moreover, while Schlöndorff seems to have read the novel in French, Ruiz initially read it in Spanish translation, and then later in the Portuguese and Italian translations before consulting the French. Ruiz is a well-known playwright himself, having written more than 100 plays. He has lived in exile in France since the 1973 coup in Chile. His *Time Regained* is also international in scope, a French-Italian-Portuguese production, with an international cast,

Table 3.5 Spanish translations of *À la recherche du temps perdu*

In Spanish, the translation history runs similar to the English: translations began as early as the 1920s, with Pedro Salinas offering *Por el camino de Swann* in 1920 and *A la sombra de las muchachas en flor* in 1922. José Maria Quiroga Plá joined Salinas, and by 1931, the first three volumes were out. After a pause during the Spanish Civil War, the following four volumes were translated and published by Argentine Marcelo Manasché, and by 1947, the Argentine publishing house Santiago Rueda made the first collection of the full *En busca del tiempo perdido* in Spanish available. These were followed shortly after that by Spanish versions of the final four volumes prepared by Fernando Gutiérrez in 1952, and then again the same volumes by Consuelo Berges in 1967–69, now published by Alianza, which became the canonical Spanish edition, with stronger reviews than the Manasché edition, still widely available in Latin America. As in many countries, there is a new wave of Proust translations in the Spanish-speaking world, with at least three new versions since 2000, referring to the corrected French editions and improving upon existing translations (Fondebrider 2010).

including the French actresses Catherine Deneuve as Odette de Crécy and Emmanuelle Béart as Gilberte; the American John Malkovich as the Barron de Charlus; the French actor Pascal Gregory as Robert de Saint-Loup; and the Italian Marcello Mazarella as Proust himself.

In his film *Time Regained* (1999), Ruiz is more imagistic and even surrealistic in his approach than Schlöndorff, and my sense is that he may well have been familiar with Deleuze's work before filming. The casting choices are exaggerated: Catherine Deneuve as Odette possesses an elegance that belies Odette's social standing; so too does Emmanuelle Béart as Gilberte, who moves all too easily in a crowd that shunned her parents' marriage. Additionally, the American John Malkovich's decadent and accented performance stresses but one aspect of the Baron de Charlus, who represents the elite of the elite; and Marie-France Pisier as Madame Verdurin is frenetically atypical as host of the dinner parties and the guest list she commands. Further, the Italian actor Marcello Mazarella, who plays Proust, poses a striking resemblance to the author, and his actions are ever so polite and observant. Ruiz was creating more dramatic stereotypes rather than naturalistic characters to underscore Proust's revelations and his vision.

Ruiz's cinema also lends itself well to the novel, in particular, the lives of the rich, their soirées, music, dress, food, drink, and lifestyle. Ruiz makes good use of narrative styles, perhaps overusing Proust as a narrator, but with the help of voiceovers, he succeeds in giving insight into internal/external thoughts and memories. Ruiz also makes generous use of flashbacks, generally triggered by sounds, and uses close-ups of facial expressions to capture emotions. As Schlöndorff before him, Ruiz has Proust remembering and rewriting at the end of his life, a convenient narrative device, but one that differs from the novel and makes the film more autobiographical. Both directors use the film to comment on European history; in Ruiz's film there is a definite Latin American skepticism of entrenched elite European behavior. In Ruiz's case, the narrator/Proust, lets others make fools of themselves as he observes them. In addition to the flashbacks, Ruiz adds freeze-frames for the symptomatic moments, such as Proust tripping on the cobblestones in the Guermantes' courtyard as he is nearly run over by a carriage, which triggers memories of a trip to Venice and all sorts of associations with joy and art in a Deleuzian sense.

In Ruiz's film *Time Regained* (1999), in addition to being a silent observer, Proust at times is shown to be quite voyeuristic; the most shocking one being Proust climbing on a stool and watching through a little window of a seedy hotel the scene in which Charlus is sadistically chained and beaten by a sailor in a gay encounter. To the use of flashbacks and freeze-frames, Ruiz adds a hallucinatory sheen, particularly in the scene from Proust's *Time Regained* when the narrator returns to a party at the Guermantes only to notice the white pallor, old age, and artificiality of the elite. Here Ruiz shows the participants as semi-transparent and translucent, blending with the aging decor, a cinematographic metaphor for the decay of the aristocracy, and his exaggerated characters find their *raison d'être*. The Schlöndorff film portrays the rich as less in control and more selfish, but the social commentary is quite similar. Ruiz also moves the camera more, circling in on the actors and objects to highlight the changing perspectives, which serves both the narrative style and the cinematic adaptation. Further, Ruiz adds acoustic cues; audible sounds, often mixed in with the soundtrack, of significant moments, such as girls laughing while playing on the beach, cued with seagulls crying from the sky, all integrated into the soundtrack. These avant-garde techniques prove successful, especially in the sense of Sherry Simon's and Gilles Deleuze's definitions of going further.

Because of the sheer number of rewritings, it is impossible in the scope of this chapter to comment on every one. However, before going on to other forms of rewriting, there is yet the *unmade* film based on *The Proust Screenplay* (1977) by Harold Pinter, in collaboration with Joseph Losey and Barbara Bray. It too begins at the end, with a shot in 1921 outside the Guermantes' home; followed by a scene in the library with the sound of a waiter knocking a spoon against a plate; then the scene in the drawing room with the aging aristocracy; and finally back outside again with the image of Proust stumbling on the cobblestones. Ruiz must have been familiar with the Pinter screenplay, and that there is an element of rewriting a rewriting going on, which may be, as Baudrillard (1994 [1981], 1994 [1992]) suggested (see Introduction in this volume), indicative of the age. The Pinter screenplay suggests a very visual film: before a word is spoken, Pinter proposes 35 visual shots. The first spoken scene returns to Combray in 1888 with the narrator's parents entertaining their guests and Marcel lingering for a goodnight kiss from his mother. Yet many of the shots of Combray set the scene for the later action, which is largely derived from the last three books.

These include Marcel interacting with Albertine in *La Prisonnière* (translated as *The Captive* in 1923 and *The Prisoner* in 2003), including Marcel's jealousies of Albertine's earlier affairs; the secretive affairs of Charlus in *La Fugitive* (translated as *The Sweet Cheat Gone* in 1927 and *The Fugitive* in 2003), including the sadistic scene of his being chained and beaten; and finally Proust's discovery of his art in the last book *Le Temps retrouvé* (translated as *The Past Recaptured* in 1927, *Time Regained* in 1931, and *Finding Time Again* in 2003). The script ends with Gilberte presenting Marcel her 16-year-old daughter from her marriage with Robert Saint-Loup, and then a series of another dozen silent images, including the steeples of Martinville and the trees at Hudimesnil. Finally, Vermeer's painting *View of Delft*, the most repeated image in Pinter's treatment, shown in fragments earlier in the script, is shown in its full form at the end.

Pinter took his screenwriting quite seriously. He spent months reading and rereading *À la recherche du temps perdu* and traveled to Combray/Illiers and Paris to get a first-hand impression. Later, he worked closely with Losey on the cinematic vision and consulted with Bray, a script editor at BBC and an expert on Proust, on the details, especially those symptomatic images. According to Pinter's introduction, his goals were twofold: (1) to depict the cultural movement toward disillusion; and (2) to disclose the writer's revelation in the art (Pinter et al. 1977: 2). Although never filmed, the Pinter script was later adapted for the theater and performed in 2000 at the Royal National Theater in London, directed by Di Trevis. Productions followed in Australia in 2002, and Denmark and Slovenia in 2004. According to reviews by Nicholas de Jongh and Michael Billington posted on the Pinter website, the set was sparse, with just a piano, a few gilded chairs, and tables with vases of lilies (Jongh 2000). As with Ruiz, Trevis as director freezes the action frequently, such as the guests at the Guermantes' party turned into a still-life tableau. Faithful to the screenplay, the production also begins at the end, as the secrets and hypocrisies of the upper classes are revealed, the Proust narrator character being both an observer and a participant. The Pinter/Trevis production emphasized the erotic jousting in the novel, always one of Pinter's strengths, showing just how haunting the suggestion of Albertine's lesbian affair can be. The biting language in the aristocratic dialogues, another Pinter strength, demonstrates just how cutting a single word can be if uttered in the right context and tone.

Transitioning to the discussion of theater adaptations, I should mention *Eleven Rooms of Proust* (2000) adapted and directed by Mary Zimmerman, who is American but who lived many years in Paris. Zimmerman picked 11 key passages from the book and walks the audience through a series of rooms configured into landscapes, salons, and artist studios, all staged in a large warehouse in Chicago. Four different narrators plus dialogue piped in over loudspeakers, give the audience acoustic passages from the novel, but the rooms, largely conceived as *places in Proust's mind*, are what lend this production its significance. From the first scene of the young narrator waiting/hoping for his mother's kiss in his bedroom as the family entertains guests downstairs, to the narrator hovering over his captive Albertine while she sleeps, the audience is drawn into the visual spaces of Proust's mind. The art, the architecture, the furniture, even the walls of the warehouse itself, take on as much importance as the text, a furthering or post-translation adaptation of text into spatial places (Boykewich 2000). I find it fascinating that the play has been reviewed by more architecture journals than by translation journals (Bordenaro 2000), showing how translation studies scholars need to broaden their horizons. Post-translation studies scholars such as Sherry Simon and Federico Montanari are beginning to work on matters of translation into architecture, including physical places such as squares, office buildings, museums, schools, and, in this case, rooms in a warehouse. There is also a new journal in the field, *Translation Spaces*, edited by Deborah Folaron, Gregory Shreve, and Ricardo Muñez Martin that envisions translation as a set of socio-cultural spaces, both physical and virtual.

One last post-translation adaptation to mention in this section is Andy Warhol's *À la recherche du shoe perdu* (1955), an illustrated book with 18 photolithographs with watercolor additions, which he produced at the time he was head of advertising at a shoe company. The book consists of the prints of images of a variety of shoes from different eras, including Belle Époque France. The self-published book represents the transition of Warhol from a commercial to an aesthetic artist, and it also uses fashion to veil certain gay tendencies.

Warhol did the artwork and lithographs; his mother did the calligraphy; friends colored in the prints, and the poet Ralph Pomeroy wrote the text. The graphics are of period-piece shoes and are exaggerated, full of elaborate, often exotic, details and hand-painted in a variety of colors. One might say that the ideas, relationships, and disguises in *Recherche* inspired Warhol, who went further by performing the text in his art. While it seems that Warhol did not read Proust and that Proust's and Warhol's art forms seem wildly divergent, there are artistic connections. For example, in *Proust/Warhol: Analytical Philosophy of Art* (2008), David Carrier compares Proust's aesthetic to Warhol's, looking at matters such as sources for their art, commentary on the current fashion, queer art-making, and their associations with fellow artists, such as how certain artists in *Recherche*, including Elstir, Vinteuil, and Bergotte, compare to Warhol. Carrier suggests that the better one understands Proust, the better one is prepared to grasp how Warhol thinks (Carrier 2008: 2).

Very few post-translation novels exist of Proust's *In Search of Lost Time*, but one worth mentioning is *Albertine* (2001), written by Jacqueline Rose. Proust was concerned that his candid portrayal of homosexuality would give him problems with the publication (it did not). Perhaps more controversial was his misogyny, especially as shown toward Albertine in *The Captive*. Not only does he bring Albertine into his home to live with him without marrying her, but he quasi-imprisons her, buying her clothes and meals, ordering

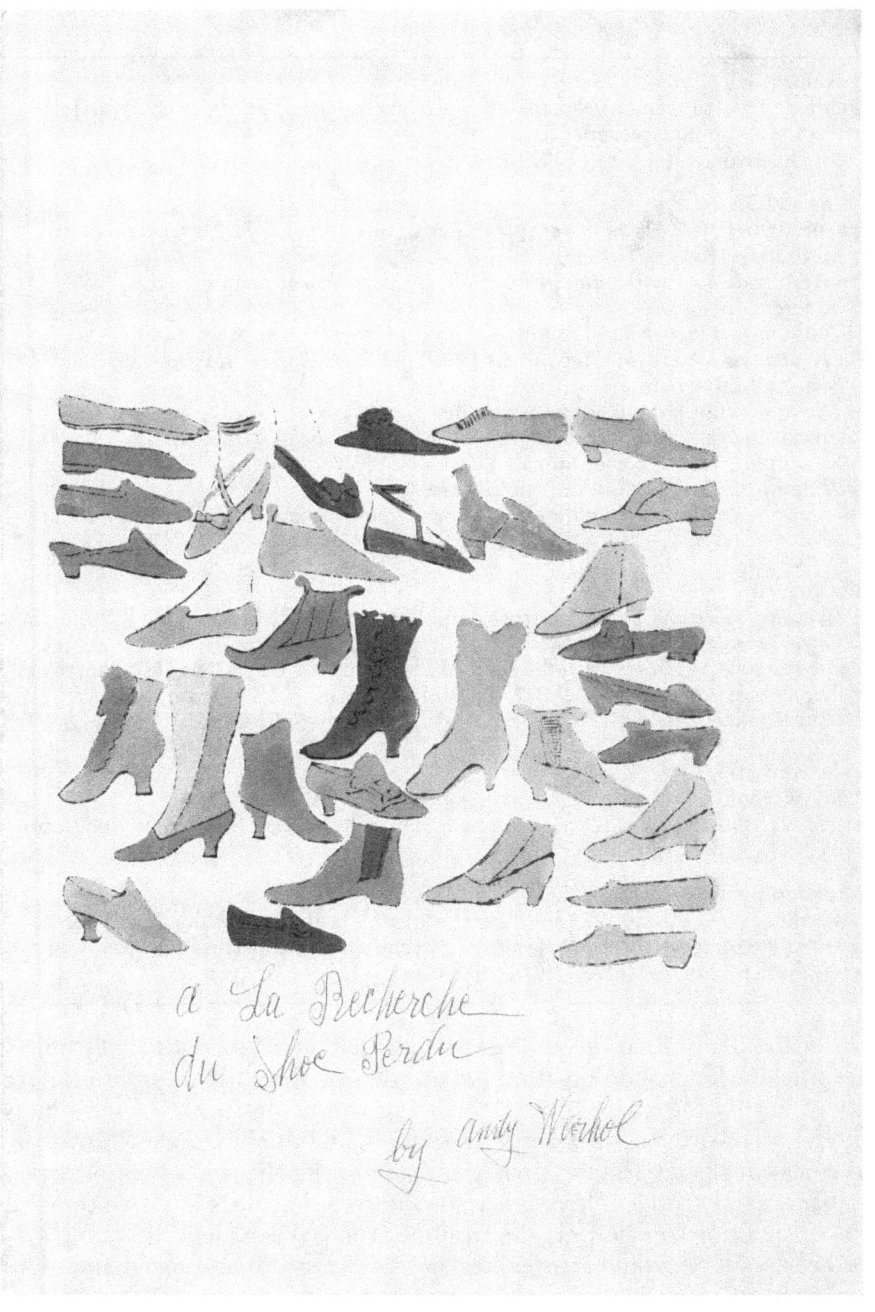

Figure 3.2 Andy Warhol, *À la recherche du shoe perdu* (1955), © The Andy Warhol Foundation for the Visual Arts, Inc. Artists Rights Society (ARS), New York.

Table 3.6 Rewritings of *À la recherche du temps perdu*

Novelizations

Stéphane Heuet (Franco-Belgian comic) *Remembrance of Things Past*, Parts I–IV (1988). Graphic novel adaptation.

Jacqueline Rose, *Albertine* (2002), novel.

Films and TV

Harold Pinter, *The Proust Screenplay*, film adaptation (1977). Never filmed. BBC radio play 1997.

Un Amour de Swann [*Swann in Love*] (1984), dir. Volker Schlöndorff w. Jeremy Irons.

102 Boulevard Haussmann (1990) TV program for BBC w. Alan Bates.

Le Temps retrouvé (*Time Regained*) (1999) dir. Raúl Ruiz w. Catherine Deneuve & John Malkovich.

Le Captive (2000), dir. Chantal Akerman.

Luchino Visconti, Suso Cecchi d'Amico. *À la recherche du temps perdu*. *Screenplay*. 1984). Never filmed.

Quartetto Basileus (1982), dir. Fabio Carpi.

À la recherche du temps perdu (2011), dir. Nina Companéez, for French TV, all seven volumes.

Theater

A Waste of Time, dir. Philippe Prowse and Robert David MacDonald (1980), Glasgow. Glasgow Citizen's Theatre.

Remembrance of Things Past, dir. Harold Pinter and Di Trevis, based on Pinter's *The Proust Screenplay* (2000), London. Royal National Theatre.

Eleven Rooms of Proust (2000), dir. Mary Zimmerman. Chicago.

Other rewritings

Andy Warhol, *À la Recherche du shoe perdu* (1955). Paintings.

My Life with Albertine (2003). Broadway musical, book by Richard Nelson, music by Ricky Ian Gordon.

Fan fiction

www.fanfiction.net/s/5949783/1/Jack-Harkness-à-la-Recherche-du-Temps-Perdu

www.fanfiction.net/s/7289539/1/A-la-recherche-du-temps-perdu-drabbles

www.fanfiction.net/s/10093799/1/A-Fraction-of-Time-and-Space

---

her in and out of his room as he desires, not letting her go out socially unless accompanied, and interrogating her at every opportunity to find out more about her past. Perhaps more devastating is how he speaks of her—he is often bored with her, finds her ugly at times, and thinks her class unworthy and her intelligence lacking—while at the same time being insanely attracted to her and incapable of letting her go. Sometimes he does not even respond to her questions, as he feels she would be incapable of understanding him or his class if he would answer. Yes, he is a closeted homosexual and more attracted to men, but he is also infatuated with Albertine. As she sleeps, he fondly gazes upon her, and the two have clearly worked out some sort of sexual gratification as part of their relationship. Proust's gender and class bias come through loud and clear. Albertine, especially contemporary images of Albertine, have been so demeaned and infantilized that thinking about her as an independent woman is nearly impossible.

Jaqueline Rose, the author of the novel *Albertine* (2001), is a professor of English at the University of London and is well known for her work in literary criticism, feminism, and psychology. In the United States, she is probably best known for *The Haunting of Sylvia Plath* (1991), in which she was one of the first scholars to criticize Ted Hughes's treatment of Plath, as well as his criticism of certain poems. Instead, Rose offers a feminist interpretation of Plath's life and work. Rose is also a translator, having translated and edited work by Jacques Lacan in the anthology *Feminine Sexuality: Jacques Lacan and the école freudienne* (1985). *Albertine* is her first and only novel. Rose sets out to correct the depiction of the woman in the novel colored by Proust's socially protected class, gender, and worldview. One of the strategies Rose employs is to lend Albertine agency in the affair: the sexual behavior is a *mutually* generated activity, one in which Albertine is also complicit, and the depravity in the bedroom with the narrator is a way for her to flaunt an alternative sexuality. In some ways, Rose suggests that it is Albertine who invites Marcel into her life when she allows him as a child to join her group of friends, indeed she is proactive in getting the other girls to change their patterns to allow Proust to join them. Rose suggests that the two are both active in finding common ground. She depicts Albertine as spontaneous and adventurous, attracted to the improperness of the relationship in her own way, a way not dissimilar to Proust's fascination with homosexuality.

The seduction, in other words, went both ways, and the Proust character in Rose's *Albertine* was just as much her captive as she his. Although Albertine obeys his rules, whims, and restrictions, in Rose's rewriting Albertine also retains her freedom: her "obedience" is viewed more like a performance, one that she is at liberty to end anytime. Moreover, after she writes a letter threatening to leave, it is the narrator who becomes increasingly dependent upon her and grows increasingly jealous of Albertine's options and relationships with others, especially women. In the meantime, Albertine is maturing; becoming more confident and knowledgeable about Parisian high society, increasingly gaining respect from Proust and others around him. She plays games, slipping away from the chauffeur just so she knows that she can, or touring Versailles on her own without Proust's consent. She thereby is able to arrive at her own impressions, such as taking an ironic note of the little hamlet behind the palace where Marie Antoinette was kept on the condition that she never leave the grounds. The final scene of *Albertine* is the most radical. Deleted is her death in a riding accident. Instead, she is shown riding a horse, going faster and faster as she rounds a meadow in ever-diminishing circles. The ride is invigorating, buoyant, free, and open. When the horse rears up at the end, Albertine has no fear of the danger of falling, nor of being translated into another state of being.

Post-translation studies are open to such retranslations and rewritings by women offering alternative perspectives to translations (1) done by men of texts written by women, more often than not from colonized cultures; (2) of canonical texts that have emphasized certain beliefs that tend to serve patriarchal cultures; or (3) merely to explore possibilities inherent but often hidden within the text. Rose's rewriting of *Albertine* falls into all three such categories. While some translation scholars feel that such rewritings extend beyond the scope of translation studies, ignoring such texts reveals a lacuna in the field and silences what might be a gendered perspective in the field. Again, the Quebec feminist translation studies scholars have taken the lead, and a lot can be learned from furthering their concepts of *réécriture au féminine*, translation and rewriting in and of the feminine, as posited by Nicole Brossard and others. Proust opens the door to further rewritings such as women rewriting men; gay men rewriting men and/or women; transgendered rewritings; and, especially, rewritings of the self and the other *within*. Translation so conceived offers a way into such spaces, not just revealing and rewriting, but allowing for a form of self-expression or self-embodiment.

Regarding the Internet and Web-based reversions, rewritings of Proust are comparatively few, mainly found in Proust reading groups, of which there are many, essentially serving as a form of an open journal articulating reactions while reading and motivating fellow readers in the group to keep going. Different readers bring different qualities to the text: women/men, young/old, gay/straight, literary/non-literary, and monolingual/bilingual reactions and interpretations. In many ways, the reading groups reveal much about the *diversity* of responses and the openness of the original, particularly by non-professional readers. In Paris, to celebrate 100 years since the publication of *Du côté de chez Swann* (1913), the year 2013 was called the "Year of Reading Proust." In addition to exhibitions of manuscripts, film screenings, roundtable discussions with notable authors, and concerts, many new reading groups were founded. One site at Goodreads has more than 1,500 members. Responses range from individuals trying to figure out what makes Proust great; readers struggling with Proust's style; creative writers posting poems inspired by Proust; members adding links to related novels, artworks, and music; and, most prominently, individual readers commenting on the impact Proust has had on their lives. To better determine the post-translation repercussions, an analysis of such reading groups can be a good place to start. What is striking is the candor and insight some of these non-professional readers have, especially on difficult topics such as love and jealousy.

Another well-known Proust reading group is run by the Center for Fiction, which founded a Proust Society in 1997, and which starts new reading groups in four-year cycles. They now support two such groups: Proust I, for first-time readers; and Proust II, for those who have read the volumes at least once. The Proust Society has distinguished critics leading the groups' discussions, but they are private and not posted on the Web for the world to see. In England, the newspaper *The Guardian* also offers a reading group for just *Swann's Way* that contains mostly subjective reactions and postings aimed at helping motivate struggling readers. There are local groups in the United States, such as a group in Seattle, as well as various national groups in Italy and Germany.

In closing this section on rewritings of *À la recherche du temps perdu*, I turn to abridgements, of which there are hundreds, including SparkNotes, Cummings Study Guides, Wikipedia, and pages from just about every teacher who has taught an introductory class on Proust. While I normally would not include abridgements in this book, regarding Proust there are so many that the abridged Proust has become a genre in and of itself. Some of these are very academic, such as Patrick Alexander's *Reader's Guide to The Remembrance of Things Past* (2009), a 400-page book with an overview, summary, synopsis and chapters on each of the books, with illustrations, list of characters, historical background, maps, photographs of Belle Époch Paris, and paintings of people who inspired Proust; or Roger Shattuck's *Proust's Way: A Field Guide to "In Search of Lost Time"* (2000), which serves as both a summary and critical engagement of the novel. Shattuck gives an overview of the novel, biographical information, a note on the various translations, a chapter on how to read such a complex novel, and several chapters on the main themes such as time, memory, and art. Both the abridgement and the criticism would be included in Lefevere's definition of translation and rewriting. Shattuck also has a section on the reception of Proust, various debates among the critics, and responses to film versions.

In addition to such fairly traditional scholarly summaries, such texts are also being abridged and parodied. For example, there is *The 14-Minute Marcel Proust*, written by Stephen Fall (2010), which was derived from his blog on the Internet while he spent a year reading the new Penguin editions, and which he has now rewritten into a book. While he has a chapter on each of the seven books, the publication has become known for its two-minute synopsis that introduces each chapter, thus two minutes times seven books equals Proust in 14 minutes. Then there is the Worldwide Summarize Proust Challenge, a faux competition to see who can summarize all seven books in less than three minutes. Patrick Alexander posits the "Summarize Proust Challenge" in 2009, ostensibly to celebrate 100 years since Proust began writing the novel, and it is both serious and slightly facetious. Alexander seems to be developing a minor industry out of Proust abridgements; in addition to his book and video, he is working on an illustrated version of all seven volumes, and he has a Twitter site #ProustTweet, which is a translation and summary of the entire seven-volume original rewritten in a series of daily tweets. At the time of this writing (December 2014), Alexander had posted more than 8,700 tweets and was up to the point where Albertine dies, the narrator is on the train returning from Venice, and Gilberte has re-established contact. What began as a kind of a joke in 2010 has turned into a fairly serious matter: Alexander finds the medium of Twitter to be a good way to reveal the inner thoughts and changing impressions of the narrator. It will be interesting to see what happens when he gets to *Time Regained*.

Another well-known abridgement is the Monty Python's Flying Circus episode titled "The All-England Summarize Proust Competition" (1972), in which the competitors, first in a swimsuit and then in evening dress, try to summarize the novel in 15 seconds. Of the final contestants, none gets beyond the first book, some not even the first page of *Swann's Way*, and all are disqualified. One contestant spends too much time talking about abstract themes; another becomes nervous, stammers, and forgets names, and a third brings out a choir of seven members each singing a summary, but they are more focused on the harmony and less on the content. In short, John Cleese and his fellow comedians, while making fun of the entire genre of Proust abridgements, contribute in a very creative fashion to that very genre.

Finally, there is even a Tumblr site cleverly called "Proustitute" for *À la recherche du temps perdu*, hosted by an eclectic critic named K. Thomas Kahn, a reviewer, and contributor to *3:AM Magazine*. The site is fascinating, containing paintings by Picasso, Rembrandt, and Whistler; poetry by Charles Bukowski, Charles Wright, and Frank O'Hara; translations by Burton Raffel; quotes by Borges, Kierkegaard, Paul Celan; and, of course, numerous citations from Proust. Kahn receives many submissions and suggestions, from which he chooses wisely. In many ways, the Tumbler site is the closest to and most distant from Proust, a multimedia collage of art, quotations, poetry, and photography, all very much connected to Proust's insights and aesthetic.

The translations and rewritings, shortenings and furtherings of Proust's *À la recherche du temps perdu* into English, despite the number that I cover here, are comparatively few in relation to postmodern rewritings of other such canonical texts. Translators and rewriters were no doubt stymied by the novel's sheer length, complex prose style, and aesthetic inventiveness. In more than 100 years, other than the hundreds of abridgements, there are but two translations, just a handful of films, a couple of novelizations, theater works, and musical adaptations. The Internet sites, while more numerous, are also not that many: a few blogs, very limited fan fiction, and one Twitter account. In the previous chapter, Goethe's *Faust* solicited hundreds of translations and film versions, numerous theater and musical adaptations, and so many spin-offs on the Internet that it is easy to lose count. With both Goethe and Proust, many translated passages erase themselves as they enter the realm of creative writing, some so distant that the connection between the original and rewritten text is difficult to discern, thereby complicating the job of the post-translation scholar. In the next chapter, I turn to *Hamlet* rewritings in China in which one can better see the role translation plays in theater and film, the emergence of new genres, and overall cultural evolution.

Bibliography

Alexander, Patrick. 2009. *Reader's Guide to The Remembrance of Things Past*. New York: Vintage.

Alexander, Patrick. 2015a. "Marcel Proust at Prousttweet." Twitter at https://twitter.com/prousttweet, accessed 15 December 2015.

Alexander, Patrick. 2015b. "Summarize Proust Challenge." YouTube at www.
youtube.com/watch?v=CdIZUomR21M, accessed December 20, 2015.

Bassnett, Susan. 1980. *Translation Studies*. London: Methuen.

Bassnett, Susan and André Lefevere, eds. 1990. *Translation, History and Culture*. London: Routledge.

Baudrillard, Jean. 1994 [1981]. *Simulacres et simulation*. Paris: Éditions Galilée. *Simulacra and Simulation*, trans. Sheila Glaser. Ann Arbor: University of Michigan Press.

Baudrillard, Jean. 1994 [1992]. *L'illusion de la fin*. Paris: Galilee. *The Illusion of the End*, 1994, trans. Chris Turner. Stanford: Stanford University Press.

Belle Époque. 2015. "Chronological Synopsis 1870–1914" at www.la-belle-epoque .de/index.html, accessed February 15, 2015.

Bhabha, Homi K. 1994. *The Location of Culture*. London: Routledge.

Billington, Michael. 2000. "The Pint-Sized Proust." *The Guardian*. November 25. Online at www.haroldpinter.org/plays/plays_remembrance.shtml, accessed December 10, 2014.

Bloom, Harold. 1997 [1973]. *The Anxiety of Influence: A Theory of Poetry*. Oxford: Oxford University Press.

Bordenaro, Michael J. 2000. "Dancing About Architecture." *Architecture Week*. September 27. Online at www.architectureweek.com/2000/0927/culture_2-1.html, accessed December 10, 2014.

Boykewich, Stephen. 2000. Review of *Eleven Rooms of Proust*, conceived and directed by Mary Zimmerman. *Artscope*, May. Online at www.artscope.net/ PAREVIEWS/Proust0500.shtml, accessed December 10, 2014.

Brossard, Nicole. 1987. *Le Désert mauve*. Montreal: l'Hexagone.

Carrier, David. 2008. *Proust/Warhol: Analytical Philosophy of Art*. New York: Peter Lang.

Carter, William C. 2000. *Marcel Proust: A Life*. New Haven: Yale University Press.

Carter, William C. 2006. *Proust in Love*. New Haven: Yale University Press.

Chevrel, Yves, Lieven D'hulst, and Christine Lombez. 2012. *Histoire des traductions en langue française: XIXe siècle (1815–1914)*. Paris: Éditions Verdier.

Compagnon, Antoine and Jean-Yves Tadié. 1999. "'The Threat to Proust': An Exchange," reply by Roger Shattuck. *The New York Review of Books*. May 6. Online at www.nybooks.com/articles/archives/1999/may/06/the-threat-to-proust-an-exchange, accessed October 14, 2014.

Davenport, Guy. 1987. "Ruskin According to Proust." *The New Criterion* 6: 64. Online at www.newcriterion.com/articles.cfm/Ruskin-according-to-Proust-7169, accessed October 3, 2014.

Davis, Lydia. 2003. "Introduction" to Marcel Proust *Swann's Way*, US edition. New York: Penguin, vii–xx.

Davis, Lydia, Marcel Muller, and Christopher Prendergast. 2006. "'Proust's Way?': An Exchange." *New York Review of Books*. April 6. Online at www.nybooks. com/articles/archives/2006/apr/06/prousts-way-an-exchange, accessed December 10, 2014.

Davis, Paul. 2002. "Reviving the Dread Deity," a review of *In Search of Lost Time*. *The Guardian*, November 1. Online at www.theguardian.com/books/2002/nov/ 02/classics.marcelproust, accessed October 14, 2014.

Deleuze, Gilles. 1972 [1964]. *Proust et les Signes*. Paris: Presses Universitaires de France. Trans. Richard Howard. 1972. *Proust and Signs*. New York: George Braziller.

Durantaye, Leland de la. 2014. "Style over Substance: Translating Proust." *Boston Review*. June 16. Online at http://bostonreview.net/books-ideas/leland-de-la-durantaye-style-over-substance-translating-proust, accessed December 10, 2014.

Evenson, Norma. 1979. *Paris: A Century of Change 1878–1978*. New Haven: Yale University Press.

Fall, Stephen. 2010. *The 14-Minute Marcel Proust*. Durham, NH: Fallbook Press.

Fondebrider, Jorge. 2010. "Sobre los traductores de Proust." Club de Traductores Literarios de Buenos Aires. August 7. Online at http://clubdetraductoresliterariosdebaires.blogspot.com/search/label/Herbert%20E.%20Craig, accessed December 10, 2014.

Forssgren, Ernest. 2006. *The Memoires of Ernest A. Forssgren*, ed. William C. Carter. New Haven: Yale University Press.

Gentzler, Edwin. 2008. *Translation and Identity in the Americas: New Directions in Translation Theory*. London: Routledge.

Godard, Barbara. 1990. "Theorizing Feminist Discourse/Translation." In Susan Bassnett and André Lefevere, eds. *Translation, History and Culture*. London: Pinter, 87–96.

Jongh, Nicholas de. 2000. "Merci for the Dreamy Memories." *Evening Standard*. November 24. Online at www.haroldpinter.org/plays/plays_remembrance.shtml, accessed December 10, 2014.

Kahn, Thomas. 2014. "Proustitute." Tumblr at http://proustitute.tumblr.com, accessed December 10, 2014.

Krebs, Katja. 2012. "Translation and Adaptation—Two Sides of an Ideological Coin." In Laurence Raw, ed. *Translation, Adaptation and Transformation*. London: Continuum, 42–53.

Kristal, Efraín. 2002. *Invisible Work: Borges and Translation*. Nashville: Vanderbilt University Press.

Lefevere, André. 1992. *Translation, Rewriting, and the Manipulation of Literary Fame*. London: Routledge.

Lefevere, André and Susan Bassnett. 1990. "Proust's Grandmother and the Thousand and One Nights: The 'Cultural Turn' in Translation Studies." In Susan Bassnett and André Lefevere, eds. *Translation, History and Culture*. London: Routledge, 1–13.

Lundell, Michael James. 2013. "Pasolini's Splendid Infidelities: Un/Faithful Film Versions of The Thousand and One Nights." *Adaptation* 6:1: 120–27. Online at http://adaptation.oxfordjournals.org/content/6/1/120.full, accessed October 9, 2014.

"Marcel Proust Reading Group." 2013. *The Guardian*. Online at www.theguardian.com/books/2013/jan/30/reading-group-swanns-way-marcel-proust#comment-21104156, accessed December 15, 2014.

Milton, John. 2009. "Translation Studies and Adaptation Studies." In *Translation Research Projects 2*, ed. Anthony Pym and Alexander Perekrestenko. Tarragona: Intercultural Studies Group, 51–8.

Moeller, Bernard and George Lellis. 2002. *Schlöndorff's Cinema: Adaptation, Politics and "The Movie-Appropriate."* Carbondale: Southern Illinois University Press.

Monty Python's Flying Circus. 1972. "The All-England Summarize Proust Competition." Season 5, episode 3. Online at www.montypython.net/scripts/proust.php, accessed December 15, 2014. See also "Summarize Proust Contest Uncensored" on YouTube at www.youtube.com/watch?v=uwAOc4g3K-g, accessed July 15, 2015.

Muhlstein, Anka. 2012. *Monsieur Proust's Library*. New York: The Other Press.

Pinter, Harold, with Joseph Losey and Barbara Bray. 1977. *The Proust Screenplay*. New York: Grove Press.

Proust, Marcel. 1954. *Contre Sainte-Beuve*. Paris: Gallimard. Trans. John Sturrock. 1988. *Against Sainte-Beuve and Other Essays*. London: Penguin.

Proust, Marcel. 1896. *Les Plaisirs et les jours*. Illustrations by Madeleine Lemaire. Préface by Anatole France and four pieces for piano by Reynaldo Hahn. Paris: Chamerot et Renouard pour Calmann Lévy.

Proust, Marcel. 1922–30. *Remembrance of Things Past*, trans. C.K. Scott Moncrieff, 6 vols. London: Chatto and Windus.

Proust, Marcel. 1931. *Time Regained*, trans. Stephen Hudson, pseudonym for Sydney Schiff, vol. 7.

Proust, Marcel. 1959 [1932]. *The Past Recaptured*, trans. Frederick Blossom. New York: The Modern Library.

Proust, Marcel. 1970. *Remembrance of Things Past: Time Regained*, trans. Andreas Mayor. London: Chatto and Windus, vol. 12.

Proust, Marcel. 1981. *Remembrance of Things Past*, trans. C.K. Scott Moncrieff, Terence Kilmartin, and Andreas Mayor, 3 vols. New York: Random House.

Proust, Marcel. 1982. *In Search for Lost Time: Swann's Way*, trans. James Grieve. Canberra: Australian National University.

Proust, Marcel. 1992. *In Search of Lost Time*, trans C.K. Scott Moncrieff, Terence Kilmartin, and Andreas Mayor, rev. D.J. Enright. London: Chatto and Windus; New York: The Modern Library. Based on the 1987–89 Pléiade edition. Vol. 7.

Proust, Marcel. 2002–4. *In Search of Lost Time*, ed. Christopher Pendergast, trans. Lydia Davis, Mark Traherne, James Grieve, John Sturrock, Carol Clark, Peter Collier, and Ian Patterson, 4 vols. London: Allen Lane. Based on the 1987–98 Pléiade edition, except *The Fugitive*, which is based on the 1954 French edition. London: Penguin Classics.

Proust, Marcel. 2013. *Swann's Way: In Search of Lost Time*, trans. and annotated William C. Carter. New Haven: Yale University Press, vol. 1.

Proust, Marcel. 1952. *Jean Santeuil*. Paris: Gallimard. Trans. Gerald Hopkins. 1956. *Jean Santeuil*. New York: Simon and Schuster. Unpublished during Proust's lifetime.

Proust, Marcel. 1954. *À la recherche du temps perdu*, ed. Pierre Clarac and André Ferré, 3 vols. Paris: Gallimard.

Proust, Marcel. 1987. *À la recherche du temps perdu*, ed. Jean Milly, 10 vols. Paris: Garnier-Flammarion.

Proust, Marcel. 1987. *À la recherche du temps perdu*, ed. Bernard Raffalli, 3 vols. Paris: Laffont,-Bouquins.

Proust, Marcel. 1989. *À la recherche du temps perdu*, ed. Jean-Yves Tadié, 4 vols. Paris: Gallimard.

Proust, Marcel. 1988–90. *À la recherche du temps perdu*, 7 vols. Paris: Gallimard.

Proust, Marcel. 1992–3. *À la recherche du temps perdu*, ed. Bernard Brun, 7 vols. Paris: Le Livre de poche.

Proust, Marcel. 1999. *À la recherche du temps perdu*. Paris: Gallimard.

Proust, Marcel. 1979 [1896]. *Les Plaisirs et les jours*. New York: French and European Publishers.

Proust, Marcel. 1987. *On Reading Ruskin*, ed. Phillip J. Wolfe and William Burford, trans. Jean Autret, William Burford and Phillip J. Wolfe. New Haven: Yale University Press.

Proust, Marcel. 2003. *Swann's Way*, trans. Lydia Davis. U.S. edition. New York: Penguin.

"Proust Reading Group." Online. The Center for Fiction at www.centerforfiction. org/for-readers/reading-proust/about-the-proust-reading-groups, accessed December 15, 2014.

Raw, Laurence. 2012. *Translation, Adaptation and Transformation*. London: Continuum International.

Rose, Jacqueline. 2001. *Albertine*. London: Chatto and Windus.

Rose, Jacqueline, ed. and trans., and Juliette Mitchell, ed. 1985. *Feminine Sexuality: Jacques Lacan and the école freudienne*. New York: W.W. Norton.

Ruiz, Raul, dir. 1999. *Time Regained*. Paris: Gemini Films, France 2 Cinéma, and Les Films du Lendemain; Rome: Blu Cinematografica; Alcochete: Madragoa Filmes.

Sansom, William. 1973. *Proust and his World*. New York: Schribner's Sons.

Schlöndorff, Volker, dir. 1984. *Un Amour de Swann [Eine Liebe von Swann; Swann in Love]*. London: Curzon Film; Paris: Gaumont Production Company, FR3 Films Productions, Societe Francaise de Production Cinematographique, Bioskop Film, Les Films du Losange, Thipol-Samreth, and Centre National du Cinema.

Shattuck, Roger. 1963. *Proust's Binoculars: A Study of Memory, Time, and Recognition in "À la Recherche du Temps Perdu."* Princeton: Princeton University Press.

Shattuck, Roger. 1974. *Marcel Proust*. New York: Viking.

Shattuck, Roger. 2000. *Proust's Way: A Field Guide to "In Search of Lost Time."* New York: W.W. Norton.

Simon, Sherry. 2012. *Cities in Translation: Intersections of Language and Memory*. London Routledge.

Skahan, Meaghan. 2013. "Bifurcating Translations: Borges's Theories of Ideas and Writing Through Translation Studies." *Portals: A Journal of Comparative Literature* 10. Online at http://portalsjournal.com/2013/bifurcating-translations-borges-theories-of-ideas-and-writing-through-translation-studies-by-meaghan-skahan, accessed October 10, 2014.

Stovall, Tyleer. 1990. *The Rise of the Paris Red Belt*. Berkeley: University of California Press.

Tadié, Jean-Yves. 2000. *Marcel Proust: A Life*, trans. Euan Cameron. New York: Penguin Putnam.

van Gorp, Hendrik. 2004 [1985]. "Translation and Comparable Transfer Operations," trans. Katheryn Bonnau-Bradbeer. In Harald Kittel, Armin Paul Frank, Norbert Greimer, Theo Hermans, Werner Koller, José Lambert, and Fritz Paul, eds. *Übersetzung, Translation, Traduction: An International Encyclopedia of Translation Studies*, vol. 1. Berlien: De Gruyter, 62–68.

Venuti, Lawrence. 1995. *The Translator's Invisibility: A History of Translation*. London: Routledge.

Venuti, Lawrence. 2007. "Adaptation, Translation, Critique." *Journal of Visual Culture* 6:1, 25–43.

Visconti, Luciano and Suso Cecchi d'Amico. 1984. *À la recherche du temps perdu: Scenario d'après l'oeuvre de Marcel Proust*. Paris: Persona.

Warhol, Andy. 1955. *À la recherche du shoe perdu*. New York: Record Offset Corporation.

White, Edmund. 1999. *Marcel Proust*. London and New York: Penguin Viking.

"The Year of Reading Proust Discussion." Online. Goodreads at www.goodreads
  .com/topic/show/1145778-group-members-reviews, accessed December 15,
  2014.
Zimmerman, Mary, dir. 2000. *Eleven Rooms of Proust*. Chicago: About Face and
  Lookingglass Theatre Company and the Goodman Theatre.

4 *Hamlet* in China

In earlier sections of this book, I looked at a number of modern and postmodern theories of translation and rewriting, beginning with Jean Baudrillard's suggestion that everything is an image of an image of previous images—all circulating and regenerating upon each other, to the point that the "original" disappears. In this chapter, I discuss the circulation of the story of *Hamlet*, first in pre-Shakespeare times, then during Shakespeare's life, and then afterward in China. One could argue that in China, the "original" has all but disappeared: most versions, both written and staged, are not based on Shakespeare's text, but on abridged and adapted versions and more focused on images than texts.

Of all the texts in the English language, *Hamlet* is probably the one that circulates the most, to the point that while many may never have read *Hamlet*, or maybe read it while in school and understood very little, nearly everyone knows the story, has seen a production or adaptation, and probably can quote a line or two. There are so many versions, abridgements, stagings, films, adaptations, novelizations, pre-versions, and sequels that it is impossible for one scholar to keep up, let alone recount in one chapter. In this chapter, after a review of the translational nature of the original Hamlet, I focus on translations and post-translations in China, where the play arrived, and the beginnings of not only a serious engagement but also perhaps where a culture-altering course is being witnessed. While there have been translations of *Hamlet* in a traditional sense in China, perhaps because of the linguistic and cultural distance, there has been less obsession with adherence to the original and more freedom to use already existing versions as the source. Indeed, the play's circulation in China begins with the adaptation of Charles and Mary Lamb's abridged children's version, first published in 1807 in the United Kingdom and then translated into Chinese as early as 1904 by Lin Shu. Many following Chinese versions, including most Chinese Opera versions, are derived from such abridgements and summaries initially put into circulation by the Lambs.

Bassnett and Lefevere wondered if anyone read *À la recherche du temps perdu* either in French or English translation and suggested that more people were familiar with translated and abridged versions. They continued to argue that translations might prove less relevant to new media productions than those images of the original texts circulating within a culture. In addition to Baudrillard, Bassnett, and Lefevere, I suggested that the Canadian theorist Linda Hutcheon's work on "adaptation" might prove helpful to an analysis of such versions. Hutcheon argued that all writing can be viewed as a form of storytelling and that storytellers/rewriters continually discover new media forms with which to circulate their work. Hutcheon has remained open to the collaborative and creative processes involved in translation, rewriting, and adaptation. Instead of referring to authors as such, Hutcheon prefers new terms such as "transmedia producers." I begin this chapter with (1) expanded definitions of translation, including "tradaptation"; followed by (2) pre-Shakespeare translations of *Hamlet*; (3) translational themes in Shakespeare's *Hamlet*; (4) the translational culture of China in the early twentieth century; (5) translations of *Hamlet* in China; and (6) contemporary tradaptations of *Hamlet* in China.

Expanded definitions of translation

"Tradaptation" is increasingly being used in adaptation studies to refer to the kind of translation, rewriting, and adaptation processes to which I am referring in this book. Surprisingly, it is frequently employed when referring to Asian and Chinese productions. Yet before I discuss its relevance in the case of *Hamlet* in China, I first mention coinage of "tradaptation" in Quebec, Canada. Not the newest of terms, the term dates back to Michel Garneau's 1978 translation into Québécois of Shakespeare's *Macbeth* (see Gentzler 2008: 49–51). The expression is also not new in translation studies scholarship either, introduced as early as 1992 in Patrick Cattrysse's *Pour une théorie de l'adaptation filmique*, which coincided with the cultural turn in translation studies. The concept was picked up and expanded, for example, in Yves Gambier's 2004 article "Tradaptation Cinématographique," used to better analyze multimedia translations. Gambier includes a fascinating account of the chain of transformations before, during, and after the film *La vie de bohème* by the Finnish filmmaker Aki Kaurismäki. In 1992, the film opened in Paris in French, with both Finnish and French actors. However, the story itself was based on an 1845–49 story called "Scénes de la vie bohème," serialized in the satirical journal *Le Corsaire*. During this same period, in 1849, several episodes were adapted for a theater piece called "La vie de bohème" by a group led by the vaudevillian Théodore Barrièrre. In 1851, the serialized story was published in a book titled "Scenes de la bohème." The tradaptation history continued with a libretto for an Italian opera by Puccini in 1896, and then a novel in French translated into Finnish in 1924 (and reissued with some modifications in 1959, 1974, and 1992). In 1943, Henri Murger turned it into a film, although Kaurismäki claims he did not see the movie. In 1990, Kaurismäki issued a new Finnish screenplay, which, in 1991, was translated into French. It was only then that Kaurismäki made his film in French, subsequently, subtitled into Finnish and shown in Finland in 1992. These successions well illustrate the labyrinthian journeys of modern cinematic versions.

Such a tradaptation history is not unusual in this day and age, and translation studies scholars working in film and media studies are well aware of the complex histories such productions have. What emerges is a series of transformations. Translation scholars are becoming increasingly adept at looking at target culture norms, including linguistic, literary, and social-political, and offering detailed descriptions of the process. Nevertheless, it is becoming difficult to identify precisely what the source text(s) might be. In addition, something is missing in this type of analysis, such as the absence of individual agency and creativity. Here the sense of "tradaptation" as used by Garneau and other Canadian playwrights, poets, musicians, feminists, separationists, and, yes, translators, comes closer to that which I wish to argue in this book. Garneau's tradaptation of Shakespeare came at a very particular moment in Canadian history during the 1970s and early 1980s when Quebec citizens were considering seceding and forming an independent Canadian-French speaking nation. A linguistic revolution highlighted the Québécois movement in which the kind of French spoken on the streets of Quebec, a popular slang called *joual*, was being proposed as a new language, a potential national language for the emerging Quebec nation. Translation was one of the leading genres in terms of the development of this independence movement and a literary/cultural base on which to stand. The translation style, however, was *not* conforming to existing linguistic norms; rather translation was *creating* them. A referendum held on Quebec separation in 1980 was closely contested until six days before the vote, when Prime Minister Pierre Trudeau promised to reform the constitution to satisfy Quebec demands for more power.

Beginning in the late 1960s, several writers were translating European classics into Québécois, including Éloi de Grandmont's translation of Shaw's cockney dialogue in *Pygmalion* (1968) and Michel Tremblay's translation/adaptation of Chekhov's *Les Belles-soeurs* (1968). Over the next decade, hundreds of plays were translated into Québécois, including French plays by authors such as Molière, Georges Feydeau, Eugène Ionesco, and Jean Racine, and English plays by Tennessee Williams, Neil Simon, Arthur Miller, Eugene O'Neill, and Edward Albee. Later plays from Italian, German, Russian, Spanish, Swedish, and Greek entered the Québécois repertoire (Brisset 1990: 39). The goal was both an attempt to appropriate European theater tradition and make it their own by developing works that better articulated repressed social and political conditions in French-speaking Canada. Garneau was one of the primary translators/creators, tradapting several of Shakespeare's plays, including *The Tempest* (1973/1982), *Macbeth* (1978), and *Coriolanus* (1989), to accomplish his goals. Tradaptation is less simply a merging of two terms into one, and more a *new* genre in and of itself. This new form of rewritten translation or, better said, refracted translation, is characterized by both a faithful translation, showing respect for the original, as well as adapting it ever so subtly, so that certain references can be understood from a minority culture within a majority culture, an almost underground or repressed culture that the mainstream ignores. As I argue later in this chapter, in China, too, with so much repression in the field of literary texts, tradaptation became a tool to import foreign texts and expand the theater repertoire, but also to disguise a secret code that spoke to audiences in a different way than the official literature could.

Michel Garneau's *Macbeth* (1978) serves as an ideal illustration, demonstrating that *joual*, or in this case more a rural, Gaspean, and antiquated Canadian French, could function as a national language. Garneau both incorporates Shakespeare's play in the local vernacular, and signals in a surreptitious way similarities between the open heath of Scotland and the *brulé* of Quebec, between the corruption of Macbeth and the oppression experienced by the Québécois under French and English Canadian domination. The farmers, hunters, loggers, and fishermen, and working-class men and women who lived in the backlands of rural Quebec identified strongly with the play, which evoked their feelings of marginalization and exile. The *images* Shakespeare used in *Macbeth*—Scotland as a bleeding country, sinking beneath the yoke of England, weeping and wounded on a daily basis—recalled the images used by not just Garneau, but also by Quebec's leading poets, such as Gaston Miron or Paul Chamberlain (see Gentzler 2008: 49–50). Garneau used a large repertoire of theater tools—language, imagery, scenery, metaphor, sound, dialect, voice, and gesture—to appeal to his Quebec audiences in a unique way, making them associate images in Shakespeare's *Macbeth* with their land, country, exile, suffering, and despair. The work's ability to communicate is uncanny in many ways; no other genre quite like it existed in Canada or elsewhere at the time. The *creative* force of Garneau's rewriting was highly original, setting the stage for a cultural revolution to follow, nearly powerful enough to unseat the government.

In " 'Tradaptation' dans le sens Québécois: A Word for the Future" (2012), Susan Knutson gives a nice overview of the evolution of the term "tradaptation" from its early Québécois period through the present. She also argues that the term is less a *mélange* and more a *new* concept for the field. While Garneau coined the term, Robert Lepage turned it into a global concept when he took *Cycle Shakespeare*, based on Garneau's three Shakespeare translations, on a world tour from 1992 to 1994, staging performances in France, Germany, Holland, Switzerland, Japan, and the United Kingdom. Suddenly Garneau's heavily localized versions with secret cultural messages aimed primarily at the Québécois audience took on a wider role: multiple cultures whose identities had been marginalized by colonial or postcolonial power structures came to identify with the Quebec situation as well (Salter 2000: 196). Several Canadian scholars began using the term, including Annie Brisset, Leanore Lieblein, Denis Salter, and Jennifer Drouin.

In "Borderlines: An Interview with Robert Lepage and Le Théâtre Repère" (1993), Denis Salter and Robert Lepage emphasize the way Garneau's scripts provide local color and produce an immediacy of an effect that, in the process of tradaptation, both decolonize and reinterrogate Shakespeare's texts. Susan Knutson argues that "tradaptation" is not a translation or adaptation but instead a conjoining not just of linguistic terms, but also of memory and intentionality, of the past with the future (Knutson 2012: 114). The theatrical experience brings into existence a new collective experience. Garneau and other Québécois translators, while adhering closely to the original, consciously released a flow of signifiers into the target culture, playing with phonemes, accents, metaphors, metonyms to allow for such cultural resonance in a variety of sign systems, including literary and linguistic to be sure, but also social, historical, musical, and political registers as well. Post-translation studies the repercussions of translations *after* the translation has been printed or staged. In this case, Garneau and his generation of translators have accomplished a great deal. They ensured the survival of a language, articulated deep psychic dissatisfactions concerning the governments under which they lived, established a literary tradition where none existed before, and offered a socio-political alternative for a minority culture, which, with Lepage's tour, connected with minority peoples all over the world. In fact, instead of representing the colonizing power, Shakespeare was retargeted toward the colonized who, more often than not, were living less in a monolingual culture and more in a *translational* culture, and thus were able to recognize the double valence of Garneau's metaphors.

After the world tour of 1992–94, Lepage brought the *Cycle Shakespeare* back to Montreal, staging it at the Montréal's Festival de Théâtre des Amériques (FTA), and bringing a global Shakespeare back to Quebec. In 1992, ironically, Canadians held another referendum on independence, which was once more defeated after a hard-fought campaign, bringing back memories of the political turmoil during the 1970s. Just after the 1994 Montreal performances, the Bloc Québécois became the second largest political party in Canada, and independence movements grew again; Garneau was relevant again, internationally and locally. Another referendum was held shortly after in 1995, losing by a mere 1 percent. Polls had shown the separatists leading up until election time. While the referendum failed, it scared the status quo so much that further changes had to be made in literary as well as political structures: translation moved to the forefront in terms of literary status and translators served as facilitators of a larger English-French cultural and art scene. In addition, the Quebec people gained much more autonomy in terms of representation in government, more progressive language rights, and increased funding for translational practice and research.

In *Translating Montreal: Episodes in the Life of a Divided City* (2006), Sherry Simon documents some of the post-translation repercussions of this volatile period in the contemporary literary, theater, and art scene. Montreal was a city divided along a north–south street known as St. Lawrence Boulevard, also known as "The Main," with the French-speaking people located to the east and the English-speaking communities to the west. The east was composed primarily of smaller houses and shops; the west characterized by larger businesses, government buildings, and monuments. According to Simon, translators served as the *travelers*, the cross-town go-betweens. Some of the translations were official, funded, and published; but many more were covert, voluntary, and unpublished. The translators would cross "The Main" and carry back to their "home" what they had learned. Translators became vital to the functioning of the city as a whole, facilitating cross-city communication. In Simon's view, translation in such a city is less something transported across a linguistic divide, and more an *underlying condition* fundamental to the lives of *all* of those living in such a divided city (Simon 2006: 17; Gentzler 2008: 5). From formal exchanges, official media, and federal law to everyday exchanges, buying and selling on the street, local signage and local conversations, translation is not an exception but the rule, less an occasional activity and instead a continuous, ongoing process.

With such a translational culture characterizing a city, it should come as no surprise that translational references began to creep into other forms of communication, such as creative writing, theater, music, and art. What Simon demonstrates in her book are the post-translation aftershocks of translation, what she calls the "provocative processes of translation" at work in the city, which include both the innovative language of everyday life and the experimental language found in the theater, cinema, and advertising (Simon 2006: 14–15). Translation becomes increasingly innovative everywhere, and soon creative writers and artists were experimenting with translational themes and markers in their *original* work. Translational poetics, creative interference, and experiments such as "non-translation," "transfiguration," and "translation without an original" began to appear in creative writing in both English and French (Simon 2006: 15). In Chapter 4 of *Translating Montreal*, titled "Paths of Perversity; Creative Interference," a pioneering essay in the development of post-translation studies, Simon shows how translation *invades* other cultural practices: translation becomes increasingly visible, an act less of conforming to existing norms and more an experimental act of invention and forming new ways of *seeing*.

The city of Montreal, Simon argues, has become a breeding ground for innovative translational practices. Here Simon expands the parameters of translation studies significantly by citing the many post-translation forms of translational activity. She first looks at creative writers using translation as a style or a theme in works by English-language writers such as Gail Scott or French-language writers such as Nicole Brossard or Jacques Brault. Simon then goes on to discuss certain writers, such as Agnes Whitfield, who have abandoned their first language in favor of their second, showing that all their writing is already *in* translation, a form of self-translation, or translation without an original. Other writers, such as Betty Bednarski, combine translation with memoire and/or criticism. As might be expected, in Simon's description, theater translators and rewriters figure heavily, including David Fennario, Robert Lepage, Robert Morin, and Michel Garneau. Simon argues that Garneau's translations of Shakespeare can be used to create new cultural artifacts, thereby recalling the *anthropofagia* movement of Haroldo de Campos and others in Brazil (Simon 2006: 157).

In her chapter on "Creative Interference," Simon catalogs some procedures used by both creative writers and translators that may be helpful for the analysis of tradaptations. Simon offers the term "transfiguration" to refer to a kind of writing that not only transforms a text linguistically or rhetorically but also introduces a form of individual transformation, enhancing the self as languages are crossed (2006: 120, 138–40). In Simon's list of new procedures, issues of identity and self-definition continue to surface. Translation impacts not just socio-cultural definitions and development, but also individuals' lives and their definitions of themselves. Deliberate "mistranslation," with false cognates, often invades creative texts for purposes of parody, but also to explore both comic and tragic *effects* of translation. "Creative interference" is viewed as a technique to avoid becoming too comfortable with the expressions in just one language and instead to create anew against those monolingual norms, carving out space for individuals oppressed by the dominant cultural conditions. Creative interference gives creative writers a tool with which to challenge easy acceptance or recognition, thereby giving readers pause to reflect on the medium, calling to mind similar to Brechtian defamiliarization techniques (2006: 127–28). Creative interference also allows for a larger vocabulary, a flexibility of syntax, and a widening of the semantic fields of association, revealing the *creative* power of translation when it enters the monolingual space.

One of the most useful terms Simon offers in *Translating Montreal* is her concept of "furtherings" (2006: 149), which refers to the translation techniques taken by the many translators of such experimental writers. Nicole Brossard is famous for encouraging her translators not to translate literally, but to go further, to feel free to rewrite in and of the spirit of the original, leading her and her translators to develop a form of feminist translation and rewriting called *réécriture au feminine*. Translation is viewed as a *communal* practice, one that allows multiple women's voices and perspectives to emerge (Lotbinière-Harwood 1991: 62; Gentzler 2008: 57–58). The many translators of Brossard's work, including Barbara Godard, Erin Mouré, Robert Majzels, Suzanne de Lotbinière-Harwood, and Daphne Marlatt, have moved to the forefront in the field of translation and rewriting as they develop into what Simon calls a formidable "writing machine" for creative variations and imaginative solutions. Brossard often works with her translators, less to be sure that the translations do not stray too radically from the original, and more to be sure that the solutions continue the innovations and insights characteristic of the original.

Finally, Simon mentions an almost irreverent form of translational rewriting called "transelation," coined by Erin Mouré in *Sheep's Vigil by a Fervent Person; A Transelation* (2001), her translations of Fernando Pessoa, the Portuguese poet and translator known for his frequent use of heteronyms. In her translations of Pessoa, Mouré both translates and authors her poetry, with each line of Pessoa provoking a line of Mouré, with the two versions printed on facing pages. The side-by-side presentation allows for what she calls a "multiplication of Pessoan *effect* and *affect*" (Mouré 2001, quoted by Simon 2006: 153, emphasis in original). Pessoa's images of rural sheep provoke images of urban cats in Mouré; Portuguese wooden carriages conjure up old cars in Quebec. Mouré is excessive, and she knows it, expanding in a playful way images and ideas stimulated by the Pessoa poem, thus the elation found within her translation.

In this book, I suggest that such tradaptations, transfigurations, creative interference, furtherings, and transelations are part and parcel of the process of translation and that the field needs to hold on less dogmatically to old definitions. Scholars such as Yves Gambier seem open to enlarging the definition of translation to cope better with film and theater translations and adaptations. In all the examples Simon cites, however exceptional, translation is a *primary* goal, but with certain creative licenses. Her inventory of the multiple forms of translation and rewriting taking place in Canada is helpful to the field, and in many parts of the world, especially those places in which oral and performative translations are more prevalent than written translations, where such processes are less the exception and more the rule. As I point out in the section below discussing *Hamlet* translations in China, in the early part of the twenty-first century, such tradaptations were prominent. Simon's work in uncovering the many facets of translation in the divided city of Montreal, especially her looking at constituent translational conditions underlying many forms of art, including translations, creative writing, art, and architecture, are increasingly applicable in many parts of the world. Multilingualism is more prevalent than monolingualism. Many peoples find themselves in a constant state of either self-translation into the dominant discourse, or, in an act of rebellion, taking the reins of translation back by turning it in opposition to the dominant culture and using it to achieve their mode of self-expression. Québécois writers, including Garneau, Scott, Brossard, and Mouré, adapted translation to facilitate their creative practices and to attain their form of self-expression, individually altered through the process of translation, and, in turn, altering the post-translation culture in which they live.

Pre-Shakespeare translations of *Hamlet*

Contrary to what is traditionally believed, Shakespeare was *not* the original author of the story of Hamlet. The tale of the murdered Danish king is an old one, passed down orally in many Scandinavian, Germanic,

Icelandic, and Anglo-Saxon cultures for hundreds of years. Traces of the story can be found in several Icelandic sagas, including *Hrólfs saga kraka ok kappa hans* [The Saga of King Hrolf Kraki and his Family] (Jónsson and Vilhjálmsson, n.d.), which dates back to the thirteenth century, although it refers to events as far back as the fifth or sixth century. Similar versions exist orally in other language traditions, including Roman, Italian, and Spanish cultures. Saxo Grammaticus, a Danish historian who lived from c. 1150 to c. 1220, first wrote down the story of "Amlethus," or "Hamlet." His *Gesta Danorum* [History of the Danes], which translates, recites, embellishes, and glorifies Danish history, runs to 16 volumes. Saxo was a learned scholar and translator, not just well versed in Roman language and culture, but also Danish, Norwegian, Old Norse, and Icelandic languages, literature, and folklore. He drew on many sources, some more reliable than others, and was not afraid to cite Scandinavian mythology, Latin historians, oral tales, and Icelandic sagas, as well as conversations with friends, patrons, and clergy. While Shakespeare scholars cite Saxo's "Amlethus" as the "source" for Shakespeare's play, Saxo was also a translator, and the translation history of his version goes back to the roots of Viking cultures. Saxo's *Gesta Danorum* history begins with the Danish culture before Christ and goes through Christian Denmark, right up to the time of Saxo himself. The biggest difference between Saxo's version of "Amlethus" and Shakespeare's *Hamlet* is that in Saxo's tale, Hamlet's revenge is successful, and he lives.

In a translation of Saxo by Oliver Elton (1894), revised by D.L. Ashliman, and titled "Amleth, Prince of Denmark," there is a Danish King named Horwendil, who, on his return from an expedition during which he kills the King of Norway, marries Gurutha. Gurutha, daughter of Rorik, bears him a son named Amleth. Horwendil's brother Feng (early Claudius figure), who is jealous of his brother's success, is also attracted to the Queen. Similar to Shakespeare's version, Feng murders the king and takes Gurutha as his wife. Amleth witnesses the events and plots his revenge, which involves a complicated game of playing dumb. Under suspicion and watched closely by his uncle, Amleth feigns madness, manifested by dullness and lethargy. The name "Amleth" or "Amlodi" in many Nordic languages often refers to "stupid," "dull," or "mad" (Gollancz 1967 [1926]: 32). The uncle repeatedly tests Amleth. Two unnamed friends (Rosencrantz and Guildenstern figures) spy on him and try to get him to reveal his intentions, but Amleth eludes them. In another trick, Feng sends a maid/harlot (an early Ophelia character) to seduce Amleth, hoping to drive him out of his lethargy. Amleth, however, is tipped off, and, although he ends up sleeping with the maid, he makes her promise not to tell anyone. Saxo's story continues, with the son going to his mother's bedchamber to accuse her of incest. An unnamed counselor (the Polonius figure) is hiding in the wings, and Amleth, upon discovery, stabs the concealed figure. Some of the language echoes in Shakespeare, as Saxo talks of "awaiting the fitting hour," "there is a place for all things," and "deeper devices of the mind" (Saxo 1894 [1185]; see also Gollancz 1967

[1926]: 115). The uncle even sends Amleth off to England with a secret letter asking the British king to kill him upon arrival. Amleth, as in Shakespeare, discovers the letter, rewrites it so that now the bearer would be killed, but in Saxo's narrative, he adds that he, Amleth, also be allowed to marry the daughter of the king of England. When he returns to Denmark, where the king's subjects are celebrating his "death," Amleth sets fire to the palace, goes to the king's chamber and slays him, thereby exacting his revenge. He then makes an eloquent speech to the people of Denmark explaining what had happened: his uncle's fratricide, the incest, and his uncle's subsequent tyrannical behavior. The people, in turn, are won over and acclaim him to be their new king. In a final twist, in Saxo's history, Amleth then goes back to England to collect his new wife. However, the king of England, who has a secret pact with Feng saying that if either of them were to be killed, the other would take revenge upon the perpetrator, is caught in a dilemma of whether to embrace his new son-in-law or to avenge Feng's death. He chooses the latter, and a complex struggle ensues between Amleth and the king of England, including a scene in which Amleth is sent on behalf of the king of England to woo Hermutrude, the queen of Scots, as a potential new queen of England. Because of Amleth's cleverness, however, she ends up falling in love with him as well. Eventually, Amleth slays the king of England, inherits his lands, and returns to Denmark now with *two* wives. He reigns successfully and wisely, until finally heroically sacrificed much later in a battle for Zealand (Saxo 1894 [1185]: 106–30).

Shakespeare's rendering contains parts of Saxo's version, including portions of the plot, the feigned madness, and Amleth's accusations against his mother. Yet, while Shakespeare has been accused of misogyny, Saxo's portrayal of women is even *more* misogynistic. In the last battle for Zealand, for example, Amleth is worried about being killed in combat and leaving his Scottish wife behind. She swears to him that she would not forsake him, nor would she ever marry again. After Amleth is slain, she, however, without compunction, immediately consents to become the conqueror's bride. Saxo concludes with a long section on women, saying "all vows of women are loosed by change of fortune," that "the faith of their soul rests on slippery foothold," and that women are "weakened by casual chances," "glib in promises," "lustful," and invariably find themselves in "pursuit of something" (Saxo 1894 [1185]; Gollancz 1967 [1926]: 163). Shakespeare's rewriting instead toned down some of Saxo's more disparaging remarks about women.

In 1514, Saxo's *Gesta Danorum* was printed in Paris. Then, in 1576, in a series of volumes titled *Histoires tragiques*, the French translator François de Belleforest (1530–83) published the Amleth story under the heading "Avec quelle ruse Amleth, qui depuis fut roy de Dannemarch, vengea la mort de son pere Horvuendille, occis par Fengon sonfrere, & autre occurrence de son histoire" [How cunning Amleth, who later became King of Denmark, avenged the death of his father Horvuendille, who was slain by his brother

Fengon, and other events in the history] (1565–76). *Histoires Tragiques* was a multivolume collection that included translations of stories by Belleforest of the Italian writer Matteo Bandello (1948 [1565–76]). The stories proved very popular and provided sources for other Shakespeare plays, including *Romeo and Juliet, Much Ado about Nothing*, and *Twelfth Night*.

Belleforest's translation of Saxo Grammaticus's "Amleth" in the English-language world has become known as "The Hystoire of Hamblet" (1608) as it was translated and published in English by an anonymous translator. The best source for a comparative analysis of the translations is to be found in Israel Gollancz's *The Sources of Hamlet with an Essay on the Legend* (1966 [1926]), which gives the reader the full Latin text of Saxo and its English translation from 1894 by Oliver Elton on facing pages, followed by Belleforest's translation into French, with the anonymous English translation also on facing pages. The "b" in Hamblet may recall the Latin "Amblethus," but is more likely merely a seventeenth-century English spelling that was common during the period. In many ways, Belleforest's translation remains very faithful to Saxo's version. The names are much the same: the Danish King Horwendil is turned into Horvendile, who is married to Queen Geruth; the son's name Amleth becomes the familiar Hamblet. The king's brother is called Fengon, who kills the king and marries the queen. Belleforest's plot is nearly identical to Saxo's, from the scene in the queen's chamber, through the accidental killing of the Polonius figure, to Hamblet being sent off to England, and his madness to escape persecution. He switches the letters, gains the promise of the king of England's daughter, and returns to Denmark. He again sets fire to the palace, goes to the king's chamber, and gains his revenge. As in Saxo, Hamblet goes back to England, escapes the king, collects his two brides, and returns to Denmark. In the Belleforest version, the queen of Scots is named Hermetrude, but in the French version, she falls in love with one of Hamblet's uncles, who then murders Hamblet, a parallel case of an uncle killing a king and taking the wife (Harrison 1968: 880).

The Belleforest translation was very popular, being issued in at least ten editions between 1570 and 1608. It was well known in London. Shakespeare could have easily read or consulted Saxo and his French was certainly strong enough to read Belleforest. The English version of Belleforest's tale was first published in 1608, therefore after Shakespeare's *Hamlet*, but some speculate that the English translation may have appeared earlier. Belleforest, while keeping the names and the plot, does elaborate extensively. The main difference is how he frames the tale: while Saxo emphasizes the heroic and virtuous deeds of the Danish kings, Belleforest considers all Nordic culture barbarous and violent. In his opening, the adjectives Saxo uses to describe the Danes include "brave," "pious," and "valiant." Adjectives Belleforest uses to describe the Danes are just the opposite: "cruel," "without faith" "uncivil," and "seeking nothing but murther" (Belleforest 1926 [1608]: 181). This framing is difficult, for Hamlet is a great Danish hero. Belleforest begrudgingly admits that Hamlet in the end "continued sober," accomplished "some good," and has gone on to "win praise" (1926 [1608]: 311). The last sentence of Belleforest's version says that despite the Danish character, such a story gives even more splendor to "our" French nation, as "our religion surpasseth their superstition," and our age is "more purged, subtill, and gallant" (1926 [1608]: 311).

Belleforest's depiction of the Danish women also increases the misogyny of the story. First, he has the uncle incestuously seducing the queen *before* killing his brother. Gerrutha in Saxo is a "fair woman," "gentle," "meek," and "unrancorous," whereas, in Belleforest, she is "wicked," "imbased," and "vile." In the bedchamber scene, Hamblet's accusation against the queen is even more brutal, as she is compared to a mare sleeping with the stallion that has run off her mate, implying the bestial nature of her sexual behavior, or "bitch" that might couple with many males. The end of the story, before Belleforest's framing devices, keeps the misogynistic tone, as all women possess a "natural slipperie loyaltie" and are "rash, covetous, and unthankful" (1926 [1608]: 309). While certainly present in the original, Belleforest has added to the negative portrayal, perhaps in keeping with his general distaste of Danish culture.

In addition to the image of women changing in translation, so too, in the French version, does the understanding of Hamlet's mood change. In Belleforest's version, Hamlet is less lethargic and more melancholic (Stabler 1966: 207). In *What Happens in Hamlet* (1951), John Dover Wilson argued that during the Renaissance, depictions of melancholia increased, and the understanding of its characteristics changed. The Renaissance arrived earlier in France than in England, and melancholia was frequently depicted in French poetry and paintings during the late fifteenth and sixteenth centuries, whereas in England it only arrived in the early seventeenth century with Robert Burton's *The Anatomy of Melancholy* (1621). The understanding of the condition was also shifting from something more physical, such as an imbalance of bodily fluids as understood in late medieval culture, to something more emotional, such as in sorrow, grief, fear, and discontent as viewed in early Renaissance culture. Other characteristics cited by John Dover Wilson included visits by spirits, thwarted ambitions, and chronic inaction until the blood fever ran high (Wilson 1951: 114–17). Indeed, this depiction of malaise and suffering had become rather fashionable in France, a sign of a higher intellectual level, which is maybe why it appears in Belleforest's translation.

While textual comparisons give evidence that Shakespeare was familiar with both Saxo and Belleforest, most scholars agree that the *main* source for Shakespeare's version was an earlier play in English, referred to as the Ur-*Hamlet*, which was performed in London as early as the 1580s, and that gained popularity in the 1590s. In 1589, for example, in a preface to Robert Green's novel *Menaphon* (1589), Thomas Nashe referred to the "Hamlets" and their "tragical speeches" (Harrison 1968: 880). Other references to early *Hamlet*s include an allusion in Philip Henslowe's *Diary* (1591–1609), a good source of information on the theater in London at the time, to a 1594 performance of *Hamlet*. Further, in his book titled *Wit's Misery*, Thomas Lodge mentions a *Hamlet* seen in 1596, which contained a ghost that cried miserably in the theater (Jenkins 1982: 83–84). Lodge also remarks that *Hamlet* was one of the plays in the repertoire of the Lord Chamberlain's Company, for whom Shakespeare wrote for much of his career. References to earlier productions are given as evidence of a pre-Shakespearean *Hamlet*, which seemed to be very popular at the time, but of which no copy remains. Some attribute it to Thomas Kyd, who was writing revenge plays at the time, including *The Spanish Tragedy*, written in the 1580s, but claims of his authorship are speculative at best. In lists of Shakespeare's plays before the 1600s, *Hamlet* was not included, so it is doubtful that these early London-staged versions were his.

I suggest that the evidence indicates that Shakespeare was rewriting from multiple sources: a translation (an Ur-*Hamlet* in English written by another playwright) of a translation (Belleforest's French) of a translation (Saxo's Latin) of an oral tale (in Old Norse, Icelandic, Danish, or Scandinavian). In Shakespeare's translation/rewriting, the changes are clear and dramatic, from the beginning in which the ghost of Hamlet's father appears to the end in which Hamlet dies. In terms of time, Saxo's and Belleforest's versions covered many years, whereas Shakespeare's takes place over a very short period. Shakespeare added several translational elements, including character doubles, such as Laertes and Fortinbras, as parallel characters to Hamlet, and the play-within-the-play, which mimics the larger action. Instead of being viewed as an historical or heroical account, Shakespeare's play is now a tragedy: in the last scene, the stage is scattered with bodies. "Modern" elements are added as well, at least, when compared to medieval beliefs, such as the inclusion of Christian ethics or humanist ideas. Indeed, viewing Shakespeare as a translator and rewriter allows scholars to glean many insights. Shakespeare's version of *Hamlet* provides a record of how certain *ideas* travel, such as changes in the conception of *revenge* in the early modern period, to the *image of women* from medieval Scandinavian to early Renaissance French, and in the perception of *psychological suffering* from dullness and lethargy in Saxo, to melancholy and emotional sadness in Belleforest, to a state of depression and suicidal thoughts in Shakespeare. Hamlet's influence on later depictions of depression continues into the present, as nearly all psychoanalysts, from Sigmund Freud to Jacques Lacan and Donald Winnicott, refer to Hamlet's psychological state frequently.

The publishing history of Shakespeare's *Hamlet* also indicates the play itself had gone through many changes before being written down and registered, and that editors over the years have continued the process of tinkering with the text. For years, beginning with the 1709 Rowe version, the preferred text was the First Folio (1623), published seven years after Shakespeare's death. In the late nineteenth century, a shift toward the earlier Second Quarto (1604) published during Shakespeare's lifetime, arose as

Table 4.1 Pre-Shakespeare and Shakespeare's versions of *Hamlet*

1100s	The story of *Hamlet* is more than 800 years old, passed down as an oral tale in Denmark, Scandinavia, and Iceland. It seems known in most Germanic languages, including Old English. Iceland saga of *Hrolf Kraki* is very similar, although the murdered Danish king has two sons.
c. 1185	Saxo Grammaticus, "Vita Amlethi" [The Life of Amleth] in *Gesta Danorum* [Danish History], includes the story of the legend of *Amleth* (Old Norse for "mad" or "not sane"), translated into Latin, and reflects Roman concepts of virtue and heroism. Widely available in London during Shakespeare's time.
1576	François de Belleforest, *Histoires tragiques*, translates and rewrites Saxo's "Amleth" into French. While fairly faithful, the tale is embellished and now twice as long. Hamlet's pensiveness and grief are introduced.
1580s	A *Hamlet* version, now lost, staged as a play in England, but not written by Shakespeare. Thomas Nashe satirizes the play in a preface to Robert Green's novel *Menaphon*.
1580s	Thomas Kyd writing and staging revenge plays in London, including *The Spanish Tragedy*.
1589	Another version of *Hamlet* plays in London, although not by Shakespeare. Possibly by Thomas Kyd.
1594	First record of *Hamlet*, sometimes referred to as Ur-*Hamlet*. No copy has survived. Ghost of Hamlet's father introduced.
1596	Shakespeare's only son Hamnet dies at age 11. (Sometimes "Hamnet," a fairly common name at the time, was spelled "Hamlet," given the inconsistent orthography of the period; the English language is still evolving.)
1596	Another record of *Hamlet*, which may or may not have been by Shakespeare.
1601	Shakespeare's father, John, dies.
1602	First record of Shakespeare's *Hamlet*. Elements from Belleforest's version included.
1603	*Hamlet*, First Quarto, sometimes called the Bad Quarto, some 1,700 lines shorter than Quarto 2. The "To be, or not to be" soliloquy is markedly different. Discovered first in 1823.
1604	*Hamlet*, Second Quarto, fullest text of the play, but with many mistakes.
1607	*Hamlet*, Second Quarto reprinted, still with the same mistakes.
1608	Belleforest translated into English, *The Hystorie of Hamblet*.
1623	*Hamlet*, First Folio published.
1709–present	Beginning with Nicholas Rowe's Shakespeare edition (1709), most editors combine the Second Quarto and the First Folio to present a full and inclusive text, which probably had little to do with any *Hamlet* performed during Shakespeare's day.

scholars and editors wanted better access to the performed version. By the 1930s, editors heavily favored the Quarto versions, making claims about accessing Shakespeare's "original intentions" (Rosenbaum 2002: 73). Then a shift back to the First Folio occurred as editors claimed an increased understanding of Shakespeare's "final intentions" (Rosenbaum 2002).

The talk about discovering an "original" *Hamlet* by Shakespeare is a bit of an oxymoron. Most editions today combine the Second Quarto of 1603 with the First Folio of 1623, with further additional editorial changes, including stage directions, updated spellings, and "mistakes" corrected. In the Second Quarto, for example, there are no divisions into acts or scenes, and even in the First Folio, the acts and scenes are carried out only until Act II, scene 2, and omitted after that. Some estimate more than 1,000 differences between the Second Quarto and the First Folio. When the Second Quarto and the First Folio contain different versions of the *same* passage, editors either select their preference or amend the selections to combine both. For example, in the Second Quarto, the *last* lines spoken by Hamlet, not insignificantly, are written, "The rest is silence" (V.ii.342); but in the First Folio. the same line reads, "The rest is silence. O, O, O, O." (V.ii.311–12). How does one decide? An editor may make one choice, a director another, and a translator a third. Some editors use neither, such as G.R. Hibbard, who, in the Oxford edition of *Hamlet* (1987), cut the Os but "translated" them into a stage direction: "He gives a long sigh and dies," which is not present in *any* of the Shakespeare versions (Rosenbaum 2002: 74).

In contemporary editions, editors use the First Quarto of 1603, often referred to as the "Bad Quarto," as it seems to be an acting copy reconstructed largely from memory and may be a piracy. While more than 1,700 lines shorter than the Second Quarto, it does have an additional 240 lines that do not appear in either subsequent version. In the First Quarto, the arrangement of the scenes is different from later versions, Polonius is called Corambis, and in the closet scene, perhaps following Belleforest, the queen denies participating in the murder of the king and promises to help Hamlet gain revenge against Claudius. Most importantly, many speeches seem to be paraphrased, including Hamlet's soliloquies. For example, in the First Quarto, Hamlet's "To be, or not to be" soliloquy begins as follows:

> To be, or not to be – ay there's the point,
> To die, to sleep –, is that all? Ay all.
> No, to sleep, to dream – ay marry, there it goes,
> For in that dream of death, when we're awaked
> And borne before an everlasting judge
> From whence no passenger euer returned –
> The undiscovered country, at whose sight
> The happy smile and the accursed damned.
> (7.115–22)

Yet Quarto One remains significant as it is the *first* one attributed to Shakespeare, and it follows more closely the Saxo and Belleforest translations. Some scholars are beginning to suggest that it represents an early version of *Hamlet* that Shakespeare rewrote into a much better play during the following years. The frontispiece states that the play had been performed at various times in London, at two universities, and elsewhere, probably by Lord Chamberlain's Men, thus the play was already in production and could very well be in process rather than a final version. The text also seems to be an actor's copy, and some stage directions are included, most of which do translate into future performances.

Confusing? The text English readers read or see performed today has very little to do with the play performed by Shakespeare and his company in the early 1600s. Rather, it has been rewritten by the editors, with different versions of *Hamlet* combined, selected, emended, conflated, updated, annotated, and stage directed so that very few editions of *Hamlet* are alike. While some of these changes might prove helpful, others seem to add to the confusion. Directors did not know on which play to base their performances, and translators did not know which text to use as their "original" because *Hamlet*, the original, exists in several versions. Lefevere would argue that such edited texts are a form of translation or, better said, a form of rewriting. When one adds the multiple original versions to the mountain of critical interpretations of *Hamlet*, determining the "source" is fraught with complexities. Fortunately, in 2006, Arden Shakespeare, one of the most respected publishing firms distributing Shakespeare's works, made a very radical decision, destabilizing notions of an original. In their Third Series of Shakespeare plays, they issued a two-volume edition of *Hamlet* (2006–7), edited by Ann Thompson and Neil Taylor, which runs over 900 pages. The first volume contains an introduction, their preferred version of the Second Quarto from 1604–5, and appendices outlining additions taken from the First Folio; the second volume contains two other texts: the extant First Quarto of 1603 plus the full First Folio of 1623. This form of publication, while longer, disentangles the competing versions and allows readers to make up their own minds.

Writers such as Borges claim that there is no true original; instead, what we are left with is a series of translations and rewritings that preceded Shakespeare's versions, continued through Shakespeare's lifetime, and have been carried forward after his death. In a post-translation context, this might be seen as less of a hindrance, as the instability of the original and uncertainty about the future of Denmark is one of the major themes of the play. "Time is out of joint" and Hamlet curses the fact that he was "born to set it right" (I.v.186–87). However, he does *not* set it right. Hamlet not only dies, but *all* of the royal family die, and the kingdom of Denmark is lost, taken over by the Norwegians, reversing one of the most significant accomplishments of Hamlet's father. All that is left is the narrative, which continues to be retold and rewritten up to the present. Shakespeare began his rewriting with the doublings of characters, providing alternatives to the traditional revenge-play storyline. In this chapter, I suggest that his doublings have only proliferated to the present. In the next section, I look at Shakespeare's doublings and duplicities, telling and retellings, arguing that a better understanding of the *translational* aspects of *Hamlet* can only enhance one's appreciation of the play.

Translational themes in *Hamlet*

Hamlet is the longest of Shakespeare's plays, the most quoted, and, for many, the most confusing. One of the complexities involves figuring out this multifaceted character of Hamlet, who feigns madness, explores various guises, and waffles in his decisions. He hesitates to act, contradicts himself, lacks conviction, is inconsistent in love, and obsessed with death. Indeed, it can be argued that there are *multiple* Hamlets; the central proposition of this section.

In rewriting the Saxo/Belleforest translations, Shakespeare added any number of doubles: characters who, in some ways, have also come to represent Hamlet. These character doubles are *not* present in early pre-Shakespeare versions of the tale; they include Fortinbras, Laertes, and Ophelia, and they all can be interpreted as different versions, or different translations, of the same character, that of Hamlet. This *translational* technique allows Shakespeare to present multiple aspects of the same character, all reflecting upon and informing each other. The technique is fragmented, creating less a definitive version and more an open and evolving one. In this context, Bassnett and Lefevere's approach of analyzing these images, or refractions, of Hamlet might prove very valuable.

The Fortinbras character, for example, serves as a shadow of Hamlet, always present but in the background. Ironically, it is he, not Hamlet, who inherits the throne of Denmark. Although Hamlet's revenge is unsuccessful, Fortinbras's revenge for Hamlet's father killing his father is. Because of the length of the play, many directors cut Fortinbras's lines, and this misses the point. Many plays end with "the rest is silence" (V.ii.342) *before* Fortinbras marches on to the stage, as if to imply that Shakespeare's ending was not intended. Directors also frequently cut the entire scene on the plain in Denmark as Hamlet travels to England, and where he encounters Fortinbras, the Norwegian prince, and his army marching through Denmark to engage the Polish army, all for a small and barren patch of land. Hamlet has a superb soliloquy at the end of this scene, in which he compares his indecisiveness to Fortinbras's strong convictions (Fortinbras means "strong arms"). Both Fortinbras and Hamlet have experienced the death of their fathers, both seek revenge, both stand to inherit their respective thrones, and both have designs on each other's kingdoms. Hamlet finds himself amazed to learn of Fortinbras's willingness to risk the sacrifice of thousands of his men, even when the reward may be so trifling. The scene is a great turning point in the play as Hamlet finally *shames himself* into action. The final part of the soliloquy runs as follows:

HAM: … How stand I then
   That have a father killed, a mother stained,
   Excitements of my reason and my blood,
   And let all sleep; while to my shame I see

The imminent death of twenty thousand men
That for a fantasy and trick of fame
Go to their graves ...
... O, from this time forth
My thoughts be bloody or be nothing worth.

(IV.iv.55–61, 64–65)

In this scene, Hamlet becomes conscious of this shadow self—this ambitious and more formidable self—and he is trying to summon the courage to translate himself into that being, to become more like Fortinbras, who provides a model for how many feel he *should* act. However, Shakespeare is clever, and the Fortinbras character provides but one option; there are more. What makes the play of Hamlet significant is that there is not just one path, just one true form of behavior, appropriate for the occasion.

Laertes, also a character absent from the French or Scandinavian versions, provides another double. Laertes is like Hamlet and Fortinbras in that he has also lost a father and seeks revenge. Additionally, both he and Hamlet love Ophelia, one as a brother, the other as a lover, and in a highly symbolic scene, the two jump into her grave, both expressing their grief in the same manner. In Laertes's rush to judgment about who killed his father, he makes an error, and falsely accuses the new King Claudius of the crime, which is a mistake that Hamlet has wished to *avoid*. Laertes first heard the news of the death of Polonius while he was in France, and he rushes back to Denmark full of wrath, seeking not just revenge upon Claudius, but to lead a rebellion and overthrow the country; he is ushered into the king's castle with a rowdy crowd of rebels. However, Laertes's anger is out of proportion and his accusations hasty, as he soon discovers that, in this case, the king is not to blame. To Hamlet, the Laertes double provides a counterbalance to that of Fortinbras; whereas one acts decisively to defend one's name and family; the other acts rashly, thereby providing a model for Hamlet to take his time and get his facts straight before enacting revenge.

Ophelia is also a "new" character in Shakespeare's rewriting, although traces of her can be seen in earlier versions: in Saxo she is more of a harlot; in Belleforest she is more of a promiscuous girl infatuated with Hamlet, but there is no mention in either earlier version of her being the king's counselor's daughter. Ophelia is viewed as a double for Gertrude; both are at first loved by Hamlet and later despised. In addition, Ophelia and Gertrude suffer terrible deaths, and neither is really at fault. Ophelia's grief at losing Hamlet and her father Polonius proves too much, and she drowns herself; Gertrude's death is also a shame, as she accidentally drinks from the poisoned cup that Claudius had intended for Hamlet. Furthermore, as a potential wife of Hamlet, when she loses her love, Ophelia does *not* take another lover or husband, as does Gertrude, but instead chooses to end her life. Hamlet accuses Gertrude of committing incest and Ophelia of not being an honest maid, but neither accusation can be substantiated. However, in both cases, in Shakespeare's rewriting, the women fare better than in earlier versions, in which Gertrude may have started her affair with the brother of the king *before* the king's death, and that the harlot/maid figure was likely unchaste.

In addition to serving as a double to Gertrude, Ophelia *also* offers up a form of a double to Hamlet. While Hamlet's madness and depression fluctuate during the play, his loss of love for Ophelia manifests itself in anger that impinges upon his interpretation of events. Ophelia's losses are overwhelming, and in one of the great descriptions of madness in literature, she truly goes insane. While in his "To be, or not to be" speech, Hamlet contemplates suicide, the Ophelia/Hamlet double *enacts* that alternative, and has come to represent that path Hamlet does not take, but nevertheless haunts the play throughout. The "image" of Ophelia's death is in many ways more moving than Hamlet's, whose death in the duel is accidental and a consequence of his attempts at revenge. Ophelia surrenders; her obsession with flowers, her folk songs, and her drowning in a form of self-burial is a real alternative ending suggested by Shakespeare only contemplated by Hamlet. Instead, at the end, he becomes just one of the many bodies strewn across the stage, representing a less heroic and tragic individual death and more emblematic of the tragedy of Denmark. The theme of alternative deaths is present throughout the play, and Ophelia's demise is one of its most poignant imaginable form, and, in some ways, has come to represent *better* the suicidal alternative.

Thus in his rewriting of the Hamlet story, Shakespeare spawned a plethora of alternative Hamlets, much like a translator might make several different versions of the same poem, all serving as viable options. Once one begins to see the *translational alternatives* posited in the play, they are everywhere to be seen: The old king of Denmark and the old king of Norway; Rosencrantz and Guildenstern; two gravediggers (repeating the same joke); two ambassadors; the Player King and Queen; or Horatio as a fellow student to Hamlet. In the chapter "Or" in *Meaning by Shakespeare* (1992), Terence Hawkes argues that Shakespeare's technique is not to posit definitive answers, but instead to offer alternatives, as in the scene in which Hamlet suggests alternatives to the shape of a cloud:

HAM: Do you see yonder cloud that's almost in shape of a camel?
POL: By th' mass, and 'tis like a camel indeed.
HAM: Methinks it is like a weasel.
POL: It is backed like a weasel.
HAM: Or like a whale?
POL: Very like a whale.
HAM: Then I come to my mother by and by.

(III.ii.367–74)

The point is less to psychoanalyze the shapes that Hamlet sees and more to recognize the "or" of the passage: Hamlet sees alternatives, and each interpretation has its possibilities. Hawkes goes on to argue that what makes his plays so rich are those very multiple alternatives. Each play contains many repetitions, retellings of the same story, images metamorphosing into related images, cycles and recycles, telling and retellings, sons replaying their fathers' roles, and daughters re-enacting mothers. One cannot help but be reminded of Baudrillard's claims that texts "circulate" rather than originate. Shakespeare has multiple "texts" circulating within the *same* play. Hawkes's essay primarily concerns *A Midsummer Night's Dream*, but one could easily apply the argument to *Hamlet*. In Shakespeare's play, there is no once-and-for-all "meaning" (Hawkes 1992: 38), which is Hawkes's purpose of the whole book. I suggest that Shakespeare not only translated and rewrote the Hamlet legend once but many times. One of the problems with English literary scholarship during the twentieth century is that scholars were looking for a true and unified meaning; so, too, did editors hope to reconstruct the one and true text. All of this scholarship has led to lively debates and wonderfully supported critical readings attempting to prove the validity of the single-text theory, but I suggest that such research misses the point. A translational analysis allows one to see and support a multiple-Hamlets approach, one more in keeping with the evidence and aesthetic of the play.

In the play *Hamlet*, the word "translation" appears twice. The first time is in Act III in the brutal "Get thee to a nunnery" scene between Hamlet and Ophelia:

HAM: … Are you honest?
OPH: My Lord?
HAM: Are you fair?
OPH: What means your lordship?
HAM: That if you be honest and fair, you should admit no discourse to your beauty.
OPH: Could Beauty, my lord, have better commerce than with Honesty?
HAM: Ay, truly. For the power of Beauty will sooner *transform* Honesty from what it is to a bawd than the force of Honesty can *translate* Beauty into his likeness.

(III.i.102–13, emphasis added)

"Honest" here refers to many things, including whether Ophelia is spying on Hamlet, but it primarily refers to her chastity. Whether or not she is indeed chaste is an open question. Most directors seem to think so, but if one goes back to Saxo, the answer is less clear, and there are many hints in Shakespeare that the two have slept together. Hamlet thinks that beautiful women, because of their very beauty, are *more* susceptible to being pursued than less beautiful women and, therefore, less likely to be virtuous or "honest." English literature students well know the ending to John Keats's "Ode to a Grecian Urn" in which he writes, "Beauty is Truth, truth beauty—that is all/Ye know on earth, and all you need to know." For Shakespeare, the beauty = truth equation does not hold. Hamlet's argument here is that whereas truth might *translate* beauty, beauty *transforms* truth. Ophelia's beauty attracts suitors, thereby making her less likely to be "honest." Hamlet feels deceived, and his anger increases as the tension in the scene escalates, to the point where he hears or suspects that Ophelia's father Polonius is also watching him and that the now dishonestly perceived Ophelia is colluding against him. His anger inflames him to the point of madness; that which once was feigned becomes overridingly real. He ends with a furious condemnation "God hath given you one face and you make yourselves another. You jig, you amble, and you lisp … to a nunnery, go" (III.i.142–48). "Nunnery" of course contains the well-known double meaning here, of a convent, but also a whorehouse. The doublings and deceptions are growing, reality and imagination blurring, and sanity and madness less distinguishable. Translations, which used to be valid, are proving false friends.

The second time Shakespeare uses "translate" is at the beginning of Act IV, just after Hamlet leaves the Queen's chamber after killing Polonius, and she has just absorbed a verbal lashing from her son. Hamlet has departed, and Claudius has just entered the Queen's bedchamber:

KING: There's matter in these sighs, these profound heaves,
        You must *translate*; 'tis fit we understand them.
        Where is your son?

                                                              (IV.i.1–3)

Shakespeare's employment of the term "translate" here is a more common one of "report" or "retell" frequently used in the play, as Gertrude is being asked to *report back* to Claudius on Hamlet's behavior. In this case, the term refers to both an intersemiotic translation of the meaning of Gertrude's sighs, but also asking for an intralingual retelling of what happened in the bedchamber. As in the "Get thee to a nunnery" scene with Ophelia, Claudius had sent Polonius to overhear the mother-son exchange, but with Polonius now out of the way, Claudius must rely on Gertrude. Instead of hearing about Gertrude's sighs or her feelings, he is more interested in hearing about Hamlet. "Translate" in this case is a form of reportage, or more accurately, espionage, which is one of the main themes of the play. Hamlet is trying to catch Claudius covering up his guilt from murdering the king, while at the same time, Claudius is trying to discover what Hamlet's true intentions are as logical heir to the throne.

Gertrude's "report" to the king is in the form of an intralingual translation; she even quotes Hamlet's cry of "A rat, a rat!":

QUEEN: Ah, mine own lord, what have I seen tonight!
KING: What, Gertrude? How does Hamlet?
QUEEN: Mad as the sea and wind when both contend

Which is the mightier. In his lawless fit,
Behind the arras hearing something stir,
Whips out his rapier, cries "A rat, a rat!"
And in the brainish apprehension kills
The unseen good old man.

(IV.i.5–12)

The translation is not entirely accurate; not only is the Queen trying to protect her son, not mentioning the fact that his madness is feigned, but in this case, she also misquotes him. Hamlet is less than decisive about Polonius's identity. When hearing a noise behind the curtain, Hamlet says, "How now, A rat!" After slaying Polonius, when the Queen asks, "what hast thou done?" Hamlet can only answer with a question, "Nay, I know not. Is it the King?" (III.iv.23–24). The Queen, in her translation, has implicated Hamlet as more culpable and madder than he really is, making it all the easier for the king to ban him from the kingdom.

This form of translation as reporting or retelling is the most frequent one in the play: of retelling events and conversations in a scheming way as a means to offer evidence. The instances are many: In Act III, scene 1, Rosencrantz and Guildenstern are returning from their first round of capitalizing on their friendship with Hamlet to glean information and report on back to the king; Rosencrantz and Guildenstern are ambivalent, feeling some friendship, but demonstrating even more loyalty to the king. In this case, Claudius learns very little. When the king asks, "Can you … get from him why he puts on this confusion?" (III.i.1–2), Rosencrantz answers, "He does confess he feels himself distracted, But from what cause 'a will by no means speak" (III.i.5–6). Another example of a similar intralingual translation occurs in Act II, scene ii, when the king asks Polonius how Ophelia has responded to Hamlet's love, Polonius does not entirely answer the question and instead offers up his side of the story, of his daughter's obedience to him and his forbidding her to see Hamlet. Polonius quotes himself in this passage:

KING: … But how hath she
Received his love?
POL: … I went round to work
And my young mistress thus I did bespeak:
"Lord Hamlet is a Prince out of thy star.
This must not be." And then I prescripts gave her
That she should lock herself from his resort,
Admit no messengers, receive no tokens;
Which done, she took the fruits of my advice.

(II.ii.125–26, 136–42)

In the same scene, Polonius tries to convince the king that the cause of Hamlet's madness is due to his love for his daughter and not the death of Hamlet's father and that Ophelia, because of his "prescripts," has not returned that love, thereby driving Hamlet insane. By now the audience is increasingly aware of Polonius's meddling and mistrusts him, but the theme of mistranslation, of false reports, or manipulating conversations and events, is growing stronger. Hamlet is particularly good at masking his true real intentions.

In "Hamlet and the Power of Words" (1995), Inga-Stina Ewbank, a Swedish-born literary critic and translator, cites many instances of this form of translation. She sees a tension between translation as in "transform" and translation as in "interpret." Very early in the play, when he is about to send Rosencrantz and Guildenstern to spy on Hamlet for the first time, the king talks about "Hamlet's *transformation*" (II.ii.5, emphasis added). Hamlet may well be transformed in this play, but the difficulty, indeed one of the major themes of the play, is in *interpreting* that transformation, as all parties, from Claudius through Gertrude and Ophelia to Laertes, have vested interests. Ewbank writes, "There is a troublesome tension—indeed often an insoluble contradiction—between the demands of 'interpretation' and those of 'change,' between original meaning and meaningfulness in another language" (Ewbank 1995: 58). Often the form of translation that Shakespeare is emphasizing is a *double* translation: Hamlet translates real events into a veiled form of madness, and others attempt to translate back from that invention to discern an underlying truth. Ewbank continues: "Hamlet himself is throughout the play trying to find a language to express himself through, as well as languages to speak to others in; and round him—against him and for him—the members of the court of Elsinore are engaging in acts of translation" (Ewbank 1995: 59). The many instances of reporting and retelling, as characters speak for or against Hamlet, can be seen as a form of translation.

In Act III, scene 4, when the Ghost, seen only by Hamlet, exits Gertrude's bedchamber, Hamlet uses the word "reword" to express this form of translation:

[Exit GHOST]
QUEEN: This is the very coinage of your brain.
        This bodiless creation ecstasy
        Is very cunning in.
HAMLET: My pulse as yours doth temperately keep time
        And makes as healthful music. It is not madness
        That I have uttered. Bring me to the test
        And I the matter will *reword*, which madness
        Would gambol from.
                    (III.iv.135–42, emphasis added)

The ability to "reword" an occurrence becomes a form of offering proof of the validity of one's rationality. The difficulty is to find a way to translate that both gives justice to the event, and retell that event in a way that communicates to another party. Shakespeare is a master of such a form of translation: taking a story that has elements of ambition, feigned madness, or melancholia; and then, using conventions from translation, interpretation, and rewriting, turn those earlier depictions in other languages and cultures into English. Shakespeare takes oral legends and their translations into classical, romance, and Anglo-Saxon languages and rewrites them in English by translating and adapting, translating and going further, and translating and recreating. Shakespeare is a genius in the way he finds the right English words for thoughts and feelings that hitherto had not been articulated. When existing words are inadequate, Shakespeare invents new terms, often drawing upon German and Scandinavian roots, but also Greek, Latin, and French derivations, to coin new words and expressions in English and to enable new ways of seeing. I view Shakespeare as a master translator: translation can serve to invigorate languages, especially when they are new or emerging. Shakespeare seemed well aware of the power of retelling and reporting in one's own words for future generations. In Hamlet's dying words, he asks Horatio to "report" him to the future:

HAM: ... Horatio, I am dead.
　　　Thou livest; *report me* and my cause aright
　　　To the unsatisfied.
　　　　　　(V.ii.322–24, emphasis added)

This reporting on events or people's lives becomes not only important to the historical record of an era, but also to the emergence of a new language and culture. "Report" (*re-* means "back" and *portare* means "to carry," resulting in "carry back") is of course very close in terms of its etymology to "translation" (*trans-* means "across" and *fero* is a form of *latum* that means "to carry," resulting in "carry across"), and very close synonyms would be "transport" and "transfer." The very meaning of "translation" in the English language is emerging at this very time out of Shakespeare's work, and his definition, as with most Elizabethan and Renaissance writers, is much more creatively oriented than existing definitions.

The best example of translation in Shakespeare's *Hamlet*, serving to both import new ideas into the English language and retell the same story is, of course, *The Murder of Gonzago*, the play-within-the-play. Scholars seem divided as to whether or not the play was a theater piece of the period or an invention of Shakespeare. It does *not* appear in earlier versions of the Hamlet story, whether in Scandinavia or France. The fictional play is ostensibly an Italian play, and here performed as a translation into Danish in the twelfth century. Whether it is an actual translation or a pseudo-translation misses the point. The fact is that the traveling players, be they English, Danish, or Italian, were a sign of the times. As seen in the *Midsummer* chapter above, traveling players performing plays in translation were a significant part of Elizabethan culture and are seminal to this particular play. The scene with the players is the longest in the play and is located squarely in the middle of Act III. Shakespeare writes, "His name is Gonzago. The story is extant and written in very choice Italian" (III.ii.254–55). Thus, the play *performs* a translation. Because Hamlet knows the play, he has probably seen it before, and *The Murder of Gonzago* is thus depicted to have enjoyed some popularity at the time.

Italian revenge plays were very popular in England, and during the late sixteenth and early seventeenth centuries, there were many *commedia dell' arte* groups traveling throughout Europe, including England. Shakespeare would have been well aware of the genre, and the dramatic possibilities that it offered; indeed, some of Shakespeare's comedic characters, his frequent use of vernacular jokes and puns, and his sympathy for the common man derive from the Italian form. In *The Elizabethan Hamlet* (1987), Arthur McGee goes so far as to suggest that the events must have been based on real occurrences in Italy that had been put into a play. He writes, "*The Murder of Gonzago* was probably a reference to a real murder when Luigi Gonzaga murdered the Duke of Urbino in 1538, and it seems to be accepted that Shakespeare's knowledge is founded on an Italian original" (McGee 1987: 107). The genre of an Italian comic-tragedy revenge play mimicking historical events was not uncommon; audiences would understand the historical references.

I contend that Shakespeare, in this case, while not translating in the traditional sense of the term, is instead *transadapting*: translating, rewriting, adapting, and going further to the point of adding "some dozen lines, or sixteen lines" (II.ii.477). The play already imitates the events of *Hamlet*, in which the uncle kills the king by pouring poison into his ear, after which he takes the king's wife as his own. In a minor twist, in *The Murder of Gonzago*, it is the nephew who murders the king, again by pouring poison into the king's ear. Before the audience can see what happens to the Player King's wife, the "real" King Claudius interrupts the production, as the events in the play too closely match the events of his life. The translation, while adapted and rewritten, speaks volumes, for it is "truer" than *all* the earlier versions; the play depicts events that no one talks about publicly or privately, and generates reactions that have been hidden or suppressed.

Hamlet is not just a witness to the play-within-the-play; he is also writer, director, and interpreter. Hamlet interrupts *The Murder of Gonzago* at times to "interpret":

HAM: This is one Lucianus, nephew to the king.
OPH: You are as good as a chorus, my lord.
HAM: I could *interpret* between you and your love if I
    could see the puppets dallying.

(III.ii.237–40)

As the chorus in classical Greek theater would interrupt the action and comment on what had happened or what was to follow, so too is Hamlet acting as a type of a chorus. He compares himself to a puppet master while interpreting, commenting upon, and explaining events, serving as a translator/ mediator between the events of the play and the audience. Hamlet also provides language for the action, exclaiming "'A poisons i' th' garden for his estate" (III.ii.254) and then begins to describe the reactions of the audience. In the First Folio, when the king rises, Hamlet bursts out, "What, frighted with false fire!" (III.ii.258). The play no longer is *The Murder of Gonzago* by an Italian playwright, but now a new version renamed *The Mousetrap* and authored, translated, adapted, and interpreted by Hamlet.

The Murder of Gonzago is not the only translation performed by the traveling actors. Before the play-within-the-play, there is another translation, this time called the "dumb show," which is a *silent* translation performed as a summary or preview of the play to follow. Shakespeare's doublings continue, and the dumb show is now a play-within-a-play-within-a-play or better said a translation (the dumb show) of a translation (the English play *The Murder of Gonzago*) of a translation (Shakespeare's *Hamlet*) of a translation (Belleforest's *The Hystorie of Hamblet*) and so on through Saxo's and the various Viking Scandinavian versions. The *mise en abyme* spirals backwards and Genette's concept of the palimpsest becomes increasingly relevant to present and future readings. The dumb show is a translation from the Italian into pantomime. Critics are bothered by this "second" translation of the same material (it actually comes before the play-within-the-play), a redundant form, in this case, testing the king twice. Instead, I suggest it is entirely consistent with the many doublings that have gone on in the play and, especially, with the translational theme as a whole. While *The Murder of Gonzago* is interrupted and audiences do not see the whole play, the dumb show enacts up until the end. In this case, the poisoner is not identified, but viewers do get to see the queen's reaction to the murder. Both she and the poisoner appear to lament the king's death. The poisoner then woos the queen, to which she at first is loath, then merely unwilling, and only at the end relenting to the overtures (III.ii.128). Hamlet's goal is not just to "catch the conscience of the King" (II.ii.540) but also to *test the queen* to see if she may be an accessory to the crime. In the scene immediately following the performance, Hamlet goes straight to the queen's bedchamber and speaks "daggers to her" (III.ii.386), all in an attempt to find out her culpability.

There is a third play-within-the-play, seldom talked about in the same vein, but it offers another parallel text to the main action. It is Pyrrhus's speech of Priam's slaughter, which Hamlet himself ably begins, and which is then eloquently finished by the First Player. This passage appears well known, as Hamlet knows portions by heart, and even Polonius feels qualified to comment. The speech is a translation of the Greek tale of the death of Priam, king of Troy, at the hands of Pyrrhus, the son of Achilles. The section in the play itself is a translation or better said a revision, of Virgil's *Aeneid*, which was in effect a retelling in Latin of parts of the Greek story found in the *Iliad*, in this case about the sacking of Troy as told by Aeneas to Dido. The speech as it is performed in *Hamlet* does not appear verbatim in Virgil unless it is from some lost section; however, Marlowe has a similar soliloquy in his play *Dido, Queen of Carthage* (c. 1593), and it appears that the traveling players were performing an analogous speech.

Most directors have the First Player overact the Pyrrhus speech in a form of parody, but I think it is important to take the traveling players seriously, as does Hamlet who calls them the "brief chronicles of the time" (II.ii.462) and urges Polonius to lend them better hospitality than he normally might. Once more, the speech mirrors the larger action: Priam is the virtuous old king and Pyrrhus, as the Hamlet figure, suffers from the loss of fathers, mothers, and daughters, which is why Hamlet may have memorized so many of the lines. As Denmark will lie in ruin at the end of *Hamlet*, so too is Troy about to be destroyed. The most significant parallel is the fact that before Pyrrhus kills the king, he hesitates:

1ST PLAY: ... For, lo, his sword
     Which was declining on the milky head
     Of reverend Priam, seemed i' th' air to stick.
     So as a painted tyrant Pyrrhus stood
     Like a neutral to his will and matter,
     Did nothing ...
     ... so after Pyrrhus' pause
     A roused vengeance sets him new a-work.
         (II.ii.415–20, 425–6)

As moving as the above scene is, even more poignant is the actor's portrayal of Aeneas's speech depicting the grief experienced by Priam's wife Hecuba, who watched the killing of her husband at the hands of Pyrrhus, and who later is given to Odysseus, the victor, which she vehemently resisted. This is the "Mobled Queen" speech, and it, too, needs to be taken seriously. The speech ends as follows:

1ST PLAY: When she saw Pyrrhus make malicious sport
     In mincing with his sword her husband's limbs,
     The instant burst of clamor that she made
     (Unless things mortal move them not at all)
     Would have made milch the burning eyes of heaven
     And passion in the gods.
         (II.ii.451–56)

Hecuba's grief is tangible; the actor's eyes tear up when he speaks the lines. Polonius, who twice interrupted the speech mocking the players asking them to please end the performance: "Prithy no more" (II.ii.458) he says. Hamlet begrudgingly agrees, but for a different reason. He is so moved by the speech, especially by Hecuba's grief and the passion exhibited by the actor, that he begins to reflect on his *lack* of passion and, by extension, cowardice. The translation and performance of Hecuba's tears are what motivates Hamlet, who has suffered analogous pain, to bring himself to action. In this case, Hamlet takes action by asking the traveling players to re-enact the murder of his father while he observes his uncle during the key scenes, thereby finding the proof he needs to execute his revenge.

Once one begins to think in terms of the translational aspects of Shakespeare's *Hamlet*, they are everywhere to be seen. The first appearance of the Ghost of Hamlet's Father at the beginning of the play serves as another form of a dumb show, foreshadowing events to follow. Horatio is asked to speak to the Ghost, as only those who speak Latin can communicate with ghosts, hence Horatio's questioning of the Ghost must be "in translation." Hamlet's back-translation of the Ghost's urging him to seek revenge is fraught with credibility issues, as he is uncertain whether the Ghost is the spirit of his "real" deceased father or a "devil" in disguise. Such uncertainty of antecedents opens the aspect of translation in a *psychological* context, the interpretation of a hallucination or a dream, and it should come as no surprise that psychologists have had a field day with *Hamlet*. In the secondary literature, it is this psychoanalytical form of "translation" when applied to *Hamlet* that predominates. "Mirrors" are metaphors for translation that reoccur frequently in the play, from the players' holding a mirror up to nature to show the characteristics of the age (III.ii.22) to Hamlet's holding a glass up to the queen to show the inmost part of her (III.iv.18). Names become repetitive, such as Hamlet and Fortinbras sharing their father's names, and, in effect, translating their legacies. Rosencrantz and Guildenstern translate each other so closely, that the king at one point mixes the two up. The gravediggers also serve as doubles of each other, but more importantly, end up translating the morbid thoughts of death that occur throughout the play into a more comic and palatable form. Acting metaphors, too, abound, and as we know, acting is a form of translation. The greatest actor in the play is Hamlet, who speaks in multiple discourses as he translates himself into various personalities and positions, feigned or real. The translations, interpretations, rewritings, and recyclings go on and on, and I argue that *that* is one of the major points of the play. I also suggest that translation studies scholars are particularly well suited to undertake such an analysis. Post-translation studies breaks down borders between original works and translations and encourages scholars to begin the analysis of translations embedded within or translational aspects intrinsic to, so-called "original" works. I suggest that once that analysis begins, many new facets of translation will be discovered that can only enrich the field.

Translational culture of China in the early twentieth century

While there is to date no published history of translation in the United States, in many countries those histories are being written, and China is no exception. Several scholars, basing their research on Ma Zuyi (1984) have documented the history of translation in China, and the majority agree that the history might be characterized by different periods of boom and bust. During those boom periods, translation has not been a secondary activity; rather, it has served to import new ideas and forms, behaving, in Lin Kenan's words, as a "catalyst for social change in China" (Lin 2002: 160). Histories of Chinese translation include *A Brief History of Translation in China up to the May Fourth Movement of 1919* (1984) by Ma Zuyi, *A History of Translated Literature in China* (1989) by Chen Yugang, and *A History of Translation Theory in China* (1992) by Chen Fukang. Nearly all agree on the main periods of high translation activity. Lin cites five periods of high translational activity:

1   The Buddhist period from 148 AD to 1037, characterized by the translation of Buddhist texts typically via translators and monks, customarily from India. The post-translation impact on Chinese original writing, religion, art, and architecture has been enormous, continuing up to the present.
2   The science and technology period from 1368 to 1644, during the late Ming dynasty, was characterized by the introduction of European scientific and technological texts, led by mostly Chinese scientists, but also helped along by Western missionaries and expatriots living in Italy, Germany, and Belgium. Again, the social and cultural changes spurred by such translations have been key and set the groundwork for the current economic and technological changes being experienced today in China.
3   The post-Opium War period in the 1840s, following England's invasion of China during the late Qing dynasty. As the feudal Qing society weakened, new ideas regarding democracy and free market capitalism took hold, and the seeds of a bourgeois revolution were planted. While the post-translation repercussions were not immediately to be seen, when measured over time, the influence on government and social relations was paradigm-changing.
4   The Russian period during the 1950s–70s was of a shorter kind, generated by shared communist ideologies and closely watched over by state bureaucrats. The selection of texts was restricted—more than ten times more Russian writers were translated than American—and the cultural influence was limited, having more impact on education and politics than on aesthetics, entertainment, art, and popular culture.
5   Finally, the current wave that began in the late 1970s when China opened up to the outside world. While it is too early to tell what the

post-translation impact will be of the current period, indications are that the changes in many fields, from economics to philosophy, from high art to popular culture, and from science to technology, are significant and promise to be long-lasting. In many ways, the long history of translation in China allows scholars to better view and assess the post-translation effects of translation in any number of fields, including literature, science, business, and politics.

The period of interest here is phase 3, during the fall of the late-Qing dynasty, the one that just preceded Shakespeare translations in China, which began in 1904 with Lin Shu's translations. Without this rich translational culture, the importation of Shakespeare would have been impossible. Not only were the Qing dynasty feudal structures crumbling, so too was the period full of traumatic events for the Chinese people, including their defeat during the Opium War (1839–42) and the Sino–Japanese War of 1895. The big shift during this period was away from the translation of science, technology, and religious texts and toward the humanities and social sciences texts. One could argue that these translations set the stage for the social revolutions to follow. The great translators of this age are well known, including Yan Fu (1853–1921), who translated works by Thomas Henry Huxley, John Stewart Mill, Herbert Spencer, Adam Smith, and other social scientists, all of which greatly influenced the thinkers of the 1911 Revolution; Lin Shu (1852–1924) who, in addition to translating Shakespeare, translated more than 180 novels into Chinese; and Liang Qichao (1873–1929), who headed the Translation Bureau. Liang was involved in training students to translate Western works and translated works by Enlightenment philosophers such as Thomas Hobbes, Jean-Jacques Rousseau, John Locke, and David Hume. Liang lived in Japan from 1898 to 1912. Consequently, many of his translations were secondary, retranslations from the Japanese, which was indicative of the times. Lu Xun (1881–1936), one of China's greatest novelists, served as a translator in the early 1900s while living in Japan. Lu was well familiar with Yan Fu's translations of Huxley and Mill and Liang's translation of Locke, Rousseau, and Hume. In 1902–3, Lu Xun's translations included several Japanese texts plus French novels such as Jules Verne's *From the Earth to the Moon* and parts of *Journey to the Center of the Earth*, translated from the Japanese. Later in the decade, after Lu Xun had studied Russian, he turned to translating short stories by many Russian and East European experimental writers, collected in *Tales from Abroad*, published in 1909. I argue that without this great age of translation activity preceding Lu's fiction career, no *Diary of a Madman* (1919) or *The True Story of Ah Q* (1921) would have been possible. Lu Xun mentions Shakespeare as early as 1907 in essays that he composed while in Japan. For example, he wrote, "a society needs ... not only Newton but also Shakespeare [because] a writer like Shakespeare can make people have a sound and perfect human nature" (quoted by Levith 2004: 3; see Zhang 1996: 101–2).

The post-translation repercussions of these translators' works are every-where to be seen, enticing Chinese creative writers to read more international texts, experiment with new forms, learn foreign languages, and author new translations. More importantly, it created a new sense of social and political purpose as Chinese citizens turned to express their desire for moderniza-tion via translations. During this period, European ideas, customs, social forms, family relations, working conditions, and social problems were all introduced, playing a role in the anti-feudal sentiment, and contributing to the social revolutions to follow. In "Translation and English in Twentieth-Century China" (2002), Eva Hung looks at the role literary translation played regarding cultural change and construction in China during this period. She writes, "Twentieth-century China saw an unprecedented attempt at culture and rejuvenation through the transfer of foreign knowledge, and translation plays a role in almost all aspects of this development" (Hung 2002: 25). In addition to importing different texts, most of the translators were interested in *transforming* Chinese society and culture, and texts were strategically chosen to serve those aims. Many of these translations, including Lin Shu's, were less translations and more rewritings, taking alarming liberties with the source texts. The approach led not only to a higher degree of readability but also allowed translators to impose their *own* ideas and social-political beliefs on to the translations, sometimes in a shockingly direct fashion. Lin Kenan's essay "Translation as a Catalyst for Social Change in China" illus-trates the direction of such historians' post-translation studies scholarship. It is not enough to merely describe the linguistic and artistic changes made in a synchronic study. More important to the field is to analyze who reads such different texts *after* they have been translated to discover who adopts those new ideas and how they incorporate such ideas in their own thinking and writing. Mao Zedong read Karl Marx in translation. He adapted his political philosophy to the Chinese situation, changing the working-class proletariat to the peasant class, which became the key to empowering the peasants and, by extension, enabling them to overthrow the rulers of the country. There are many translation and rewriting elements in Mao's politi-cal texts, although scholars do not call them as such.

How can such post-translation effects be discerned and measured? It is difficult, to be sure. In *Translingual Practice: Literature, National Culture, and Translated Modernity: China 1900–1937* (1995), Lydia He Liu points out that an analysis of the technical linguistic shifts in translation is not enough, nor is a study of the history of translation that helpful, although certain patterns can be discerned. Rather, the problem goes deeper; she argues that there is a need to investigate the "conditions of translation" (Liu 1995: 26) and "discursive practices" that develop from the interlin-gual exchange. Rather than "translation," Liu prefers the term "translingual practice," the process by which new words, meanings, discourses, and modes of representation "arise, circulate, and acquire legitimacy" (1995: 26). She maintains that translation is less a neutral event and instead one constantly engaged in social and political struggles. The "Power Turn" in translation studies, as posited by myself and Maria Tymoczko (Tymoczko and Gentzler: xvi), helps in such an analysis. Questions raised include: under what circumstances do translations have the most impact, what forms of translation are the most successful, how can translators penetrate reified worldviews, and how does translation relate to cultural dominance or resistance? The power turn predates the post-translation turn in translation studies, but the two are deeply interrelated.

Liu goes further than describing power relations linguistically or institutionally. Rather, she proposes that translation is the very place in which differences are encountered and social authorities are challenged, because it is in such contested spaces that new words and meanings emerge. She writes:

> I hope the notion of translingual practice will eventually lead to a theoretical vocabulary that helps account for the process of adaptation, translation, introduction, and domestication of words, categories, discourses, and modes of representation from one language to another and furthermore, helps explain the modes of transmission, manipulation, deployment, and domination within the power structure of the host language.
>
> (Liu 1995: 26–27)

For Liu, limiting the field of study to traditional definitions of translation does not prove adequate to gleaning an understanding of how new terms, categories, and modes enter into a culture. She needs a larger term, which she calls "translingual practice," one that includes adaptation, introduction, and domestication as well as translation to study those post-translation effects. Her goal is not to come up with a term that better describes that process, but one that *explains* the transmission, deployment, and eventual domination of such terms and concepts. Moreover, in that tricky terrain, things are not always what they seem. Many histories are linear, as Lin Kenan's seem to indicate, and the importation of ideas and terms so crucial to Western culture, such as Enlightenment concepts of free speech, individual liberty, free will, natural man, and democracy, remain foreign to the Chinese. While from one person's viewpoint, they may seem enlightening and progressive; from another, they are colonizing and manipulative. An uncritical adaptation of such beliefs can be colonizing as well, and Liu fears the uncritical adaptation of many modernist ideas and beliefs do not serve China well. Questions Liu poses include not just how did Western ideas transform China, for better or worse, but also how do the Chinese *name* those very ideas. What language do they use to talk about such new concepts? What rhetorical strategies do they employ when talking about those new ideas? How are the ideas legitimized? How are discursive practices in any number of fields, from literary studies to social formations to government practices changed as a result? (Liu 1995: 28–29). While most feel that real progress has been made in China with the fall of the feudal Qing and the rise of the new republic and communist state, there have been costs to Chinese traditions, cultural beliefs, and, especially, to the very *language* itself. The progression is not linear, from feudal to capitalist to communist, from West to East, from classical to modern. Instead, the course has been bumpier, with multiple confrontations involving both progress and sacrifice. While some in China welcomed Western ideas and concepts, others fought to preserve older values and ideas once those Western ideas began to proliferate. Shakespeare translations find themselves right at the cusp of such transformations: while introducing a new form of theater and a myriad of new ideas into China, it comes with a cost to more traditional Confucian thought and historical theatrical forms, which have been irrevocably altered through such a confrontation.

Translations of *Hamlet* in China

In China, translators have taken up Shakespeare's plays and translated them both linguistically and culturally to produce an entirely different *Hamlet*; one that may, in many ways, be just now reaching its fulfillment. In *Shashibiya: Staging Shakespeare in China* (2003), Li Ruru gives a history of *Hamlet* translations and productions in China, stressing not just conformity to social and literary norms, but also considering the individual thoughts and ideas of the respective translators and adapters. The early translation history is characterized less by linguistic or literary fidelity, and more by connections to the various images of the play, or, especially after the communists took over, the perceived ideology of the play. In fact, most early translators did not use any of the Shakespeare texts—neither of the first two Quartos or the First Folio, nor any later edited conflated versions. Instead they drew from Chinese versions based on Charles and Mary Lamb's summary. Further, later versions also did not derive from Shakespeare's English, but rather via secondary translation from Japan. Finally, after Mao Zedong took over, socialist criticism held sway, and translations came to emphasize Shakespeare's realism, criticism of feudal conditions, and sympathy for middle- and lower-class characters. Thus, I suggest, in conformance with Bassnett and Lefevere's ideas about translation that, from the beginning of *Hamlet* being imported into China, translation and rewritings predominated, and those were heavily influenced by the image and ideology of the text.

The play *Hamlet* arrived late in China, beginning in 1903 with the anonymous translation of a selection of Charles and Mary Lamb's *Tales from Shakespeare* into a classical Chinese fiction style. The volume was entitled *Strange Tales from Abroad* [*Xiewai qitan*], with *Hamlet* being titled *Hamlet takes Revenge by Slaying his Uncle*. A year later, in 1904, Lin Shu completed a complete version of the Lambs' *Tales*, this time into classical Chinese but significantly abridged. The Lambs' version contained no poetry, no soliloquies, no play-within-the-play; it was a summary more than a translation. As Lin Shu did not speak English, he had an assistant named Wei Chunshu read him the story, and then he *rewrote* the story with Chinese characters, settings, and beliefs. Thus, Lin was rewriting from a summary (by Wei) of a summary (by the Lambs), with Shakespeare far removed. Lin's title for *Hamlet* was *A Ghost's Summons* [*Guizhao*]. Lin also translated quickly: 20 plays in 20 days. Lin concentrated on the plots of the plays, but he also made significant changes: for example, Hamlet is married to Ophelia, and he is the author himself of the *Murder of Gonzago* play-within-the-play (Levith 2004: 6). Nevertheless, Lin's translations were very popular and reprinted many times, serving as the only version available in China for decades, and still regarded as a model for excellent Chinese prose. Lin Shu's translations also greatly influenced subsequent stage versions for generations, in which actors were merely given an outline of the plot and then improvised. Even the first Chinese opera of *Hamlet* was based on Lin Shu's version.

With the May Fourth Movement, during the 1920s, there was a resurgence of translated plays from the West, including work by Ibsen, Shaw, Gorky, and Shakespeare. In 1922, Tian Han published the first full-length translation of *Hamlet* [*Hamletgleite*]. Tian studied in Japan from 1916 to 1922, so he also became familiar with *Hamlet* versions in Japanese. His translation was into a traditional Chinese, and allusions to Chinese classics abound. However, Tian was a well-known poet (one of his poems provides the lyrics for the Chinese National Anthem) and playwright (he wrote more than 80 plays), and his translations reveal much about his ideas. According to Li Ruru (2010), Tian's uncle was assassinated while working for Sun Yat-sen, and Tian's personal grief and sense of injustice gets translated into the character of Hamlet. Tian also wrote a critical preface to the play talking about the importation of modern theater into China and the uses of *huaju* style, or "spoken" drama, as opposed to a more traditional *xiqu* style, or "melody" theater, which included song, dance, and even martial arts. Thus, Tian was doing *more* than a linguistic or literary translation; rather he was importing a whole *new* genre, using translation to *change* the literary system. As Lin Kenan has argued in "Translation as a Catalyst for Social Change in China" (2002), translation served as one of the most powerful vehicles not only to introduce new works, but also to import whole new forms of expression. Lin shows the post-translation impact of such importations on the future not only on translation, but on theater, creative writing, and social engagement in twentieth-century China during its various stages of social evolution.

Translations continued throughout the mid-twentieth century, really up until the Cultural Revolution in 1966. In one surprising case, the United States became involved. In the early twentieth century, at the very end of the Qing dynasty, a rebellion occurred called the Yihetuan Movement, known in English as the Boxer Rebellion. Primarily characterized as a peasant movement, the uprising targeted foreigners, missionaries, and Christians across northern China. Many in the Qing government and the Imperial Army supported the faction. However, an eight-nation international alliance, headed by Japan, the United States, and the United Kingdom, intervened to suppress the rebellion and establish a more stable government. In the ensuing treaty, strict stipulations were imposed, including the execution of those in the government who had supported the rebellion, the stationing of international troops in Beijing, and reparations to be paid to the West. In 1924, the United States forgave the Chinese their debt, and some of that money went into *translation*, including the hiring of five scholars to translate Shakespeare. One of those hired was Liang Shiqiu, a professor of English at the National Shandong University in Qingdao (Levith 2004: 8). By 1936, Liang had completed his *Hamlet*, and while others dropped out of the project, he continued his work for the next 30 years, finally publishing his *Complete Works of Shakespeare* in Taiwan in 1967–68. As he felt that the poetry was too difficult to translate well, Liang translated the plays into prose, nevertheless keeping many of the rhyming couplets. While Tian's translations were difficult to perform on stage, Liang's were written to facilitate the actors speaking the lines. Unlike some of the previous translators, Liang did a lot of research for his translations, not only on Shakespeare but also on German and British romantic literary traditions.

During the late 1930s, a major literary debate broke out between Liang and the famous novelist Lu Xun over the social qualities of the play and the role Shakespeare translations should have in the development of China, again illustrating the importance of translation in its literary evolution. So, too, in his "Talks at the Yenan Forum on Art and Literature" (1942) did Mao Zedong criticize Liang for his upholding "bourgeois" over "proletarian art and literature," labeling Liang as a "counter-revolutionary" (Mao 1967 [1942], quoted by Levith 2004: 9). The support by the Americans of the translation project could not have helped Liang's reputation.

In 1935, Zhu Shenghao, who had studied both English and Chinese literature, began translating Shakespeare, finishing 30 of the 37 plays, and translating right up until the day he died in 1944 at the age of 32. His translations, first published in 1947, were the most successful of the group of mid-twentieth-century translators. His *Complete Works of Shakespeare*, which contained 27 plays, became the main edition used on the Mainland for the next 50 years, and his translations were the ones most often utilized for stage productions for decades. However, more remarkable is his story. During the Sino–Japanese War (1937–45), his manuscripts were destroyed not once but twice; nevertheless, Zhu persevered, rewriting and retranslating while ill and bedridden, right up until his death, demonstrating his individual will (Li 2003: 49). Zhu's work provided a basis for a *Complete Works of Shakespeare*, with the missing plays translated by fellow faculty and classmates, which was later published in Taiwan in 1978. During the late 1930s and early 1940s, Sun Dayu was also translating Shakespeare, beginning with *King Lear*, which he finished in 1935. Sun was one of the first translators to translate into poetry, inventing a new form called the "sound unit" [*yinzu*] to correspond to Shakespeare's blank verse. While Sun's *Lear* is well known and praised by Chinese critics, both for his significantly better understanding of the English than his predecessors and for his stronger command of the Chinese language, there is little evidence of his translations of additional plays. *Hamlet* is referred to in Sun's Preface, citing the difficulty of translating the verb "to be" in the famous soliloquy, as Chinese does not have a similar adequate term (Levith 2004: 13). Translations of Shakespeare were improving in China; Japanese intertexts and prose summaries were increasingly criticized. Nevertheless, Sun suffered under the changing political climate, and his translations were not published until much later, with the tragedies coming out in 1965, just before the Cultural Revolution.

Beginning in 1949, at the start of the communist period in China, Shakespeare translation went through periods of limited acceptance to full rejection. The primary concern, as might be suspected, had to do with the ideology of the plays. The leading translator of the period was Bian Zhilin, who was a poet, having written modernist symbolic poetry in the 1930s and 1940s; a translator of English and French literature, publishing translations of William Shakespeare and André Gide; and an essayist, having written a very influential essay on *Hamlet* in 1957. After establishing himself as a poet in the 1930s, he turned to translation and the study of international writing after World War II. Bian's translation of *Hamlet* first appeared in 1956. In his essay on *Hamlet* in 1957, he showed concern with the ideology of the play and used a Marxist approach for his interpretation. Hamlet was viewed as a distraught individual fighting against the social conditions of the times, including resisting feudal structures that limited his choices. Bian's translation was republished in 1958 and has had a strong influence on Shakespeare's reception in the People's Republic of China. Hamlet's rebellion against the king and queen was well suited for a Marxist interpretation, reinforcing Lefevere's point about the importance of ideology in translation. Bian's translation was used in Lawrence Olivier's 1948 film *Hamlet*, which was dubbed into Chinese in 1958, and which, to my knowledge, is still the version shown in China today.

After the success of Bian's translation, newer *Hamlet* versions were few. In 1966, the Cultural Revolution began, and anyone associated with Western and bourgeois ideas was suspect. Creative writers and translators, especially those interested in Western literature and literary forms, suffered terribly. Sun Dayu was taken away, and Tian Han died in prison during this period. The translation history of *Hamlet* in China is thus fraught with both literary and ideological manipulation, and most of the translators from Lin Shu on, were rewriting and adapting as they translated. Traditional translation scholars might find reason to criticize such a style of translation, but many of these translations enjoyed enormous success, introducing *Hamlet* to large segments of the Chinese population, connecting audience members of all ages to the story, and, perhaps most importantly, introducing new ideas and forms of expression that led to cultural and political change. It is hard to say how much of the existential

Table 4.2 Translations of *Hamlet* into Chinese

Date	Description
1599–1602 Shakespeare's *Hamlet* First Quarto 1603 First Folio 1623	Shakespeare's longest and most influential play. The Hamlet legend was well known in Scandinavia before arriving in England. Based on Saxo Grammaticus's version (Danish scholar writing in Latin about history of the Danes) of *Amleth* in the thirteenth century, then translated and retold by François de Belleforest (French writer and translator) in French, Shakespeare might also be viewed as a translator. There may have been a British Ur-*Hamlet* performed in London in the 1590s before Shakespeare wrote his play, but scholars are uncertain.
1807 *Hamlet* in *Tales of Shakespeare*, translated and abridged by Charles and Mary Lamb	Children's version in prose and illustrated. Charles Lamb was a poet and essayist, and a member of literary circles with Coleridge and Wordsworth. The Lambs' version was very popular at the time, and its popularity continues, as it has never been out of print. Charles adapted the tragedies, and Mary the comedies. They produced about 20 plays.
1904 Lin Shu *Bao dachou Hanlide shashu* [Hamlet Revenges Slays Uncle] and *Gui zhao* [Ghost's Command]	Based on Charles and Mary Lamb's translations. Lin Shu knew no English or any foreign languages. His translations were very popular, and have been reprinted many times. Classical in style, refers to *wenmingxi* [traditional drama] productions. Lin's version was the only one available for 20 years, and was still popular after Tian Han's version in the 1920s. All early stage versions were also adapted from Lin Shu. Actors were often only given an outline and much improvisation was needed. Focused on usurpation and revenge. Assimilated Western ideas and themes into Chinese, such as filial piety, chastity, and karma.
1919 May Fourth Movement	Resurgence of translations of many plays from the West. Many modern socially conscious plays by Ibsen, Shaw, and Gorky were translated into Chinese during this period. New and emerging *huaju* [spoken drama] develops in China.
1922 Tian Han (Tian Shouchang) *Hamletgleite*, published in Young China Association series	First full-length translation of *Hamlet*. Focused on Hamlet's suffering. Tian studied in Japan 1916–22. His father was assassinated while working with Sun Yat-sen. Tian's personal loss recalls Hamlet's grief. Prose. Traditional Chinese with allusions to classics. Tian became a well-known creative writer, writing 80 plays, many traditional, and hundreds of poems.
1930 Shao Ting *Tian chou ji* [Heaven/hatred/story]	Focused on Hamlet's revenge. Style of classical Chinese poetry, sometimes at the loss of semantic references.

(*continued*)

Table 4.2 (*cont.*)

Date	Description
1938 Liang Shiqiu Taiwan	First *Complete Works of Shakespeare*. Only edition available in Taiwan for many years. Prose style, but with many couplets kept in rhyme. Liang aware of romantic tradition, including Germans Goethe and Schiller, as well as Coleridge and Hazlitt. Big debates with Lu Xun over Shakespeare: romantic vs. realistic; individual vs. society; bourgeois vs. working class. Last published translation of *Hamlet* for some 30 years.
1930s–50s Sun Dayu Not published until 1988	Invented new concept of *yinzu* [sound group]. Sun imprisoned as a rightist during the late 1950s. Concentrated on tragedies. Taken away during Cultural Revolution in late 1960s.
1947/1978 Zhu Shenghao People's Republic	Translated 30 Shakespeare plays. Manuscripts were destroyed during the Sino–Japanese War. Finished project on deathbed at 32. Zhu was the main contributor to the only version of the *Complete Works of Shakespeare* published in the Mainland prior to 2001. Most performances of Shakespeare used Zhu's versions. Very evocative and imagistic.
1956 Bian Zhilin People's Republic	More concerned with ideology of the play, using a Marxist approach. Wrote an essay on the play in 1957 analyzing the historical background and Hamlet as an individual against larger social forces. Strong influence on subsequent translations. Used in the dubbed version of Laurence Olivier's *Hamlet*. Influenced by Russian Shakespeareans and Marxist scholarship: *Hamlet* well suited to a Marxist interpretation and safe for critics.
1966–76 Cultural Revolution	No translations, although Mao thought that Shakespeare could be performed as a progressive writer depicting conflict during the feudal era in England. Mao also founded many popular theater groups around the country. Hamlet could be seen as a clear-minded and heroic individual overcoming moral and social decay under feudal structures.

thought, individual rebellion, will to take action, and, of course, opposition to aristocratic corruption got through in these early Chinese versions, but my guess is, although hard to empirically measure, that it was quite a lot. Translation often works in a secretive, hidden fashion: one small seed can bear fruition years from the date it originated (Gentzler 2008: 10). *Hamlet* figures prominently in post-Cultural Revolution theater and film productions, as we shall see below.

Rewritings and transadaptations of *Hamlet* in China

The first theater production of *Hamlet* in the People's Republic after the Cultural Revolution occurred in 1984, and it was based on Zhu Shenghao's translation. Staged at the Shanghai Theater Academy and directed by Chen Mingzheng and An Zhenji, it had a Marxist bent, connecting with the views of the working classes. However, it was also influenced by Lawrence Olivier's 1948 film, which was banned in China until after the Cultural Revolution, and the Old Vic English-language production, which performed *Hamlet* in Beijing and Shanghai when visiting in 1979. During the 1980s, nearly a dozen different productions of *Hamlet* were carried out on Chinese stages, others were adapted to Chinese opera.

One production was an experimental production of *Hamlet* [*Hamulaite*], staged in 1989, directed by Lin Zhaohua and Ren Ming, and translated by Li Jianming. Taking place just after the June 4 shut-down of the Tiananmen Square protest, the production at the Lin Zhaohua Drama Studio was small, with only eight performances, and tickets were not sold but freely distributed. The show depicts Hamlet as an ordinary citizen of Beijing, as "one of us" (Li 2010). Hamlet is no longer viewed as a prince fighting against feudal corruption, but just an ordinary citizen in contemporary Beijing facing other ordinary citizens and coping with everyday life. The stage is quite empty; the only piece of furniture is a chair, which might be viewed as a throne, but is like an old dentist or barber's chair.

The set is minimal. No props are used, with just a couple of exceptions: Hamlet reading a book, a gravedigger using a shovel. Costumes are simple, mostly black, gray, or brown with loose-fitting sweaters, or simple black or brown jackets, representative of everyday dress in today's Beijing. The women are dressed just a bit brighter, with Gertrude in a subdued red and Ophelia in beige. A simple white cloth serves as a backdrop, the floor is loosely covered with a gray cloth, and a couple of ceiling fans rotate above. Lighting is also minimal, sometimes the stage is faintly lit from above, or just a few spotlights shine on the actors' faces. With the drab colors, the actors' clothes absorb the light, leaving their faces and gestures illuminated. After decades of productions in which the British and Elizabethan foreignness was emphasized, often with period-piece costumes, make-up, and even artificial noses, this dressed-down version is welcome.

Significantly, Lin switches several characters' roles, and *three* different actors play Hamlet. The first two Hamlets switched back and forth between Hamlet and Claudius, but the third Hamlet figure is quite complex, playing characters of Polonius, Fortinbras, and the Gravedigger as well, recalling some of Shakespeare's translational doubles outlined above. The "To be, or not to be" soliloquy, for example, is spoken by Hamlet, Claudius, and Polonius, emphasizing the idea that Hamlet can be *anyone*. The production is small, and the viewers limited, but the idea has had major repercussions (Li 2003: 83–99). In the West, this production is sometimes known as the

Figure 4.1 Gravedigger scene from Lin Zhaohua, *Hamlet* [*Hamulaite*] (1989).

"Tiananmen Square *Hamlet*" and has come to represent the protesters in Beijing during the Tiananmen uprising living under repressive conditions. That may be an oversimplification, as it could be interpreted as an individual's constructive criticism against generic corruption, or even an apolitical drama about individual anxiety and uncertainty. The fact that Hamlet doubles as Claudius suggests that Hamlet possesses elements of the corrupt king in him, as does the king entertain elements of Hamlet as well, such as doubt and resistance. Chinese authorities were clearly divided on how to proceed with the protests, as were many of the populace. That may be the point of Lin's production: the co-existence of conflicting emotions and the very lack of a clear solution, as shared by all actors in the drama. In the end, it is not clear who killed whom: did Hamlet kill King Claudius, or did Claudius kill Hamlet? In China, many in and out of government were troubled by the unsettling events leading up to Tiananmen, during the protests, and, of course, disturbed by the bloody aftermath. Lin himself was deeply moved by such events, although he claims not to delve into politics. In China, after decades of Shakespeare being used as an ideological tool, such distancing from official and unofficial stances is a welcome change. Lin also stayed relatively close to the text; the language carries the show: actors speak quickly, but without the improvising, posturing, or ideological manipulation characteristic of previous versions.

Experimental versions continued in China during the 1990s, with the 1992 production *Shamlet*, directed by Li Guoxiu, and first staged in Taiwan, and then following soon at the 1994 Shanghai International Theater Festival. As the title indicates, this production is more a comedy/parody of *Hamlet* and depicts the struggles of an emerging theater group trying to mount any production. Shakespeare is parodied, as is the figure of Hamlet, but more importantly, the play serves as a satire of the director and players in Taiwan (Shanghai) and the problems of their lives, including difficulties in their relationships, and their multitude of obstacles while trying to stage the play. Their problems are only distantly echoed in the play: one character has a bad credit rating; a second is afraid of being poisoned; and a third worries that his wife loves another man. Shakespeare's *Hamlet*, in fact, becomes the play-within-the-play, thereby exponentially raising the levels of self-satirization present in Shakespeare, but further emphasized in *Shamlet*. During the production, many things go wrong, including actors forgetting lines, and in the case of those cast in multiple roles, even forgetting which character they are playing. While the production has its absurdities, it is not just a farce; rather, it serves as a comment on the schizophrenic nature of the theater world and larger society. Not only are characters doubled within the play of *Hamlet*, but also they are once more doubled outside of the theater. Li's play has a self-reflexive, postmodern feel to it, casting doubt upon unified meanings or established interpretations of the play.

In "*Shamlet*: Shakespeare as a Palimpsest" (2014), Alexa Huang also suggests that the play raises questions about the mediated nature of historical experience. Borrowing from Genette, Huang invokes the palimpsest metaphor, to which *Hamlet* productions seem well suited. By this time in China, audience members are familiar with the story, having read at least a couple of abridged versions, seen parts or all of the Olivier film or the Jacobi version, and maybe attended a live performance in either English, Chinese, or both. Thus, any director's new production involves a form of rewriting or in Huang's words, "repositioning," "recycling," and "reassigning." She writes, "Because of the multiple layering of texts, contexts, translations, and performances that grow larger every year, 'Shakespeare' has become a palimpsest on which performers constantly erase, re-write and gloss" (Huang 2014). Interestingly, Huang tells us that the director Li did *not* have access to the English texts of *Hamlet* and instead worked from Franco Zeffirelli's 1990 film *Hamlet* starring Mel Gibson, plus two different Chinese translations by Liang Shiqiu and Zhu Shenghao. Such an indirect translation and rewriting from secondary sources well demonstrates Bassnett and Lefevere's point when they ask if anyone ever reads the canonical work in the original, instead finding themselves more familiar with abridged versions, summaries, translations, or film versions. Bassnett and Lefevere had in mind everyday readers; yet in this postmodern age, the same questions can be posed to theater directors.

In 2000 a hybrid version appeared in China, titled *Hamlet, Hamlet*, directed by Xiong Yuanwei, a multimedia version with film characters speaking English and stage actors speaking Cantonese. The choice of *Hamlet*, the most famous play of the British colonial power, and the use of a bilingual version, hints at both English and Chinese being the future official languages of Hong Kong. In addition, *Hamlet, Hamlet* gives some indication of the attempt to use theater to help bridge the two merging cultures as Hong Kong integrates into the People's Republic. The play, a joint production of the Mainland and Hong Kong theater companies, was shown during the millennial celebrations marking the unification of Hong Kong and the Mainland. Matters became quickly complicated given the different theatrical traditions, economic scales, political systems, and the fact that spoken Cantonese is not the same as Mandarin. Still Hamlet's uncertainty, his hesitations, and his doubts translate well to the anxiety regarding the evolving social-political conditions of Hong Kong. The play is presented in a form of simultaneous translation, as the film projected above the stage is Olivier's 1948 *Hamlet* (subtitled and not dubbed); the English actors' voices can be heard, and the live actors on stage speak in translation in Cantonese (Li 2010). Thus, the title itself, *Hamlet, Hamlet*, refers to the fact that the play is in English and Chinese, yet there is a blurring of boundaries between the original and translation, for the "real" actors are performing the "translation," and the film characters above, with subtitles functioning as surtitles, are performing the "original." Doubles are on the screen and on the stage, giving the audience at least two versions of the same scene to consider.

The play *Hamlet, Hamlet* begins in a contemporary Hong Kong, with Hamlet and Ophelia watching the Olivier film while the audience can only hear the English. Ophelia interrupts by saying to Hamlet that he has already seen this movie many times, but Hamlet makes the connection between the situation of Hamlet in Denmark as prefiguring the current situation in Hong Kong. Hamlet then switches on a video recording of another *Hamlet* performance, this time in Cantonese, but the acting is very similar to the Olivier film. Gertrude even smiles the same. At other times, the stage action deviates from the film. For example, according to Li Ruru (2010), while the duel scene between Hamlet and Laertes is playing above, on stage Horatio dies trying to save Hamlet, followed by Marcellus machine-gunning Claudius's soldiers to stop them from killing Hamlet. Hamlet survives in the staged version and then delivers part of the "To be, or not to be" soliloquy, but does not finish. The audience is left wondering which play to follow, Xiong's or Olivier's. However, that is the point in the postmodern world. The image of the Olivier version is very powerful and remains in the peoples' minds, especially in China, no matter what stage version is being watched. Olivier's version, too, is an adaptation. The stage production of *Hamlet, Hamlet* finishes before the film. When the action is over, the film still runs, a metaphorical

Table 4.3 Rewritings and adaptations of *Hamlet* in China

Date	Description
1979 Old Vic production with Derek Jacobi as *Hamlet* tours China.	First professional play from the West to be staged in Mainland China. Simultaneous interpretation available through earphones. Reaction mixed, as the play differed greatly from the Chinese audience members' expectations.
1984 Stage production based on Zhu Shenghao's translation and Bian Zhilin's Marxist interpretation. Performed in Shanghai.	First production after the Cultural Revolution in the People's Republic. Presented conflicts of feudal society. Emphasized naturalism. Connected with views of the working class. Also influenced by Olivier's 1948 film, which was banned in China until the late 1970s.
1989 Stage production directed by Lin Zhaohua; translation by Li Jianming. Performed in Beijing.	Experimental. Lin had worked with Gao Xingjian (Nobel Prize 2000). Reflects tragic events in 1989 Beijing. Staged in Beijing in 1989, 1990, and 1994, and toured abroad in 1995. The first production at Lin Zhaohua Drama Studio. The first production not to use white-face for European characters. Hamlet depicted as an everyday Beijing citizen. Very fast dialogue. No heroes or nobles, just ordinary Beijing people. Hamlet as "one of us." Actors change roles at times: Claudius speaks Hamlet's lines; Hamlet speaks Claudius's lines. Soliloquy shared by three actors. Small production. Limited viewers.
1992 *Shamlet (Shamuleite)* Dir. Li Guoxiu (Taiwan). Performed at Shanghai International Shakespeare Festival in 1994.	Comedy/parody of revenge. Uses transliterations: Shakespeare = Shashibiya. Plot about a bumbling theater group in Taiwan, who misread the title of the play. Absurd. Many reversals and unresolved problems. Lots of mistakes and puns that take on double meanings. *Hamlet* becomes a play-within-the-play. Li translated, directed, and acted in the play.
2000 *Hamlet, Hamlet* (in Cantonese) Dir. Xiong Yuanwei Performed in Hong Kong.	Xiong Yuanwei is from the Mainland, but *Hamlet, Hamlet* was performed by three Hong Kong companies in Cantonese. Millennial celebration and unification of Mainland China and Hong Kong. Multimedia with film and stage. Explores uncertainty about what the future might bring. Title reflects two Hamlets: the classical image of the English actor shown on video above the stage, and the live Chinese actor on the stage. Part of the "to be, or not to be" soliloquy moved to the end, "Whether tis nobler …" leaves an open question for the audience about the future.

(*continued*)

Table 4.3 (cont.)

Date	Description
2000 *Shei sha si le guowang* [Who Kills the King?]. Directed by Gu Yian. Performed in Hong Kong.	No exact equivalent for "to be" in Chinese, so the focus is on the killing of the king, in this case Hamlet's father. Three characters plan to kill him—his brother, wife, and son. Each act ends with "to be, or not to be" speech, but with different Chinese translations for each one. Different theatrical styles for each act: puppet show, Chinese opera, Western opera. In last act everything is dark, and actors are dressed in black.
2006 *The Banquet* Film directed by Feng Xiaogang First screened at the Venice Film Festival. Distributed worldwide.	Adaptation of Shakespeare's *Hamlet* and Ibsen's *Ghosts*. First Chinese film version. Feng is from Beijing, but the film was distributed by the Hong Kong Media Company. Box office success, very commercial. Zhang Ziyi plays Gertrude, Empress Wan. Ambitious, strong-willed. Set in late Tang dynasty China, with much turmoil following a prosperous period. Hamlet and Gertrude are lovers from early age, but Hamlet's father marries her first. Claudius kills his brother, and marries Gertrude, who still loves the prince. All die in the end. Hamlet has little ambition, and instead studies art and music.
2006 *Prince of the Himalayas* Film directed by Hu Xuehua (Sherwood Hu, born in Shanghai; lived 20 years in USA). Film released in China, Australia, and USA. Also adapted as a play and staged in Shanghai.	In Tibetan. Less of a commercial success but had good reviews. Set in the highlands of Tibet, and the actors are Tibetan. The location is beautiful, in the high mountains. Traditional rituals, pure, noble thoughts. The struggle by heirs to the throne in feudal Denmark parallel nicely with ancient feudal Tibet, and much of the original plot is retained. But there are some changes. Gertrude is in love with Claudius, but the older King Hamlet takes her away and marries her first, yet continually suspects her of infidelity. Hamlet is named Prince Lhamoklodan, and is the son of Gertrude and Claudius. Ophelia gets pregnant by Hamlet and dies giving birth. Beautiful scenery and the imagistic cinematography.
2011 Shanghai Peking Opera performs *Hamlet* at Edinburgh Theater Festival.	There is a long history of Peking Opera performances of Shakespeare's *Hamlet*, dating back to the early 1910s when traditional Chinese opera versions based on Lin Shu's abridged versions appeared. Body movements, dance, make-up, costumes, and gestures accompany the "translations" into song of the main scenes of the play.

comment on the age; the audience does not know what to do, highlighting the uncertainty of the future for the region.

While Shakespeare and directors in the West may be fond of doubling characters and creating mirror images in sets and scenes, in China, in the post-translation era, *tripling* seems increasingly characteristic. Li Ruru (2010) discusses a 2000, experimental version titled *Shei sha si le guowang* [Who Kills the King?], directed by Gu Yian, that has *three* characters seeking to kill the king, who in this case was a still-living Hamlet's father. The three antagonists are his brother, his son Hamlet, and, his wife as well, all trying to poison him, albeit for different reasons. As in Shakespeare, the brother both thirsts for power and lusts after the wife; Hamlet in this production is not only the rightful heir but also is ambitious; Gertrude, on the other hand, has grown tired of the old king and has fallen in love with the younger brother. There are also three "to be, or not to be" soliloquies, presented at the end of each of the first three acts, each of which employs a different translation into Chinese, showing the multiple possibilities for translation. As there is no verb "to be" in Chinese, the phrase is impossible to translate, which is one of the points of the play. Also, three different theatrical styles are used in each of the first three acts: the first a puppet show, the second a Chinese opera, and the third a Western opera, which show the arbitrariness of performance. The fourth and final act has the actors all dressed in black and performing on a dark stage. Further versions of the "to be, or not to be" lines emerge. In "Hamlet in China: Translation, Interpretation, and Performance," Li Ruru provides translations from the final scene:

KING: All right. Nowadays Denmark has become a huge hell. Everyone wants me to die and you have used questions, which can be piled up as high as a mountain, to pressurize me. I cannot even breathe. What can I do? What can I do?

KING'S BROTHER: To live or not to live, this is a question.

QUEEN: Life or death, it is the exact question.

PRINCE: Existence or destruction, this is a question that needs to be considered.

[Note: each of the above three lines uses a different Chinese translation of "To be, or not to be"]

(Li 2010)

Finally the king, experiencing his own existential crisis about whether he has accomplished anything during his reign and weary of fighting against his antagonists, instead chooses death and drinks the poison himself, the ultimate translation of "To be, or not to be."

In 2006, not one but two films of *Hamlet* were made in China: the very popular *The Banquet*, released in the United States as *Legend of the Black Scorpion*, directed by Feng Xiaogang, and the more obscure *Prince of the*

Himalayas, directed by Hu Xuehua [Sherwood Hu]. *The Banquet* is set in the late Tang dynasty China in the late tenth century when it was crumbling and as various members of the imperial family vied for power. The film diverges significantly from Shakespeare's play, as there are no soliloquies, no Horatio or Fortinbras, and no suicide by Ophelia. However, many Shakespeare scenes are played with a high degree of insight, such as the ghost of Hamlet haunting the action; the bedchamber scene, highlighting Gertrude's incestuous feelings for Hamlet; the play-within-the-play attempting to catch the king; and, especially, Hamlet's hesitation to act throughout. From the beginning, Prince Wuluan (the Hamlet character) has had a romantic longing for Little Wan (the Gertrude figure) since childhood, but the prince's father intervenes and marries her first. The prince then goes off to southern China to escape, writing poetry, and studying music, dance, and theater. Three years later, the emperor has been murdered and his brother Li (the Claudius figure), who also intensely loves Wan, takes the throne and marries Little Wan, who now becomes Empress Wan. Prince Wuluan returns, and the power struggle ensues, and many in the royal palace get involved, not just Wuluan and Emperor Li, but Empress Wan as well, for it is she who conspires to poison the emperor. In the final scene is the banquet, from which the title derives, where all the antagonists gather, and where the murdering begins with poisoned wine and flying knives.

The film *The Banquet* is fascinating for many reasons, perhaps most importantly for its use of intersemiotic translation. Much of Shakespeare's text gets translated into images: the dark inner central palace versus the light of the snow in the north, where the king's messengers attempt to exile Hamlet, or the artists clothed in white in the beautiful bamboo forest in the south where Hamlet goes to study art, in contrast to the dark, black uniforms and helmets of the imperial army attacking them. Costumes, sound, lighting, and music carry much of the meaning, and dance comprises significant portions, such as the dance and song Qing Nü (the Ophelia character) performs in the banquet scene, with Wuluan (the Hamlet figure) as one of the masked dancers. The best example of intersemiotic translation would be the play-within-the-play as the actors do not speak, and all the meaning is communicated by gesture, pantomime, masks, and movement. Shakespeare had a dumb show, but here the silent theater becomes the main event, with no prologue, spoken drama, or Hamlet jumping up to explain the action. The play-within-the-play is more reminiscent of Chinese opera than *commedia dell'arte*. In fact, the director Feng Xiaogang draws from not just Chinese theater, song, and dances for his translations, but also employs Greek choruses, Noh Theater, and Kurosawa filmmaking. Probably the largest change that Feng makes is that, compared to Shakespeare, Belleforest, or Saxo, the women are significantly empowered. Qing Nü (the Ophelia character) does not go insane or commit suicide: instead, she fights for her love until the end, and indeed, her constancy in love is one of the more redeeming aspects of the play. In the final scene, to honor Wuluan (Hamlet), she sings a poem written by him, and, as there are no soliloquies, it is conceivably his most memorable "speech" of the film. Moreover, Empress Wan (the Gertrude character) is the most powerful of the lot; in fact, the play is narrated from her point of view. It is she who loves three men; she who attempts to poison the king and take over the kingdom herself; and, after all three of her loves have died, it is she who decides to go it alone, becoming emperor, not empress in the end.

The second film version, Hu Xuehua's [Sherwood Hu] *Prince of the Himalayas* (2006), sticks close to the plot of *Hamlet*, with the son Lhamoklodan (the Hamlet figure) returning to find his "Uncle" Kulo-ngam (the Claudius figure) having taken over the throne and now married to his mother Queen Nanm (the Gertrude figure). The play presents many aspects of Shakespeare closely, including the appearance of the ghost of Old Hamlet, Po-lha-nyisse (the Polonius character) spying on Hamlet and reporting back to the king, Lhamoklodan feigning madness, the harsh treatment of Odsaluyang (the Ophelia character) driving her mad and drowning herself, the duel with Lassa (the Laertes character) with the poisoned sword, and the queen mistakenly drinking the poisoned wine. Thus, the plot stays relatively close to Shakespeare's play; the names of the characters have a close phonetic connection to the English names, and many lines are fairly literally translated.

Yet other aspects of *Prince of the Himalayas* are more radically rewritten and adapted. The location is distant from Denmark or England; now set in the highlands of Tibet, the scenery is beautiful, an outdoor palace of sorts. The actors are Tibetan and traditional Tibetan rituals, such as weddings and funerals, are included. Particular aspects of the plot are changed as well. Lhamoklodan (Hamlet) is *not* the son of the older king and the queen, but of Uncle Kulo-ngam and the Queen Nanm, and the old king conspires to kill them both. At the end the old king forces Nanm to marry him, resulting in living 17 years in an unhappy marriage. At the end of their married life, the old king suspects her of an affair with his brother and threatens to kill her. Thus, the uncle's killing his older brother the king is a *good* act, an attempt to save the lives of the queen and their son. Indeed, Kulo-ngam (Claudius) has many redeeming qualities: he is shown as a loving father, but one who silently endures because of his secret murder of his brother. Further, the Hamlet and Ophelia characters are sleeping together, as the Ophelia character becomes pregnant and later dies in childbirth. The film is intense; there are no comic interludes such as the gravediggers, nor much punning or wordplay.

In *Prince of the Himalayas*, Hu Xuehua rewrites the dilemma that faces Lhamoklodan (Hamlet). Rather than confronting "to be, or not to be," the choice Lhamoklodan faces in *Prince of the Himalayas* is between revenge and forgiveness. In the opening scene, Kulo-ngam (Claudius) is shown asking forgiveness from the gods for the murder of the king. Immediately introduced is a new spirit, the Wolf-Woman, who appears in the initial scene instead of the ghost of the old king.

Figure 4.2 Wolf Woman from Hu Xuehua [Sherwood], dir. *Prince of the Himalayas* [*Ximalaya Wangzi*] (2006).

The Wolf-Woman is a major addition: she prophesizes the bloodshed to follow, advises Hamlet to forgive Kulo-ngam, leads the theater troupe, and even serves as a doctor when Hamlet is wounded. The ghost of the old king appears to Lhamoklodan in the very same way, and with the same language, as he presented himself to Hamlet in Shakespeare, and the murdered king wants Hamlet to take revenge in this case for personal reasons and not for some large concern for justice. Thus, the old king advises revenge, while the Wolf-Woman pleads for forgiveness. Hamlet, caught in the middle, prefers to die rather than to continue in such a state of maddening conflict. He climbs to a mountaintop in the hope of freezing to death, and when he survives, decides not to fight back during the duel with Lassa. The "To be, or not to be" speech is moved to later in the play, after the Lassa and Lhamoklodan fight during Odsaluyang's funeral. The translation in the subtitles runs "Who am I? Where do I come from? How do I fight against this sea of troubles? To die, to sleep, and by sleep we say to end." Only at the end does Hamlet learn that his true father was the Claudius figure and not the old king. Thus, in this case, Hamlet's hesitations are *justified*, which may be the point of the film. The Claudius figure also chooses death, killing himself with his sword, hoping to reunite with his family in the afterlife. The deaths in *Prince of the Himalayas* are different than in the West; here they are a form of death with honor in an attempt to preserve the good name of the family, more sacrificial in nature than an eternal cycle of vengeance.

Finally, the most noticeable change, a second Hamlet appears, saved by the spiritual female figure of the Wolf-Woman. The baby Hamlet, the son of Lhamoklodan and Odsaluyang, may be interpreted as representing hope for the future, or, from a different cultural perspective, a form of good karma rewarding the benevolent acts of *refusing* to take revenge. The Buddhist twist is powerful, veiled but apparent throughout the film in the often reflective acts of Kulo-ngam. The Wolf-Woman's prophecy, the repeated calls by characters for forgiveness from the gods, and the dramatic depiction of the heavenly landscape hint that Kulo-ngam may be Lhamoklodan's father. The stunning photography of the Himalayan Mountains, with the snow shimmering, mists rising, birds circling, and rivers flowing, takes on a spiritual dimension, becoming a character of its own. Hu's images work slowly, as viewers' recollections of the dark and decaying atmosphere of Denmark in their minds is gradually displaced by another emerging vision.

Just as Shakespeare introduced a humanist alternative to the medieval notion of revenge, so too does Hu introduce a humane alternative to twentieth-century massive acts of violence and greed. Shakespeare's *Hamlet* has a raw, nihilistic edge to it; no one lives; bodies are buried rather than resurrected and the kingdom crumbles, given over to the foreigner Fortinbras. Hu's *Prince of the Himalayas* has a less tragic vision. It seems as if Hamlet, Gertrude, Claudius, and Ophelia are forgiven, with a new Hamlet, a rebirth, arriving on the scene. In a further fascinating twist, Ajisuji (the Fortinbras character) is a *woman*, who in the last scene is shown holding the baby, perhaps suggesting that she may mother the child in the future. In many ways, Shakespeare translations and rewritings can put a culture on a map, and with this *Hamlet* translation, the Tibetan language and culture achieve a major boost. While Lin chose to locate his *Banquet* in a royal Tang Dynasty palace and culture, Hu chose to locate his play in a remote tribal village in the Himalayas, which has its majestic qualities. The palace is not nearly as large, the costumes are not ornate or elaborate, but are rather more practical and fit for the natural elements. The national and transnational implications of the translation are large, lodged mainly in questioning the purpose of all the jealousies, conspiracies, and vengeful mandates contained in the play and offering an alternative based on spiritual beliefs in the region, in harmony with natural elements, and pointing toward a more peaceful resolution.

Hamlet arrived in China in an abridged form and was adapted to the local Chinese culture from the beginning, a rewriting process that has continued to the present. Lin Shu's shortened and prosaic version became the foundation for subsequent versions, and yes, while there were fuller translations in a traditional sense, these translations, too, were adapted for artistic and ideological purposes. It was not long before more experimental, socially engaged, and artistically creative versions appeared. In all of these more recent theater and film productions of *Hamlet*, the scenes, settings, locations, dress, and music, in short, the *image* of Hamlet, despite its different incarnations, becomes as important as the text itself. Some say that Kurosawa's *Throne of Blood* (1957) is the best production of *Macbeth* ever, including the best Royal Shakespeare versions in London and Stratford. International productions of *Hamlet*—including the anti-feudal and increasingly socially progressive versions in China—are circling back and in turn influencing the play's twenty-first-century reception in English. Even those productions not traveling well, such as Lin's 1989 post-Tiananmen *Hamlet*, are having an impact in theater and scholarly international circles. These Chinese *Hamlet* productions well illustrate Baudrillard's suggestion that in today's global world, texts circulate rather than originate. More than the influence of the *translated* text, it is the influence of the *images* of that text upon the stage or in the film that enhances reception. I think that in her discussion of *Shamlet*, Alexa Huang is exactly right about the palimpsestic nature of translation, especially of such canonical works, and as new layers are applied in the present, the original will only recede further into the past. Genette's focus upon the relations between texts and multiple ways they reread and rewrite one another is perhaps a more fruitful approach to better understanding *Hamlet* translations and rewritings in China. So too does Hutcheon's thinking about the original as an already adapted text help with unpacking the layers. Finally, Garneau's concept of tradaptation allows for increased local appeal while at the same time connecting to minority cultures worldwide. In addition to being an author, Shakespeare was an actor, and he, too, was well aware of the layering, borrowing, rewriting, and adapting processes. The incorporation of Chinese aesthetics, theatrical traditions, and local innovations are invigorating the contemporary scene of *Hamlet* productions, and I suggest such transnational revisionings may be more influential than a strict linguistic equivalent for Chinese as well as international audiences. Translation scholars need to look beyond the linguistic and literary to the music, lights, set, costumes, gestures, make-up, and facial expressions to better understand this new intercultural and intersemiotic age of translation. As the media changes, so too do the performance options increase, and more dynamic theories of translation and internationalization are needed for the future.

Bibliography

Bandello, Matteo. 1948 [1565–76]. *The French Bandello: A Selection. The Original Text of Four of Belleforest's Histoires tragiques*, trans. François de Belleforest, ed. Frank Scott Hook. Columbia: University of Missouri.

Barthes, Roland. 1977 "The Death of the Author," trans. Stephen Heath. In Stephen Heath, ed. *Image-Music-Text*. London: Fontana, 42–48.

Bassnett, Susan and André Lefevere. 1990. "Proust's Grandmother and the Thousand and One Nights: The 'Cultural Turn' in Translation Studies." In Susan Bassnett and André Lefevere, eds. *Translation, History and Culture*. London: Pinter.

Baudrillard, Jean. 1994a. *The Illusion of the End*, trans. Chris Turner. Stanford: Stanford University Press.

Baudrillard, Jean. 1994b. *Simulacra and Simulation*, trans. Sheila Faria Glaser. Ann Arbor: University of Michigan Press.

Belleforest, François de. 1926 [1608]. "Hystoire of Hamblet." In Israel Gollancz, ed. *The Sources of Hamlet, with an Essay on the Legend*. London: Oxford, 165–311.

Benjamin, Walter. 1968a [1955]. "The Work of Art in the Age of Mechanical Reproduction," trans. Harry Zohn. In Hannah Arendt, ed. *Illuminations*. New York: Harcourt, Brace and World, 217–52.

Benjamin, Walter. 1968b [1955]. "The Task of the Translator," trans. Harry Zohn. *Illuminations*. New York: Schocken, 83–110.

Bian Zhilin. 1957. "Shashibiya de beiju 'Hamuleite' [Shakespeare's Tragedy Hamlet]." *Wenyi yanjiu jikan*. December, 79–137.

Bloom, Harold. 1997 [1973]. *The Anxiety of Influence: A Theory of Poetry*. Oxford: Oxford University Press.

Brisset, Annie. 1990. *Sociocritique de la traduction: Théâtre et altérité au Québec (1968–1988)*. Montreal: Les editions du Préambules. Trans. Rosilind Gill and Roger Gannon. 1996. *A Sociocritique of Translation: Theater and Alterity in Quebec 1968–1988*. Toronto: University of Toronto Press.

Burton, Robert. 2001 [1621]. *The Anatomy of Melancholy*. New York: New York Review of Books Classics.

Cattrysse, Patrick. 1992. *Pour une théorie de l'adaptation filmique*. Berne: Peter Lang.

Chen Fukang. 1992. *Zhongguo yi xue li lun shi gao*. Shanghai: Foreign Languages Publishing House.

Chen Yugang. 1989. *Zhongguo fan yi wen xue shi*. Beijing: Publishing House of Foreign Languages Teaching and Research.

Derrida, Jacques. 1985. "Des tours de Babel." Translated by Joseph Graham. In Joseph Graham, ed. *Difference and Translation*. Ithaca: Cornell University Press, 165–248.

Entell, Bettina. 2002. *Post-Tian'anmen: A New Era in Chinese Theater: Experimentation during the 1990s at Beijing China National Experimental Theater/CNET*. Doctoral Dissertation. University of Hawai'i.

Ewbank, Inga-Stina. 1995. "Hamlet and the Power of Words." In David Scott Kasten, ed. *Critical Essays on Shakespeare's Hamlet*. New York: G.K. Hall, 56–78.

Feng Xiaogang, dir. 2006. *Ye Yan. The Banquet*. Beijing: Huayi Brothers and Hong Kong: Media Asia Films.

Gambier, Yves. 2004. "Tradaptation Cinématographique." In Pilar Orero, ed. *Topics in Audiovisual Translation*. Amsterdam: John Benjamins, 169–81.

Genette, Gérald. 1997 [1982]. *Palimpsests: Literature in the Second Degree*, trans. Channa Newman and Claude Doubinsky. Lincoln: University of Nebraska Press.

Gentzler, Edwin. 1993. *Contemporary Translation Theories*. London: Routledge.

Gentzler, Edwin. 2008. *Translation and Identity in the Americas: New Directions in Translation Theory*. London: Routledge.

Gillespie, Stuart. 2001. *Shakespeare's Books: A Dictionary of Shakespeare Sources*. London: Athlone Press

Gillies, John, Ryuta Minami, Li Ruru, and Poonam Trivedi. 2002. "Shakespeare on the Stage in Asia." In Stanley Wells and Sarah Stanton, eds. *The Cambridge Companion to Shakespeare on Stage*. Cambridge: Cambridge University Press, 259–83.

Gollancz, Israel, ed. 1967 [1926]. *The Sources of Hamlet with an Essay on the Legend*. London: Oxford.

Harrison, G.B. 1968. "Introduction to *The Tragedy of Hamlet, Prince of Denmark*." In G.B. Harrison, ed. *Shakespeare, The Complete Works*. New York: Heinle and Heinle, 880–84.

Hawkes, Terence. 1992. *Meaning by Shakespeare*. London: Routledge.

Hu Xuehua [Sherwood], dir. 2006. *Prince of the Himalayas [Ximalaya Wangzi]*. Shanghai: Shanghai Film Group.

Huang, Alexa. 2009. *Chinese Shakespeares: Two Centuries of Cultural Exchange*. New York: Columbia University Press.

Huang, Alexa. 2014. "*Shamlet*: Shakespeare as Palimpsest." MIT Global Shakespeares: Video and Performance Archive. Online at http://globalshakespeares. mit.edu/blog/2014/07/20/shamlet-shakespeare-as-palimpsest-by-alexa-huang/, accessed February 23, 2015.

Hung, Eva. 2002. "Translation and English in Twentieth-Century China." *World Englishes* 21(2): 325–35.

Hutcheon, Linda. 2006. *A Theory of Adaptation*. London: Routledge.

Hutcheon, Linda and Siobhan O'Flynn. 2012. *A Theory of Adaptation*, revised edn. London: Routledge.

Jenkins, Harold, ed. 1982. *Hamlet, Prince of Denmark*. The Arden Shakespeare. London: Methuen.

Jónsson, Guðni and Bjarni Vilhjálmsson, eds. n.d. *Hrólfs saga kraka ok kappa hans*. Online at www.heimskringla.no/wiki/Hrólfs_saga_kraka_ok_kappa_hans, accessed March 30, 2015. Translated by Jesse L. Byock. 1998. *The Saga of King Hrolf Kraki*. London: Penguin.

Kaurismäki, Aki, dir. 1992. *La vie de bohème*. Helsinki: Sputnik Oy.

Kennedy, Doris and Yong Li Lan, eds. 2010. *Shakespeare in Asia: Contemporary Performance*. Cambridge: Cambridge University Press.

Knutson, Susan. 2012. "'Tradaptation' dans le sens Québécois: A Word for the Future." In Laurence Raw, ed. *Translation, Adaptation, and Transformation*. London: Continuum. 112–23.

Lamb, Charles and Lamb, Mary. 2013 [1807]. *Tales from Shakespeare*. Mineola, NY: Calla Editions.

Lefevere, André. 1992. *Translation, Rewriting, and the Manipulation of Literary Fame*. London: Routledge.

Levith, Murray J. 2004. *Shakespeare in China*. London: Continuum.

Li Guoxiu, dir. 2006. *Shamlet*. Taipei: INK.

Li Ruru. 2003. *Shashibiya: Staging Shakespeare in China*. Hong Kong: Hong Kong University Press.

Li Ruru. 2010. "*Hamlet* in China: Translation, Interpretation and Performance." MIT Global Shakespeares: Video and Performance Archives: Essays and Written Interviews. Online at http://globalshakespeares.mit.edu/blog/2010/04/05/hamlet-in-china-translation-interpretation-and-performance, accessed January 15, 2015.

Lin Kenan. 2002. "Translation as a Catalyst for Social Change in China." In Maria Tymoczko and Edwin Gentzler, eds. *Translation and Power*. Amherst: University of Massachusetts Press, 160–83.

Lin Zhaohua, dir. 1995 [1989]. *Hamulaite*. Beijing: Beijing People's Art Theater. Online at http://globalshakespeares.mit.edu/hamulaite-lin-zhaohua-1995, accessed April 29, 2015.

Liu, Lydia He. 1995. *Translingual Practice: Literature, National Culture, and Translated Modernity: China 1900–1937*. Redwood City, CA: Stanford University Press.

Lotbinière-Harwood, Susanne de. 1991. *Re-belle et infidel: La traduction comme pratique de réécriture au feminine/The Body Bilingual: Translation as a Rewriting in the Feminine*. Montreal: Les éditions du Remue-ménage; Toronto: Women's Press.

Ma Zuyi. 1984. *Zhongguo fanyi jian shi*. Beijing: China Publishing Corporations of Translations.

Mao Zedong. 1967 [1942]. *Talks at the Yenan Forum on Literature and Art*. Beijing: Xinhua News Agency.

McGee, Arthur. 1987. *The Elizabethan Hamlet*. New Haven: Yale University Press.

Mouré, Erin. 2001. *Sheep's Vigil by a Fervent Person, A Transelation*. Toronto: Anansi.

Qi Shouhua. 2012. *Western Literature in China and the Translation of a Nation*. New York: Palgrave Macmillan.

Raw, Laurence, ed. 2012. *Translation, Adaptation, and Transformation*. London: Continuum.

Rosenbaum, Ron. 2002. "Shakespeare in Rewrite." *New Yorker*. May 13: 68–77.

Salter, Dennis. 2000. "Between Wor(l)ds: Lepage's Shakespeare Cycle." In Joseph I. Donohoe, Jr. and Jane M. Koustas, eds. *Theater sans frontières: Essays on the Dramatic Universe of Robert Lepage*. East Lansing: Michigan State University Press, 191–204.

Salter, Denis and Robert Lepage. 1993. "Borderlines: An Interview with Robert Lepage and Le Théâtre Repère." *Theater* 24(3): 71–79.

Saxo Grammaticus. 1514 [1185]. *Hamlet from the Historia Danica of Saxo Grammaticus*, trans. Oliver Elton. In Israel Gollancz, ed. *The Sources of Hamlet, with an Essay on the Legend*. London: Oxford, 93–163.

Saxo Grammaticus. 1894 [1185]. "Amleth, Prince of Denmark" in *The First Nine Books of the Danish History of Saxo Grammaticus*, Books 3 and 4, trans. Oliver Elton. London: David Nutt, 106–130. Revised by D.L. Ashliman. Online at www.pitt.edu/~dash/amleth.html, accessed March 31, 2015.

Shakespeare, William. 1968. *The Complete Works*, ed. G.B. Harrison. New York: Heinle and Heinle.

Shakespeare, William. 1974. *The Riverside Shakespeare*, ed. Frank Kermode, G. Blakemore Evans, Anne Barton, and Harry T. Levine. Boston: Houghton Mifflin.

Shakespeare, William. 1978. *Macbeth*, trans. Michel Garneau. Montreal: VLB.

Shakespeare, William. 2006–7 [1603 and 1623]. *Hamlet: The Texts of 1603 and 1623*, ed. Ann Thompson and Neil Taylor. London: Bloomsbury Arden.

Shakespeare, William. 2006–7 [1604–5]. *Hamlet*. The Arden Shakespeare, 3rd Series, ed. Ann Thompson and Neil Taylor. London: Bloomsbury Arden.

Simon, Sherry. 2006. *Translating Montreal: Episodes in the Life of a Divided City*. London: Routledge.

Simon, Sherry. 2012. *Cities in Translation: Intersections of Language and Memory*. London: Routledge.

Stabler, A.P. 1966. "Melancholy, Ambition, and Revenge in Belleforest's *Hamlet*." *PMLA*, 18(3): 207–13.

Tymoczko, Maria and Edwin Gentzler, eds. 2002. *Translation and Power*. Amherst: University of Massachusetts Press.

Wilson, John Dover. 1951. *What Happens in Hamlet*, 3rd edn. Cambridge: Cambridge University Press.

Xiong Yuanwei, dir. 2000. *Hamlet, Hamlet*. Hong Kong: Amity Drama Club, Shatian Spoken Drama Theare, and Fourth Line Theatre.

Xiong Yuezhi. 1996. "An Overview of the Dissemination of Western Learning in Late Qing China." *Perspectives: Studies in Translatology* 4(1): 13–27.

Zeng Lin. 2013. "Encounter Between Languages: Liang Qichao's Translation and Translingual Practice." *New Zealand Journal of Asian Studies* 15(1): 77–91.

Zhang Xiaoyang. 1996. *Shakespeare in China: A Comparative Study of Two Traditions*. Newark: University of Delaware Press.

Zhu Wen and Zhang Junchuan, eds. 1992. *Shashibiya Cidian*. Hefei: Anhui Arts and Literature Press.

Conclusion

This book began with a discussion of translation studies as it transitioned to post-translation studies and offered the views of a series of scholars, including Bassnett and Lefevere, Arduini and Nergaard, Simon and De Campos, Baudrillard and Derrida, and Genette and Hutcheon, whose work influences my own. The theory is based on poststructural, postcolonial, and postmodern ideas that emerged in the 1970s and 1980s and has had a significant impact on many disciplines but were largely excluded from translation paradigms. Comparatively, the post-translation turn is a rather late one. I then demonstrated the post-translation hypothesis through a selection of case studies, from Shakespeare's *A Midsummer Night's Dream*'s success in traveling from Elizabethan England to Germany and back to the English-speaking world; to Goethe's *Faust* triumph in romantic and classical Germany to its postcolonial turn in the twentieth century; through Proust's revolutionizing Belle Époque literary and artistic conventions in France and then the postmodern impact of the translations on creative writing; and finally to the abridgements, transadaptations, and performances of *Hamlet* in China, whose post-translation repercussions are still too recent to analyze.

The case studies presented were strategically chosen as symptomatic of their respective centuries: seventeenth, eighteenth, nineteenth, and twentieth. In each chapter, I looked at the translational culture that lay behind their "original" creation, the translational aspects contained within the seminal source texts, traditional translations that followed, and finally, post-translation rewritings that continue to shape the respective receiving cultures today. I propose expanding the boundaries of "translation studies" to include translated texts as well as pre-original and post-translational texts seldom studied by the field, but which I suggest have far-reaching implications, especially upon cultural formation. Baudrillard's claim that texts no longer originate, but circulate in a process of "rewriting everything" (Baudrillard 1994b [1992]: 12) forms an underlying premise, which the latter parts of each chapter well demonstrate.

I also have been attracted to a new set of terminology with which to analyze the multiple forms translations now assume. Gerald Genette's study of the many types of translation and rewriting—imitation, parody, pastiche, caricature, and even plagiarism—have become useful categories for post-translational analysis. Productive, too, have been the terms with which Genette describes translations and rewritings—transtylization, augmentation, reduction, prosification, and versification (Genette 1997 [1982]: 214–28). Haroldo de Campos's neologism such as *"transcriação," "transluminação," "transfusão,"* and *"transluciferação"* are proving valuable in the analysis of Brazilian, Latin American, and Third World translated texts, many of which allow for a more creative latitude (Campos 1981: 180, 208–9). When I first lobbied for the usefulness of terms such as "cannibalization" in 1993 in *Contemporary Translation Theories*, many translation scholars thought I was offering fashionable literary-critical terms that would be short-lived. Instead, they have held up well, particularly in postcolonial approaches to the study of translation. Sherry Simon's network of new terms to study the post-translation effects of translation on newly emerging original works— creative interference, furtherings, transelation—are also proving useful for describing how translations enter into the realm of various artistic practices (Simon 2006: 127–53).

This investigation goes beyond just advocating for a new set of terms with which to better describe translational elements; rather, I suggest that the discipline is changing in a fundamental way. Hutcheon and O'Flynn's question of whether such a turn in translation is one of degree or kind remains a very real question (Hutcheon and O'Flynn 2012: xix). It may be that if indeed the change is in *kind*, we may have to rename and restructure the discipline. Since Antoine Berman (1984) and Lawrence Venuti (1995), many modern scholars have posited the two-voiced nature of translation, i.e., that the translator is no longer invisible, but that his or her voice can also be heard in addition to the author. In the post-Venuti world of translation, rather than the translator's visibility being a negative trait, it has become a to-be-expected, if not entirely positive, aspect of any translation. In this book, I maintain that translation is much more than double-voiced; rather, the voices are multiple, a translation of a translation of a translation, extending back diachronically. This book has illustrated many such trajectories. The Faust translations and rewritings in Chapter 2 of this volume serve as just one example. The Germanic oral tales, followed by puppet plays performed by traveling players, to several pre-Goethe written versions, culminate in Goethe's masterpiece. Goethe's *Faust* then was translated into many European languages, adapted into an opera in French by Charles Gounod, and followed by the many post-Gounod rewritings of *Faust*, including Estanislao del Campo's poem *Fausto* (1866), and French writer Gaston Leroux's novel *The Phantom of the Opera* (1909–10). The novel, in turn, was adapted into the 1925 Rupert Julian film starring Lon Chaney, and then further rewritten for the stage by Andrew Lloyd Webber in 1986. Extracts of Gounod can even be found in *The Adventures of Tintin* by Georges Remi (pen-name Hergé), which in turn have been translated into more than 70 languages. The voices of translation and rewriting are many indeed.

Thus, Genette's concept of a palimpsest is useful when seeking to unpack the process of rewriting and retranslation. Some of the translations may be more or less faithful or imaginative, derivative or creative, but they all contribute to a text's reception going forward. Further, translations are increasingly communicated via different technologies, as new media forms allow for an increasing variety of means for representation and translation. Arduini and Nergaard (2011: 15) suggest that the field should be open to *trans*disciplinary change, i.e., that the discipline needs to transform itself in order to adapt to the new and increasingly hybrid objects of study.

One objection frequently made against such postmodern analyses in translation studies is that they are elitist, falling into an art-for-art-sake category. Herein may lie a difference between postmodernism and post-translation. Many of the post-translation rewritings, while they may undermine traditional definitions of translation, are doing much more than offering largely meaningless alternatives or unlimited semiosis. As I hope to have shown in William Kentridge's version *Faustus in Africa* (1995), the translation serves as a form of translating or writing *back* to the original and its reception in Germany, perhaps righting wrongs (re-righting), or in this case, re-emphasizing elements present in Goethe's text, but effaced by that palimpsest of authoritative rewritings in its German critical reception. Regarding post-translation versions of Proust's *À la recherche du temps perdu*, the rewritings and adaptations—from Volker Schlöndorff's film *Un Amour de Swann* (1983) through Jacqueline Rose's *Albertine* (2001)—aimed at making the text *more* accessible to everyday readers, taking the text out of the hands of the literary elite and broadening its interpretation and reception. *Albertine* serves as a good example of a parody of Proust, rethinking and redrawing a character not fully sketched by a literary establishment, lending her a women's agency denied in most interpretations. So too in China, did the 1989 production of *Hamlet* [*Hamulaite*], directed by Lin Zhaohua, return the play, once considered academic and elitist in China, to the ordinary citizens of Beijing, with Hamlet depicted as "one of us." Indeed, in many post-translation rewritings, the elitist charge does not hold; instead, I suggest that Bassnett and Lefevere's emphasis on institutions of power and ideology move to the fore (Bassnett and Lefevere 1990; Lefevere 1992), and the politics of the rewritten original must be closely scrutinized.

A second charge levied against post-translation studies approaches is that they may kill off existing translation studies programs. Translation studies is not the only discipline threatened by such poststructural volleys, and certainly my field of comparative literature has been killed off and reborn any number of times. As one of those new disciplines emerging in the 1970s and 1980s, the early pioneering scholars—Lambert, Holmes, Bassnett,

Hermans, Lefevere, Toury, Tymoczko—had to work hard to map out a discipline, define the object of study, and develop acceptable methodologies for textual analysis. Once the discipline became successfully located within academia, along came a new generation of scholars attacking the very model. While translation studies as a discipline enjoys a 30-plus year history in many Western countries, in other countries and cultures, such as in India, Southeast Asia, or Middle Eastern cultures, the discipline is new. The argument presented in this book does *not* call for a dismantling of existing translation studies research paradigms; indeed, they still hold central relevance. Rather I call for *expanding* the boundaries, allowing for an analysis of pre-original culture and conditions, the translational nature of original writing, and, especially, the post-translation repercussions of translation, not just on later translations, but on creative writing, any number of the creative arts, and a variety of disciplines. I hold that translation forms and transforms aspects of *all* disciplines, from literary and linguistic, through political and philosophical, to religious and ethical. This study is a call for interdisciplinary collaborations and international connections; it calls for an openness to the ideas and insights of scholars working on translational issues from *outside* the discipline; and, at last, it wants to foster an openness to the idea that such considerations might change the field from within.

A third criticism is that a renaming is unnecessary and that those scholars who have taken the cultural turn have been open to such post-translation analysis all along. I find that this critique is largely valid. Certainly my mentors Susan Bassnett and André Lefevere have always been open to a plurality of approaches with which to study translations (Bassnett and Lefevere 1998: 138). Unfortunately, the field has not been as open to new voices as envisioned at the time, and the poststructuralist, postmodernist, or intersemiotic scholars of translation are few. I sense that something quite new and exciting is occurring, not just in the field of translation studies but in many other fields taking a translation turn, thereby increasingly exposing the limitations of certain Euro-American investigations. I mentioned in the Preface and Acknowledgments that the idea for this book began at a conference in Brazil called *Transfusão* [Transfusion], which was a gathering of academics and artists and included many performances that were hybrid in nature and open to creative interference. Thus, Cole Porter songs were not just translated to conform to the English, but performed with Brazilian musicians, reinvigorated in a *tropicalismo* vein.

I closed the Preface with an allusion to a Con-Fest (conference-festival) that I attended in Delhi, India. This meeting was again a combination of academics and artists open to creative rewritings and hybrid art forms, from oral storytelling, to film and theatrical performances, to embroidery and wall hangings. In "In Our Own Time, On Our Own Terms" (2006), Harish Trivedi suggests that there is a striking absence of written translation in India. Much of the translation instead is internal, oral, or even unspoken, as many languages are mutually intelligible. Translation, as understood in the

West, arrived with European colonization. He suggests that the Hindi word *anuvad* associated with translation suggests a temporal process, more of a "speaking after" rather than a "carrying across." In many cultures, the very definition of translation has always included the "speaking after" aspect advocated by those taking the post-translation approach to the study of translation. While such a turn exponentially expands the corpus of objects for study, I suggest that such an expansion is healthy and that doing so may allow scholars to glean additional insights not only into the practice of translation but also into the nature of the very object of study for the discipline.

A final question that arises from these considerations is where scholars are to find such post-translational texts. Sometimes one has to turn away from traditionally translated texts and move on to a whole new set of corpora entirely. For example, many creative writers have written about translation in their fiction, memoirs, biographies, and autobiographies. While not empirical texts per se, the fictional form allows both for a distance from and candor about translational matters. A group of scholars, including Rosemary Arrojo, Klaus Kaindl, Nitsa Ben-Ari, Brian Baer, Judith Woodsworth, and Susanne Jill Levine, has begun the analysis of the translational elements within *original* writing. Calling for the "fictional turn" in translation, which began perhaps with Borges's *Ficciones* (2008 [1944]), the term entered translation studies circles with Else Vieira's "(In)visibilidades na tradução: Troca de olhares teórico e ficcionais" [(In)visibilities in Translation: Exchanging Theoretical and Fictional Perspectives] (1995–96), in which she coined the phrase "the fictional turn" in translation studies. Vieira referred to the short story "*O espelho* [The Mirror]" (1962) by João Guimarães Rosa, who plays with the idea of the mirror as not only reflecting reality, but also incorporating various indigenous beliefs associated with mirrors. Thus, Rosa's fiction moved from the realm of realism to magic realism and served as a metaphor for faithful translation shifting to creative translation. Vieira, situating her work in the ideas of Charles Sanders Peirce and Jacques Derrida as well as Susan Bassnett and Nelson Ascher, suggests that there is always a covering/discovering aspect to translation, manifest more in *fictional* works that in translation studies itself (Gentzler 2008: 108–9).

Arrojo, Kaindl, Ben-Ari, Baer, Woodsworth, Levine, and others have been meeting at conferences since 2011 and sharing their research on what has become known as "Transfiction." They report on their findings in the volume *Transfiction: Research into the Realities of Translation Fiction* (2014), which covers translational elements in fiction and film. From *Don Quixote* (2015 [1605, 1615]), through Borges's *Ficciones* (2008 [1944]), and to works such as Eva Hoffman's *Lost in Translation* (1990), Brian Friel's *Translations* (1991), Salvador Benesdra's *El Traductor* (1998), Jonathan Safran Foer's *Everything is Illuminated* (2003), Leila Aboulela's *The Translator* (2006), and Ludmila Ulitskaya's *Daniel Stein, Interpreter* (2012), the scholars reveal the central role of translation in cultural formation. With enhanced means of travel and communication, movement and migration are rising, and more and more people find themselves in a *state* where translation is a fundamental necessity. Indeed, translation seems not to be a secondary, but instead a leading theme by which authors articulate various aspects of movement, migration, exile, displacement, adaptation, and integration. No longer limited to a supporting character, the translator has become a main figure in fiction, poetry, drama, and film. Michael Cronin wrote a book called *Translation Goes to the Movies* (2009) in which he looks at films such as Sofia Coppola's *Lost in Translation* (2003), Sydney Pollack's *The Interpreter* (2005), and Alejandro González Iñárritu's *Babel* (2006), all of whom foreground translators or translational concerns. Such fictional portrayals allow the author or director to delve into issues of translation and identity and add variables that both complicate and humanize the translator figure. Many translation studies programs continued to limit their studies to translation encounters that take place under fairly ideal conditions, and the ethics of the profession—neutrality, faithfulness, and objectivity—actually end up distorting a full picture. The translators presented in fiction, coming from civil war, refugee camps, contested neighborhoods, massive poverty, racial fears, and police brutality, often have higher concerns than fidelity. Survival is at stake. Personal ethics, family loyalties, community solidarity, and spiritual beliefs, often conflict with, or at times override, the ethics of the profession.

Shakespeare criticism has been particularly rife with post-translation artifacts and analysis. For example, in *Tempests After Shakespeare* (2002), Chantal Zabus discusses any number of rewritings of Shakespeare's play. Indeed in the introduction, entitled "On Rewriting," Zabus discusses nearly four decades of *Tempest* rewritings and how the major characters—Caliban, Miranda, and Prospero—have come to represent postcoloniality, postpatriarchy, and postmodernity respectively. From Africa to the Caribbean and Latin America, Caliban has come to represent a colonized indigenous insurgent. In Canada and the Caribbean, Miranda (and at times Ariel) have come to embody a challenge to patriarchy. For the United States and Britain, Prospero has to deal with eroding power and changing conditions, emblematic of the postmodern condition. Caliban rewritings include Aimé Césaire's *Une tempête* (1974 [1969]), in which Caliban and Prospero are seen as equals; George Lamming's, *The Pleasures of Exile* (1992), in which Caliban migrates from his native kingdom to the "island" of Prospero (Milan/London); and David Dabydeen's poetry collection *Coolie Odyssey* (1988), where Caliban successfully sleeps with Miranda, the empire doing more than just writing back. In the rewritings, wide ranges of palimpsestic layers are uncovered, revealing indications of incest, rape, suicide, drowning, and murder rediscovered in the original text. The rewritings are too many to mention, but the number of Canadian Miranda rewritings struck me. Zabus goes so far as to suggest that Miranda has become a "national symbol," coming to represent Canada's filial relationship to England (2002: 105). To pick just a few examples, in *Prospero on the Island* (1971), Audrey Thomas uses aspects of Miranda to depict development of the Canadian female artists; in Suniti Namjoshi's poem "Snapshots of Caliban" (1989), Miranda is rewritten as a lesbian; and in *The Measure of Miranda* (1987), Sarah Murphy shows Miranda as a powerful voice in the realm of dominant male politics. The Miranda rewritings suggest a counterdiscourse and moral alternative to the male-dominated cultural and political conditions in Canada.

The sheer volume of rewritings of Shakespeare has exploded the boundaries of written texts and has entered the realm of electronic reproduction. Electronic databases of Shakespeare post-translation versions are on the rise. Three that inform my work have been the Massachusetts Institute of Technology (MIT) Global Shakespeares, the University of Warwick's Global Shakespeare Project, and the Asian Shakespeare Intercultural Archive (A|S|I|A). The MIT Global Shakespeare site contains hundreds of videos and performances and has open access. At the time of this writing, more than 400 international videos have been posted—everything from Cheek by Jowl's 2011 production of *The Tempest* in Russian, to the National Theatre of Egypt's 2002 production of *King Lear*. In addition to the wealth of videos of full productions and excerpts from productions, MIT Global Shakespeare offers synopses, reviews, comments, scripts, interviews, critical articles, and online links to further articles. MIT's Global Shakespeare online site is connected to the University of Warwick's Global Shakespeare Project, which is developing a range of research projects to better analyze Shakespeare internationally, provide a location for students and scholars to conduct research, hold conferences and forums on international topics, and help support teachers of Shakespeare.

While the MIT Global Shakespeare site contains both mainstream and progressive versions of Shakespeare's plays, the Asian Shakespeare Intercultural Archive (A|S|I|A) is decidedly more *engagé*, intending to diversify Shakespeare's reception and to allow a more incisive comparative analysis. The A|S|I|A also offers videos, such as Lin Zhaohua's 1989 *Hamlet* cited in Chapter 4 in this volume, but also posts data on the creation of the production, responses to the event by different groups of spectators from a variety of backgrounds, a discussion of the various forms and languages employed in the production, and the contexts on which the production was based, from Shakespeare to other related productions. Significantly, A|S|I|A holds that translation is "at the root of Shakespeare and Asian theater." All the videos are accompanied by scripts in (1) the performance language; (2) the script's translation into English; and (3) translations into Chinese and Japanese. In the future, Korean translations will also be offered. This commitment to translation, to sharing resources with non-English-speaking scholars and acknowledging the central role translation plays in such adaptations is unparalleled.

Contributions to post-translation analysis are beginning to appear in the discipline as well. In *Translation Effects: The Shaping of Modern Canadian Culture* (2014), edited by Kathy Mezei, Sherry Simon, and Luise von Flotow, contributors look at the impact of translation not just on poetry, fiction, media, and the arts, but also on politics, legislation, and judicial decisions, especially as they pertain to First Nations. From oral histories to the translation of treaties, to literary and theater events, the authors point out the numerous effects translations have had on Canadian life and culture. They argue that many texts bear little resemblance to the facing-page translations characteristic of many essays, literary texts, or official decrees; rather, they take the form of movies, theatrical productions, translation in courtrooms and hospitals, in cafés and on the streets. They argue that professional definitions of translations have obscured the awareness of these other forms of translation, which are more prevalent, touch more lives, and have a stronger impact on cultural development than officially mandated translation. Contributions range from discussions of forms of Native American translations, different approaches by different genders, the role of minority languages such as Yiddish or *joual*, the impact of translation on immigrants, and, especially, the effect of translation on social policies and cultural change. In translation studies scholarship, many distinctions maintained do not hold: the borders between literary and non-literary texts are increasingly fluid, distinctions between textual translation and transculturation dissolve, and legislative acts contradict daily practices. While many of the effects are anticipated, some are unintended byproducts. Some are easily observable, such as the impacts of Bible translation; others are difficult to discern, such as a viewer's aesthetic experience. In addition, generalizations are difficult, as some translations have different effects on different peoples. The volume well illustrates the centrality of translation on the evolution of Canadian society.

In the Introduction to this book, I suggested that while many translators strive for a linguistically accurate translation, more important to the translators is the introduction of a new *idea* or artistic *form* into a culture. While translation scholars have gotten very good at describing and evaluating translations, the analysis of the successful transmission of the ideas in any given text is harder to measure. In many ways, in this book I call for a focus on the democratization process of the reception of translations. The plethora of rewritings not only carry translations forward into new genres for new generations, but they also give us an insight into the ideas, responses, and opinions of a much more diverse group of readers and viewers. The range of popular translations and rewritings offers a window into the social-psychological space of the *reader* and how translated ideas are received.

In *Literary Translation and the Rediscovery of Reading* (2012a), Clive Scott begins to address such questions. First, he expands the corpus of the objects for translation studies, calling for a shift from the overemphasis on interlingual translation to an increased emphasis on *intralingual*—rewriting within the same language—and *intermedial* translation, or translation across media, which is precisely the claim I am making in this book. Further, he suggests that criticism has tended to avoid dealing with the individual input by the reader because of its idiosyncratic and subjective nature. Yet these impressions, often triggered by personal associations, old memories, and unpredictable intertexts, are precisely those aspects that reveal what the reader finds useful and why. Scott calls for the return to an *autobiographical* analysis by unpacking the reader's or the translator's voice and increasing the focus on paralinguistic elements—sound, speed, volume, silences, intonation, selection, and emphasis. The goal is to reveal *how* a reader experiences the text. Scott thus sees translation not just as a textual act, but also as a "pre-textual act," i.e., the source text is already an inadequate transcription of a previous oral performance, and as a "post-post textual act," i.e., a translation of the *memory* of reading a text (Scott 2012a: 2).

Thus, post-translation studies is not bound by fixed objects—source and target texts—but is more fluid and includes looking at the pre-textual components, the multilingual aspects and multicultural ideas that comprise an original. A source text, according to Scott, is never static, but always in the process of composition and revision, a "process of potentially infinite extension" (2012a: 3). Post-translation studies also looks at interlingual translation, not by excluding subjective impressions, often dismissed as anomalies by scholars, but instead by opening itself to those very personal idiosyncrasies that are part of every translation. Importantly, post-translation looks at the after-effects of translation in the target culture. Scott is particularly strong on the analysis of the post-translation impact of any given source text, calling for research on the text's "post-publication life in the minds of countless readers, in different editions, imitations, adaptations, merchandising, and so on" (2012a: 3). Finally, Scott adds a fourth dimension, calling for the analysis of the text's entry into and becoming part of the mind of the *individual* reader. Scott hopes to unpack how translation *changes* an individual reader's worldview. Difficult as that may be, in a sequel to *Literary Translation and the Rediscovery of Reading* called *Translating the Perception of Text: Literary Translation and Phenomenology*, Scott undertakes that task, which is more driven by psycho-physiological perception than direct linguistic reference. Translations are analyzed less by one-to-one comparisons and more by unpacking the multiple layers of a palimpsestic series of texts in "an endless process of inclusive modulation" (Scott 2012b: 62).

A translated text enriches a reader in countless ways, to the point that it is absorbed into that person's very being. Inasmuch, translation is one of the most revolutionary acts: bringing across an idea or form from another culture and offering the possibility to *change* people's lives. Because translations themselves are metaphoric, multilingual, and multisensory, so too must translation studies include multisensory forms of analysis. I suggest the field begin viewing translation in a more postmodern vein: as a creative, experimental, and avant-garde act, at once self-reflective and self-generative. Translation studies finds itself on the cutting edge of time, with the potential to adapt, shift, grow, and expand into the future. The repercussions of translation can be seen everywhere—in print, art, signage, fashion, food, and media—and in every discipline—literature, politics, architecture, anthropology, philosophy, and religion. Translation ensures the regeneration of texts, the means through which ideas can be exchanged, and the processes by which languages evolve and grow. In a world of increased movement and migration, translation allows individuals to come to terms with themselves, understand their multilingual identities, and articulate their personal stories. Further, translation reaffirms such fundamental values as cultural diversity and individual creativity. To capture these cultural complexities, I suggest that translation studies' definition and discourse must change. Translation studies needs to reinvent itself, coming up with more inclusive parameters, more fluid theories, and more incisive socio-psychological analysis, to better understand translation and rewriting in the post-translation age. I hope that this book has offered a step in that direction.

Bibliography

Aboulela, Leila. 2006. *The Translator*. New York: Black Cat.

Arduini, Stefano and Siri Nergaard. 2011. "Translation: A New Paradigm." *Translation; A Transcisciplinary Journal*. Inaugural issue, 8–17.

Asian Shakespeare Intercultural Archive. Online at http://a-s-i-a-web.org, accessed February 5, 2016.

Bassnett, Susan and André Lefevere, eds. 1990. *Translation, History and Culture*, London: Pinter.

Bassnett, Susan and André Lefevere. 1998. *Constructing Cultures*. Clevedon: Multilingual Matters.

Baudrillard, Jean. 1994a [1981]. *Simulacres et simulation*. Paris: Éditions Galilée. *Simulacra and Simulation*, trans. Sheila Glaser, Ann Arbor: University of Michigan Press.

Baudrillard, Jean. 1994b [1992]. *L'illusion de la fin*. Paris: Galilee. *The Illusion of the End*, 1994, trans. Chris Turner, Stanford: Stanford University Press.

Benesdra, Salvador 1998. *El Traductor*. Buenos Aires: Ediciones de la Flor.

Berman, Antoine. 1984. *L'épreuve de l'étranger: Culture et traduction dans l'Allemagne romantique: Herder, Goethe, Schlegel, Novalis, Humboldt, Schleiermacher, Hölderlin*. Paris: Gallimard. Trans. Stefan Heyvaert. 1992. *The Experience of the Foreign: Culture and Translation in Romantic Germany*. Albany: SUNY Press.

Borges, Jorge Luis. 2008 [1944]. *Ficciones*. New York: Rayo.

Campos, Haroldo de. 1981. *Deus e o Diabo no Fausto de Goethe*. São Paulo: Perspective.

Cervanates, Miguel de. 2015 [1605, 1615]. *Don Quixote de La Mancha*. Madrid: Real Academia.

Césaire, Aimé. 1974 [1969] *Une tempête: d'après "La Tempête" de Shakespeare: adaptation pour un theater négre*. Paris: Éditions du Seuil.

Coppola, Sofia, dir. 2003. *Lost in Translation*. San Francisco: American Zoetrope.

Cronin, Michael. 2009. *Translation Goes to the Movies*. London: Routledge.

Dabydeen, David. 1988. *Coolie Odyssey*. London: Harsib.

Foer, Jonathan Safran. 2003. *Everything is Illuminated*. New York: Perennial.
Friel, Brian. 1981. *Translations*. London: Faber and Faber.
Genette, Gérald. 1997 [1982]. *Palimpsests: Literature in the Second Degree*, trans. Channa Newman and Claude Doubinsky. Lincoln: University of Nebraska Press.
Gentzler, Edwin. 1993. *Contemporary Translation Theories*. London: Routledge.
Gentzler, Edwin. 2008. *Translation and Identity in the Americas: New Directions in Translation Theory*. London: Routledge.
Global Shakespeare Project. Coventry: University of Warwick and London: Queen Mary University of London. Online at www2.warwick.ac.uk/fac/cross_fac/iatl/activities/projects/globalshakespeare/, accessed Febuary 2, 2016.
Hoffman, Eva. 1990. *Lost in Translation: A Life in a New Language*. New York: Penguin.
Hutcheon, Linda and Siobhan O'Flynn. 2012. *A Theory of Adaptation*, revised edn. London: Routledge.
Iñárittu, Alejandro González, dir. 2006. *Babel*. Hollywood: Paramount.
Kaindl, Klaus and Karlheinz Spitzl, eds. 2014. *Transfiction: Research into the Realities of Translation Fiction*. Amsterdam: John Benjamins.
Kentridge, William, dir. 1995. *Faustus in Africa*. Cape Town: Handspring Puppet Theater.
Lamming, George. 1992. *The Pleasures of Exile*. Ann Arbor: University of Michigan Press.
Lefevere, André. 1992. *Translation, Rewriting, and the Manipulation of Literary Fame*. London: Routledge.
Lin Zhaohua, Lin, dir. 1995 [1989]. *Hamulaite*. Beijing: People's Art Theater. Online at http://globalshakespeares.mit.edu/hamulaite-lin-zhaohua-1995, accessed April 29, 2015.
Mezei, Kathy, Sherry Simon, and Luise von Flotow, eds. 2014. *Translation Effects: The Shaping of Modern Canadian Culture*. Montreal: McGill-Queens University Press.
MIT Global Shakespeare. Online at globalshakespeares.mit.edu/#. Accessed February 5, 2016.
Murphy, Sarah. 1987. *The Measure of Miranda*. Edmonton: NeWest Press.
Namjoshi, Suniti. 1989. "Snapshots of Caliban." In *Because of India*. London: Onlywoman Press, 85–102.
Pollack, Sydney, dir. 2005. *The Interpreter*. London: Working Title Films.
Rosa, João Guimarães. 1962. "*O espelho* [The Mirror]." In *Primeiras estórias*. Rio de Janeiro: Livaria José Olympio Editoria, 71–78.
Rose, Jacqueline. 2001. *Albertine*. London: Chatto and Windus.
Schlöndorff, Volker. 1983. *Un Amour de Swann [Eine Liebe von Swann; Swann in Love]*. London: Curzon Film; Paris: Gaumont Production Co.
Scott, Clive. 2012a. *Literary Translation and the Rediscovery of Reading*. Cambridge: Cambridge University Press.
Scott, Clive. 2012b. *Translating the Perception of Text: Literary Translation and Phenomenology*. London: Modern Humanities Research Association and Maney Publishing.
Simon, Sherry. 2006. *Translating Montreal: Episodes in the Life of a Divided City*. Montreal: McGill Queens University Press.
Thomas, Audrey Callahan. 1971. *Munchmeyer; and Prospero on the Island*. Indianapolis: Bobbs-Merrill.

Trivedi, Harish. 2006. "In Our Own Time, On Our Own Terms: 'Translation' in India." In Theo Hermans, ed. *Translating Others*, vcl. 1. Manchester: St. Jerome, 102–19.

Ulitskaya, Ludmila. 2011. *Daniel Stein, Interpreter: A Novel in Documents*, trans. Arch Tait. New York: Overlook Duckworth.

Venuti, Lawrence. 1995. *The Translator's Invisibility: A History of Translation.* London: Routledge.

Vieira, Else. 1995–96. "(In)visibilidades na tradução: Troca de olhares teórico e ficcionais." *Com Textos* 6(6): 50–68.

Zabus, Chantal. 2002. *Tempests After Shakespeare.* New York: Palgrave.

Index

Taylor & Francis eBooks

Helping you to choose the right eBooks for your Library

Add Routledge titles to your library's digital collection today. Taylor and Francis ebooks contains over 50,000 titles in the Humanities, Social Sciences, Behavioural Sciences, Built Environment and Law.

Choose from a range of subject packages or create your own!

Benefits for you

>> Free MARC records
>> COUNTER-compliant usage statistics
>> Flexible purchase and pricing options
>> All titles DRM-free.

REQUEST YOUR **FREE** INSTITUTIONAL TRIAL TODAY

Free Trials Available
We offer free trials to qualifying academic, corporate and government customers.

Benefits for your user

>> Off-site, anytime access via Athens or referring URL
>> Print or copy pages or chapters
>> Full content search
>> Bookmark, highlight and annotate text
>> Access to thousands of pages of quality research at the click of a button.

eCollections – Choose from over 30 subject eCollections, including:

Archaeology	Language Learning
Architecture	Law
Asian Studies	Literature
Business & Management	Media & Communication
Classical Studies	Middle East Studies
Construction	Music
Creative & Media Arts	Philosophy
Criminology & Criminal Justice	Planning
Economics	Politics
Education	Psychology & Mental Health
Energy	Religion
Engineering	Security
English Language & Linguistics	Social Work
Environment & Sustainability	Sociology
Geography	Sport
Health Studies	Theatre & Performance
History	Tourism, Hospitality & Events

For more information, pricing enquiries or to order a free trial, please contact your local sales team:
www.tandfebooks.com/page/sales

Routledge
Taylor & Francis Group

The home of
Routledge books

www.tandfebooks.com

For Product Safety Concerns and Information please contact our EU
representative GPSR@taylorandfrancis.com
Taylor & Francis Verlag GmbH, Kaufingerstraße 24, 80331 München, Germany